THE BIG TEST

ALSO BY NICHOLAS LEMANN

The Promised Land: The Great Black
Migration and How It Changed America

Out of the Forties

The Fast Track

THE BIG TEST

THE SECRET HISTORY OF
THE AMERICAN MERITOCRACY

Nicholas Lemann

FARRAR, STRAUS AND GIROUX
New York

Farrar, Straus and Giroux
19 Union Square West, New York 10003

Copyright © 1999 by Nicholas Lemann
Distributed in Canada by Douglas & McIntyre Ltd.
All rights reserved
Printed in the United States of America
Designed by Lisa Stokes
First edition, 1999

Library of Congress Cataloging-in-Publication Data

Lemann, Nicholas.
    The big test : the secret history of the American meritocracy / Nicholas Lemann. — 1st ed.
        p.   cm.
    Includes index.
    ISBN 0-374-29984-6 (alk. paper)
    1. Educational tests and measurements—United States—History—20th century.
2. Ability—United States—Testing—History—20th century. 3. Intelligence tests—
United States—History—20th century. 4. Educational Testing Service—History. 5. Elite
(Social sciences)—United States. 6. Chauncey, Henry, 1905–   . I. Title.
LB3051.L44   1999
371.26'0973—dc21   99-32036

To Alex and Theo

The traits of American character were fixed; the rate of physical and economical growth was established; and history, certain that at a given distance of time the Union would contain so many millions of people, with wealth valued at so many millions of dollars, became thenceforth chiefly concerned to know what kind of people these millions were to be. They were intelligent, but what paths would their intelligence select? They were quick, but what solution of insoluble problems would their quickness hurry? They were scientific, but what control would their science exercise over their destiny? . . . What interests were to vivify a society so vast and uniform? What object, besides physical content, must a democratic continent aspire to attain?

—HENRY ADAMS
History of the United States of America During the Second Administration of James Madison

book 1

THE MORAL EQUIVALENT OF RELIGION

1
Henry Chauncey's Idea

It is February 4, 1945. A man named Henry Chauncey is sitting in an Episcopal church in Cambridge, Massachusetts—an old, gray, simple, graceful building on the Cambridge Common, where George Washington first took command of troops in the American Revolution. It's the Sunday morning before his fortieth birthday. He is perfectly at home here. Descendant of Puritan clerics, son of an Episcopal minister, graduate of the country's leading Episcopal boarding school, Chauncey, in his tweeds and flannels, wearing his gray hair neatly plastered across his forehead, is a full-fledged, born-in member of a distinct American subculture. In the seventeenth-century graveyard next to the church lie his forefathers.

One of the central tenets of this particular subculture is that you don't put on airs. You imagine a kind of ordinary decency to be your chief quality. Chauncey's life, like the life of everyone else who is in the church this morning, has its good points and its bad points. He is trying without complete success to switch from cigarettes to a pipe. Money is a bit of a problem, and so, in all honesty, is his marriage. On the other hand, he is optimistic and he believes in things, which is a great temperamental blessing. He never complains; one doesn't. He is a respectable man trying to do his best.

Bursting through the tight seams, though, is something grander and more ambitious in Chauncey. First of all, he looks like more than what he is, which is merely an ill-paid assistant dean at Harvard College. He's tall, barrel-chested, big-jawed, and moon-faced, almost simian, with bushy black eyebrows and a commandingly vigorous physical presence—the kind of person who ought to be put in charge of something. Notwithstanding the appealing modesty, his group, as every one of its members knows very well, occupies a highly favored—from today's point of view, almost unimaginably favored—position in American society. High-Protestant men of the Eastern seaboard occupy the White House, all the great university presidencies, the captaincies of finance and the professions, and many other leading positions, and each has rough access to the others. What any member of the group, including even Henry Chauncey, thinks and wants matters a great deal more than what members of other groups think and want.

The Second World War is now drawing to its conclusion, which, it is clear at last, will be a total victory by the Allies. The war has made the United States into the greatest power in the world, the central and essential civilization that, Americans hope, will serve as a model of how to organize a society properly. The United States is not only unusually influential at this moment but also unusually malleable. The war has put the country into flux, and basic arrangements can be altered now in a way that would be impossible in normal times. For a man of Henry Chauncey's social class, entering the prime of life, with direct experience of the drama and scale of wartime, the mind fills practically unbidden with utopian dreams about the shape of the postwar world and the part one might take in realizing them. Chauncey knows that big changes in American society are coming, and that they are going to be made swiftly, out of public view, by a tight group of men quite a number of whom he knows personally. The imminent prospect of joining in this is exhilarating. So, as he prays and listens and sings through the comfortable and familiar service, Henry Chauncey is thinking expansively about his future and the country's.

After the service he goes home, takes out a diary he has recently begun keeping (and filling with portentous, idealistic musings about the new age that is dawning), and writes:

> Finally, I decided to take the plunge. From a safe and respected job I am embarking on an opportunity whose development depends very much on what I do.
>
> During Church this morning a thought occurred to me which though not new was amplified in its implications. There will undoubtedly in the near future be a greater emphasis on taking a census of our human resources in terms of capacities for different kinds of employment. . . . This project requires consideration from a lot of angles but men of vision in the field of testing, vocational guidance, government, economics, education could be consulted individually and eventually in groups and a program eventually developed. Men with whom this might

be discussed might even be so high in authority as . . . President Roosevelt himself.

This is what Henry Chauncey wants to do in (for, really!) postwar America: he wants to mount a vast scientific project that will categorize, sort, and route the entire population. It will be accomplished by administering a series of multiple-choice mental tests to everyone, and then by suggesting, on the basis of the scores, what each person's role in society should be—suggestions everyone will surely accept gratefully. The project will be called the Census of Abilities. It will accomplish something not very different from what Chauncey's Puritan ancestors came to the New World wanting to do—engender systematic moral grace in the place of wrong and disorder—but via twentieth-century technical means. The vehicle through which he hopes to achieve all this is an aborning organization called the Educational Testing Service, purveyor of a test called the SAT. You've heard of it? The residue of the Census of Abilities is the standardized tests that you took in high school and college, that you probably prepared for and sweated over because it seemed they would determine your fate in life. Right now, Chauncey is about to become the first president of the Educational Testing Service. That's the plunge he's taking.

The way that Henry Chauncey's thoughts were running near the end of the Second World War is pertinent not just as an example of the tenor of that moment, and not just because Chauncey was on the point of founding an important American institution. American society was, in fact, at a crossroads—Chauncey may have been dreaming, but he wasn't fantasizing. A quiet but intense competition was taking place over the future structure of the country. Chauncey had a part in it, generally because he belonged to the group that decided things back then, and particularly because he was connected to a powerful patron, James Bryant Conant, the president of Harvard University.

Chauncey believed in progress and wanted to be part of it. He was sure that an expansion of mental testing, which seemed to him to be a science with limitless possibilities, was the proper avenue. But he was an agnostic on the question of what form, exactly, the progress should take. Conant was not. He had a plan fully worked out, which he had recently proposed in a series of righteous, almost inflammatory magazine articles: to depose the existing, undemocratic American elite and replace it with a new one made up of brainy, elaborately trained, public-spirited people drawn from every section and every background. These people (men, actually) would lead the country. They would manage the large technical organizations that would be the backbone of the late-twentieth-century United States and create, for the first time ever, an organized system that would provide opportunity to all Americans. Conant assumed, in fact, that picking a new elite in just the right way would enhance democracy and justice almost automatically. It was an audacious plan for engineering a change in the leadership group and social structure of the country—a kind of quiet, planned coup d'état.

Chauncey's wishes and Conant's both came true: the United States did embark on the world's largest-scale program of mental testing, and one consequence of this (though not the only one) was the establishment of a new national elite. The machinery that Conant and Chauncey and their allies created is today so familiar and all-encompassing that it seems almost like a natural phenomenon, or at least an organism that evolved spontaneously in response to conditions. It's not. It's man-made. The organized way we have of deciding who winds up where in American society exists because, in the intense maneuvering of the period before, during, and just after the war, one particular system triumphed over other, alternative systems.

Here is what American society looks like today. A thick line runs through the country, with people who have been to college on one side of it and people who haven't on the other. This line gets brighter all the time. Whether a person is on one side of the line or the other is now more indicative of income, of attitudes, and of political behavior than any other line one might draw: region, race, age, religion, sex, class. As people plan their lives and their children's lives, higher education is the main focus of their aspirations (and the possibility of getting into the elite end of higher education is the focus of their very dearest aspirations). A test of one narrow quality, the ability to perform well in school, stands firmly athwart the path to success. Those who don't have that ability will have much less chance than those who do to display their other talents later.

The placing of such a heavy load on higher education has had many other effects. A whole industry has grown up to help people get into college and graduate school. Educational opportunity has become a national obsession. There is a politics of it, a jurisprudence of it, and a philosophy of it—none of which was the case fifty years ago. To improve it is the fundamental promise made by most candidates for public office. It is the fundamental good that parents try to get for their children. Preoccupation with it is the chief theme of the first quarter of Americans' lives. It is the object of elaborate work, hope, scheming, manipulation, and competition.

Those who do best under this system make up a distinct class, with its own mores and beliefs and tastes and folkways. They don't serve as the unquestioned leadership of the United States, as Conant and Chauncey would have expected; they're at least as much resented as admired. They aren't perceived by others as people who have earned their position in completely open and fair competition (though that's the way they perceive themselves) or who are primarily devoted to the public interest. But still, they are Conant's and Chauncey's children, precisely the products of the ideas they had and the moves they made after the end of the Second World War.

One way to understand the current shape of American society is as its being the result of Conant's, Chauncey's, and their allies' concerted attack on a specific problem, which was so successful that the problem no longer exists. So much force was marshaled against that one problem, though, that in addition to its being solved, practically everything else was changed, too— which created new problems. The story of what happened has to begin with the original problem, or else it doesn't make sense.

Here is what American society looked like, from the point of view of Conant and Chauncey, at the close of the Second World War.

They took it as a given that the essence of American greatness was a quality that Alexis de Tocqueville had remarked upon early in the nineteenth century: social equality, of a kind that would be unthinkable in any other country. Because the United States didn't have a rigid class system, it could take full advantage of its people's talents and at the same time generate intense social cohesion across a range of physical space and a variety of ethnic origin that elsewhere would have been considered insuperable.

But during the early twentieth century American society had taken an ominous turn. Conant and Chauncey accepted without question the view of Frederick Jackson Turner, the historian of the American West who was a Harvard professor in their younger days, that what had made the United States democratic and classless was the availability of open land on the Western frontier. Now the frontier was closed, the country had become industrial, and the cities were crowded with immigrant workers, many of whom were socialists—or who, at the very least, believed that group unity, rather than individual opportunity, was the highest good.

Even worse, a distinct American upper class had emerged. It was very much on display at Harvard and other leading universities, where, up to the start of the Second World War, rich heedless young men with servants, whose lives revolved around parties and sports, not studying, set the tone of college life. The plurality of Harvard students had come from boys' boarding schools in New England, the kind where parents could register their sons at birth; pretty much anybody who went to one of these schools, and was not "a little slow," and could pay the tuition, could go to Harvard, or to Princeton, or to Yale. Even the faculty was disproportionately made up of proper Bostonians, rather than modern academics.

Harvard and institutions like it fed into another series of institutions: law firms, Wall Street financial houses, the Foreign Service, research hospitals, and university faculties. These, too, had begun to look like the province of a hereditary upper class. All the good places were reserved for members of a certain group—the all-male, Eastern, high-Protestant, privately educated group to which Henry Chauncey belonged. No Catholics or Jews were allowed, except in rare cases that required of them a careful extirpation of any accent or other noticeable expression of their alien culture. Nonwhites weren't in close enough range of membership in the elite to be excluded. And even the fieriest social reformers of the day didn't think to suggest that women ought routinely to participate in running the country. Snobbishness, small-mindedness, and prejudice were the worst aspects of the elite institutions, but even at their best they were preoccupied with a vaguely defined personal quality called "character," and tended to ignore intelligence and scientific expertise. But these, precisely, were the traits Conant thought most vitally necessary in postwar America.

What could you do to dethrone this upper class and restore the United States to its true democratic nature? It was a question without an obvious answer. Using the educational system to create a fair society, which seems today like the way to do the job, looked then like a distant, unrealized, possibly unrealizable dream.

At the close of the Second World War, the United States had been the world's leader in trying to educate a large part of the citizenry for more than a hundred years. During the nineteenth century Americans created, not without a struggle, the free public elementary school as a basic social institution and, during the first half of the twentieth century, the high school. These institutions weren't well enough established to be taken for granted as they are now. In 1940 the country still hadn't passed the milestone of graduating more than half its teenagers from high school. The idea that there might be a way of evaluating all American high-school students on a single national standard and then making sure that they went on to colleges suited to their abilities and ambitions—most people would have regarded that as a wild, futuristic fantasy, although Chauncey and Conant were among a handful of people who knew that, technically, it could be done.

Colleges were the same story as public schools. The United States provided far more people with higher education than any country ever had— about one in four young people entered college and one in twenty stayed long enough to get a degree. But these students were the ones whose parents had enough money to send them to college; American higher education's size didn't mean that it was open to everyone. Neither was it established that professors should be respected, well-compensated, formally trained experts dedicated to advancing the frontiers of knowledge by conducting rigorous, objective research. During the late nineteenth century, hundreds of American scholars had gone to Germany to receive strict academic training (because that was the only country where it was available) and came back imbued with the goal of setting up German-style research universities here. It was an appealing picture, Herr Doktor Professor as scientific figure sitting atop a formal university hierarchy and consulted by government and industry, but by the Second World War it had scarcely been achieved.

Most leading private universities, like Harvard, drew their students and faculty from a local or regional pool and had a genteel, belletristic quality. In most cases their students were male. In private higher education, women usually went to women's colleges whose announced purpose was to prepare them for supporting roles in life. Most African-Americans who went to college went to black colleges, which were also segregated by sex. State public universities were, in contrast, open to just about anyone (except those in the South), but most were expected by their state legislatures to impart the educational basics to all comers first, and conduct advanced research second.

Within the inner and higher chambers of American society a struggle was under way to reform   literally   re-form—schooling at all levels. It had been going on all through the Depression and war years, spiritedly, sometimes bitterly, without attracting public notice. All the participants shared Chauncey's and Conant's assumption that education was going to change dramatically and was going to turn into the mainspring of American society, the repository of the country's distinctive greatness.

This book tells, for the first time, the story of the new system that emerged after the Second World War: where the ideas animating it came from, how it was put into effect, what other choices were rejected, what compromises were made along the way, and how the new leaders' lives and their roles in the country's drama turned out.

Whatever Tocqueville thought, the United States has always been a country with an elite, or a series of elites, overlapping, competing, and succeeding one another. Henry Chauncey did not share Conant's animus against the American elite of the mid-twentieth century. That was because he was a member of it. Indeed, the story of the Chauncey family makes a good capsule history of the progression of elites in America.

The Chauncys (as the name was originally spelled) were never just ordinary folks, and they were never holders of a simple unprepossessing idea of the world. Originally they were Norman noblemen who came to England in the conquest of 1066 and wound up as barons in Yorkshire. In the 1400s they were dispossessed and moved down a notch, into the ministerial class. The Chauncy who moved to America, Charles Chauncy, born in 1592, was educated at Cambridge and became a professor of Greek there, but he was mainly a devout and opinionated Puritan minister who spent his life getting into disputes with church authorities. In 1629 he was hauled before the high commission court for publicly criticizing the Church of England's policy of allowing sports, games, and recreation on Sundays. In 1635 he was thrown into prison for publishing a lengthy treatise protesting the placing of a railing around the communion table. He won his release by writing a weak recantation—though according to a family history written by one of his descendants, he "deeply bewailed his sinful compliance" until his dying day.

In 1637 Chauncy left England for the Massachusetts Bay Colony, where, even in a community of fellow Puritans, he stood out as a vehement critic of what he regarded as excessive religious laxness. He created "much trouble," in the words of Governor John Winthrop, by expressing the view that "the children ought to be dipt and not sprinkled" at their baptism. In 1654, worn down by that controversy and other tribulations of American life, Chauncy resolved to return to England, where the Puritans had taken power and the bishop who had tormented him "had given his head to the block." He changed his mind, however, when he was made president of Harvard College, on condition "that he forbear to disseminate or publish any tenets concerning immersion baptism."

Everybody thinks of America as a country where people came to escape formal social structures—a place with a genius for disorganization. Charles Chauncy represents another strain that has been present in American society all along. No amount of anachronistic pretzel-twisting can make him into a populist or a democrat. He was self-consciously a figure at the top of society. He did come here to escape an order that he found oppressive—but only because he hoped to help create a new order that would be stricter and therefore more virtuous than the old one.

But where Puritans like Chauncy do connect to the modern American creed is in their idea that the state of grace was individual and irrespective of social rank. This was a radical notion, and it led in the direction of a society run by people who had earned their places by good works, rather than by an upper class selected by birth. The last controversy of Charles Chauncy's theologically combative life was over the Halfway Covenant, a Puritan doctrine that granted the privilege of automatic baptism to the grandchildren of members of the elect. Chauncy was dead set against it. Initiation into the state of grace, he felt, ought not be conferred by inheritance.

Charles Chauncy died in 1671, having well established his family in New England. The best-known Chauncy of the 1700s was one of his great-grand-sons, also named Charles Chauncy, who for decades was minister of the Presbyterian First Church of Boston. This Charles Chauncy was the leading opponent of the Great Awakening, the ecstatic revival movement that was led by the young, charismatic, showy Congregational minister Jonathan Edwards out on the wild frontier surrounding Northampton, Massachusetts. In 1742 Edwards published his credo, *Some Thoughts Concerning the Present Revival of Religion in New England*. The next year Chauncy published a censorious rebuttal, *Seasonable Thoughts on the State of Religion in New England*, which lengthily disapproved of preachers like Edwards who, in dealing with their flock, "aimed at putting their Passions into a Ferment."

The Chauncy sternness is unmistakable. The family remained in its traditional position of being as ambitiously idealistic as anybody about the national enterprise, about the quest for the good, but in believing that there had to be a disciplined, orderly, restrained means to that end. Jonathan Edwards represented a trust in the good instincts of all people, however unruly that mass might be; Charles Chauncy, belief in a trained, systematic elite. By this time, though, most of the descendants of the original Puritans, including Chauncy, were bound up in the prosperous commercial culture of New England's cities and towns. They were migrating from their original Congregationalism into more conventional Protestant denominations, and from the ministry into trade.

In the nineteenth century the Chaunceys (as they now spelled it), without losing their moralism, became rich. They were early exemplars of what one of their twentieth-century relatives, Joseph Alsop, the Washington columnist, called "the WASP ascendancy." The first family member named Henry Chauncey, who was born in 1795, went into foreign trade. During the 1830s he moved to Chile. As if to provide evidence for Max Weber's future theories about the connection between Puritanism and capitalism, he took pains to persuade his family back home that his main concern in business was with virtue, not money. He wrote his father-in-law in 1835: "Be assured that I have not been influenced by a desire of great wealth, no part of my ambition is to be thought rich, if I have enough to give my children a good education, to carry us through and a few dollars to help those that are in need is all I require." Nonetheless, Chauncey returned to America with a substantial fortune. He lived in a mansion on Washington Square in New York City.

Henry Chauncey left his money to his children, which ruined them. They lived splendidly in New York, whiled away days at their clubs, and pursued expensive hobbies. His son Frederick, the grandfather of our Henry Chauncey, created a series of beautifully illustrated little notebooks about his recreations—*Birds Shot, Fish Caught*—and worked as a merchant. In 1884 his business failed because Frederick's partner had secretly and disastrously speculated with its funds. Frederick soon caught pneumonia following a game of racquets and died at the age of forty-seven. His wife and four children fell into a pathetic existence that sounds like the subplot of an Edith Wharton novel. Socially impeccable but broke, they lived in a modest apartment on the Upper East Side, supported by subventions from relatives. Mrs. Chauncey took the position that because of their misfortunes, none of the children should ever marry or leave home.

The only one who disobeyed her was Henry's father, Egisto Fabbri Chauncey (named, before the terrible truth came out, after Frederick Chauncey's dishonest partner). He entered the ancestral family profession, the ministry, although as an Episcopalian he was affiliated with the American branch of the Church of England, the very institution the Puritans had come here to escape. His son Henry Chauncey was born in 1905. In his baby book, carefully preserved, there was a place to write down what "people are reading"; Mrs. Chauncey listed Thomas Dixon's *The Clansman* (one of the books on which the movie *Birth of a Nation* was based), Edith Wharton's *The House of Mirth*, and Jack London's *War of the Classes*, indicating a country that was still, despite the best improving efforts of two and a half centuries of Chaunceys, in a state of upheaval over matters of race, class, and social exclusion.

The Chaunceys, however, were not in the slightest daunted in their quest for a perfected, orderly America. The year after Henry's birth Egisto Chauncey received a call to become rector of St. Mark's Church in Mount Kisco, New York, a bosky country retreat for the rich. This was where Henry Chauncey spent his early childhood, impecunious compared to everybody else, but righteous. The Reverend Chauncey built a new home for St. Mark's—a substantial (but not luxurious) bluestone structure in the Gothic style, designed by the firm of Cram, Goodhue, and Ferguson, the leading church architects of the day. Over one of the doorways he had painted a motto, taken from the Book of Proverbs: "Where there is no vision the people perish."

Let's give a name to the elite that Henry Chauncey was born into: the Episcopacy.

After the Civil War the United States industrialized, and industry generated new fortunes. The makers of them constituted a rising group that was repugnant to the old New England mercantile elite to which the Chaunceys belonged. The warfare between the old and new groups is a staple of late-nineteenth-century fiction and social comment.

What's most curious about their rivalry in retrospect is that, having appeared during the 1870s and 1880s to be unalterably bitter, it quickly went away. The two groups merged into one. The wholesale conversion of many on both sides to the Episcopal Church—the newly rich often switching over from being Methodist or Baptist, the old rich from being Unitarian or Congregationalist—was a crucial part of their smooth coming together. Between 1860 and 1900, Episcopal Church membership in the United States grew by 318 percent. Episcopalianism had two main appealing features: to the new capitalists it offered an opulence of ritual and setting and to the old mercantilists it provided a link to England, which—at a time when mass uncontrolled immigration from other places was changing the character of the United States—for them had gone from being the place their ancestors had fled to the mother country.

Not every member of the elite was an Episcopalian, though nearly every member was a Protestant. There was room for some variability of denomination. Still, it is remarkable how overrepresented at the top of the society that one numerically small order was. Along with the rise of the Episcopal Church itself, a series of subsidiary institutions sprang up at the end of the nineteenth century to facilitate the blending of the old and new elites, especially through intermarriage: country clubs, suburbs, debutante cotillions, and boarding schools emphasizing gentlemanliness. In this last category, the pre-eminent institution was the Groton School, founded in Massachusetts in 1884. This was where male Chaunceys were educated before they went to Harvard.

The founder of Groton was another Puritan descendant, Endicott Peabody. Raised a Unitarian in Salem, Massachusetts, Peabody as a teenager moved with his family to London, where his father had gone to work in banking with Junius S. Morgan, J. P. Morgan's father. The years in England made Peabody into an Anglophile, an Episcopalian, and a devotee of the British boarding school. After graduating from Trinity College, Cambridge, he returned to the United States, worked briefly and unhappily on Wall Street, became an Episcopal minister, spent a year preaching in the unlikely venue of Tombstone, Arizona, and then, at the age of twenty-seven, started Groton. J. P. Morgan was the crucial member of the board of directors, and two Chaunceys were among the original students.

Peabody exemplified one of the oddest aspects of late-nineteenth-century America, which was that this country, having become rich, powerful, and unified, was overcome with a pathetic cultural insecurity with respect to Europe, especially England, that it had successfully resisted back when the United States had been a shaky proposition. It is hard to imagine that even Queen Victoria could have been as Victorian as Endicott Peabody—a man who refused to let divorced people set foot on his campus as late as the 1930s, whose idea of great literature was Kipling, and who required all his boys to take cold showers every morning, to wash in long metal basins, to live in doorless, ceilingless cubicles, to attend church services every morning, and to shake his hand every evening (every boy, every evening) and say, "Good night, sir!" before going to bed.

And yet, Peabody's time-frozen and transplanted little patch of mid-nineteenth-century British upper-class culture was a fully successful American institution, not least because of Peabody's great personal force, never ruffled by doubt. (Although Groton is located in a small, out-of-the-way place in rural Massachusetts, it is well to remember, wrote Peabody's biographer, a typically awestruck protégé, that "Bethlehem was a little town in an obscure corner of an empire.") During the early and middle decades of the twentieth century, when high-Protestant men who had gone to expensive private schools in the Northeast seemed to run just about everything that mattered, Groton graduates were able to operate at the headiest heights of the great world without Peabody's importance to them diminishing in the slightest from the schoolboy level.

Just before taking the oath of office so that he could begin to dismantle the form of capitalism whose extremest beneficiaries had sent their sons to Groton, Franklin Roosevelt felt the need to kneel before Endicott Peabody—whom he had imported to Washington for the occasion, even though Peabody had, of course, voted for Hoover—and receive a blessing. Peabody also had officiated at FDR's wedding, and those of many other Grotonians, and sent congratulatory notes when his sons were born (along with a Groton registration form—the Groton student body was made up of 70 percent alumni sons well into the New Deal). FDR was merely the best known of a long list of influential Grotonians who considered themselves to be protégés of Peabody: Achesons, Alsops, Bundys, Harrimans, and Whitneys, in addition to Roosevelts and Morgans.

To be cynical about Groton, which Peabody never was, its purpose was to prevent very rich boys from turning into playboys or pantywaists. It trained them not to become prosperous (that they would be prosperous was already certain) but to be good and useful. It did this by inculcating the idea of "service," meaning turning one's orientation away from immediate gratification and toward higher (though not exactly self-abnegating) pursuits. Groton conferred upon its students the ability to act with confidence and faith in their disinterestedness and God's approval—even, or especially, while they were exercising great power. It's easy to see this creed as a convenient (but not consciously so!) adaptation of the Puritan tradition to the needs of the ruling group in a modern industrial society: there is the same core idea of a small, disciplined, elect group operating under a virtually theological mandate, but with the added note of obligation to exercise power over the mass. The motto Peabody chose for his school was *cui servire est regnare*, which means "to serve is to reign."

The basic form of social organization at Groton was the prefecture system, borrowed from English public (which is to say private) schools and probably best known today as the subject of countless exposés by bitter upper-class Englishmen: the headmaster and other teachers ceded great disciplinary power to a small coterie of handpicked older boys. But at Groton, or anyway in the literature of Groton, where irony and disillusionment had not the smallest handhold, the prefects were never obsequious to the head or cruel to the other boys. In the words of Peabody's biographer: "The highest honor and most responsible position in the school was that of senior prefect. He lived in state, with a huge study and bedroom adjoining, saw the Rector daily, and was the instrument through which many policies and desires were carried out."

Henry Chauncey was senior prefect at Groton. He got the job because he was an embodiment of Endicott Peabody's ideas about Christian young manhood, in which intellectual brilliance and artistic creativity—hollow virtues associated with people who are not doing things but merely offering their commentary on the world—were far less important than leadership, character, spirit, faith, manners, and athletic ability. The completeness with which Chauncey absorbed the Groton creed, which once lodged in his mind was there for life, comes across in a self-description he jotted down one night shortly after he graduated:

> Now one of my biggest ideas, which isn't new or astounding, is that schools & colleges, especially the former, should aim to develop character as well as to teach knowledge. . . . A person to be a good Xtian doesn't need to carry his philosophy around with him openly wherever he goes, but with it in the background and with common horse sense and a love of one's fellowman in the foreground a happy life just naturally follows.

One big difference separated Chauncey from most of his fellow Grotonians. His family had no money. As an Episcopal minister from a distinguished family, his father (Groton '92, Harvard '99) was theoretically the social equal of the people he had gone to school and college with, and he was certainly immune from any gross, overt exclusion, but sending Henry to Groton could be accomplished only by cobbling together subventions from relatives. During Henry's Groton years Egisto Chauncey was rector of Trinity Episcopal Church in Columbus, Ohio, the big downtown cathedral across the street from the state capitol building. After Groton, Henry came to Columbus and enrolled at tuition-free Ohio State, a public state university of the kind that no Grotonian had ever attended. Then Endicott Peabody set things aright by making an arrangement with Clarence Dillon, the Wall Street financier (and father of C. Douglas Dillon, a Grotonian and future Secretary of the Treasury), under which Dillon would make up the difference, $700 a year, between what the Chaunceys could afford to pay and what it would cost to send Henry to Harvard. It was through this kind of informal, invisible scholarship system that the Episcopacy took care of its less fortunate members. After a year Henry left Columbus for Cambridge.

By all appearances, Henry Chauncey chose simply to ignore the financial provisionality of his membership in the elite and adopt the Rector's view of life without reservation. He was an enthusiastic, improving, unshaded person. If it seemed unfair to him that he should be poor when all his friends were rich, if he felt a compensatory pull toward importance (assuming he could find some realm where an aggressive embrace of the good counted for more than money), these feelings were so deeply buried that he wasn't aware of them. He had somewhat improbably emerged, from a family of stern American founders that had nearly spun itself out in a congeries of impecuniousness and celibacy, as a paragon of energetic self-confidence, a full six inches taller than his father.

2 The Glass Slipper

Sometimes a person grows to maturity inside a tightly con-strained milieu and then, exposed to the outside world for the first time, is struck with unexpected force by something from completely beyond his experience: a book, a lover, a mentor, an avocation. In such cases, the mystery is what it was about the new thing that made it so powerful. It must have linked itself to something that is already deeply set into one's makeup, else how to explain the instant, overwhelming impact—but what?

That happened to Henry Chauncey during his year at Ohio State University. What took him by storm—and retained its power for his whole life—was mental testing, a new applied science that was, in both its substance and its tone, antithetical to the creed of the class in which he had been raised.

The French psychologist Alfred Binet devised the first test of intelligence in 1905, the year when Henry Chauncey (who over his lifetime was to do more than anyone else in the world to engender the use of intelligence tests) was born. Binet's test consisted of a series of written questions presented to schoolchildren—involving, for example, identifying the emotion meant by a pictured facial expression, or counting coins—from the answers to which he claimed he could derive a rating of their "mental age."

Binet meant his test to be used to identify slow learners so that they could be given special help in school. The American promoters of his idea—men like Lewis Terman at Stanford University, who gave the name "intelligence quotient," or IQ, to the ratio of mental and physical age, and Edward Thorndike at Columbia—thought of the IQ test as a much more significant and widely applicable scientific breakthrough. They believed it could quickly, almost miraculously, measure the innate capacity of the brain, a quasi-biological quality that they considered the essential human attribute in the modern age. Terman and Thorndike were tireless advocates of the widest possible use of IQ testing by American educators, so that students could be assessed, sorted, and taught in accordance with their capabilities.

Not only mental testing but psychology itself was an infant science when Chauncey was in college. Terman and Thorndike, pioneer figures, were in the prime of their careers. They were protégés of the founders of American psychology—Terman had studied with G. Stanley Hall and Thorndike with William James—and they were busily sending protégés of their own out into the higher education system, often to found psychology departments at universities. A student of Thorndike's, Herbert Toops, was at Ohio State, and Henry Chauncey's cohort of freshmen was the first to be given a "psychological examination" devised by Toops. Something about the test so intrigued Chauncey that he signed up for a course on psychology that had a section on mental testing. At the end of his first semester, he dropped by the office that had administered the Toops exam to find out what his score was.

"What were your grades?" he remembers being asked.

Two A's and a B, he reported.

"That is just what your test score predicted."

Chauncey was bowled over. It was magical: the idea that the mysterious, inaccessible human mind would now yield its contents to psychologists who knew the right few questions to ask. Testing touched upon the deepest mythic themes: the ability to see the invisible (what was inside people's heads), the oracular ability to predict the future (what someone's grades would be in courses he hadn't even chosen yet).

Mental testing would have been the last thing Endicott Peabody touted to his boys at Groton, and not just because it was so new. His idea of what students should learn was the classics and English history and literature—not much science except mathematics, and certainly not social science, which was emerging only during the later years of his headmastership, because it was not only sweaty and technical but also based on the principle that man could understand matters that it was given only to God to master. And the idea that intelligence as measured by mental tests was of primary importance would have been anathema to Peabody, who valued other qualities far more and who always made sure that Groton boys put in more hours on the athletic fields than in class. What testing seemed to connect to in Chauncey was something deeper, something predating the environment in which he had been educated: perhaps a Puritan attraction to improvement of the human state through system and order, and perhaps also a desire to break out of the

Groton world's tight confines (especially tight for someone penniless like himself). Testing was momentous and young, and he might become a part of it. A modest eleemosynary good life lived out at a church or a school seemed pallid by comparison.

When Chauncey arrived at Harvard after his year at Ohio State, he studied whatever he could about testing, though it wasn't much. Harvard was a broader and more intellectual institution than Groton, but not as much more as you might think. It was governed—as it still is—by the Harvard Corporation, a board all of whose members were then Episcopalian gentlemen from Boston. Since 1909 Harvard's president had been Abbott Lawrence Lowell, who was the grandson of a member of the Harvard Corporation (and a cousin of one of the founders of Groton) and who had been put in charge of Harvard specifically to ratchet back the trend toward cosmopolitanism and scholarship that his predecessor, Charles William Eliot, an admirer of the German university model who valued scholarly research above all else, had begun. Lowell's official biographer gave this explanation for why the members of the Corporation happened to pick him:

> There were personal relationships involved. Francis Cabot Lowell was Lawrence Lowell's brother-in-law. Dr. Cabot was a distant relative of Mrs. Lawrence Lowell's. Major Higginson's closest friend whom he never ceased to mourn was Charles Russell Lowell. Mr. Adams was the namesake of his uncle who disapproved Eliot's administration of the College quite as much as Lowell did.

Harvard in the 1920s didn't have a psychology department. Chauncey majored in philosophy because that was the department that offered what few psychology courses there were. He also found courses at Harvard's graduate school of education that touched upon psychology and testing. On the whole, though, he was that familiar character, the young man who is firmly on a track to do something and can't quite figure out how to get off it. He was destined to hold a respected position within the subculture that had educated him, not to be a future tycoon in the unknown world of educational testing. He was more outstanding as an athlete and clubman than as a student, which was standard for a Grotonian at Harvard. He was such a good baseball catcher that the Boston Braves tried to recruit him. In football he electrified the crowd at the 1926 Harvard-Yale game by throwing what one of his classmates later called the "greatest of all forward passes, and also the most aristocratic," to his friend William Saltonstall, another Puritan descendant and a future boarding-school headmaster.

Sitting in the stands that day was Richard Gummere, headmaster of the Penn Charter School in Philadelphia. He was so impressed by Chauncey's performance on the field that he offered him a job as a teacher and coach— that was how things worked then. Chauncey spent a year at Penn Charter, then returned to Harvard to take graduate courses in history and do minor administrative chores part-time. In 1929 he took a job as an assistant dean. Assistant deans at Harvard were generally young men of a certain type: athletic, of good character, graduates of a boarding school and Harvard, and probably on their way to a headmastership at some well-respected private school.

But soon Chauncey had a road-to-Damascus experience that reawakened his interest in testing, and in projects beyond the scope of what someone in his position would ordinarily have encountered. He attended a lecture by an educational researcher named William S. Learned, who described an ambitious study he was conducting for the Carnegie Foundation for the Advancement of Teaching.

After the lecture, aflame, Chauncey went home and wrote out by hand a five-page letter to Learned. "I am interested in the complete reorientation and reorganization of secondary school aims and methods," he declared, pretty grandly for a twenty-six-year-old. More immediately, he had another idea: "It is less complicated and more possible of fruition in the near future. It is concerned with the application of objective tests to college admission. . . . I myself should be only too glad to be of any help in such a venture should it be projected."

That was in January 1932. In November of that year Abbott Lawrence Lowell announced his retirement. In April 1933, the Harvard Corporation selected James Bryant Conant, a chemistry professor, to succeed Lowell. In the fall of 1933 Conant took office, and almost immediately he called in Henry Chauncey and gave him the opening Chauncey had been looking for.

In pursuing what he thought of as a pure, uninflected interest in mental testing, Chauncey had wandered unwittingly right into the middle of a big fight over the future of education in America.

The fight had a peculiar form because of the peculiar position of the Episcopacy during the 1930s.

In the institutional world, the Episcopacy's power was as great as it had ever been. That meant decisions of great moment for the life of the country could be made from within a very tight, private circle. But in the world of advanced thought, the obsolescence of the old elite was taken for granted and the question at hand was how to unseat it and what to replace it with.

Hard science, aesthetic modernism, and political liberalism were on the march. The 1929 stock market crash and the Great Depression had severely shaken the confidence (and damaged the prosperity) of the elite, and made its leadership of the country look inept. Hence this curious situation in the early 1930s: the linked issues of what would succeed this old elite and how American education should be organized were being debated from within the deepest inner confines of the Episcopacy itself.

Harvard was a good example of the phenomenon. An institution whose governing boards, administration, faculty, and students were overwhelmingly drawn from the upper classes of Protestant New England, it had nonetheless just made a conscious departure in picking Conant as its president. To an outsider Conant wouldn't have appeared very different from his predecessors. He was a Bostonian descended from Puritans, a graduate of Harvard College, and a Harvard faculty member. He most definitely was not a man of the upper crust, though. He had grown up in middle-class Dorchester, his father was an engraver, his parents' religion was Swedenborgian, he had been educated at a private school called Roxbury Latin that admitted students by competitive examination, and his academic field was chemistry rather than literature or history. He burned with a fierce disapproval of the old ways at Harvard, and his first goal as president was to loosen them.

The institution that, along with Harvard, had the greatest influence on higher education was even more dramatically private and tightly controlled. That was the Carnegie Foundation for the Advancement of Teaching. The Carnegie Foundation was one of several organizations created by the fortune of Andrew Carnegie, the self-educated Scottish immigrant who in the late nineteenth century personified America's unlimited opportunities. During his lifetime, Carnegie endowed public libraries all over the country, so that ambitious children from humble backgrounds could improve themselves as he had done. Now, with Andrew Carnegie himself gone, the foundation was continuing his mission by promoting education more generally; a small, well-connected staff in New York was thinking in the most ambitious way about what form America's educational system should take.

Four distinct ideas about the future of education, each implicitly leading to a different kind of new social order, were competing with each other.

One was progressive education, whose adherents believed that schools should promote the individual blossoming of each student as a creative thinker and an active, skeptical citizen, rather than treating young people as drones whose empty heads should be filled with prescribed material in a disciplined environment. The founding father of progressive education, John Dewey, was the most revered figure in American education, and the movement was at the peak of its influence in the late 1920s and early 1930s. The Carnegie Foundation was funding a project called the Eight-Year Study, organized by the Progressive Education Association, in which thirty high schools across America, more of them private than public, would experiment with looser, more creative teaching methods, and colleges would agree to accept their graduates even if they lacked conventional course credits. The means to this last end would be new college entrance examinations, which would test intellectual ability rather than rote knowledge.

The idea of progressive education, and of the Eight-Year Study, was to end traditional teaching and curriculum in high school and college and, down the road, to create a more liberal-minded, freethinking, tolerant class of leaders, who would build a fairer society.

Just about exactly the opposite was the idea that tough, uniform standards should be imposed on American schools. But the Carnegie Foundation was promoting that idea, too, by funding another, even broader research project called the Pennsylvania Study. It was this study that Henry Chauncey had heard Carnegie's William Learned lecture about at Harvard.

By the time Chauncey heard the lecture, Learned and his partner, Ben D. Wood, a professor at Columbia University Teachers College, had been at work for nearly five years on their investigation of educational conditions in Pennsylvania. They hadn't published any results yet, but already their findings were clear and dramatic. The high schools and colleges of Pennsylvania were in a shocking mess. Any student who amassed the proper number of credit-hours, just by sitting in class, could obtain a high-school diploma. Colleges would accept any high-school graduate who could pay the tuition, and then the same process would begin again: you merely had to show up and accumulate your quota of credit-hours, and you'd graduate. Nobody along the way, in Pennsylvania or anywhere else in the United States, endeavored to find out whether students were learning anything.

When Learned and Wood finally did so, by administering standardized achievement tests that Wood devised, they discovered enormous disparities among students. There was nothing like a uniform level of knowledge among college sophomores or among high-school seniors. Many students who hadn't continued on after high school tested higher than many who had completed more than a year of college. And among college students, the lowest scorers by far were the very people who were going to be entrusted with this benighted system in the future—education majors.

The idea animating the Pennsylvania Study was to establish a body of material that all students in high school and college should be required to master, test them on it, and ruthlessly weed out the student population on the basis of the test results. Then the United States could become a technocracy, led by a coterie of college graduates who would be highly skilled experts.

A third idea about the future of education had IQ tests, those shiny new miracles of psychology, playing the key role. True believers in IQ tests thought they should be given to all American children, so that the high scorers could be plucked out and given the best schooling and the average and low scorers consigned to a briefer, more limited education. Standard-setters like Learned and Wood wanted to reward students who had demonstrated mastery of a body of knowledge; the IQ testers wanted to reward pure inherent brainpower, as they believed it was revealed by IQ test scores.

The study of human intelligence had always attracted people with a certain cluster of beliefs, even before there were IQ tests around for use as evidence. They thought of intelligence as being by far the single most important human trait, and therefore the one around which society should be organized; they believed it was genetically inherited; they believed that the world's darker-skinned races were inferior in intelligence to its lighter-skinned ones; and they were concerned that unintelligent people were reproducing at a more rapid rate than intelligent ones, which would ultimately bring down the IQ of the entire human species. All these views can be found in *Hereditary Genius*, by Francis Galton, Charles Darwin's cousin and a pioneer geneticist, which was published in 1869, thirty-six years before Binet administered the first IQ test; and they can be found in *The Bell Curve*, by Richard Herrnstein and Charles Murray, who claim to have come to them only reluctantly on the basis of irrefutable evidence provided by IQ testing, which was published in 1994.

Galton coined the word "eugenics" to mean the use of selective breeding techniques to improve the intelligence, and other attributes, of the human race. There was a time—roughly speaking, 1890–1920—when eugenicist views were common among enlightened Americans. That was also the time when immigration to the United States was high and unrestricted. Theodore Roosevelt and Oliver Wendell Holmes, Jr., flirted with the eugenics movement—Holmes endorsed government sterilization in a Supreme Court decision, with the memorable phrase "three generations of imbeciles are enough." One of the Carnegie philanthropies funded a "Eugenics Record Office" on Long Island. Edward L. Thorndike, the influential educator and testing pioneer, was a eugenicist. Eugenics was a small, rare point of overlap between a corner of the Episcopacy, which had trouble seeing America's new immigrants as fully capable, and a corner of social science.

During the First World War the IQ-testing cause took a great leap forward when Robert Yerkes, a Harvard professor, persuaded the Army to let him administer IQ tests to nearly two million recruits, partly as a way of choosing officer candidates and partly to help the IQ movement build up a record of statistical evidence. This was the first large-scale administration of a mental test in history. Yerkes, his chief assistants, and the literature they produced analyzing the results of the Army tests all had a strong eugenicist cast. Walter Lippmann, the country's most brilliant young political writer and the rare Establishment figure of the day who strongly opposed eugenics and IQ testing, called Yerkes and his colleagues "the Psychological Battalion of Death."

The idea of the IQ testers was not to reform education, especially higher education, so much as to reserve it for highly intelligent people, as indicated by IQ scores, lest their talents be wasted. Society should be classified according to brainpower, and the brainiest people should be its leaders.

Curiously, all three camps—the progressives, the standards imposers, and the IQ testers—had, for all their differences, one thing in common: at a time when dramatically fewer Americans than now were being educated in high school or college, none of them championed the expansion of education. For the IQ testers, selection of the intelligent few was the overriding goal. For the standards imposers like Learned and Wood, schools and colleges seemed to be scandalously overpopulated with students who had no interest in or capability for learning. Even the liberal progressive education camp was focused much more on reforming a handful of high schools across the country, most of them private day schools for the rich whose students went on to Ivy League colleges, than on bringing the benefits of progressive education to all Americans.

The fourth camp, the education expanders, was only faintly visible to people in the Harvard-Carnegie orbit, because it was headquartered off in the faraway mists of the Midwest. Every so often George Zook, the head of the American Council on Education, the trade association dominated by the big public universities, would issue a thunderous, clumsy call upon the nation to send more of its young people to college. From the point of view of Ivy League figures like Chauncey, Conant, and William Learned, such statements were like heavy shells lobbed far past the heart of the battle. The expansionism of the state universities was eternal, and it was irrelevant to what they thought were the urgent issues at hand.

The most interesting man in the education-expansion camp was E. F. Lindquist, a psychology professor at the University of Iowa. In 1929, Lindquist started a program called the Iowa Academic Meet, colloquially known as the Brain Derby, which was a statewide academic competition meant to confer upon good students some small portion of the prestige that college athletes had. Lindquist was really up to something more important, though. Within a year, the Iowa Academic Meet was only the most public aspect of a much bigger operation called the Iowa Every-Pupil Testing Program, under which all public-school students in the state were given achievement tests that Lindquist and his staff devised. Within a few years, other states in the Midwest were adopting the Iowa tests. (Today they're a familiar nationwide institution.)

These tests were part of a broad, optimistic, democratic view of education. Their purpose was similar to Alfred Binet's when he devised the IQ test: to let teachers know which students needed special attention. Lindquist wanted to educate more students, not fewer, and to use tests to further the goal. In 1936, in his contribution to a report on testing, he heatedly condemned the use of tests to select gifted students or to impose uniform standards on the schools, because that would be "excellent and beneficial for one particular type of boy and girl and young man and young woman, namely, those of superior bookish ability . . . those same standards, because of their uniformity and rigidity, are thwarting and damaging to all other kinds and degrees of capacity." Between high school and college, he wrote in a late-in-life memoir, the need was "not for a test that would skim the cream off the top of a distribution of applicants, but rather for one that would help screen out the few who might least profit from college opportunities." State schools like the University of Iowa ought to be essentially free, open-admission institutions. And their professors ought to be primarily teachers, not scholarly researchers.

For the education expanders, the governing fable was that of the ugly duckling: schools should be used to transform unlettered Americans, as many as possible, into people who read and thought and had training and skills and therefore who could get on in the world more successfully. They didn't believe that education should be used to generate a national elite, so the question of how to define the elite didn't matter to them. The three other camps, for all their heartfelt differences, were working on variants of the fable of Cinderella. The educational system would fit glass slippers on the feet of a lucky few, who would be whisked away to college and trained to lead American society; the dispute among them was over the design of the slipper.

The reason the competition among the four camps mattered so much was that in the coming years American education, which had been overwhelmingly local, was going to become more national; otherwise there could be no national labor market and the economy couldn't modernize. There had to be an overall governing principle. So whoever won would score a highly consequential victory—would get to configure the basic form that life took for most Americans for the rest of the twentieth century. As out-of-public-view as the competition was, the stakes were very high, including the stakes for the public. It was like a slow-motion, invisible Constitutional Convention whose result would determine the American social structure.

Henry Chauncey, a vigorous, unsophisticated young man in his twenties, was not well versed in these arguments about the future of education in America. He didn't have a strong opinion as to which of the four camps was right. What he believed in was testing. He thought the technique itself was so revolutionary, so automatically good, as to make the question of what it was used for a minor one. That could be worked out later! What mattered was to expand testing as much as possible. In the mind of Henry Chauncey, scientific progress, of which the development of mental testing was a prime example, far outranked the byplay of ideas about society. He didn't see that in choosing a particular type of test, one would perforce also be choosing a social vision about what the United States would be like. To Chauncey, if it was a test, it was beneficial to mankind.

So, from Chauncey's point of view, what was most important about the competition over the future of American education was not the immense differences among the various camps, but the one thing they all had in common: they all involved more testing.

3
Native Intelligence

Just after the beginning of the 1933–34 academic year, his first as president of Harvard, James Bryant Conant invited Henry Chauncey and another young assistant dean, Wilbur J. Bender, to lunch at his presidential residence. He told them he needed their help in setting up a new scholarship program.

Unlike Chauncey, Conant had a precise idea about the form he wanted education to take—at least at Harvard, and soon enough in the whole country. Although Harvard didn't look to outside appearances like an institution in crisis, Conant was quite unhappy about the state it was in.

Most of the students at Harvard College came from New England or New York and were graduates of private schools. As a group, these young men were not notably studious. Paying students were in short supply during the Depression, and to be admitted was not much of a feat if you had the money and the right background (unless you were Jewish, that is—all of the most prestigious private universities in America maintained informal but strict ceilings on the number of Jews they would admit, Harvard being unusual only in President Lowell's willingness to announce publicly that this was his policy). Rich young men at Harvard conducted a life barely recognizable today as that of college students. At a time when a quarter of the American workforce was unemployed and desperate, they lived in private apartments, attended by butlers and maids, in a district called the Gold Coast, went to debutante balls in Boston, did not customarily attend classes, and enrolled briefly in special tutoring schools at the end of each semester so they would be able to pass their exams.

Harvard did offer some scholarships to students from modest

backgrounds, but Conant thought they were regarded by the nonscholarship students as "badges of poverty" rather than of honor. The scholarships were conditional both on financial need and on maintaining a certain academic average. A scholarship student whose grades fell had to leave Harvard. Room and board weren't included, which meant that many of the students on scholarship came from Boston and lived at home with their parents, or supported themselves by waiting on the more fortunate students in the dining halls.

Conant told Chauncey and Bender that he wanted to create a new kind of scholarship at Harvard, a full four-year grant that would cover tuition, room, and board, with minimal conditions and no work requirements. The recipients would be indistinguishable from other Harvard students—or, if they were distinguishable, they would occupy a higher place than the rest, not a lower one. You wouldn't have to be from a poor family to get one of the scholarships. It would be an honor based solely on academic promise. A rich recipient would be declared a winner and given no money.

It's worth spending a moment soaking in the newness, strangeness, even borderline impracticability of Conant's idea. Harvard and other American colleges did not operate on the principle that an undergraduate's high academic performance equaled valor. Students who were extremely studious were considered a little peculiar—they were anything but the great gods of campus life. And even if you did want to change the ethos dramatically and begin to seek out and reward academically outstanding young men, how would you do it? How could you tell which high-school seniors, in all the vastness of public education in the United States, which was under the purview of 15,000 local school boards each free to set its own standards, were the most likely to perform brilliantly at Harvard?

The job that Conant gave to Chauncey and Bender was to figure out a way to select public-school students, initially just from the Midwest, soon from all over the country, for his new scholarship program. This was one of those path-setting moments in which small decisions are made from which great consequences later flow. The means of selection that Chauncey and Bender settled upon would become not just a way of handing out a few scholarships to Harvard, but the basic mechanism for sorting the American population.

To the extent that Harvard already had an admissions screening device, it was a weeklong battery of essay examinations in various subjects, called the "college boards." These exams were offered by the College Entrance Examination Board, a tweedy, clubby association of a few dozen private schools and colleges that had been founded in 1900 to perfect the close fit between New England boarding schools and Ivy League colleges. The boarding schools wanted a uniform admissions test that all the colleges would accept, and the colleges wanted to impose some curricular order on the schools so their students would arrive reliably prepared.

From Conant's point of view, the problem with the college boards was that they were so much a test of mastery of the boarding-school curriculum that they couldn't be used to size up the Midwestern public-school boys he wanted to bring to Harvard. Even getting to a place where the test was administered would be impracticable for the kind of bright lad from modest circumstances whom Conant had in mind. All through the 1930s, Harvard's way of working around the limitations of the college boards was to admit automatically anybody who came from the South or the West and was in the top seventh of his high-school class. Some of these men did well and some of them didn't; Conant wanted to be sure that his new scholarship boys did very well. So Chauncey and Bender had to find a new admissions test.

In 1933 testing was still so new that it was possible for two novices in the field to meet everybody who mattered and to learn everything that was known in the space of just a few weeks. Before the year had come to an end, Chauncey and Bender had traveled to Princeton and met Carl Campbell Brigham, a psychology professor there and author of the Scholastic Aptitude Test.

Brigham was a handsome, nattily dressed, hot-tempered man who had drunk his way through Princeton as an undergraduate, class of '12, and then, to the great surprise of his friends, become a social scientist, an expert in the infant field of intelligence testing. During the First World War, Brigham worked as an assistant to Robert Yerkes, administering the Army IQ tests. When the war ended he settled into teaching at Princeton and worked up a book based on the findings of the Army tests.

Like so many IQ testers, Brigham was an ardent eugenicist, a warm friend not just of like-minded academic colleagues but also of the most prominent self-appointed race theorists of the day, men like Madison Grant (author of *Decline of the Great Race*) and Charles W. Gould (author of *America: A Family Matter*), who felt the country was at the brink of disaster because of immigrant dilution of the "native stocks." Brigham thought the results of the Army tests offered strong support to the eugenics movement. In 1922, just after he had finished his book, correctly anticipating that he would be attacked by liberals, he wrote to Yerkes: "I am not afraid to say anything that is true, no matter how ugly the facts may be, and am perfectly willing to stake whatever position I have on the outcome. If the 'Conclusions' are published approximately as they stand, I shall invest everything that I can scrape together on short-term life insurance in the hope of leaving an estate."

Brigham's book, *A Study of American Intelligence*, trafficked in the prevailing eugenicist theory of the day, which held that there were three distinct white races in Europe—in descending order of intelligence, Nordic, Alpine, and Mediterranean—and that the United States had been initially and successfully populated by the highest but was now being filled up with the lowest. Mediterraneans were not only immigrating but also reproducing in alarming numbers. On the Army IQ tests, Nordics scored higher than Alpines, who scored higher than Mediterraneans. The test results as a whole were like a photograph of American culture, so faithfully did they reproduce the social order. Officers scored higher than enlisted men, the native-born scored higher than the foreign-born, less recent immigrants scored higher than more recent immigrants, and whites scored higher than Negroes. There were ironclad natural laws at work here, Brigham felt, and he warned that wishful thinkers who pretended otherwise were deluding themselves—writing, for example: "Our figures, then, would rather tend to disprove the popular belief that the Jew is highly intelligent." Brigham's stern conclusion was this: "American intelligence is declining, and will proceed with an accelerating rate as the racial admixture becomes more and more extensive. . . . These are the plain, if somewhat ugly, facts that our study shows."

During the years after the war, Brigham and other pioneer intelligence testers turned their attention to schools—after the armed forces, the institutions that had to evaluate and process large numbers of people most quickly, and therefore fertile ground for testing. Lewis Terman devised a "National Intelligence Test" for elementary-school students that, thanks to energetic promotion by a commercial test publisher, had more than half a million takers a year during the 1920s. E. L. Thorndike, at Columbia, constructed an intelligence test for students there, which the University of Pennsylvania also adopted. Yale also administered intelligence tests to students—as an experiment, not for admissions purposes—during the early 1920s. Brigham, too, focused on colleges and universities. He administered a version of the Army test to Princeton freshmen, and to applicants for admission to Cooper Union, an all-scholarship technical college in New York City.

In all these cases the tests were, essentially, IQ tests: the questions had multiple-choice answers from which the student had to choose, and, like the Army test, they relied heavily on vocabulary questions. The main difference was that they were made more difficult. Brigham had found that Princeton students, even in those days of easy admissions and selection primarily on "character" rather than academic ability, scored higher than any other identifiable group on the Army test, which, he wrote a colleague in 1926, "breaks down as a finely differentiating measure at the upper end of the scale." He went to work on upgrading the questions, and by 1926 the Army test had metamorphosed into the SAT.

If you took an early version of the SAT, you would encounter some questions involving mathematical calculations and some involving the identification of shapes and facial expressions—but the bulk of the test was devoted to word familiarity, the eternal staple of intelligence testing. The SAT has changed remarkably little over the years; although the questions on the original version had a boarding-school, English-lit veneer that is gone now, the basic format will be familiar to the many millions of Americans who have taken the test. A few samples from the original version convey the SAT's inimitable way of being simple and confusing at the same time, its tendency to induce uncontrollable, anxious second-guessing on the part of the taker:

Pick out the antonyms from among these four words:
                obdurate   spurious   ductile   recondite

Say which word, or both or neither, has the same meaning as the first word:
                impregnable   terile   vacuous
                nominal   exorbitant   didactic

Find the wrong word and change it to the right word in the following passage:

In the citron wing of the pale butterfly, with its dainty spots of orange, he sees beyond him the stately halls of fair gold, with their slender saffron pillars, and is taught how the delicate drawing high upon the walls shall be traced in tender tones of orpiment, and repeated by the base in notes of graver hue.

Someone who had never heard of such tests and was given one out of the blue might find incredible the proposition that three hours of this kind of questioning could bring to light the dimensions of the mind, and that a total of answers gotten right and wrong could be used to decide what place in society a person should occupy. But to test-makers, the SAT and tests like it had the aura of a great breakthrough.

Testers are looking for two main qualities in a test, which they call reliability and validity. Reliability is demonstrated by the similarity of a person's scores on different administrations of the same test. Tests that require a student to write essays (rather than to choose among a number of printed possible answers), like the college boards, are highly suceptible to the subjective judgment of the grader and to the mood of the taker on the day of the test, so they have low reliability. Multiple-choice, objectively scored tests like the SAT produce much higher reliability.

Validity is shown in a test's ability to predict some future outcome. In the case of tests for high-school seniors, the outcome would be grades in the first year of college. In those early days of scattered results and experiments conducted by proselytizers for testing, some of the validity figures for intelligence tests being bandied about were almost incredibly high. On a scale of .00 (no relationship between test scores and first-semester grades) to 1.00 (complete congruence of the two), intelligence tests were said to produce validities of .60, while the college boards were down in the .20 range. Carl Brigham was one of the more restrained and careful voices, but he was still an enthusiast. In 1924 he acknowledged that in his experiments, the validity of intelligence tests wasn't appreciably higher than that of the college boards, but he explained this away by saying that his subjects—high-living, raccoon-coated Prohibition-era Princeton and Yale students—had so many "social distractions" that they didn't "work to their full capacity" like Thorndike's more sober test subjects at Columbia.

Brigham had good contacts at the Army, because of his war experience, and at the College Board, because of its involvement in Princeton admissions. So he was able to arrange for formal administrations of the SAT soon after its metamorphosis from the Army intelligence test was completed. The official date of the introduction of the SAT into American life is June 23, 1926. Under the auspices of the College Board, 8,040 high-school students, mostly in the Northeast, took the test that day and had their scores reported to the colleges they wanted to attend. The Army at the same time decided to let Brigham use the SAT to test applicants to West Point, and in 1930 the Navy followed its lead and had Brigham test Annapolis applicants. Applicants to Yale and Princeton who took the college boards also took the SAT, and, more sporadically, some applicants to Harvard took it. The Yale Law School adapted the SAT into a test for its applicants. In all these cases, the SAT was being used not to decide who was admitted, but to build up a validity record by correlating the scores with the takers' freshman grades. By the time Henry Chauncey and Wilbur Bender met him in 1933, Brigham had data to support the idea that the SAT could predict academic performance.

At the same time that he was promoting the SAT to universities, Brigham was undergoing a momentous intellectual change. He had come to the view that the central tenet held by IQ testers, including, previously, himself—that the test measured a biologically grounded, genetically inherited quality that was tied to ethnicity—was false.

In 1927, only a year after the unveiling of the SAT, Lewis Terman, the giant of American intelligence testing, invited Brigham to speak at a conference he was putting on in Boston. Brigham declined, making what would become a preoccupying point for him: that most of the experimental work on IQ was being done by true believers who began by announcing their conclusions (IQ tests were supremely reliable and valid, so much so as to represent one of the great scientific advances in history), and then conducted their studies in an atmosphere of wild unobjectivity. In 1928 Brigham appeared before a meeting of eugenicists and publicly recanted his earlier views.

Soon Brigham had come to the point of specifically renouncing his best-known book, *A Study of American Intelligence*. In 1930 he published a formal retraction, calling it "pretentious" and "without foundation." His next book, published in 1932, was titled, pointedly, *A Study of Error*. He also began trying to put some distance between the SAT and IQ testing. At the outset the SAT score had been a single number, like the intelligence quotient, and Brigham had published a crude scale for converting it to an IQ score. He was persuaded by his assistant, however, to divide the SAT score into two parts, one for verbal and one for mathematical ability, and to drop the conversion scale.

Brigham thought that the enthusiasm of the leaders of the IQ-testing movement had led them to make an unwarranted and dangerous leap. They assumed that because they could produce a reliable test result, what the test measured must be a biological trait of the brain, although there was no physical evidence for the truth of this belief. "The more I work in this field, the more I am convinced that psychologists have sinned greatly in sliding easily from the name of the test to the function or trait measured," he wrote in 1929 to Charles Davenport, head of the Eugenics Record Office and an old friend, who had sent him a manuscript on differences in test scores by race. "I feel we should all stop naming tests and saying what they measure . . . if we are to proceed beyond the stage of a psycho-phrenology."

Five years later, in an unpublished manuscript, Brigham put it even more bluntly:

> The test movement came to this country some twenty-five or thirty years ago accompanied by one of the most glorious fallacies in the history of science, namely, that the tests measured *native intelligence* purely and simply without regard to training or schooling. I hope nobody believes that now. The test scores very definitely are a composite including schooling, family background, familiarity with English, and everything else, relevant and irrelevant. The *"native intelligence"* hypothesis is dead.

The implication of Brigham's new view was not that testing should be abandoned. He believed in tests as "a ready method of interview" (rather than as "a measure of some mysterious power"), and he kept working on the SAT. Instead, the implication was that brakes ought to be applied to the natural enthusiasms of psychometricians who, in Brigham's experience, could be counted on always to claim their tests were measuring an essential, innate human quality, always to want to put tests into wide use prematurely, and always to overstate their results. "Practice has always outrun theory," Brigham wrote, " . . . this is a new field and . . . very little has been done which is right. As new information comes in and new methods are developed, practically everything that has gone before seems full of errors." It was one thing for us to have ginned up a massive testing operation for the Army during wartime—"emergencies demand the sacrifice of individual ambitions"— and quite another to try to replicate it during peacetime for education. "A college being a humanitarian institution cannot afford to make mistakes against the individual," Brigham wrote.

But at the same time that the SAT's inventor was developing powerful doubts about it, machinery for making the use of testing widespread, even universal, was being put into place. The ironic result was that Carl Brigham's test was hitched to a test promotion and administration structure he disapproved of, built by people he had no use for.

It is easy to imagine who, in Brigham's mind, would have personified the dangers of overenthusiasm for testing: among the older generation Lewis Terman and Edward Thorndike and, among the younger, William Learned and Ben Wood, who were conducting the Pennsylvania Study for the Carnegie Foundation. Henry Chauncey knew Learned, of course, from having heard him lecture in 1932, and he and Bill Bender met Wood soon after

being assigned by Conant to investigate testing. In the Learned-Wood partnership, Wood was the technical expert. During the early 1930s, he and
Brigham were figures of equivalent eminence in testing, and were bitter professional enemies.

"In all too many of the social science fields there is a large proportion of
the slightly maladjusted," Henry Chauncey once wrote in his diary. Ben Wood
was a case in point. The eleventh of thirteen children, Wood had been raised
on the arid Texas-Mexico border, where his parents had moved, for the dry
air, after his mother had contracted tuberculosis. He spent the first six months
of his life in, as he put it, "a marsupial sanctuary inside my mother's clothing," and his early childhood living in a supposedly disease-proof six-by-six-
foot cage set on stilts out in the desert. When he was a young boy, a servant
whom he had asked for a glass of water mistakenly gave him kerosene instead,
and the result of his drinking it was that he was unable to speak normally. In
addition he was subjected to regular beatings by his father and his brothers.

Thickly bespectacled, eccentric, and opinionated, the adult Wood
believed that testing would purge the educational system of its pervasive
idiocy, which he had first encountered when he enrolled as a freshman at the
University of Texas and was required to take remedial Spanish even though
it was his first spoken language. After Texas, Wood joined the Army, where,
like Brigham, he helped to administer IQ tests to recruits. Through that work
he encountered Edward Thorndike, and after the war he went to graduate
school at Columbia as Thorndike's student. Wood soon took Thorndike's
place as the leading promoter of standardized educational testing.

Wood was, if anything, even more energetic and enthusiastic than the
Chief (as he called Thorndike), though his main passion was achievement
testing rather than IQ testing—testing, that is, of mastery of a body of
knowledge rather than of innate mental ability. Thorndike, like most early
IQ theorists beginning with Galton, left a record of published opinion about
the inherent intellectual abilities of the races and the need for selective
breeding. Wood did not. During the 1920s Wood was enormously influential. He persuaded the New York State Regents to put him in charge of constructing objective exams for high-school students in the state; and he
became William Learned's partner in conducting the Carnegie Foundation
study of education in Pennsylvania; and he founded the Cooperative Test
Service, which sold tests to elementary schools and colleges; and he began to
work with Thomas Watson, the founder of IBM, to develop a machine that
could score thousands or even millions of tests in the mass administrations
that were sure to come. (A few years later, in 1935, Wood also created the
Graduate Record Examination for the Carnegie Foundation.)

What most annoyed Wood about American education was that it was illogical and disorganized. There was no real system to prepare students for college. The colleges themselves were run for the benefit of the professors, who taught whatever they wanted to and declared students to be educated merely because they had signed up for and passed a certain number of courses. Even so, most students who entered college didn't graduate. And of the college students who did finish, the very worst went on to become teachers. (Despite the fulfillment of Wood's fondest dreams about the institution of mass testing, all of this is still true.) Wood wanted to establish what he called "self-education," a system by which students would move through schools on the basis of their own objectively demonstrated achievement, without reference to such foolishness as credit-hours and semesters.

Wood was most definitely not an educational expansionist. At a time when only 6 or 7 percent of American eighteen-to-twenty-four-year-olds were enrolled in institutions of higher learning (as against today's 65 percent), Wood believed that a third of the college population didn't belong there; indeed, he thought that the high-school population could use some weeding out, too, and that the country was crazy to try to educate everyone, even idiots and imbeciles, through age eighteen. Wood wanted to see new people, talented and obscure as he had been, provided with higher education, but only in limited numbers. In 1933 he wrote to his dean at Columbia, Herbert Hawkes:

> Another point on which I think we should force the radicals down to brass tacks is their attitude regarding the fact of individual differences. . . . Do they really believe that more than twenty per cent if that many of the high school population has the basic ability to learn principles and apply them to new problems? . . . The lunatics must answer these questions or clear out.

What Wood had in mind was the institution of a great national testing apparatus that would do two things: select the very best students for advanced education; and take away the absolute arbitrary power of teachers by creating a way for students to show they had mastered a subject.

Wood and other promoters of testing knew that even if they conquered all the technical problems of test construction, and even if they overcame all the bureaucratic opposition to testing, they still had a great obstacle standing between them and their plans. That was the administrative difficulty of testing large numbers of people. One advantage of a multiple-choice test was that a roomful of people could take it simultaneously—but then it still had to be scored by hand, one by one, by error-prone humans. As the Pennsylvania Study drew to a close, though, a long-held idea of Wood's, that thousands or even millions of tests might be scored instantly by machine, was finally coming true, thanks to the work of an obscure garage inventor.

In 1931 a young high-school science teacher named Reynold B. Johnson in the town of Ironwood, Michigan, began experimenting with an electrical machine that could grade tests. He got a prototype working, barely, and the local newspaper did a story about him that was picked up by the Associated Press and attracted attention all over the country. As a result, he gave the machine a name, the Markograph, and had an advertisement made up showing it being caressed by a pretty girl.

While in Minneapolis exhibiting the Markograph at the National Educational Association convention, Johnson was struck by an inspiration. As a farm boy in Minnesota, he had tormented his older sisters' dates by scratching pencil marks on the outside of the spark plugs on their Model-T Fords. Because lead conducts electricity, the pencil marks drew the sparks away from the spark plugs when they tried to start their cars and the engine couldn't ignite, ha-ha. Why not use the same principle in a test-scoring machine? If students were made to mark their answers in pencil on a separate sheet, then the sheets could be fed into a machine that could electrically sense whether the answers were in the right spaces.

Johnson went right to work on a new machine that could detect pencil marks. By the end of the summer of 1933, he had a working model. Meanwhile, because of the Depression, he was laid off by the school in Ironwood. Newly married, he tried to support himself as a substitute teacher and by selling duplicating machines on the road. He was beginning to think he'd better find something else to do with his life when out of the blue a telegram arrived from an executive at IBM who had seen one of Johnson's Markograph-and-girl publicity shots and wanted him to bring the latest version of the machine to New York. Johnson leaped at the offer.

There was one last hitch. IBM had been working on a test-scoring machine since 1928, at the suggestion of Ben Wood, with no success. But the team doing the work was convinced it was on the verge of a breakthrough. Its goal was to buy and shelve Johnson's machine and then keep going with its own. Johnson was so desperate for money that selling his machine to IBM was fine with him, especially if IBM also gave him a job. In July 1934 he sold IBM the rights to his machine for $15,000. In August, Wood, who had met Johnson on his trip to New York, intervened, writing a personal letter to the head of IBM, Thomas Watson, at his summer estate in Maine to advise him that his underlings were about to deep-six Johnson's machine and prevent him from joining the IBM staff, too. Watson stepped in, Johnson was hired, and in 1936 an IBM machine descended from the Markograph was used to score tests for the New York State Regents and the Providence, Rhode Island, public schools. Next Wood used the machine to score the test results in his Pennsylvania Study, so as to demonstrate that the mass testing he had been calling for was now technically possible.

Chauncey and Bender's assignment, to find a way to select the winners of Harvard's new scholarships, came down to a decision about which of the two testing figures they would throw in their lot with, Ben Wood or Carl Brigham. They picked Brigham and the SAT. For Chauncey, Brigham was the comfortable choice—he was the official testing expert of the College Board, which had an apparatus for administering tests, and Harvard was the Board's most influential member—but there was a more important reason for using the SAT. Ben Wood was an achievement tester, and President Conant was adamantly opposed to using achievement tests in his scholarship program. He wanted to use aptitude tests—meaning, really, IQ tests. Chauncey had learned that whenever he discussed a test with Conant, Conant would ask him whether it measured aptitude or achievement, and if the answer was achievement, Conant wasn't interested. Even in the case of the SAT, Chauncey had to allay Conant's suspicion that it might be a wolf in sheep's clothing, an achievement test that merely called itself an aptitude test.

    What Conant didn't like about achievement tests was that they favored rich boys whose parents could buy them top-flight high-school instruction. He wanted to award his scholarships to very bright boys from every corner of the social structure—little Conants. Although he was never a eugenicist or a public crusader for IQ testing, Conant believed in the native intelligence hypothesis that Carl Brigham was now rejecting. If you were going to test, why not test for the key quality? So, although Chauncey didn't care to choose sides in the debate about the future of American education, Conant had already made his choice. He was in the intelligence testing camp, and, as events began rapidly unfolding, that made a great deal of difference to the future shape of American life.

    In January 1934, Conant instructed Chauncey and Bender to use the SAT, in addition to transcripts and recommendations, to select ten young men from the Midwest (the possibility of selecting women, who would enroll in Harvard's sister college, Radcliffe, apparently not occurring to any of them) for scholarships to attend Harvard that fall.

Chauncey was good at organizing things. With Bender he devised application forms, visited public high schools all over the Midwest, and did anoint ten Harvard National Scholars for the class of 1938. At their graduation four years later, eight of the ten were elected to Phi Beta Kappa. In 1935 and 1936 Chauncey and Bender repeated the exercise—finding, for example, a future Nobel Prize winner in economics, James Tobin, who was the son of the sports information director at the University of Illinois and a senior at Champaign High School.

The program had an effect far beyond just the addition of ten students a year to the Harvard student body. Casting the net for the Harvard National Scholarships brought in many more students than just the winners, which helped make Harvard a more national university. More important, the program enabled Conant to begin undermining the view of what it meant to be a "college man" that had prevailed in earlier decades. What most Harvard students thought of academic accomplishment was on display in a series of articles on Conant's scholarship program that appeared in *The Harvard Crimson* in 1935: CONANT PRIZE SCHOLARS NOT BOOK WORMS RUNNING STRAIGHT A'S IN MOST OF COURSES—INTERESTED IN OUTSIDE ACTIVITIES. The headline must surely have failed to reassure precisely because it was trying so hard to do so.

After three successful rounds of scholarships, Henry Chauncey decided to take a further step and enlist the other Ivy League schools in a system to make multiple-choice mental tests the admissions device for all scholarship students. Chauncey secured the participation of Princeton, through Carl Brigham; Columbia, through Ben Wood; and Yale, through Albert "Baldy" Crawford, a young dean there who was a testing enthusiast and protégé of Brigham's. (Such minor figures could get their colleges to join because, to university presidents other than Conant, this looked like a minor matter. It involved only a small group: scholarship students. Only in hindsight does it signal a wholesale change in the tenor of the institutions.) Wood agreed to devise a battery of achievement tests in various subjects—multiple-choice tests, not essay examinations like the college boards—that high-school students could take in the afternoon, having taken the SAT in the morning. Each applicant would pay ten dollars to take the tests, so the program would not be expensive for the colleges. On April 24, 1937, the Scholarship Examinations were administered at 150 sites all over the country to 2,005 high-school seniors.

And Conant kept pressing, too. After these Scholarship Examinations had gone off successfully, he took the much more dramatic step of proposing publicly that a new national testing agency be created to operate all the leading standardized educational tests: Brigham's SAT, all the tests Ben Wood had developed, and whatever other worthwhile tests existed. The agency would become the home of research on and development of future tests. Wood had been pushing this idea for years, but Conant's imprimatur gave it real force. The new agency would, obviously, have the potential to reach past the confines of the Ivy League. It would form at least the embryo of a national personnel system, and it could affect exponentially more lives than those of a few thousand aspiring Ivy League scholarship students. The timing seemed propitious, besides, for the long-gestating Pennsylvania Study by Learned and Wood, a clarion call for more testing, was about to be published.

But a serious obstacle soon materialized. Carl Brigham was opposed to the new testing agency.

In December 1937, in an educational journal called *School and Society*, an article by Brigham appeared in which he lengthily and wittily complained about its potential dangers ("it is probably simpler to teach cultured men testing than to give testers culture"). What worried him most, because of his long experience with the incaution of testers (including himself, in his younger days), was that any organization that owned the rights to a particular test would inevitably become more interested in promoting it than in honestly researching its effectiveness.

Just after the article came out, William Learned took Brigham to lunch to try to bring him around. Brigham didn't think much of Learned to begin with, had been growing irritable owing to high blood pressure, and had recently had a heart attack. Evidently the lunch did not go well. On January 3, 1938, Brigham wrote what was, given the politesse that then prevailed in organizational life, an amazingly ill-tempered five-page single-spaced letter to Conant opposing the idea of a merger of all the testers. He called the old Army IQ test "atrocious" and the Pennsylvania Study "propaganda," and—his key point—warned that "the very creation of powerful machinery to do more widely those things that are now being done badly will stifle research, discourage new developments, and establish existing methods, and even existing tests, as the correct ones."

He went on:

> If the unhappy day ever comes when teachers point their students toward these newer examinations, and the present weak and restricted procedures get a grip on education, then we may look for the inevitable distortion of education in terms of tests. And that means that mathematics will continue to be completely departmentalized and broken into

disintegrated bits, that the sciences will become highly verbalized and that computation, manipulation and thinking in terms other than verbal will be minimized, that languages will be taught for linguistic skills only without reference to literary values, that English will be taught for reading alone, and that practice and drill in the writing of English will disappear.

A month later, Brigham wrote Conant again to apologize for his outburst: "The bitterness and unjustice of my personal remarks were totally unwarranted and entirely foreign to my make-up. I should have had sufficient insight to recognize my own unbalanced state, but these conditions sneak up on one so gradually that correct insight at the time is apparently impossible to achieve." Still, Brigham remained opposed to the new testing agency, and his opposition was enough to keep it from being created.

So the testing field remained scattered, and the SAT remained an Ivy League device used mainly for testing scholarship applicants. At its first administration, in 1926, there had been 8,026 takers; at the eleventh administration, in 1936, there were 9,437. With the advent of the Scholarship Examinations the number began to grow, but slowly. When the United States entered the Second World War, it was still less than 20,000 a year.

Carl Brigham's health continued to deteriorate. On January 24, 1943, at the age of fifty-two, he died. The roadblock was removed.

4 The Natural Aristocracy

If it seems, by today's standards, unusually ambitious for James Bryant Conant, president of Harvard, to have taken it upon himself to set scholarship policy for the whole Ivy League—well, Conant was soon setting his sights much, much higher than that. Within a few months of the first administration of the Scholarship Examinations, Conant had written a highly prescriptive article called "The Future of Our Higher Education," which was published in a national magazine. The grand title actually understates the article's breadth, for Conant had strong opinions about elementary and secondary education, too. And not long after that, Conant began producing blueprints for a sweeping remaking of the basic structure of American society. For someone with theories about the ideal shape of the world, Conant had an unusual degree of institutional power; and for someone with institutional power, he had an unusual degree of intellectual reach. His power and his reach together allowed him to have an influence far beyond what a private citizen can usually achieve.

By the late 1930s Conant had found a kind of sacred text containing an idea, from an impeccable source, about what the United States should be, and he liked to think of himself as being luckily situated to put it into effect. It was a letter that Thomas Jefferson wrote to John Adams in 1813, when they were both ex-Presidents. The letter is long and carefully thought through, but in Jefferson's writing it is a freestanding document, an isolated statement of a late-in-life idea; it doesn't represent the centerpiece of his thinking. The person for whom it was a centerpiece was Conant. He was using Jefferson for justification as much as for inspiration.

Jefferson wrote to Adams:

I agree with you that there is a natural aristocracy among men. The grounds of this are virtue and talents. . . . The natural aristocracy I consider as the most precious gift of nature for the instruction, the trusts, and the government of society. . . . May we not even say that that form of government is the best which provides the most effectually for a pure selection of these natural aristoi into the offices of government?

He went on to describe, ruefully, a failed attempt he had made long before to persuade the Virginia legislature to establish a system of universal public education. He presented this as a scouting operation for natural aristocrats, who would be picked through a series of educational winnowings and sent on to the University of Virginia. "Worth and genius would thus have been sought out from every condition of life, and compleatly prepared by education for defeating the competition of wealth and birth for public trusts," Jefferson wrote.

Imagine how thrilling this letter must have been for Conant when he came across it! What Jefferson called "an artificial aristocracy founded on wealth and birth" was in control of the United States, as far as Conant could tell from his perch at Harvard. But now, finally, 125 years after Jefferson's letter, there was the possibility of creating a true natural aristocracy to govern America. The Depression had made it difficult for anybody to argue that the people running the country were doing a perfectly good job, and Franklin Roosevelt had engendered a spirit in which reformist schemes of every kind were being promoted. And by now we had the kind of public-school system Jefferson hadn't been able to put across, through which natural aristocrats might be found. Moreover, science, which Conant believed in no less wholeheartedly than Jefferson, now offered in mental testing a way of selecting the country's deserving new leaders. The SAT, in other words, would finally make possible the creation of a natural aristocracy.

Conant was absolutely clear in his mind about how to set up the system over which the natural aristocrats would reign. Everyone would go to elementary school and high school. Then would come a strict selection. The brightest students would be sent on to college at public expense. Some portion of the rest might go to two-year junior colleges, but Conant insisted that the country should not increase access to four-year colleges. Indeed, the college population ought to be reduced: "there are too many rather than too few students attending the universities of this country." At the very least we should weed out "perhaps one-half" of the people in college, and put "others of more talent in their place." He proudly laid out the story of the Harvard National Scholarships as proof that his plan was practicable.

In other words, Conant was not at that point very interested in the cause of expanding educational opportunity, except for members of a tiny cohort of intellectually gifted men. He had in mind an updated version of Jefferson's unsuccessful proposal for public education in Virginia, which would have given every child three years of free schooling. At the end of that time, Jefferson wrote in *Notes on the State of Virginia*, in every school district "twenty of the best geniuses will be raked from the rubbish annually and be instructed, at the public expense." ("I was never so tactless as to quote these particular words, of course," Conant wrote many years later, after the system he had in mind had been safely set up.) Conant's central cause—or, as he preferred to put it, "Jefferson's ideal"—was creating a new American elite, drawn from every region and background, and disabling the current, suffocatingly narrow one. The new elite's essential quality, the factor that would make its power deserved where the old elite's had been merely inherited, would be brains.

The idea of a nation's being ruled by an elite whose members were selected early in life without reference to their station of birth and then elaborately trained by educators for positions of governance that they would hold for their adult lives (but couldn't hand down automatically to their children) actually long predates Conant and, for that matter, Jefferson.

In *The Republic*, Plato proposed a system in which society would be run by a class of "guardians" who would be taken away from their parents at the age of ten, raised by teachers, and then would become the rulers of the state. That guardians must be drawn from all classes was an essential point for Plato: "a golden parent will sometimes have a silver son, or a silver parent a golden son," he wrote. "If the son of a golden or silver parent has an admixture of brass and iron, then nature orders a transposition of ranks. . . . For an oracle says that when a man of brass or iron guards the state, it will be destroyed." Another point Plato was very clear on was that the guardians would be lifelong government officials, concerned only with the good of the state and indifferent to private wealth. He called this ideal system "aristocracy," meaning, literally, rule by the best.

Until the nineteenth century, the closest thing to a Platonic aristocracy was the mandarin system of Confucian China, under which, beginning in the second century B.C., future high officials were trained in a special national school. Beginning in the sixth century A.D., mandarins were selected by examination. In the late eighteenth century, several European nations developed systems for the selection (without regard to family background) and university training of high-level civil servants, technicians, and military officers. A civil-service system, with hiring by examination, began in the United States in 1883, but, perhaps because American society is more commercial than European society, career government employees and the national elite have always been two separate groups; people with every glittering opportunity before them almost never choose to spend their whole lives as government employees.

That Thomas Jefferson settled upon the phrase "natural aristocracy" in 1813 is evidence that the word "aristocracy" had become slightly, but not wholly, corrupted by that time. Ralph Waldo Emerson, another American prophet whom Conant liked to cite, wrote an essay titled "Aristocracy" in 1848 in which he demonstrated a Jeffersonian comfort with the word, as long as it did not denote inherited privilege: "The existence of an upper class is not injurious, as long as it is dependent on merit." In fact, to Emerson, the ideal society would be the right kind of aristocracy, the Platonic kind—if there were only a good way of determining the membership. Playfully, he expressed the wish that there could be an "anthropometer" to gauge everyone's merit: "I should like to see that appraisal applied to every man, and every man acquainted with the true number and weight of every adult citizen, and that he be placed where he belongs, with so much power confided to him as he would carry and use."

Conant presented himself as the enemy of aristocracy, but that was because the word had come to mean rule by inheritors of wealth—what Plato would have called "oligarchy." Setting up an aristocracy in the Platonic sense of the word was exactly what he had in mind. He had not the slightest doubt that rule by a selected few was the ideal social form, so long as it was the right few, chosen for the proper quality. And he had at his disposal, in the SAT, the anthropometer that Emerson had dreamed of.

Conant's resurrection of Jefferson's idea was so successful, and has by now worked its way so completely into our assumptions about how American society should be organized, that it's hard to imagine that any sensible person could object to it. But the first person to be exposed to it, John Adams, thought it was a terrible idea.

On November 15, 1813, Adams sent off a long, witty, mocking reply to Jefferson's natural aristocracy letter. Adams first pointed out that there are many talents and they are already amply rewarded; Jefferson's idea that there is only one talent that really matters (educational genius) and its holders alone should be put in charge is inflexibly narrow and unrealistic. Then he got to the real issue, which was that a statesman of the young United States shouldn't be holding up any kind of aristocracy as the ideal. What did it matter whether it was chosen fairly or unfairly? Slipping into sarcasm, he wrote:

> Your distinction between natural and artificial aristocracy does not appear to me well founded . . . both artificial aristocracy, and monarchy, and civil, military, political and hierarchical despotism, have all grown out of the natural aristocracy of virtues and talents. We, to be sure, are far remote from this. Many hundred years must roll away before we shall be corrupted. Our pure, virtuous, public spirited federative republic will last for ever, govern the globe and introduce the perfection of man, his perfectibility being already proved by Price, Priestley, Condorcet, Rousseau, Diderot, and Godwin.

Adams ended his discussion, and put Jefferson away, by writing: "Your distinction between the aristoi and the pseudo aristoi will not help the matter. I would trust one as soon as the other with unlimited power."

If Conant was aware of these objections, he wasn't troubled by them. Soon he was taking a further step in his campaign to remake American society into a natural aristocracy. He positioned himself, improbably, as the modern-day champion of opportunity for all Americans, not just the handful who would be picked for the new elite—as the legatee of Andrew Jackson as well as Thomas Jefferson.

During the early 1940s, Conant wrote about half of a book that was never published, titled *What We Are Fighting to Defend*. In it he dramatically (and fatefully) broadened his horizons, from the question of how to identify a few extremely bright students and send them to the best colleges on scholarship, to the question of the future of democracy in America. By this time the war had taken over Conant's life. He was spending most of his time in Washington (he left Harvard in the care of his provost, Paul Buck), where he belonged to a small group of scientists who were advising President Roosevelt on such high-level and secret matters as the development of the atomic bomb. Although Conant thought of himself as analytical rather than emotional, how could anyone in his position not have found his thinking taking an apocalyptic turn?

The main theme of the book was that the United States, historically a classless society, had recently developed a hereditary aristocracy, whose existence put the whole national project into peril. It was essential that we reverse this process, and the only means with which to do the job was public education—"a new type of social instrument whose proper use may be the means of salvation of the classlessness of the nation . . . a means of recapturing social flexibility, a means of approximating more nearly the American ideal."

Conant had not abandoned his earlier ideas about educational selection and sorting, so, in hindsight, the obvious question about the central idea of his unpublished book is: How can you build a classless society through the mechanism of relentlessly classifying the entire population? Conant did think about this. His answer was that the goal of all the testing and selecting he proposed would be simply to direct each person to the most approporate place for service to the nation and full use of individual talents. There would be no connection, he insisted, between educational sorting and the tokens of class that he abhorred, such as money, social superiority, and prestige. He wrote: "We must proceed from the premise that there are no educational privileges, even at the most advanced levels of instruction . . . there should be no hierarchy of educational discipline, no one channel should have a social standing above the other."

Was this touchingly naive, or wilfully naive, or just unpardonably naive? Whichever it was, Conant held roughly the set of views he first set down in *What We Are Fighting to Defend* for the rest of his life, and never imagined that he and Henry Chauncey actually might be creating a new kind of class system even more powerful than the old one. Soon he began unveiling his new vision bit by bit, most notably in a series of three articles for *The Atlantic Monthly*.

In the decades since Conant wrote this material, historians and sociologists have built up a body of statistical research on the issue that preoccupied him, social mobility in the United States. The data don't support Conant's premise that mobility was radically decreasing at mid-century: there was much more class stratification in nineteenth-century America, and less during the 1930s and 1940s, than Conant believed. It's also noteworthy that what to us would seem the most obvious departures from the American democratic ideal during the 1940s—legal segregation in the South, informal segregation elsewhere, and the relegation of women to a secondary position in society—went unmentioned by Conant in his writings during the war. He was intensely focused, to the point of being blindered, on an idea of a class-bound present that was the product of an extreme extrapolation from what he saw at Harvard, and an idea of a classless past that came from an unquestioning acceptance of the views of Frederick Jackson Turner, who had been the dominant American historian at Harvard during Conant's undergraduate days.

Turner was a man with a simple, powerful theory: that the open Western frontier had guaranteed the distinctive quality of American society, opportunity for all. (It's a sign of the quality's distinctiveness that Turner, rather than any of the great European social theorists, seems to have invented the terms "social mobility" and "equal opportunity.") He burst on the scene as an influential figure in 1893, when he seized upon the Census Bureau's declaration in the 1890 census that there was no longer a line beyond which open land was available for settlement. Turner's entire work, therefore, was elegaic. From the beginning, as much as he was glorifying the frontier he was mourning it—and warning of the peril that its disappearance posed to the stability of the United States in the future. "Even in the dull brains of great masses of these unfortunates from southern and eastern Europe the idea of America as the land of freedom and of opportunity to rise, the land of pioneer democratic ideals, has found lodgement," he wrote, displaying the alarm about immigration that was characteristic of leading citizens of the day, "and if it is given time and is not turned into revolutionary lines it will fructify."

Three or four generations of historical revisionism have made Swiss cheese out of Turner's thesis, but Conant believed in it completely. His wartime writings are shot through with quotations from Turner and references to the dire social consequences of the closing of the frontier.

What could replace the frontier? To Turner, and also to Conant, the obvious and only answer was public education. Like the frontier, this distinctive American institution could give every citizen the opportunity to rise in the world.

In one of the *Atlantic* articles, Conant referred casually to "our newly erected system of public education." Indeed, the public school then did still seem like a recent, not yet fully exploited institution. In 1813, Jefferson was complaining to Adams that public education hadn't ever taken root in Virginia. In 1848, Horace Mann, in his famous "Twelfth Annual Report as Secretary of the Massachusetts State Board of Education," pleaded in almost desperate tones with the burghers of the most liberal state in the union to establish public elementary schools; Conant's father was alive then. In 1900, only 6.3 percent of seventeen-year-olds were high-school graduates; when Conant was writing the figure was just reaching 50 percent. As for higher education, what bothered Conant was that its students were selected mainly on their parents' ability to pay for tuition, room, and board. The idea of college as a provider of education and therefore of opportunity regardless of a student's background was a dream, not a reality.

In the new, classless American society Conant hoped for, everyone should start on an equal footing, and the abler graduates would rise to high positions strictly because they deserved to. They should not, however, be able to confer special advantages upon their children; America could use "the powers of government to reorder the 'haves and have-nots' every generation to give flux to our social order." And how would such a society be achieved and managed? Through public education. "Abilities must be assessed, talents must be developed, ambitions guided," Conant wrote. "This is the task for our public schools." And, he might have added, for Henry Chauncey and the SAT.

The last and most impassioned of Conant's *Atlantic* articles was published in May 1943, a few months after Carl Brigham's death. In "Wanted: American Radicals," he invented an alter ego, the American radical, who had views much more extreme than Conant-as-Conant was willing to own up to: he was "a fanatical believer in equality," but, unlike his European (meaning, to Conant, Marxist) counterpart, our radical would strive for "equality of opportunity, not equality of rewards." The American radical's "political ideal" was, of course, Jefferson; Conant used language lifted right out of the natural aristocracy letter (Jefferson: "laid the axe to the root of pseudo-aristocracy"; Conant: "wielding the axe against the root of inherited privilege"). Unless America could find "the equivalent of those magic lands of the old frontier," it might—once the war was over—become vulnerable to the other kind of radicalism, because "there will be many who will become frustrated and embittered."

Conant felt the danger of class stratification so urgently that he called upon the government "to confiscate (by constitutional methods) all property once a generation." That was truly a radical idea, and one that was hardly in the interest of Harvard University, which then as now subsisted on income from an endowment built by contributions from inherited fortunes. (It was no surprise that Conant's article displeased his superiors on the Harvard Corporation.) Indeed, Conant, head of America's leading private university, went so far as to proclaim that the American radical "will be little concerned with the future of private education."

Conant's central notion had not changed in the decade he had been president of Harvard. He wanted to unseat the Episcopacy and replace it with a new elite chosen democratically on the basis of its scholastic brilliance, as revealed by scores on mental tests. What had changed was the breadth of his rhetoric and the reach of the system he believed should be created. Now, he thought, education should be not just an elite-selector but also the official repository of opportunity in America. That was a new idea, not just for Conant but also for the country.

Plato's guardians, the Chinese mandarins, Jefferson's natural aristocrats, and Conant's new SAT elite all had in common that they were supposed to devote their lives to public service and be unconcerned with financial gain. Conant once wrote, by way of arguing for a program of government scholarships for his late-twentieth-century natural aristocracy, that "the taxpayer has a duty to supply the talented with the education necessary for the development of that talent. Why? Because such educated talent will later serve the taxpayer by serving the entire nation." As Conant originally conceived it, the new elite would be a governing class, like the people chosen by the examination systems of France or China. The SAT was not meant to be what it is almost universally taken to be today, a means of deciding who would reap America's rich material rewards. That was a separate topic, and one that interested Conant very little.

Traditionally, opportunity in America, that distinctive national preoccupation, came to people in an informal, unorganized way, and certainly outside school and college. College was assumed to be for privileged people who had no interest in rising in the business world, or for people training for one of the prestigious but then not very remunerative professions—law, medicine, the church, diplomacy, or the armed forces. Conversely, worldly success was assumed not to require educational credentials. "The first thing that strikes one in the United States is the innumerable crowd of those striving to escape from their original social condition," Tocqueville wrote. "Every American is eaten up with longing to rise." How to fulfill the longing? Not through elaborate formal education, certainly: "at the age when one might have a taste for study, one has not the time; and when time is available, the taste is gone."

Benjamin Franklin, the original personification of someone who had benefited from unlimited opportunities, began his career as an uneducated apprentice. Even into the twentieth century, the celebrity representatives of the possibility of success for the common man usually had the same life story, little formal education and apprenticeship as the first step on the road to wealth. Andrew Carnegie began as assistant to Thomas Scott of the Pennsylvania Railroad. Edward Bok, the founder of a publishing empire, who like Carnegie came to America as a penniless small boy, had only seven years of formal education and got his start by writing letters to famous men who happened to be staying at the Fifth Avenue Hotel in New York asking if he might come by to get advice about how he could become as successful as they were. Bok's autobiography, an inspirational best-seller in the early twentieth century as Franklin's autobiography had been in the mid-nineteenth, was published only fifty years before his grandson, Derek Bok, was made president of Harvard.

The self-made man in American novels and stories was, similarly, a figure with negligible education, who often regarded school as being positively an impediment to success. Horatio Alger's popular novels about poor ambitious lads had that theme, with a fortuitous meeting between the eager young hero and a powerful self-made older man being the device that usually got the plot rolling. Frank Cowperwood, the title character of Theodore Dreiser's *The Financier*, leaves school at thirteen because "I don't want to be a boy. I want to get to work." The youthful Jay Gatsby keeps a self-improvement checklist of the kind recommended by Franklin in his autobiography, but Fitzgerald does not tell us that he had any noticeable education.

Writers of popular advice books about success in America sounded the same note about the irrelevance of education. Elbert Hubbard—an eccentric communitarian, utopian, craftsman of fabrics and furniture, and pamphlet publisher who was the greatest propagandist for success of the early twentieth century—constantly downplayed the importance of formal education. In his lecture "A Message to Garcia," which at one point nearly every middle-class American heard or read, he instructed his audience: "It is not book-learning young men need, nor instruction about this or that, but a stiffening of the vertebrae which will cause them to be loyal to a trust, to act promptly, concentrate their energies: do the thing." In one of Hubbard's innumerable inspirational pamphlets, he reported proudly, after a visit to Andrew Carnegie, "Mr. Carnegie has given no money to universities," because "all the great and fashionable universities are given over to cigarettes, booze, bromide, and the devious ways of dalliance."

Frederick Jackson Turner, professor though he was, presented the frontier-opportunist-hero of the halcyon days as having been uneducated: "The West was another name for opportunity. Here were mines to be seized, fertile valleys to be preempted, all the natural resources open to the shrewdest and the boldest." Nineteenth-century society was "a mobile mass of freely circulating atoms, each seeking its own place and finding play for its own powers and for its own original initiative."

It is true that all through American history educators have used the rhetoric of opportunity. But they have used it to argue for free public schools, paid for by the taxpayers' money, open to all, and aimed at equipping students with basic learning and with practical skills to help them get on in the world—not to argue for selective private institutions of higher learning, like Conant's Harvard. Horace Mann, who as Commissioner of Education for the state of Massachusetts made himself the most influential figure in nineteenth-century American education by successfully championing the free, open "common school," was a liberal reformer whose passion for schools primarily concerned their promotion of democratic ideals. But, because he knew that idea alone wouldn't get taxpayers to open their wallets, he consistently promoted the practicality of public education as well. Mann wrote in 1841: "Education is not only a moral renovator, and a multiplier of intellectual power, but . . . also the most prolific parent of material riches . . . I have novel and striking evidence to prove that education is convertible into houses and lands, as well as into power and virtue."

Abraham Lincoln was another champion of useful education for ordinary people. In 1859, in a speech in Wisconsin, he put forth the novel proposition that "henceforth educated people must labor," puzzled over what kind of labor they would perform, and settled upon scientifically advanced agriculture: "The mind, already trained to thought, in the country school, or higher school, cannot fail to find there an exhaustless source of profitable enjoyment." This kind of thinking led to the Morrill Act creating the land-grant college system, an early piece of federal social legislation that Lincoln signed into law in 1862. Along with the already established state universities, these land-grant colleges constituted the first attempt in the history of the world to extend higher education to the common man. Land-grant colleges, like public schools, were supposed to be broad-gauge providers of opportunity. The idea of economic opportunity being not provided but *distributed*, selectively handed out, through education—an idea taken so much for granted today that we don't even think of it as a distinct idea—was not even part of the discussion.

What Conant was proposing, therefore, was to take a deep-seated wish in world history—a governing elite selected on the basis of merit, not parentage—and the most deep-seated wish in American culture, opportunity for everyone, and conjoining them in a new kind of educational system. Linking the two wishes, with the implicit promise that the new elite would formally take responsibility for making sure that all Americans had equal opportunity, was what was new. If Conant's aim had been only to select a new elite or only to provide educational opportunity to all, life in the United States in subsequent years would have proceeded much more simply. Trying to accomplish both at once, within the same system, was the tricky part.

If there was going to be a new elite selected formally, why should its membership be determined solely by academic performance and IQ? Could it be counted upon to devote itself to public service, as planned, or might it convert its anointment into personal gain? Would the men and women not chosen accept the goodness of the system and the leadership of the new elite? Could such momentous changes in American society be put into place without public debate? These are excruciatingly difficult, possibly even unanswerable questions—but that would not become clear for quite a while.

5
Victory

Henry Chauncey wanted to serve in the Second World War, but he was too old and too settled for active duty at the front. In 1932 he had married Elizabeth Phalen, a minister's child like himself (Unitarian) and an accomplished violinist, trained at the Juilliard School, in New York City. They soon had two sons, the first named Egisto after Chauncey's father, the second named Henry after Chauncey himself. During the 1940s they had a daughter, Ann, and another son, Donald. So Chauncey was not in a position to go off and fight.

Modestly paid and parsimonious, he felt he could not afford to buy a house in Cambridge, so, to Elizabeth Chauncey's frustration, the family moved from rented home to rented home in the Boston suburbs—Lincoln, Watertown, Lexington, Lexington again, back to Lincoln. It wasn't the life of an established man entering middle age. At Harvard, he might be an excellent administrator, and a direct descendant of the second president, and a former star athlete, but fundamentally he was only a dean and wouldn't ever be anything more.

But a war generates new chances. The first big step toward the widespread use of mental tests in America had come during the First World War, with the Army intelligence test. The Second World War presented another chance to test on a scale previously unimagined. Wartime requires that millions of people be evaluated and routed quickly; multiple-choice testing can be an important weapon in the military arsenal. Every Army inductee, ten million men in all before the end of the war, took an adapted IQ test called the Army General Classification Test, and was assigned in part on the basis of the result.

Practically every American of note who had anything to do with testing was involved with the armed forces in some way during the war. Leaving aside the patriotic reasons, where else would you want to be than in the vicinity of a once-in-a-lifetime chance to advance your field dramatically? The competition over the future of testing and education was likely to be settled during those years. Just as it was understood that the place where Soviet and Western Allied armies met in Europe would determine who would control what territory after the war, testers knew that whoever brought off large-scale tests in wartime would be in an advantageous position when peace came. That gave their maneuverings a special urgency.

Two important matters were at stake. The organizational one was which of the many outfits offering tests would prove to be the best, most efficient, and most knowledgeable, for it surely would then be entrusted with testing after the war. The substantive matter was what exactly the tests would measure, and what the results would be used for. Would they test IQ, or some other supposedly inherent quality of mind, or would they test the accumulation of learned skills? Would the test scores be used to select a small high-performing group for special treatment, or to weed out the lowest scorers? These were wartime questions that were also questions about the shape of postwar America.

On the Sunday in December 1941 when the Japanese bombed Pearl Harbor, a group of College Board officials happened to be having lunch together in Princeton. Princeton was the home of the College Board's mental-testing operation; the main office, home of the board's traditionalists, was in New York. The boys in Princeton were talking, as they often did, about how nice it would be to abolish the old College Board essay examinations and use the SAT for all applicants, not just scholarship students. In the middle of this the telephone rang with news of the raid. Within two weeks, the essay exams had been suspended for the duration of the war—too administratively complicated for use during a national emergency. They were never resumed. So all that had to happen was for the United States to enter the war—and the SAT immediately became the admissions device for the most prestigious private colleges in the country, something that would previously have been an unthinkably radical step.

During Carl Brigham's terminal illness, he had gradually been replaced at the helm of the College Board office in Princeton by his deputy, a young psychometrician named John Stalnaker—another of the figures in the testing world whom Henry Chauncey had befriended. When the United States entered the war Stalnaker and the College Board had themselves made testing consultants to the Navy, first on a series of minor issues, then on a major one.

The Navy established a program called V-12, in which young men deemed to have the potential to perform advanced technical jobs would be inducted and then sent to college for special training, rather than directly to war. The Navy asked Stalnaker to develop a selection test for the V-12 program.

From Henry Chauncey's point of view, the V-12 test was a big chance. For the widespread use of testing that he dreamed of to come to pass, he had to find a client bigger than Harvard or the College Board, and he had to demonstrate that a multiple-choice test could be given under secure conditions and scored reliably for many, many more takers than the SAT had had to date. The breakthrough would be to give a test to lots of people at many sites all at once, on one day, under secure conditions, and then do a quick reporting of the scores to a central authority. That was what the V-12 program offered. Recognizing how high the stakes were, Chauncey and Stalnaker began to move with the ferocious assurance of people who realize their moment in life has arrived and they'd better capitalize on it.

On February 1, 1943, Stalnaker scrawled a handwritten note to Chauncey from Washington:

> Dear Henry
>   Write to me at once at Room 3732 Navy Annex. . . . This is *at last* a real job. Here is hoping that you are 38 and can write up your record to sound very convincing on testing and selection. You should get a lt. commander commission and take charge of the testing & selection if all goes well. . . . Hurry.

Chauncey hurried. His and Stalnaker's primary worry was not that the Navy would back away from the test, but that it would pick somebody else (like the American Council on Education) as its testing agency. Chauncey decided he had to enlist Conant to ensure that the College Board would get the V-12 assignment. Chauncey worked up his nerve and took the highly unusual step of calling Conant at home in the evening and saying he needed to see him immediately.

Conant was a forbidding figure. When he became president of Harvard at the age of forty, he had been considered informal and fun-loving, but that had quickly faded; with his gray three-piece suits, his heavy, neatly parted gray hair, his steel-rimmed spectacles, his thin horsey face, and his overpowering seriousness, he had an air of overwork and distraction by important matters he wasn't free to discuss. But now Conant said he was on his way to Washington: if Chauncey came there they could get together on the Sunday night before Conant's Monday morning meetings.

When Sunday came, Chauncey got on a train to Washington and began working furiously on the material he would present to Conant. His train stopped at the North Philadelphia station; he grabbed another train, booked himself into a roomette so he could concentrate, and kept working. When the conductor came by to collect tickets, he told Chauncey he was his way to Harrisburg, not Washington. In a panic, Chauncey disembarked at the next stop, left a message for Conant that he'd be late, and found a series of trains that would take him back to Philadelphia and then to Washington. Had he blown it? No. Rather than being furious and canceling the meeting, as Chauncey had feared he would, Conant greeted him with perfect calm, as if nothing was amiss. It was not given to Henry Chauncey to see exactly how things were done at Conant's level, but not long after he made that frenzied dash to Washington, steadied himself, and stated his case, the Navy awarded the contract for the V-12 test to the College Board.

Chauncey now had less than two months to develop a test and have it printed and shipped out without any leaks of the contents; to line up testing centers all over the country, find and train people to run them, and set up regional offices to receive and score the answer sheets; and to establish a re-scoring operation in Princeton to double-check the results so that there would be no mistakes. (These last were staffed by grandmotherly women operating hand-cranked calculators, because Chauncey didn't feel the IBM scoring machine was yet up to the task.) He went to Chicago to do all this while Stalnaker remained in Washington.

For a month Chauncey lived one of those strange temporary wartime lives in a big empty hotel on the lakefront on a floor all by himself. Staying on another floor was a theatrical troupe. He spent his days at Chicago Plano-graph, his printer, or at R. H. Donnelley, his distributor, making sure that no errors got through and that not a single copy of the test fell into unauthorized hands. They kept the printed test booklets in a warehouse on skids casually draped with cloth, like a shipment of bootleg liquor, so that nobody would realize their importance—a matter of life and death, quite literally—and walk away with a copy. In the evenings Chauncey would sit alone in the hotel's vast dim dining hall watching the actors practice. The Army abruptly decided to use the same test for a program similar to V-12, which increased the stakes—and the pressure on Chauncey.

On April 2, 1943, the Army-Navy College Qualification Test—containing mostly questions adapted from the SAT plus a new section called "common-sense science" that Chauncey had added because he felt it would turn up gifted farm boys with limited vocabularies—was given to 316,000 high-school seniors all over the country. Everything went well, evidently in a spirit

of not just grim efficiency but full-bore home-front ebullience. At a testimo-
nial dinner afterward for Chauncey, the College Board staff sang him this
ditty:

He plans 'em, he makes 'em, he hands 'em out too.
He scores 'em, reports 'em, a one-man test crew.
Then with brow deeply furrowed, with thumbs in his vest,
He calls from Chicago, "I gave the wrong test!"

Chauncey spent the whole 1943–44 school year working for the Navy
and supervised three more administrations of the test, but the first was the
largest and most significant. It stands as an unremarked watershed event in
American history, especially when coupled with the publication of Conant's
"Wanted: American Radicals" article just a couple of weeks later. By demonstrating that an SAT-like test could be successfully administered at one sitting to a group larger (by a factor of forty!) than had ever taken it before,
Chauncey had made a nationwide multiple-choice personnel scan of the
entire American population into a real possibility. Such a project, if put into
effect, would be a far cry from an Ivy League scholarship examination. It
would affect everybody, the whole life and form of the country. It would be
the practical means of realizing Conant's ambition of creating a social structure for the future that would (to his mind, at least) represent the long-
delayed fulfillment of Thomas Jefferson's dreams.

In June 1944 Chauncey returned to Harvard with a slightly grander title,
assistant to the dean of the faculty and chair of the Committee on Scholarships—but, inevitably, being back was a letdown. Then John Stalnaker
made a career decision he would regret for the rest of his life: he left the College Board testing office in Princeton to become dean of students at Stanford
University. With Carl Brigham dead and Stalnaker gone, somebody had to
come in as the head of testing for the College Board. Chauncey was the obvious choice for the job. He spent the end of 1944 and the beginning of 1945
agonizing over whether to take it.
   What Chauncey would have really liked would be to talk at length with
Conant about the future of testing and his place in it, but during this period
Conant seemed especially distant. When it came time for Chauncey to make
up his mind, he requested and was granted an appointment; he found
Conant sitting in a chair grimacing from back pain. He laid out his dilemma,
hoping that Conant would tell him which job offered the better chance to
pursue the shining promise of testing. Instead Conant asked Chauncey how

much of a raise he had in mind—as if money was the reason Chauncey was restless! Disappointed (even though he didn't believe one should become disappointed), Chauncey tried to respond rationally rather than emotionally. He went home and devised a chart, assigning points to the College Board job and to his deanship in a series of categories and then computing the totals. The College Board job won by a score of 36 to 32.

So the Chaunceys moved to Princeton. It wasn't clear what would happen next. At the least, the College Board would now be administering the SAT to many more people than it had before the war. At the most, Chauncey would have a far, far greater and more exciting job to do. Conant would revive his old idea of combining all the testing agencies in America into one; the office Chauncey was now running would become the one big testing organization for the whole country; and Chauncey's idea about testing every American on every human quality and creating a scientized social utopia might be realized. Chauncey thought of this as the opening of an era, if all went well, just as industrialization had opened an era after the Civil War. Shortly after making his decision, he wrote in his diary: "The stage of development in which testing is now in is the same as the railroads were in the 1850s—a lot of separate small lines. The big developments were to come in the next two decades." His assignment, to continue the railroad analogy, would be to establish a standard gauge, in people.

To understand what happened next requires clearing the mind of preconceptions.

What we now believe is that at the end of the war, the United States self-consciously committed itself to greatly expanding opportunity for ordinary Americans, by making it possible—for the first time, anywhere, any time—for most people to go to college. We wouldn't operate our universities for young aristocrats, the way the British did, or for a select group of future scholars, scientists, and upper bureaucrats, like the French. We would hand out the tickets broadly and unselectively, trusting in the capacities of ordinary people, so that they could be used for general upward mobility. The vehicle for this commitment was the GI Bill, which with spectacular success put millions of men on their way to the middle class of a democratized American society.

That is not the way it looked at the time.

President Roosevelt signed the GI Bill (officially, the Servicemen's Readjustment Act of 1944) on June 22, 1944, just at the time that Henry Chauncey was finishing his Navy work and returning to Harvard to contemplate his future. Legislation conferring some kind of reward upon veterans after a war is a standard feature of American government. The Republican Party established its political dominance in the late nineteenth century by setting up generous pensions for Civil War veterans. The stinginess of the veterans' benefit package after the First World War had led to a political upheaval, the Bonus March on Washington in 1932, which many government officials of the 1940s had witnessed and did not want to reprise. The GI Bill therefore provided a rich menu of benefits, including not just money for college education but also cut-rate mortgages, free train tickets home, and medical care. College was not supposed to be the main item on the list; nobody had any inkling of how many veterans would use the GI Bill to educate themselves.

The bill's education program was put under the direction of the Veterans Administration rather than the federal Office of Education. That was a sign that it was supposed to be a short-term transitional program, using campuses as a decompression chamber for battle-scarred soldiers. In the Senate hearings on the bill, the commander of the American Legion, the key organization lobbying for it, warned that "in this war we have had a much greater load" of veterans who were "mentally unstable" than "we have ever had in the history of warfare." Men who had been trained "in all kinds of destructive processes from hand-to-hand combat to the gigantic bombing operations over land and sea" might "require a period of guidance and adjustment after hostilities cease which a well-regulated and sympathetic educational system will provide."

James Bryant Conant, who in "Wanted: American Radicals" had proclaimed, stirringly, "the demobilization of our armed forces is a God-given moment for reintroducing the American concept of a fluid society," was a (or maybe the) leading opponent of the GI Bill. The fluid society that he wanted to create after the war should, he thought, be run by a small and carefully selected natural aristocracy; giving every veteran a free, universally redeemable ticket to higher education, which Conant believed was already overpopulated, was virtually the opposite of what he had in mind. Even after the bill had passed, Conant hoped to get the government to rescind the aspect of it that most bothered him: its lack of a procedure for weeding out college freshmen at the end of their first year and allowing only the most able to continue—"clearly a disaster," he wrote Chauncey. Conant thought the instrument of the government's effort to remake American society after the war should not be the GI Bill but the presidential commission appointed in 1944, on which both he and Chauncey served, which established the National Science Foundation: this provided federal funding to enable natural aristocrats to lead a national research and development effort, especially in defense technology.

Chauncey himself hardly noticed the GI Bill, because it did not involve any testing and no one in his circles thought of it as an educational reform. Even the American Council on Education and the rest of the education-expander camp was disappointed with the GI Bill, because it had put education under the purview of the Veterans Administration. When a Boston newspaper criticized Conant for opposing the GI Bill, Chauncey loyally fired off a letter to the editor that makes it clear that the very thing we now revere the bill for having done—flinging wide the gates of the universities to the common man—was exactly *not* what he and Conant wanted for postwar America:

> Equality of opportunity in the early days of our country did not mean that every boy became the president of a bank, a railroad magnate or the captain of a ship. But each boy did have the opportunity to rise to such positions if his talent and industry qualified him.
>
> Today the lower rungs of the ladder are educational. Climbing these rungs involves the same competitive element entailed a century ago by the ladder of economic opportunity.

Conant and Chauncey were far from thinking that the question of education and social reform for postwar America was settled by the GI Bill. As the war ended, they were full of plans to settle the question themselves in quite a different way. Conant wanted to create a new elite, Chauncey wanted to create an enormous testing regime in service of no social goal more particular than progress, and together they began to push, hard.

It made matters easier for them that at that juncture America did not in any way resemble the society Conant had envisioned in "Wanted: American Radicals." A small, tight-knit group of men, who trusted each other and thought alike about most matters, still ran everything in their world. If you had your hands on the right few levers—and Conant and Chauncey did—you could quietly effect substantial changes without going through the arduous business of passing laws and persuading the general public.

Back in the 1930s, Chauncey had made the acquaintance of Devereux Josephs, a Philadelphia investment banker and fellow graduate of Groton and Harvard. Now Josephs was the president of the Carnegie philanthropic empire in New York, the country's leading institutional promoter of standardized testing. And William S. Learned, the researcher whose lecture on testing in 1933 had galvanized Chauncey, was Josephs' subordinate. And Conant, having been president of Harvard for more than a decade and having been at the center of the war effort (scientific division), was at the apogee of his influence in the public world.

In June 1945, with the war over in Europe, Devereux Josephs sent Chauncey a brief note reestablishing their acquaintance: "I am sure that you are going to be in New York from time to time. Will you make sure to come in and see me? I have an idea that you might be helpful to me, although I have nothing particular in mind at the moment."

Chauncey came in and saw him.

In October 1945, with the war over in Japan, William Learned sent Chauncey a note, which even better than Josephs' captures the tone of languid, casual power that characterized the Episcopacy in its heyday: "Can you not arrange to take time for a leisurely talk some day when you are in New York and not under special pressure? I suggest that you stop at our office about twelve or twelve thirty and have luncheon with me over at the Century Association. Almost any day will suit me and the sooner the better."

Chauncey arranged to take time for a leisurely talk.

What was afoot, at least superficially, was the minor question of the College Board's taking over the administration of the Graduate Record Examination, then as now the standardized test for entry into academic graduate school, and another exam called the Pre-Engineering Inventory Test. But this was merely a pretext for reopening the subject of a new national agency to control all the leading tests. Carnegie had the ability to put across big changes in the educational world, simply because it had money. As Paul Buck of Harvard told Chauncey: "No college will quickly turn down a proposition by the Carnegie Foundation because of their hope of getting funds at some future date."

In March 1946 Chauncey had an exciting meeting with Conant—exciting because the faint uninterest in testing that he had sensed in Conant before seemed to have disappeared. "He spoke with great conviction about the use of tests for guidance and selection as the most important movement in education at the present time," Chauncey wrote afterward in his notes. "He feels that a large gilt-edged testing organization is needed and desirable." The new agency could promote research on the best testing techniques, and help to persuade schools all over the country to adopt standardized testing.

Conant and Devereux Josephs were the men with their hands on the levers in education. If they wanted a new testing agency, Chauncey thought, then surely there would be a new testing agency, with himself as the head.

Then things went awry.

Josephs dispatched his assistant to Washington to clear with the American Council on Education the idea of the College Board's taking over the Graduate Record Exam. The head of the ACE, the overbearing George Zook, was dead set against it. It would be an insult to the ACE, Zook thought. For him, the ACE was the leading educational organization in the country, and why should it agree to turn over the test to the tiny, regional, elitist College Board without consultation? "Even if we were to decide to go ahead we might have an open feud, a fight in which Zook might go out and make a tong war," the man from Carnegie told Chauncey. And if a full-scale new agency were created, "they would actively propagandize against" it.

Devereux Josephs put his plans on hold and appointed a special committee, headed by Conant, to investigate further. His doing this was a sign of how important it was to him to make peace with the ACE, which in turn was a sign of how big his plans for testing were. He and Conant needed the ACE on board. Without it, their new testing organization would inescapably be small and regional, not big and national. In that spring of 1946 Harry Truman appointed Zook to head a President's Commission on Higher Education. He may have been little respected in the Harvard–Carnegie–College Board world, but Zook was officially America's leading higher educator. Conant and his allies wanted to make a deal that would include Zook (so that their new organization would stand supreme over educational opportunity in America) but at the same time leave him powerless (so that the principle of selecting a new, high-IQ elite, which Zook had no interest in, would be preserved).

In October 1946 Conant's committee completed its work and issued its report, and it came as a terrible shock and disappointment to Henry Chauncey. It did recommend that a new national testing agency be established—but as a branch of the American Council on Education! The College Board, employer of Henry Chauncey, would hand over all its tests to the new agency and then cease to exist.

Suddenly Chauncey and his College Board colleagues, once so excited about the prospect of a new testing agency, were dead set against it. Objections that Carl Brigham had raised nearly a decade earlier and that Chauncey had always dismissed became compelling. The new testing organization would be a monopoly, undemocratic, and sure to become unresponsive to the needs of the public. Its research, rather than being objective and scientific, would be canted toward producing material touting the superior qualities of its own tests. Why did there have to be a big new agency, anyway, when everything was going just fine already? As one of Chauncey's lieutenants wrote to him, raising objections quietly in private that in the years to come would be raised loudly in public by all manner of social critics: "When an organization of this sort becomes big and powerful, it cannot admit itself in error. So much money and so many reputations are involved that if the tests turn out to be no good, evidence of the fact is almost certain to be suppressed, or else the criteria of goodness are themselves called in question."

In an almost desperate mood, Chauncey again went to see Conant, who taught him a comforting lesson in the subtleties of academic politics. "In general, I found Mr. Conant very reassuring on the questionable points in the plan, particularly with regard to the relationship to the A.C.E.," Chauncey noted afterward. Conant explained that he didn't really envision the ACE's being put in charge of testing or the College Board's being abolished; instead, he was trying to mollify the ACE by giving it a symbolic victory. It was Conant's plan to have the College Board control the testing. Never mind how it looked, the College Board would in effect be taking over the ACE. Furthermore, with the ACE tied in to the new testing agency from the beginning, the only meaningful potential competitor was eliminated. Nobody could ever effectively challenge its dominance. "Mr. Conant felt that the A.C.E. really got nothing out of the organization as set up except kudos," Chauncey wrote. "There would be no tangible advantages for them."

The College Board decided to return to the negotiating table, but not to take Conant at his word completely. Instead it proposed an alternative deal to have the new agency be independent, not an arm of the ACE. When in March 1947 Devereux Josephs announced that Carnegie would withdraw its funding if the ACE wanted the new agency to be under its control, the fate of George Zook was sealed, because not only were his testing programs operating at a loss but the whole ACE was in a financially precarious position.

Chauncey went to see Zook and present the terms. Zook vaingloriously insisted that he still should be the one to appoint the directors of the testing agency, and that it should still be an ACE subsidiary. Then Devereux Josephs had a little talk with Zook. Josephs was of course a gentleman, devoted to public service, but at the same time he realized that at certain key moments when much is at stake, one must to do what is necessary to move matters forward. So, quietly, between the two of them, he offered Zook a bribe to fold his hand: $50,000 a year for three years, in the form of a grant from Carnegie to the ACE.

On April 17, 1947, Josephs' assistant sent Henry Chauncey a telegram: ACE COMMITTEE WILLING ACCEPT LATEST PLAN.

One hitch remained. Now that the ACE had capitulated, there was grumbling on the College Board side. The deal was now at least palatable, but why was it necessary? The Board's tweedy admissions officers weren't sure they preferred the SAT to the old essay examinations, and they didn't share Conant's fervor to topple the Episcopacy and reform the United States either. Now they were being asked to give up the College Board's cozy little testing office for the good of the country, to contribute a good portion of its cash reserves to a new testing agency, to share the income from its tests, and to accept equal representation with the ACE on the new agency board.

On October 9, 1947, a College Board meeting was given over to the airing of complaints about the merger. "Counsel of fear," a frustrated Chauncey wrote in the notes he took as the meeting progressed. "If your attitude had dominated history of this country we would still be clearing the forests with axes." Another meeting was scheduled for October 29. Devereux Josephs told Chauncey that if the College Board didn't approve the merger then, Carnegie would pull out and the deal would be off. There was nothing for Chauncey to do but go back to Conant for help one more time. At the October 29 meeting, the admissions deans who made up the usual attendance at College Board meetings were astonished to see Conant in all his magnificence, as well as the president of Princeton, the president of Cornell, and the president of Brown. All these grandees had shown up personally to argue for the merger. Helpless before such a display, the deans voted unanimously to approve.

On December 11, George Zook's Commission on Higher Education submitted its report to President Truman. The report was written as a clarion call to expand American higher education—not for Conant's purpose (or, as Conant would have it, Jefferson's purpose) of selecting and training a new elite, but to promote democracy and provide opportunity for all. The number of students enrolled in institutions of higher education by 1960, the report said, should be 4.6 million—triple what it had been in 1940. A third of every age cohort should graduate from college. Government should substantially finance this expansion by paying for students' tuitions: the first two years of college should be entirely free. All discrimination in higher education, especially against Negroes, should be vigorously stamped out.

There was no mention in this report of using standardized tests to pick out a few students for special training; instead, what it called the "most important" educational test, the ACE Psychological Examination, might be used to identify the few who would have trouble with college work. But by then George Zook had already lost the game. The long-running competition over the future of education was over.

Of course, it looked—and it may still look—as if the education-expander camp had won. The Zook report and the GI Bill could be held up as evi-

dence. But that appearance was deceiving. American colleges and universities did expand after the war, to sizes hitherto undreamed of. It was easier to
go to college here, and fewer options were foreclosed if you didn't go to a
selective one, than anywhere else in the world. But within the expansion,
though not obviously on display, a set of principles opposed to those of the
Zook report and the GI Bill were put in place. High-school students were
sorted according to "scholastic aptitude" as measured by the SAT, which
was very close to IQ. The highest scorers were separated out and enabled to
go to selective colleges, ideally without regard to whether or not they could
afford the tuition. If you wanted to go on to graduate school, you had to take
another aptitude test and go through another selection process. The government did not turn universities into extended versions of public school—free
to all, the same for all. Instead, higher education became a big system with
a small inner core reserved for a high-IQ version of Plato's guardians or Jefferson's natural aristocracy. This expanded higher education was good for
the new elite—it put them at the head of a large, all-encompassing system,
poised to make their claim to national leadership.

The true winner of the competition, then, was the IQ-testing camp. With
the merger in place and the SAT enshrined as the country's test for college
applicants, the United States had become the world's leading user of IQ tests.

But every victory contains hidden perils. Conant, without realizing it,
had set the stage for a fundamental clash. He had helped to enshrine the idea
that an absolute, formal guarantee of opportunity for all—not just for people
with high IQ scores—was the central premise of American society. But he
had also created a system for serially ranking people by a supposed innate
worth expressed in the scores made on standardized intelligence tests, on the
basis of which their place in society—their prosperity and their prestige—
would be apportioned. This was the fundamental clash: between the promise
of more opportunity and the reality that, from a point early in the lives of
most people, opportunity would be limited.

Exactly one week after the Zook report was submitted, the Educational
Testing Service was chartered, with Chauncey as president and Conant as
chairman of the board. (Chauncey later thought he might have chosen the
name because it echoed that of his father's alma mater, the Episcopal Theological Seminary.) On January 1, 1948, ETS opened for business in Princeton. The ACE Psychological Examination was immediately discontinued.

Most people connected to the College Board chose to see what looks now
like a crushing victory on their part—in which a handful of private Northeastern colleges maintained what Chauncey privately called "a bread and
butter monopoly" over educational testing in the United States—as an act of

self-abnegation. Hadn't the College Board handed over a good portion of its cash on hand to ETS, while the ACE had contributed nothing? Hadn't the College Board given its tests and part of their income stream to a new organization it did not control? "It seems to me . . . an almost unparalleled action in that the Board itself voted to surrender, without any hope of material reward, so much of its assets of all kinds, in the hope that education as a whole may profit," wrote Edward Noyes, dean of admissions at Yale and head of the College Board, to Devereux Josephs. Forever after, this view of what had happened in the merger—public-spirited sacrifice by the College Board, rather than bureaucratic triumph—remained firmly lodged in Henry Chauncey's memory. "It was in the spirit of self-denial for the benefit of testing as a whole that they agreed to participate," he wrote decades later. This formulation allowed him to build his empire aggressively, secure in the conviction that there was no element of self-interest in his behavior.

Which brings to mind the old Groton motto: To serve is to reign.

During the summer of 1948, while on his first vacation since the establishment of ETS, Chauncey read an article in a publication called *The Scientific Monthly* that troubled him considerably. The article, "The Measurement of Mental Systems (Can Intelligence Be Measured?)," was by two well-known liberal educators: W. Allison Davis, who had written *Children of Bondage*, a book about young Negroes in the South, and Robert J. Havighurst, whom Chauncey knew slightly from military testing work during the war. They argued that intelligence tests were a fraud, a way of wrapping the fortunate children of the middle and upper middle classes in a mantle of scientifically demonstrated superiority. The tests, they said, measured only "a very narrow range of mental activities" and carried "a strong cultural handicap for pupils of the lower socioeconomic groups."

Like most people familiar with testing, Davis and Havighurst treated educational aptitude tests like the SAT as being the same thing as IQ tests. And they didn't approve. Such tests, they said, measured primarily "academic or linguistic activities," called them intelligence, and then validated the score against school performance. The process was "circular," because the validation was too similar to the test itself: "a teacher's rating of a pupil is an estimate of the pupil's performance on the same kind of problems as those in the standard tests."

Although he was not generally a defensive person, Chauncey reacted touchily to the *Scientific Monthly* article. "They take the extreme and, I believe, radical point of view that any test items showing different difficulties for different socio-economic groups are inappropriate," he wrote in his diary, and went on to take a mildly hereditarian position on intelligence tests:

> If ability has any relation to success in life parents in upper socio-economic groups should have more ability than those in lower socio-economic groups. And if there is anything in heredity (such as tall parents having tall children) one would expect children of high socio-economic group parents to have more ability than children of low socio-economic group parents.

But to Chauncey's way of thinking, the real point was that the issues Davis and Havighurst were so upset about would soon be forgotten; testing and ETS were going to move beyond aptitude into a new era, when testers would achieve a broad, nuanced understanding of the whole spectrum of human abilities. Yes, it was disturbing that aptitude-test results so strongly reflected social inequities. During the war, Chauncey had himself been quietly shocked and mystified when he saw, as the public and the test-takers had not, that overall statistics on the Army-Navy College Qualification Test showed far-below-average scores for Southerners, Negroes, and the poorly educated. But he felt certain that something much bigger than aptitude testing was aborning. It was just too bad that aptitude testing was the only part of the great development that was then visible. Chauncey was thinking of writing a book or an article explaining all this, which would be called "The Dawn of Social Science."

It wasn't just Chauncey who believed a new age was dawning. The founding period of ETS represents one of the periodic high points of faith in the power of reason. In philosophy, in psychology, in physics, in anthropology, in medicine, in sociology—all across these fields of inquiry, expertise and logic were taken to be almost limitlessly fruitful. The first computer had just been unveiled. The new United Nations would end war. The disease that had crippled the privileged President Roosevelt was on the verge of being eliminated as a threat even to the poorest of the poor. No problem, no source of woe, no unsolved mystery, seemed immune to the miraculous good effects of human intervention through technology and organization.

Chauncey, typically, put an especially enthusiastic, romantic, boyish forward spin on the conventional wisdom of the moment. For centuries, he believed, the best scientific minds had turned their attention to the physical world, which once had been understood only in a mystical way, and they had relentlessly gotten to its underlying order and rationality. Now, at long last, the same process was beginning for the social world—for human capacity and interaction. "We seem . . . to have arrived at the period in Man's history when human affairs can be studied as impartially and scientifically as physical phenomena," he wrote in his diary. Just as the Manhattan Project had split the atom, the Educational Testing Service, with its research department made up of the best minds in the field, would decode the mind. Many more people than just aspiring college and graduate students would be tested, and for many more qualities. ETS would measure all abilities, not just aptitude or intelligence. It would map and code the personality. This new knowledge would help human affairs to take on a new conformation: rational understanding would replace prejudice, hatred, emotion, and superstition. Human nature itself would be reformed.

There was a match between this shining moment for Chauncey—poor boy who had been educated in schools for rich boys, administrator in a university run by scholars, now in middle age finally being put in charge of something—and the moment for social science. As one of Chauncey's diary entries in 1948 put it:

> Psychology, the Cinderella of the Social Sciences. The day when the prince will arrive to take her to the ball is not far off.
>   unappreciated, despised

Chauncey was aware that in the past the principal way people had sought to understand their condition was through religion, his family's traditional vocation. But religion, he thought, however noble its aims, could never be fully effective in improving society because it was not scientific. And being unscientific, it had impeded progress: "the social sciences are at last freeing themselves from the bondage in which they have been held by ethics, religion, prejudices, value judgments," Chauncey wrote. And, on another day: "Our mores should not be derived from ethical principles which stem from religion but from a study of man and society."

Once social science had completed its work, Chauncey believed, the question of ethics ought to be reintroduced. He was sufficiently pious to find it unthinkable to jettison moral principles in favor of data. He wanted moral principles to be in place, and he wanted to be sure they rested on a firm scientific base, as hadn't been possible before. Experts could be assembled who would sift through the discoveries of social science and use them to form a new, better set of fundamental precepts. Chauncey called this the "hierarchy of values." Then, once it had been determined, we would have to find a way to inculcate it in the populace. How? "Only Plato had the answer, the institutionalization of all children from birth." But that was impracticable; for now, in an expanded educational system, Americans would "set about to indoctrinate the youth of the country with this set of values. Freedom of thought would still remain, as one of the values that are included in the framework, but the anarchy that presently exists to the confusion and unhappiness of most people would be replaced by a sense of order."

Back in 1922, Walter Lippmann had predicted that if intelligence testing ever really caught on, the people in charge of it would "occupy a position of power which no intellectual has held since the collapse of theocracy." And indeed it was true that, as head of the Educational Testing Service, Chauncey hoped to perform a quasi-ministerial function. It would be an improvement upon, a modernization of, the work that past Chaunceys had done to help form America. In his diary, as he struggled to put into words what he had in mind, he kept making the same twist on a famous phrase of William James's. "What I hope to see established," he wrote in one such passage, "is the moral equivalent of religion but based on reason and science rather than on sentiments and tradition."

6

IQ Joe

Even if Chauncey could not immediately establish ETS's position as the moral mainspring of modern America, in his mind the nobility of the goal infused everything the organization did, and he pursued its more narrow interests with a religious fervor.

In the early going, the contrast between the expansiveness of ETS's mission and the precariousness of its daily existence was striking. The offices were just a few rooms opening onto a back alley in Princeton. The staff was small, young, and underpaid. Worry about money was in the air.

The day when everybody had to take standardized tests to get into college or graduate school was still far off in the future. ETS was running several money-losing testing programs inherited from other organizations; the market for the SAT was still quite small; ETS achievement tests for high-school seniors, first offered in the late 1930s, were even more sparingly used; admissions tests for professional schools were barely under way. The Law School Aptitude Test was first offered in February 1948, two months into ETS's existence, and a few months later ETS was given a contract to develop the Medical College Aptitude Test. Meanwhile it had to maintain its headquarters and staff in Princeton as well as a branch office in Berkeley, California, that Chauncey had established in 1947, before ETS was even chartered, as a sign of his national ambitions.

ETS was supposed to be (and really was, in Chauncey's mind) an institution devoted to public service and disinterested scientific research on testing, completely devoid of self-interest. It was chartered as a nonprofit organization, which meant that it had no shareholders and paid no federal income tax, but the initial endowment from Carnegie was nowhere near enough to operate it. So ETS had to support itself commercially. Eventually it would live on the fees the test-takers paid, but at the moment there weren't enough of them to cover the bills; many more universities would have to be persuaded to require all their applicants to take ETS tests. The research division had to confine itself mainly to performing validity studies of these tests, which could be used to persuade more schools to require them. But even after making every possible economy, ETS was operating at a loss. Two years into its existence, Robert Merry, a professor at the Harvard Business School whom Chauncey used as an advisor, wrote to him: "Basically I favor a rather drastic cut back in your present situation. . . . I would still like to urge keeping constant pressure on your project directors for more direct promotional work. You need to work just as hard on increasing receipts as on cutting your expenses."

Chauncey needed to come up with a way of making money quickly or he would have to begin dismantling his great organization just when he wanted to be building it. The obvious answer was a big government contract, proba-bly from the armed forces. That was where Chauncey had contacts from his war work, and at the time no civilian government bureau had a charter broad enough to justify hiring ETS to do anything of real scope.

Ever since his fortieth-birthday epiphany in church in 1945, Chauncey had wanted more than anything to conduct a great national Census of Abili-ties. The Census of Abilities would be the perfect marriage of testing's scien-tific potential and the spiritual guidance that Chauncey wanted to provide. ETS as an organization was ideally situated to carry out such a census, and the federal government was the natural client. So Chauncey began making inquiries among his military contacts about the possibility of launching the Census of Abilities. This would save ETS in the short run and bring the United States to a utopian state in the long.

Unfortunately, Chauncey couldn't get anything beyond polite expres-sions of mild interest from anyone in the Pentagon. "One can certainly get an idea of the frustration of scientists during the war when their ideas were turned down out of hand by low level officers," he wrote after one unsuc-cessful pitch meeting. He resolved, however, to press on. In January 1950, Chauncey sent his number-two man at ETS, William Turnbull, this expres-sion of undimmed commitment to the Census of Abilities:

> After several years of reconnoitering around the foothills of Mount Everest, I believe that the general nature of our campaign and the route that seems most promising in our effort to attain the summit are reason-ably clear. At least I believe there is little to be gained from further

reconnoitering in the foothills . . . we had better begin the climb without further ado.

Somehow Chauncey wangled an an appointment with Stuart Symington, a dazzling young man in the Truman administration, later a U.S. senator from Missouri, then working in the Pentagon. He sent Symington a detailed proposal and then called on him on July 6, 1950. What Chauncey didn't know was that Symington had in hand a memo from a member of his own staff saying: "We are not impressed . . . with the proposal to conduct a census of abilities without any relation to the job to be performed." This may explain the tenor of the meeting, as recounted in notes Chauncey made the next day:

> He was about fifteen minutes behind-hand on appointments but greeted me with apologies in a very friendly manner. He is a strikingly good-looking and pleasant person.
> Hardly had I explained how I happened to be there than he, after one question on what I meant by human resources, suggested that I write him a letter stating what I had in mind. . . .
> With that I bowed out, having taken about five minutes of his time and learned how top government executives operate.

So much, in 1950 at least, for the Census of Abilities.

Another big testing project, of quite a different nature, was actually in the offing. One of the main questions in postwar American society was who should serve in the peacetime armed forces. The United States could not afford to let its military establishment return to being the drowsy husk that it had been in the 1930s. For the first time in their history, Americans needed to maintain a large standing army in peacetime, and, because the threat from Communism was seen as both internal and external, one had to find a way of doing this that would be socially unifying rather than divisive. President Truman appointed a commission to study the matter, and it issued a report recommending that all young men be required to undergo six months of military training. James Bryant Conant was a leading supporter of universal military training, and President Truman endorsed the idea. But Congress, in 1948, stopped one step short and required merely universal draft registration, to be administered by the Selective Service System.

The head of the Selective Service System was General Lewis B. Hershey. Hershey, who ran the draft from 1941 until 1970, artfully maintained the persona of a country boy, a rumpled, cracker-barrel philosopher; he often spoke of his humble upbringing in rural Missouri by his illiterate parents, and he liked to deliver lengthy, homespun discourses that rambled from military issues to the nature of farm life and back again. Just as ETS was opening its doors, Hershey appointed a series of scientific advisory committees to the Selective Service System, on one of which Henry Chauncey served. By the end of 1948 Chauncey could see that Hershey and his committees were heading in the direction of recommending a large-scale draft-deferment test for college students. Up to that time, the mass administration of standardized mental tests had been strictly a wartime phenomenon. This new test would be by far the biggest peacetime testing program ever and, potentially, the financial salvation of ETS.

On its face the idea behind the test was gruesomely undemocratic. College students, still a small, well-off fraction of the American adolescent population, would be given an IQ test. As if to underscore the class implications of the situation, they would have to pay out of their own pockets to take it. High scorers on the test would be deferred from the draft, and low scorers, along with all the other boys who weren't in college, would have to do military service. Rather than giving only a few specialists like doctors and ministers military exemptions, as was traditional, all males with a high IQ, whether engineer or poet, would receive blanket deferments. "Hershey . . . emphasized that . . . people were deferred, not for a specific responsibility, so much as for their potential worth," Chauncey wrote after a meeting with the general.

Draft deferment had an odd upside-down bureaucratic politics. The elite of higher education were against it for being too elitist: the presidents of Harvard, Yale, Princeton, MIT, and the University of Chicago were among its opponents. Support came from jes'-folks General Hershey, whom it would make into a national personnel czar, and from the state universities, which had an irresistible financial incentive to keep students on their campuses, since they got per capita subsidies from their legislatures. But the arguments made by both sides were pure Cold War. Conant and his Ivy League allies said deferments would weaken the country by fomenting class divisions. Hershey and his scientific advisory committees said Americans had to be sure not to squander the talents of men who might go on to make breakthroughs in weaponry.

On June 25, 1950, Communist North Korean troops invaded South Korea, an ally of the United States. The Cold War had become hot, and soon American troops would be on their way to fight in Asia. The debate over draft deferment had to be settled right away.

General Hershey's committees issued their report in December 1950. "We, the citizens of the United States, now face the greatest test in the history of the Nation," it began. Using the lurid language of crisis, it tried to anticipate and answer all the arguments against the deferment test. To subject all college students to the draft "would virtually stop the production of superior scientific, professional, and specialized personnel," it said. It was important to exempt all high-scoring students, not just those on a small list of militarily essential fields, because to specify such a group "calls for an omniscience which sane men hesitate to claim." The committees acknowledged that the college population was not democratically selected or representative of all classes, but that didn't mean "that an unwise manpower and Selective Service policy should be adopted because of an inadequate national policy with regard to the distribution of educational opportunity."

As soon as the report was issued, Conant drew the battle lines by announcing the formation of a Committee for the Present Danger, an organization of eminent Establishmentarians concerned about the Cold War. Conant's committee favored universal military service (not just training anymore) and opposed the deferment test.

On March 19, 1951, the Selective Service System signed a contract with ETS to test up to a million college students. In every sense this was Henry Chauncey's big test.

Always in the past Chauncey had been the implementer of other people's ideas, operating out of view while someone better known conducted the public maneuverings. Now he had to step up to the podium. Conant, founding chairman of the ETS board of directors, was now the leading opponent of what had become ETS's biggest program by far; and General Hershey, the draft test's sponsor, was as inept as a front man as he was skillful as a bureaucrat, so he had to be kept out of view as much as possible. Truman, who hadn't gone to college (the last American President of whom this was true) and who originally favored universal training, could hardly speak out in favor of college deferments with a straight face. That left Chauncey.

Chauncey went to work on taming General Hershey's excesses and moderating the test's most disastrous public-relations aspects. He instructed Hershey to stop referring to it as an IQ test: "The test should not be looked upon or referred to as an 'intelligence' test. There are many kinds of intelligence; the ability revealed by this test is more properly called 'scholastic aptitude.' This means nothing more than the ability to do well in school or college." He put a stop to the plan to charge the takers a fee, which was the financing mechanism for the ordinary educational tests, and persuaded Hershey to pay for them with government funds. He devised a scoring system that would bring to mind school grades rather than mental testing: the median score would be 50 and the deferment cutoff 70, different (if only cosmetically) from IQ tests, where the median was 100. Inside ETS, Chauncey managed an overnight doubling of the organization's workload. The test had to be constructed, the printing and scoring arranged, and security at the testing sites planned at a level commensurate with the importance of the test's results—quite literally a matter of life and death. (All test-takers were fingerprinted, and the FBI helped to guard the sites.)

The backdrop to these arrangements was an immense public outcry against the deferment test that began as soon as Truman signed the executive order authorizing it. The editorial cartoonist of the *Sacramento Bee* drew Joseph Stalin walking into his propaganda department, wearing a self-satisfied grin and holding a piece of paper that said: "PRESIDENT TRUMAN ADVOCATES DRAFT DEFERMENT FOR COLLEGE BOYS—U.S. TO INITIATE CASTE SYSTEM." The *Philadelphia Inquirer*'s cartoon showed THE AVERAGE GUY standing on the ground looking at JOE COLLEGE up on a pedestal labeled SUPER-CITIZEN FAR ABOVE THE CRASS AND SORDID DEFENSE OF COUNTRY. A local draft board in Oregon resigned in protest. The one in Grand Rapids, Michigan, announced it would refuse to issue deferments on the basis of the test scores. Conant wrote a stinging article in *Look* magazine, which was owned by a member of the Committee on the Present Danger, Gardner Cowles; even more uncharacteristically, he submitted to a radio interview with another member of the committee, Edward R. Murrow, the famous CBS News broadcaster, who got him to agree on the air that the test "stinks." Murrow later delivered a radio commentary of his own:

> If this rule had been applied in earlier days, people like the Wright Brothers, Mark Twain, Phil Murray, Andrew Carnegie, Henry Ford, Thomas Edison, and Harry S Truman among others [including, he didn't say, Murrow himself] wouldn't have had a chance of being deferred, because none of them went to college. . . . We have never proceeded in this country on the basis of giving preference to an intellectual elite.

Hanson Baldwin, military affairs correspondent of *The New York Times*, wrote that the plan would create an "oligarchy of brains" which "does not fit well into the democratic concept," and that it would create an elite that was good at book learning while ignoring "character and leadership," which were more important. The IQ testing movement had been dogged from the very beginning by the charge that high-IQ people were merely intelligent misfits, scrawny, nearsighted, and weird; several commentators now revived this line of argument, using as exemplars of the kind of people you get when you favor intelligence America's two leading domestic villains of the day, the brainy traitors Klaus Fuchs and Alger Hiss.

Through the spring and summer of 1951, Chauncey was constantly onstage, speaking, conferring, and being quoted. Calmly, patiently, reassuringly, he explained that the test was for draft deferment, not exemption; that making a score of 70 didn't mean a man had an IQ of 70; that one could not improve one's score by cramming; that people in the top half of their college classes would be deferred no matter what their test scores were; that the nation desperately needed to keep the pipeline of scientific talent flowing. He was deft not only at handling the erupting controversies but also at preventing potential new controversies from becoming public.

One difficulty in national standardized testing is that, by producing a serial ranking of everybody who takes the test, it brings to light wide disparities in the scores of different types of people; low scores can look like an accusation of inherent inferiority and produce intense resentment. In 1951, ETS was quite worried about one low-scoring group: Southerners. Only 42 percent made the cutoff score of 70 on the draft test, as against 73 percent of New Englanders, for example. One could imagine entire colleges in the South being wiped out as their low-scoring students were drafted and went off to be soldiers, and Southern politicians declaring war on the test. Within ETS, the idea of a regional quota system, which would allow Southerners to win deferments with lower scores than Northerners, was bandied about. Chauncey resisted that and pushed instead for keeping the truth about the regional score disparities private; luckily for him, it never leaked out.

Another of Chauncey's talents was an amazing ability to calm down angry people. In 1946, just after he had taken over the College Board testing office, the hard-boiled managing editor of *The New York Times*, Edwin James, called him in to complain that the tests were "pink," the evidence being that his daughter had taken one with a reading comprehension passage saying that newspapers sometimes soften their coverage of companies that are advertisers. Chauncey listened politely while James ranted and raved, agreed with him on a few minor points, gently defended the tests, and left, having defused the potentially disastrous situation of *The New York Times*'s being implacably opposed to testing. Chauncey never lost his temper when someone prominent criticized the draft-deferment test. Instead he would try to meet with the person and explain his position—ideally in Princeton, so that the meeting could be combined with a tour of ETS's operations and then a dinner at the Chaunceys' home or at a charming inn out in the nearby countryside of Bucks County, Pennsylvania. If the critic was an educator, he might be offered a place on one of ETS's many advisory boards, from which he could express his concerns. And, as a backstop for his own efforts, Chauncey hired ETS's first professional public-relations consultant.

Had Chauncey been less adept, the test's opponents might have succeeded in getting it postponed or even canceled. But because of his surefootedness, along with the forward momentum the test already had, the test moved ahead on schedule. After the first administrations in the spring and summer of 1951 had gone off smoothly, the tone of press coverage began to change, with less emphasis on the idea that the test was introducing a class division between, as one cartoonist put it, GI Joe and IQ Joe, and more on the wonders of testing and its importance as a weapon in the Cold War. This was the case even though two-thirds of the takers of the test scored high enough to be deferred. ETS overnight became a familiar institution and Chauncey a member of that class of people who are regularly and reverentially quoted. THEY KNOW ALL THE ANSWERS was the headline on a story about ETS in *Collier's* magazine. SELECTIVE SERVICE TESTS? HARDER TO MAKE THAN TAKE said the King Features Syndicate over a story, accompanied by a picture with this caption: "Henry Chauncey, youthful looking president of ETS, is the man at the helm of many of the tests taken by young Americans." A magazine called *Pathfinder* said: "Now ETS is recognized as the No. 1 testing organization in the U.S." The stories often discussed—in the gee-whiz tone that was characteristic of press coverage of industrial technology during the 1950s—IBM's automatic scoring machine, which was being used for the first time on a mass educational test.

The terms of the contract between ETS and the Selective Service System were unusually favorable to ETS. Because of this, and because the testing went so smoothly, ETS made a windfall profit on the contract: from a total payment by the government of $1.2 million, ETS cleared $900,000, an amount just below half of the organization's total annual revenues in those days. This money instantly solved ETS's financial crisis.

The draft-deferment test put ETS on its financial feet, made its reputation, and established several principles. Because of its need to be self-supporting, and because of Henry Chauncey's drive and absolute sense of moral mission about his organization, ETS could be counted on to work fiercely to increase the use of its tests. It would operate in a professional manner, but the push would always be to test more rather than to ponder the merits of testing, though that was supposed to be its job. In most countries a government agency performed ETS's function, which meant more sensitivity to public debate and less financial pressure. But ETS was set up in a way that guaranteed its first priority would be to work aggressively to expand testing; if it didn't it would go broke. The institutional pressures on ETS set up a situation in which first its tests became ubiquitous and consequential, and then the public debate about them took place. In fact, the public debate did not begin for decades.

The draft-deferment test demonstrated that the United States would, under the right circumstances, accept a mass IQ test. The test had bureaucratic forces in its favor: being far cheaper and easier than any other kind to administer and score, IQ tests were alluring to organizations like the Pentagon and universities, which had to process large numbers of people quickly. Organizing universal military service would have been far more difficult and more expensive. Chauncey had shown that the public's immediate and vehement hostility to IQ tests could be gotten around by modulating the presentation a little—speaking more demurely of "aptitude," presenting the test as a scientific breakthrough meant to serve a high public purpose, and at the same time downplaying the impact of the score on the takers' lives.

Conant's original idea had been to replace the old national elite with a small group of academically gifted men—it didn't occur to him, even at the height of his democratic fervor, to go searching for intelligent women, too—whom aptitude tests would help to discover, wherever they happened to be and whatever their family or social circumstances were. As he became more involved in national affairs the idea broadened: the new elite would sit at the head of a great system that would restore the United States to its full promise. For the whole mechanism to work, it was essential that people accept this new elite as deserving, selfless, valuable, and dedicated to the public good. Even Plato had recognized that, insisting that the guardians devote their lives to the welfare of the state and be unconcerned with personal gain. To Conant the spectacle of well-to-do college men being deferred from required military service, to the great resentment of everyone else, under a transparently trumped-up justification, was deeply disturbing.

So after 1950 Conant tended to distance himself from the testing juggernaut he had helped to create during and just after the war. ETS "wasn't a vital part of my undertaking," he told an interviewer in 1967. "It was peripheral from the start." He didn't want posterity to regard him as someone who believed that mass aptitude testing could solve America's social problems. Once ETS had been set up, though, it turned out to be remarkably hardy, especially with Henry Chauncey in charge. He invested testing with a fervor based on his belief in what it might one day become, and on the severity of the world crisis, rather than on what it actually was. The tests were an administrative miracle. Their friends were institutionally strong and their enemies were diffuse.

In his passion to seize upon an opportune wartime moment to establish what he saw as the modern version of Jefferson's natural aristocracy, Conant had left some key points unaddressed. He had ignored Carl Brigham's warnings about the dangers of having a single all-powerful organization in charge of both research on the proper use of tests and the commercial promotion of existing tests. He had not found a way of selecting his natural aristocrats on the basis of any criterion but the IQ test score; this was far from Jefferson's own idea of "virtue and talents." He had not established a means of ensuring that they would dedicate themselves to serving their country, as he, like Jefferson, had imagined they would. He had envisioned his new social order swiftly and in private, and he had not generated public assent to it. So what developed was something he didn't fully approve of: an organization devoted above all to advocating the use of its tests as widely as possible, and unable or unwilling to hesitate over the question of what larger purpose the tests served. Testing was creating a favored elite, that was clear, but not necessarily along the lines Conant had in mind.

After the first year of administrations of the draft-deferment test was over, Chauncey went to Washington to discuss the future with General Hershey. Everything had gone so well that Hershey felt emboldened to carry the principle behind the test further than he would previously have dared. He told Chauncey he was making provisional plans to eliminate the draft deferment for fathers, which had been sacrosanct even during the Second World War. Chauncey's notes of the conversation say: "The present thinking is that there will be a given cut-off date and after that time no individuals who have become fathers or who receive certificates of their wife's pregnancy will be deferred. . . . The problem is going to resolve itself as to a decision between students and fathers." The Korean War, and the draft, wound down soon enough so that Hershey never had to make that decision, but it was obvious what its results would have been: fathers with low IQs would have had to go off and fight and maybe die so that brainy single men could stay in college. Everyone then imagined that the Soviet Union, with no elections and no free press, must be handling its personnel decisions with even more heartless efficiency.

A few years later, one of ETS's public-relations consultants sounded the alarm about the long-term danger that making such decisions posed to the organization:

> During the Korean crisis the findings of Educational Testing Service played what was in many cases a life and death role, since it was called upon to determine which young men should be permitted to continue their educations and which inducted into military service. . . . As an institution of national scope dealing in the guidance of human lives, it

has no close parallel in our society. Under the circumstances it is well to remember that the idea of any center of power, perhaps particularly one which classifies people, is historically viewed with misgivings by Americans. It has gotten both governmental and private institutions into trouble again and again.

But that was retrospective wisdom. In 1951, Henry Chauncey had the survival of ETS to think about, and that of the nation. Perhaps somewhere down the road creating a protected group on the basis of a test score might stir up social resentments, but in a time of crisis, what choice did he have?

7

The Census of One Ability

Henry Chauncey loved everything about testing, including taking tests. He had himself, his colleagues, and his family tested whenever he came across a new test that intrigued him. One test he took in the early days of ETS, constructed by a leading personality psychologist, Gordon Allport, was called "A Study of Values." You had to rank pairs of statements on a zero-to-three ascending scale of importance. For example:

> If you were given certain topics on which to write an essay, would you choose: a) the role of church-going in religion, or b) the defects of our present educational system?

Chauncey's answer was 0, 3. Or:

> Is a person who analyzes his emotions likely to be less sincere in his feeling than one who is not so reflective?
> a) Yes; b) No?

His answer there again was 0, 3.

Then there was a section in which you had to rank a series of qualities in order of their value to you. One question asked husbands about wives and wives about husbands. As the most preferred quality in a wife, Chauncey picked "likes to stay at home and keep house." As the least preferred, he picked "is gifted along artistic lines."

The marriage of Henry and Elizabeth Chauncey had long since taken on the aspect of a domestic Cold War. She was a serious musician. He had no interest in the arts; he found reports on educational policy fascinating but couldn't read a novel or even sit through a concert or a movie. After he became president of ETS, he thought he should do a certain amount of official entertaining, the way a university president would; she had no interest in playing the role of First Lady of testing. In the summer of 1952, Chauncey, characteristically believing that if there was a problem, testing could solve it, wrote a memo to himself that said:

> It seems to me that in the personality domain we are missing per-haps the simplest and perhaps the most important problem that we could tackle and that is marriage compatibility. . . . This, of course, would have to be a large scale investigation, but it certainly should be one with tremendous potentiality for the improvement of the happiness of mankind.

The following year, after a flurry of charged, marital-endgame late-night phone calls and abrupt comings and goings, Elizabeth told Henry that she wanted a divorce.

In American society of the 1950s, divorce was more shocking and less easily accomplished than it is now. Chauncey obtained assurance from the ETS board that he could continue to serve as president despite the end of his marriage, and during the summer of 1953 he moved to Wyoming, which had much more lax divorce laws than New Jersey, to live long enough to establish residence there. Chauncey's Harvard roommate operated a dude ranch called the Tepee Lodge; Chauncey moved in and earned his keep by doing odd jobs around the place, one of which was driving guests to and from the nearest air-port, in Sheridan. One guest whose plane he met was a briskly energetic young woman named Laurie Worcester, who had recently graduated from Smith College and gone to work as an editorial assistant at *Life* magazine.

It was typical Chauncey good luck that while in exile in the remote reaches of the West for the purpose of getting divorced he should meet and fall in love with someone from a proper Eastern background. He and Laurie were soon making plans to marry. Her father, a dour corporate lawyer in New York, was not thrilled with the idea of his daughter marrying a divorced man more than twice her age whom she barely knew. It was decided that they would visit a psychologist, who would determine whether she was really in love or just in the grip of a father fixation. Fortunately he gave the match his blessing.

Henry and Laurie Chauncey quickly had four daughters. Some of the flavor of the Chaunceys' life together can be gotten from a letter Laurie wrote in 1957 in response to a best-husband contest in *The Ladies' Home Journal*:

> It's an objective fact that he is the most remarkable man alive. "Alive" is a pretty feeble word to use for the combination of vitality and humanity that is unique with Henry. . . . P.S. What would I change in my husband? Frankly, it would be nice if he knew Mozart from Bach, and could at least pronounce a couple of modern artists' names. If he read some of the novels I read, he could share the nightmares they give me instead of saying, "I told you so."

Laurie's advent ushered in a golden age for Henry Chauncey and ETS.

ETS was an unusual organization that had been formed in an unusual way. It was private but it performed a quasi-public function; it had the contradictory mission of researching testing and promoting testing; the creation of just a handful of quietly influential people, it was positioned so as to have great power over the lives of millions. There had never been anything quite like it. But Henry Chauncey's mission couldn't have been more straightforward in his own untroubled mind: it was to make ETS as big and influential and prosperous and prestigious as he possibly could.

The year after his remarriage, Chauncey discovered a four-hundred-acre farm a few minutes outside Princeton that was for sale at a favorable price, and he persuaded the ETS board to buy it as a permanent home for the organization. The Chaunceys moved into the farmhouse and began to build an elaborate, idealized campus for ETS, with managed forests and nature trails, lawns, plantings, flocks of birds swimming in an artificial pond, new houses for the top executives, and low-slung modern buildings named after the pioneers of educational testing, Conant and Brigham and Thorndike and Wood.

The ETS campus had the feeling of a college without the annoyance of students, alumni, or rich donors. A set of distinct institutional rhythms developed. Truckloads of test booklets and answer sheets would arrive discreetly by the back entrance to be scored—each truck trailed by a car whose driver's job it was to make sure that no ETS material fell into the road where somebody might find it. Dozens of would-be academics for whom life had not worked out perfectly found employment at ETS writing new questions for the SAT and the other tests. They rode to work on the company shuttle bus from Princeton and ate lunch in the company cafeteria. The psychometricians—royalty in the new organization—conducted their studies, published papers, and flew off to conferences. Squadrons of high-school teachers arrived during school vacations to grade the Advanced Placement exams. The company paid better than most colleges and universities, provided excellent benefits, and never fired anyone. It was exciting to work there. ETS was at the forefront of an important new development; one executive said later that the farm outside of Princeton felt like the Silicon Valley of its day.

Every year at the company picnic Henry Chauncey would put on a chef's hat and cook hamburgers for all the employees. He presided over ETS's Annual Conference on Testing Problems, which attracted all the top people in the field. He conducted tours of ETS for visiting dignitaries—government officials, foreign leaders, important people in the press, officials of universities who were thinking of joining the College Board and using ETS's tests. The U.S. government sent Chauncey on lengthy visits to Australia and New Zealand and, twice, to Russia.

Chauncey became the educational version of a captain of industry, in tweeds rather than pinstripes. In his fifties his most distinguishing physical feature was thick black eyebrows under a full head of gray hair, and he was still fit, vigorous, and actively athletic. Although he had not personally invented the leading new psychometric techniques or educational doctrines, he had a good understanding of what they were, and could put them across to civilians better than the inventors themselves usually could. He seemed to know everyone worth knowing, to exemplify the principle that between Chaunceys and most important people, there was only one degree of separation. Back in his assistant dean days, stopped by the police in Maryland for practicing his lifelong vice of speeding, he had astonished his captors by using his one phone call to complain to the governor. At ETS, one of his lieutenants remembered that every time an influential person seemed to be blocking the organization's onward march, "He'd say, 'I'll call him up! I'll go see him!' We'd joke: How long does it take people to get on the phone when they hear Henry Chauncey is on the line?"

Testing, despite the new presence of ETS, was still a little like medicine in the late nineteenth century, with small private companies sending out unqualified snake-oil salesmen to gull unsuspecting local school boards into buying second-rate tests. ETS itself, however, was absolutely respectable and trustworthy, and Chauncey personified these qualities. Nobody could be more the opposite of a moneygrubbing fly-by-night operator than the Puritan-descended, public-spirited, gain-oblivious figure that Chauncey presented. ETS could be trusted not to roll out tests that were not ready. Although Chauncey could not hire the top tier of real giants of testing to work at ETS (they wondered what a mere assistant dean was doing running the world's most important testing organization), he was terrific at identifying and successfully wooing (often over lunches at the plummy Century Club in New York) the best people from the next tier down. Unlike many men who had been raised and schooled in the same milieu, he hired without regard to ethnic or class background, and when testing experts on the ETS staff told him he shouldn't do something, he paid attention and didn't do it.

The number of Americans enrolled in institutions of higher education passed 2 million in 1951, 3 million in 1957, and 4 million in 1961. ETS was perfectly positioned to ride this wave. In 1955, just five years after warning Chauncey that he ought to cut back drastically, Robert Merry, his advisor from Harvard Business School, wrote him: "Realistically I can see no way for ETS to avoid substantial growth because of the importance of its position in supplying the market." The College Board had expanded to three hundred members during the 1950s, and almost a third that many schools had adopted the SAT as a requirement without joining the College Board. In 1957 the number of students taking the SAT every year passed half a million (and, for the first time, they were told their scores). That same year, *Life* magazine published a portentous five-part series proclaiming the arrival of "The Age of Psychology in the U.S.," with generous attention given to the miraculous new field of educational testing. "All indications are that the expansion of psychology and psychiatry up to now—as spectacular as it has been—is only the beginning," *Life* told its readers.

Such was the mood just before the Soviet Union seemed to demonstrate its technological superiority to the United States by successfully launching Sputnik, the first space satellite, on October 4, 1957; after Sputnik, the education boom redoubled with a sense of almost wartime urgency. In 1958 Congress passed the National Defense Education Act, which authorized regular federal funding of universities under the familiar Cold War rationale that we needed to be training as many scientists and engineers as the Soviet Union undoubtedly was. Academics correctly understood the law to be the harbinger of much more government funding for colleges and universities in the future and, therefore, of further growth. The United States, without having formally or legally decided to do so, was well on its way to creating mass higher education—unknown anywhere else in the world and undreamed of even by university educators only a few years earlier. Universities were becoming institutions bearing the heaviest possible load of the American people's aspirations and frustrations.

Only one problem consistently gnawed at Henry Chauncey as he ran ETS, and that was the narrowness of what the ETS tests measured and of the use to which the scores were put. He had agreed to run ETS because he thought mental testing was a scientific miracle that would soon reveal all the ancient mysteries of the mind, and as soon as it did, he wanted to mount the Census of Abilities—to assess all Americans on all dimensions, and to use the information gained not just to place them in colleges and universities but to plot the whole course of their lives. That was his dream.

So, as well as things were going, Chauncey still found it frustrating that ETS's basic activity was nothing more than administering the SAT and the graduate and professional school admissions tests. All these were variations on the same theme of academic aptitude; they were linear descendants of the early IQ tests. The idea was beginning to take root among the students who took the tests and their parents that they measured inherent worth and were determinants of success in life—that the test score was the contemporary equivalent of the "virtue and talents" that Jefferson thought would qualify the members of a natural aristocracy. Yet from a technical point of view, all the tests were meant to do was predict a student's grades six months into the future; every question (in testing parlance, "item") was designed with this single goal of grade-predictiveness in mind. Every college that was considering using an ETS test wanted to see just one number, the "predictive validity coefficient," which measured the fit between the score and first-year grades. The ETS research department's bread-and-butter work was cranking out validity studies comparing test scores with first-year grades.

Back in the early days of testing, there were scattered reports of extremely high validities, which often came from promoters of testing like Ben Wood and William Learned. But now the numbers were dropping. Most ETS tests settled into validities, on a zero-to-one scale, in the .4 range. The predictive validity of grades was usually a little higher, and if you combined grades and test scores (an exercise Henry Chauncey had invented when he was an assistant dean at Harvard), you got a higher predictive validity than from either one alone, somewhere around .5. That was certainly enough to make the tests useful, but still, all the SAT by itself did was explain about 15 percent of the variance in first-year grades in college, which was a pretty slender achievement, hardly commensurate with the magnificent role Chauncey had envisioned for testing.

Chauncey pushed consistently to get beyond merely helping universities to predict the first-year grades of their applicants and into the empyrean realm of the Census of Abilities. There were two sides to the project: developing tests to measure qualities other than scholastic aptitude and finding customers for them. The SAT and the graduate school tests had decent validity and outstanding reliability (meaning the constancy of a person's score over repeated administrations of the test). Any new test, measuring a different quality, would have to meet these high standards. The main existing ETS tests had a built-in, and growing, market in the universities. If ETS found it could test effectively for new qualities, it would still have to find someone who wanted to use the tests.

From the moment he came across testing as a young man, Chauncey had been keeping an eye out for new tests with miraculous qualities. It's impossible in retrospect to go through the list of tests that attracted his enthusiastic attention over the years without feeling a measure of gratitude that each of them did not become a basic requirement as the SAT did. To Chauncey, though, each was as magical in its possibilities as the SAT had been, at least until somebody talked him out of that position; it was very difficult for him to imagine bad consequences flowing from something as good as testing.

When Chauncey first heard about the Rorschach test, a series of ten ink blots printed on white cards that were used to elicit revealing fantasies from the test-taker, he located a Harvard professor who was familiar with it and took him to lunch at the Faculty Club to find out more, but he was persuaded that the Rorschach couldn't be used in admissions work because it had to be lengthily, individually administered by an expert. Also during his Harvard days, Chauncey became intrigued with the work of a popular psychologist, scorned in academe, named Johnson O'Connor. O'Connor had developed a test of creativity in which the taker would be asked such questions as "What would happen if the level of the ocean would rise six feet?" and "What would happen if no trees grew more than two feet tall?" Then he would count the words in the response, and whoever had the most words got the highest creativity score. Like many early figures in testing, O'Connor was not interested in grounding his work in experimental proof, so getting Harvard to use the creativity test was not possible, but Chauncey always felt O'Connor had been onto something.

During the war Chauncey heard about a test of practical judgment that had been developed by a man in Illinois. He immediately ordered a copy and administered it to himself, and for years he needled the ETS staff about whether they could find a way to measure this quality, which surely was just as important as scholastic aptitude. At one point Chauncey had the idea that ETS should start a TV quiz show (that institution being one of the fads of the expert-worshipping 1950s), around the theme of practical judgment. The questions would be submitted by ordinary people—who better to measure practical judgment?—the most productive of whom ETS could then hire as item writers. (This was one of Chauncey's enthusiasms that his staff ignored. A few years later, when it turned out that the most popular quiz shows had been rigged, ETS got an offer to produce the questions for a new show that its involvement would certify as clean, which it declined.)

Another cause of Chauncey's was to develop a test that measured persistence. After V-E Day he dispatched a psychometrician on the College Board staff to Germany to find out whether Nazis had come up with anything in the field of testing that might be of use to the free world, as they had in rocketry. The man returned with news of a persistence test invented by a psychologist named Pauli: takers had to add columns of figures for an hour, under observation, and the length of time before their attention flagged was the basis for their score. Chauncey also maintained a long-running interest in graphology (handwriting analysis) and somatyping (the study of physical characteristics such as body type as indicators of psychological traits), but it was so obvious that getting the ETS research staff interested in these would be a lost cause that he didn't even try. His main effort to broaden the spectrum was in the area of personality testing.

One of the fabulous characters of psychology at mid-century, when it was professionalizing but still had a place for the inspired amateur, was Henry A. Murray. A child of a leading New York family and inheritor of a real-estate fortune, Murray went to Groton and Harvard (he was a classmate of Devereux Josephs at both) and then became a medical doctor. On an Atlantic crossing in the 1920s he read *Moby-Dick*, which struck him with thunderbolt force. On the spot he decided to drop medicine and become a psychologist. Although he never got a Ph.D. he became a professor at Harvard. Murray was a tall, polite, dapper gentleman who, despite appearances, was entirely preoccupied with the dark underworld of obsessions, compulsions, and ungovernable desires—that was why he was so drawn to Herman Melville's work. Over the years he developed a schema of twenty-six fundamental human needs, many of which have a dark, furry, Middle European feel: *n* Dominance (to use his shorthand), *n* Exhibition, *n* Abasement.

For many years Murray, without ever ending his marriage, carried on a tormented, intense love affair with one of his assistants, Christiana Morgan, a Swiss woman who had studied under Carl Jung. Together Murray and Morgan developed the Thematic Apperception Test, consisting of a series of black-and-white drawings printed on stiff cards, about which the test-taker is asked to tell stories. Most of the pictures are purposely unsettling, because Murray and Morgan believed that the stories they elicited would then come from deep within the unconscious. An unconscious naked woman with big breasts and flowing hair lies on a bed; next to the bed stands a man in business attire, turned away from her, his face buried in the crook of his arm. A teenage boy dressed in a suit stands in an operating theater where a doctor holds a knife poised over a woman's abdomen; a large rifle floats across the edge of the picture. A woman stands in a doorway, looking shaky, with her head in her hand. A beautiful, seductive woman embraces a handsome, super-masculine man, but he turns away with a look of dread on his face. A witch or crone stands just behind a woman who may not notice her but nonetheless appears troubled.

During the war Murray was brought into the government by General William Donovan, head of the Office of Strategic Services, the American espionage agency, to devise ways of selecting spies. One of his tests had a would-be intelligence agent being asked to build a small bridge across a stream with the help of an assistant. But the assistant was actually a double agent, working for Murray, with instructions to screw up the job. Murray would hide in a nearby barn—all this took place on government-owned land in Maryland that is now Camp David, the presidential retreat—and watch through a crack in the door to see whether the candidate could be made to lose his cool. (Evidently Murray wasn't personally much of an expert at spotting a spy: he testified as a character witness for Alger Hiss.) When peace arrived, Murray applied to Devereux Josephs at Carnegie for a substantial grant to continue his work on the Thematic Apperception Test, the OSS tests, and other personality studies. Josephs turned him down, so, with his own money and on a smaller scale, Murray founded the Harvard Psychological Clinic, which he installed in an old house in Cambridge on whose front door he had painted a white whale.

Every so often Chauncey would invite Harry Murray down to ETS to consult with the research staff on the possibility of ETS's getting into personality testing. In the early days of their relationship each man convinced himself that the other was a secret ally, which represented a wild misreading in both cases: Murray thought Chauncey's true interest was in depth psychology; and Chauncey thought Murray would want to develop multiple-choice tests that could be used to dispense practical career guidance to the masses. Finally Chauncey was forced to admit defeat. In 1950 he wrote, exasperated:

> After our two days with Harry Murray . . . I personally am convinced that the laborious and subjective methods that he uses are not going to result in a clear-cut delineation of personality and its genesis much less in any effective measurement of personality traits. . . . I am oppressed by the effort that has been made to analyze sentiments and their foci. . . . I personally am not so much interested in obtaining an absolutely complete understanding of each individual as I am in identifying and measuring some important factors that will be useful on an actuarial basis in the prediction of success.

Some good came from the Murray-Chauncey relationship. ETS got a contract to devise a test for prospective Foreign Service officers, partly because the State Department viewed Murray's testing program for the OSS as having been a success. Murray introduced one of his assistants from the OSS days, John Gardner, to Devereux Josephs, who made Gardner his successor as head of the Carnegie Corporation and therefore the leading philanthropic protector of ETS. Finally, Murray sent ETS one of his assistants, a man named Sylvan Tompkins, who had developed a child of the Thematic Apperception Test called the Picture Apperception Test. The test consisted of sets of pictures printed three on a page. The taker was asked to weave the three pictures into a single story. When Chauncey took the test, Tompkins analyzed his answers and told him that he always made the first picture represent a problem, the second a solution, and the third a leisure activity. This was much more in the range of what Chauncey considered a useful test result than anything Harry Murray had come up with; and his impression of Tompkins became even more favorable when they went to the track together and Tompkins won a lot of money, simply, he said, by applying his psychological theories to the horses. Alas, as Chauncey later remembered it, "Sylvan and the psychometricians in the ETS research department were like oil and water," so nothing came of his enthusiasm for Tompkins.

The successor to the OSS, the Central Intelligence Agency, also impressed with what Henry Murray had done during the war, became another of ETS's clients. Chauncey was unable to persuade the CIA to have a selection exam for agents—in its early days the CIA stood out even among Establishment institutions in its insistence on hiring only through an informal network, on the theory that spies had to be absolutely trustworthy (hence, certified gentlemen, which perforce meant nonethnic) and financially incorruptible (hence, preferably, rich). So, rather than a test, it used a word-of-mouth system that brought it young men who had gone to private boarding schools; one was young Henry Chauncey, Jr., who worked for the CIA when he was a student at Yale in the 1950s, having been recruited by a professor of literature named Norman Holmes Pearson, who was the agency's leading talent spotter. But ETS did perform seven studies under contract to a CIA front called the Society for the Investigation of Human Ecology. These were part of a CIA project called MKULTRA, which is best known for having administered LSD to unwitting subjects, one of whom jumped out of a window and died, but which from the ETS point of view was one of the few sponsors it ever found for its personality research.

During the 1950s ETS had dealings with such big names in educational theory as Jacques Barzun, Jean Piaget, Clyde Kluckhohn, Jerome Bruner, and B. F. Skinner, but never with a usable test as the result. The final and lengthiest effort to construct an ETS personality test began when Chauncey agreed in 1957 to have ETS act as institutional home for the Myers-Briggs Type Indicator, a test produced by a self-taught psychologist in Swarthmore, Pennsylvania, named Isabel Briggs Myers.

If a 1950s Dr. Frankenstein had been sent into the laboratory with orders to devise the creature most likely to be regarded with contempt by the ETS research department, he couldn't have done much better than Isabel Myers. An unsuccessful writer of fiction who had never taken a psychology course, a woman in an all-male world, and a person so doggedly persistent as to be unaffected by years of criticism from respectable authorities, Myers had been inspired to write her test by reading the work of Carl Jung on psychological types. She created four axes on which to plot the personality, which she took from Jung: Extraversion/Introversion, Sensation/Intuition, Thinking/Feeling, and Judgment/Perception. For the Myers-Briggs Type Indicator, the test-taker answered a series of multiple-choice questions about personal preferences and then was assigned to one or the other side of each axis. Henry Chauncey, for example, who took the Myers-Briggs Type Indicator and had his whole family take it, too, was an ENFP, Extraversion-Intuition-Feeling-Perception.

The first principle of psychometrics is that all distributions bunch up in the middle, in the familiar form of a bell curve. The Myers-Briggs test assumed that on each axis the distribution would bunch up at the ends: most people would be either introverts or extraverts, rather than something in between the two. That was one problem. Another was that, like most personality tests, the Myers-Briggs was not reliable—people would take the test twice and get different scores—and, at first glance, there was no obvious number, like the first-year grade point average, against which to validate the results. Also, the Thinking/Feeling axis and possibly the others, too, seemed to people at ETS to correspond to male-female differences rather than to personality types. "It's almost like astrology. We made fun of it," one ETS psychometrician said.

Chauncey, however, had a soft spot for the Myers-Briggs. For all the time he had devoted to meeting the great men of personality psychology, he had never been able to obtain the rights to a personality test that was not individually administered. The Myers-Briggs was therefore his last, best hope for creating the testing side of the Census of Abilities; it provided, as he put it, "a platform along with aptitude test scores for investigating additional qualities." Besides, as a nonpsychometrician himself, he believed that those without credentials might have more to offer to testing than the experts realized.

For years Chauncey assigned one or another young ETS executive to work with Isabel Myers, always generating a disastrously bad relationship. Matters reached a nadir during a period when Myers' keeper at ETS was a man named Lawrence Stricker, who tried to get published a research paper he had written called "Description and Evaluation of the Myers-Briggs Type Indicator," in which, as Myers wrote Chauncey, "he assumed a role not unlike a New York dramatic critic determined to close down a scheduled production even before its opening," and which also, for good measure, reproduced many of the questions (always a closely guarded secret in the world of testing) for all the world to see. Myers threatened to sue Stricker for copyright infringement, and Chauncey gave her a new supervisor. Soon this man reported to Chauncey, hopefully, that because Myers' mother and husband were both gravely ill, "she seems to be trying for the first time the role of wife, mother, and woman—and enjoying it very much. It is the professional exuberance that has been curbed."

The relationship limped along for the better part of two decades, Chauncey unwilling to let go of the Myers-Briggs because he didn't want ETS to be merely an aptitude tester, Myers unwilling to leave ETS because its unimpeachable respectability meant something to her. She tried to market the test to possible clients, and so did Chauncey. The CIA used it experimentally a few times. At one point the Association of American Medical Colleges was interested, and at another point the nursing schools. Finally, after Chauncey had retired, an ETS vice president called Myers in and told her ETS was not going to publish her test anymore. She put her head down on his desk and cried.

As a business matter, letting the Myers-Briggs test go was the worst decision ETS ever made. Today the Myers-Briggs is the quasi-official New Age standardized test. Published by the Consulting Psychologist Press and used by practicing psychologists and by employers who consider themselves psychologically aware, it has more takers every year than the SAT.

The problem of finding customers for the Census of Abilities continued, for Chauncey could never generate interest in it within the federal government. The obvious next candidate was big business. Wouldn't a company want to use tests to find out as much as possible about the potential of their prospective employees, just as universities wanted to know what kind of grades their prospective students would likely get? ETS made plans to start a Personality Research Center, which would conduct an "executive study" to find out what made for a successful businessman. Chauncey found a test he thought he could market to corporations, one that classified people according to the order of importance they gave to Ideas, Things, Men, and Economic Symbols (that is, money). Someone who was an ITME would then be assigned to the company's research department, an EMTI to sales, a TIEM to engineering, and so on.

Chauncey, typically, went straight to the top of American business to get support for the Personality Research Center. He put together an advisory board with representation from the likes of IBM, Chrysler, Westinghouse, and Procter & Gamble, but what was more notable was how cool a reception he got in the corporate world. The titans of the American economy did not believe they needed tests. David Rockfeller of the Chase Manhattan Bank turned down Chauncey's offer of membership on the advisory board. Chauncey had an appointment with John Hay Whitney, the venture capitalist, who had been at Groton with him, but afterward he wrote in frustration: "This conference was one more misadventure in relation to John Hay Whitney." Benjamin Buttenweiser of the Wall Street firm of Kuhn, Loeb "indicated his disapproval of esoteric subject matter." Cruelest blow of all, even Devereux Josephs, the man substantially responsible for the existence of ETS, who had gone on to become president of the New York Life Insurance Company, "felt we did not have something that had appeal to individuals or business."

These businessmen's lack of enthusiasm was matched within ETS by practically everybody but Chauncey. One ETS executive admitted to Chauncey that he had been "dragging my feet on this project," because he was uncomfortable with the idea of people's fates being determined by scores on a personality test. Another wrote Chauncey: "I think we might begin a low pressure campaign to disabuse the public of its favorite notion that there is some sort of magic key to the problem of appraising and predicting personal effectiveness and that we are the boys who expect to find the key in a matter of two or three years." Although Chauncey pushed ahead at least to the point of once holding a conference to discuss the executive study, the idea of a Personality Research Center gradually faded away and was completely gone by the end of the 1950s.

ETS made one more grand attempt to move beyond aptitude testing. Beginning in 1952, a team began work on a Test of Developed Ability: a single, massive six-hour examination that would replace the SAT and the ETS achievement tests as the basic requirement for prospective college students. Unlike most of the new tests that Chauncey had proposed for ETS, the Test of Developed Ability was not the work of an outsider who couldn't operate within the ETS system; it was produced, laboriously, by ETS itself, with close attention paid to reliability and validity. It had three two-hour sections: humanities, social studies, and science. Each section tested factual knowledge to some extent and reasoning ability to some extent, but there was almost nothing of the old IQ test standbys, such as having to identify antonyms and analogies. The social studies test even had an essay portion. The main emphasis was on having to solve new problems in a given academic specialty, rather than on proficiency with abstract word and number relationships.

The Test of Developed Ability would have represented a decisive symbolic break for ETS with its origins in IQ testing. In operation, perhaps, it might have been used in the same way as the SAT, as a means of deciding whom to admit to fancy colleges, but in appearance its purpose was merely to help higher education to guide students to whatever they'd be best off studying. The claim ETS made for the test was that it would be better than the SAT at predicting which principal subject a student would do well in; this would serve a different purpose from measuring general academic worth. ETS was still a new organization, and people in higher education, especially at the state universities, still grumbled about how Conant and his allies had hijacked educational testing and set up a national IQ operation to feed the Ivy League. The Test of Developed Ability might have quieted the grumbling.

The embodiment of the populist, public-school critique of ETS was E. F. Lindquist—father of the Iowa Every-Pupil Tests, which by then were given to public-school students all over the country, developer during the war years of the high-school equivalency test that dropouts can take to obtain a "General Education Diploma" that they can show to prospective employers, inventor of a test-scoring machine, and the head of an important academic program in testing at Iowa State. Chauncey fully realized how important Lindquist was: before ETS was a month old, he offered him the job of vice president for programs, but Lindquist turned it down. Now he was the most influential testing figure who wasn't connected to ETS in some way.

Lindquist thought of himself as being far above Chauncey in professional eminence, and, at the same time, he played the Midwestern populist to Chauncey's Eastern elitist. Chauncey tested for private universities, Lindquist for public ones. Chauncey tested for selection, Lindquist for guidance. Chauncey's tests were used to anoint the top few, Lindquist's to reject only the hopelessly unprepared and to help teachers work with the rest more effectively. Lindquist's dissatisfaction with the rapid growth of ETS and the SAT became increasingly audible through the 1950s; the Test of Developed Ability might not have satisfied him but it might well have appeased him.

In 1956 the Test of Developed Ability was administered experimentally twice. In 1957 two ETS officials published confident articles about it. It seemed to be moving forward. But in 1959 the president of the College Board noted curtly in his annual report that "the TDA battery as a whole did not find favor with the colleges as an admissions instrument and was shelved."

The trouble with the Test of Developed Ability was that it lacked the SAT's convenience. It was longer and therefore more complicated to administer, and because of the essay section it could not be entirely machine-scored. The projected per-test cost of development would be six dollars, as against three dollars for the SAT. As always, pure aptitude testing was cheaper and more convenient than any other kind. It also had a political advantage: because it supposedly measured each student's innate ability, aptitude testing did not threaten high schools with the prospect that the quality of their teaching might be rated. Anyway, by the late 1950s the SAT had developed a large enough constituency of users that to persuade everyone now to drop it in favor of something new would be a big, expensive project.

The death of the Test of Developed Ability had two consequences, one tangible and one more spiritual but no less important. The tangible one was that Lindquist started his own testing organization in 1959, American College Testing, to compete with ETS by marketing the kind of examinations he believed in, primarily to nonselective public universities. ACT is still ETS's leading rival; ACT tests almost the same number of high-school seniors every year as ETS. The spiritual consequence was that Henry Chauncey stopped thinking of ETS as being in the process of moving beyond aptitude testing. He had clung tenaciously for more than a decade to his idea of the Census of Abilities. Now it was dead. Henceforth ETS would be in the business of conducting a census of just one ability—"scholastic aptitude," a close relative of IQ—and endeavoring to make it as widely consequential as possible. That wasn't Chauncey's original intention, and it wasn't a decision that Americans had made in any organized way, either. It was the result of a peculiar combination of Conant's ideas and a series of accidents and bureaucratic imperatives. Still, there it was: a definite new system, one that, if it spread as widely as Chauncey wanted, would affect the life course of practically everybody in the United States.

8 The Standard Gauge

Henry Chauncey's situation was not unlike that of the industrialists of the late nineteenth century. He was trying to build a big, national, rational organization in an atmosphere of intrigue, corruption, competition, and disorder. To do this required administrative and political skill and also a certain ruthlessness, or at least an unshakable conviction that the rise to a near-monopoly position by one's own company would be good for humanity. With the fading away of the Census of Abilities, Chauncey's real mission was to get as much of the United States as possible to accept the SAT and the other ETS aptitude tests as a uniform standard—to make them, to use his metaphor, into the human equivalent of the railroad standard gauge, which had made nationwide commerce possible.

It wasn't an easy job.

ETS had the advantage of owning the copyright to all the most prominent tests in higher education and of inheriting from the College Board all the most prestigious private universities in the East as clients. It had the disadvantage of lacking an imprimatur from the government or the public for the almost official role it supposed itself to be playing. In order to become a national rather than Ivy League organization, it had to extend its reach in a westward and public-university direction, before anyone else did so first, and without encountering some disabling opposition to the idea of a private organization's setting up mental tests as a basic mechanism for distributing educational opportunity in America.

Testing, in the 1950s, was still a new, raw business, full of bare-knuckles players and shoddy practices. All over the country, former school superintendents were setting themselves up as test publishers to make a little money. They sold tests to their former districts, with no validity or reliability studies to assure the quality. Test security was negligible. Typically the tests themselves were left in schoolhouse closets and drawers for years, and the publishers made money by selling the answer sheets anew for each new administration of the tests. Rumors abounded of school superintendents being given stock or other financial inducements in return for choosing one or another test.

The United States had, and still has, the most decentralized educational system in the advanced world. Public elementary and secondary schools were and are under the direct control of about 15,000 local school boards made up of ordinary elected citizens. Fifty state departments of education had some sway over those local school districts, but usually not the power directly to order them to use a certain curriculum or administer a certain test, or even to force them to use reputable tests instead of disreputable ones. Most public universities in the 1950s were open-admissions, and their officials didn't see why they needed to adopt a test like the SAT. Within ETS, people thought that making the SAT a national device would involve a long, arduous campaign.

ETS was lucky, though, in this way: in the early going its main competitor and its main public critic were, respectively, inept and peculiar.

The number-two organization in testing was Science Research Associates in Chicago. Although Henry Chauncey was so congenitally cheerful that he bore no one ill will, if he had been forced to pick one person to dislike, it might well have been the head of SRA, Lyle Spencer. Like Chauncey, Spencer was a big, handsome, impressive man, in a flashier way than Chauncey; he was well connected in education (his father had been president of the University of Washington), had held an important job in testing for the Army during the war (assistant head of research), but was not a trained psychometrician. To Chauncey's mind the salient difference between them was that SRA, having been set up as a new business, was a for-profit company, and ETS, having descended from the College Board, was nonprofit. Both of them were commercial operations, but SRA had stockholders who expected to get dividends and to see the value of their shares grow. Therefore, it was clear to Chauncey, Lyle Spencer had gone into testing to get rich, not to serve the public. SRA, for example, used to sell a two-part reading-skills test to elementary schools on which the second test was easier than the first, so that superintendents were guaranteed to be able to claim that their students had dramatically improved. ETS did not do that kind of thing.

In 1954 Henry Chauncey's old boss from the wartime period at the College Board, John Stalnaker, now jealous of ETS's success, got involved with a rival testing program called the National Merit Scholarship Corporation.

Its idea was to give a national test to high-school students and, mainly on the basis of the scores, select a few of them to be given full four-year college scholarships. As was the case with ETS tests, the National Merit program was easy to sell to colleges and universities because it was a means for them to get top-quality students without cost: corporate sponsors paid the bills, in order to be good citizens and to get good publicity—the country needed just this kind of program to compete more effectively with the Soviet Union for technological advantage.

Stalnaker contracted with ETS to devise the National Merit test. He was a petulant, demanding client. Worried that ETS would market the same test he was using, under a different name, to a separate, competing set of corporate sponsors, and so try to drive National Merit out of business, he demanded that ETS promise to give National Merit exclusive use of the test. ETS refused. Stalnaker took his business to SRA. The next year, as if to rub salt in the wound, he announced that his contract was up for bid again, got Chauncey to come out to Chicago to present an elaborately prepared five-year proposal, but signed on with SRA anyway for another two years. Then Stalnaker delivered a speech at the American Psychological Association's annual convention in which he said it would be very dangerous to have one "mammoth agency" in testing that could "stifle research." And when Lindquist decided to start the American College Testing program to compete head-on with ETS, he signed on with SRA to line up clients and handle the administration and scoring.

Naturally, ETS maintained a keen interest in the doings of SRA all through the 1950s. "You might find it interesting and might collect a certain amount of information if you drop in on SRA," one ETS executive wrote to a staff member in 1951. Three years later, the same executive wrote Chauncey that while paying a call on General Hershey, he had managed to get a peek at SRA's bid for the Selective Service test, which was going to be administered again: "Nothing remotely compared to ETS." Yet SRA got the Selective Service contract. Afterward an ETS field representative reported that SRA was sure to lose money on it and that "a Jewish crowd" had taken over management of SRA and set up "luxuriant offices" in Chicago. Shortly after that, Chauncey met quietly with a former SRA official to find out more. He learned, according to his notes, that "Spencer's weaknesses are power and money," and that there was bad blood between Spencer and his biggest financial backer, Irving Harris, then a hair-products king, now a leading Chicago philanthropist (and, by the way, Jewish).

Almost from the moment that ETS was chartered, SRA and the other leading test publishers—a loose-knit group of ten private companies that constructed and sold tests, mainly to public elementary and secondary schools—had been grumbling that its nonprofit status gave it an unfair advantage. ETS did not have to pay taxes or dividends, as they did, and it could get grants from foundations and government, as they could not. They were all in the same business, competing for the same contracts, but the nonprofit ETS had both an aura of prestige and a lower cost of operation that enabled it to underbid the competition. ETS took in more money than it spent—what was the difference between that and making a profit?

After the great success of the Selective Service test in 1951, the other test publishers seemed to know exactly how much ETS had made on it, which led Chauncey to suspect that they were surreptitiously getting information from someone at the Internal Revenue Service. In 1958, the IRS notified ETS that it had launched a formal investigation of its nonprofit status. Not long after that Chauncey had a meeting with John Stalnaker, who mentioned the investigation. How did he know about it? He said Lindquist had told him. But Chauncey thought "the situation may be more complex than that, since SRA may also have taken a hand" in getting the IRS to investigate and then might have told Stalnaker. Specifically, Chauncey believed that Newton Minow, a prominent Chicago lawyer who had been on SRA's board (he was later to go to Washington as Kennedy's head of the Federal Communications Commission), was prodding the IRS to prolong the investigation of ETS on behalf of his friends at SRA.

Chauncey adeptly handled the IRS investigation, which dragged on into the mid-1960s. ETS's unusually powerful local congressman in New Jersey, Frank Thompson, gave him advice and aid. At one of their meetings in Thompson's Washington office, Chauncey complained about the IRS investigation, and Thompson just picked up the phone, called the number-two man at the Treasury (that is, the superior of the commissioner of the IRS, Mortimer Caplin) and, with Chauncey listening gratefully, passed the complaints on to him. And when Caplin left government to practice law, ETS hired him as its Washington counsel. Finally the IRS ruled that ETS could remain tax-exempt.

SRA, it turned out, appeared much more formidable from a distance than it actually was. Lyle Spencer sold it in 1960 to IBM, which was hoping to make money in computerized tests, but the organization it bought was weak and understaffed, and SRA faded from ETS's end of the educational testing scene.

In 1956 *Life* published an article—glowing, like nearly all press coverage of testing in the 1950s—about John Stalnaker's new National Merit Scholarship program. It included a box about the kind of question that would be on the scholarship examination. They were the old vocabulary standbys, antonyms and synonyms and the like; in a few questions the test-taker was asked to pick "the pair of words that are related."

Soon an angry letter arrived in Stalnaker's mailbox from Banesh Hoffmann, a professor of mathematics at Queens College and a well-known writer of books and magazine articles on science for a popular audience. Hoffmann was a physicist as well as a mathematician (he had worked as an assistant of Albert Einstein), and in addition he was an amateur grammarian deeply devoted to *Fowler's English Usage*. Fowler prefers the usage "pair of words that *is* related," presuming that the singular "pair" is the subject, not the plural "words."

Perhaps mischievously, Stalnaker told Hoffmann that he really ought to take his complaints to the people who had written the test, Henry Chauncey and the Educational Testing Service. One Saturday morning in the dead of winter Hoffmann drove down to Princeton, presented himself at the reception desk of ETS, and asked to see Mr. Chauncey. The receptionist called Chauncey at home, Chauncey came down to the office, and the two of them had a long, contentious talk. "Hoffmann is a very bright mathematical physicist," Chauncey wrote in his notes on the meeting. "He combines disbelief in objective tests generally with a Philadelphia lawyer's ability to twist words." Chauncey had correctly sized up Hoffmann as being an implacable enemy of ETS, but he let his natural optimism get the better of him. "Although inherently opposed to tests, I think he is not beyond the possibility of becoming convinced of their usefulness," he wrote. "We might just as well attempt to do a personnel job on him now and get it over with!" He directed that Hoffmann be sent a copy of the SAT, with a view to his becoming, possibly, a paid critic of test items.

Within a couple of weeks, Hoffmann had sent back a dyspeptic thirty-page critique of the SAT. Most of it was given over to obsessively precise quibbles over grammatical usage. For example: "You say that among *all* the questions following a passage there is only *one* correct answer. Of course, you *mean* one per question. But you do not *say* that at all. How could such sloppy wording have gone undetected through all your checking processes?" Hoffmann's overall worry was that the SAT, and tests generally, discriminated against "the bright student" who operated at a higher level of precision than the people who had written the test and so would be "torn between the actual meaning and the meaning probably intended." His tone was one of maximal alarm: "the situation seems to me appalling," he wrote to one ETS executive.

It was difficult for people at ETS to take Hoffmann entirely seriously.

They knew that their vulnerable flank was the argument that the tests were unfair to disadvantaged students—that had been the main line of attack against testing at least since Walter Lippmann made it in the early 1920s, though in the 1950s it was not often heard. Nobody had ever made Hoffmann's argument before, and it seemed fanciful. The whole point of the SAT, the hidden agenda to the extent that there was one, was to find the very people Hoffmann thought it discriminated against: those with unusually high IQs. On the other hand, some of his grammatical points were well taken, if petty, and he was a well-known professor, an established voice in the intellectual life of the United States. A few months after he wrote his letter, Hoffmann was invited to Princeton for a luncheon with ETS executives and a tour of the facilities.

Hoffmann turned out to have far more tenacity than ETS had bargained for. The visit to Princeton did not win him over, as it did most critics. He continued to complain loudly and constantly about ETS. In 1962 he published a book called *The Tyranny of Testing* and afterward became a familiar presence on television public-affairs programs. The damage Hoffmann did to ETS was not that his precise argument about discrimination against geniuses caught on; it did not. Instead, it was that he upset the previous arrangement according to which standardized testing was a seamless scientific miracle, from what the outside world could see, extremely technical but wholly admired by those few who could understand it. Here was an established scientist who obviously looked down on the psychometricians at ETS as second-rate. It had a bubble-bursting effect. It was not helpful to ETS, either, to have test questions floating around in the academy; it eroded the mystique of testing when the debate descended to the level of an argument over whether intelligence and leadership potential could be determined, not by some unspecified powerful technical means, but by asking students whether "signed" was the opposite of "anonymous."

It wasn't just Banesh Hoffmann who generated grumbling about ETS. A coterie of old College Board people were annoyed over how completely and suddenly mental testing, something they never believed in, had become a force in admissions. There were other testing companies that had been at the other end of rough, if lordly, treatment by ETS. When one big king takes what had been the domain of many small dukes, he inevitably makes enemies. By the mid-1950s, when professional educators wrote articles or gave speeches, they often sounded the note that testing had excesses that ought to be avoided. In 1957 John Gardner—head of Carnegie, Henry Chauncey's close friend, ETS board member and financial backer—wrote an article published in *Harper's* magazine in which he made a passing reference to America's need for "the wisdom to avoid a tyranny of the aptitude tester." Chauncey shot off a letter to him: "Had it not been for our recent conversations . . . I could only have written 'et tu Brute.' "

They had lunch. Gardner was a more cautious, even more nervous, man than Chauncey, lacking Chauncey's expansive tycoon's self-confidence. For a number of years he had been quietly warning Chauncey, over lunches at the Century Club, that a certain amount of negative sentiment toward ETS, because of its imperial aggressiveness, was brewing within the Establishment. Whitney Griswold, for example, since 1950 the president of Yale, was known to be hostile to testing, and he was not alone: "the negative attitude toward ETS was not an isolated incident or unusual but fairly prevalent among psychologists, testers, and educators," Chauncey wrote in his notes on one conversation with Gardner. ETS, Gardner felt, should find a way to win these people over. After his *Harper's* article was published, Gardner explained to Chauncey that he personally was not suspicious of testing but was concerned that other influential people were becoming so. The work of the testing critics ought to be nipped in the bud. "He felt that the job was largely one of immunizing those whom such individuals might try to poison," Chauncey wrote. Otherwise their whole great work might be threatened.

Chauncey hired a series of public-relations consultants to attend more closely to ETS's image, and it seemed to work. Gardner commissioned two studies of standardized testing, first a private confidential one (which actually everybody in the testing world knew about) and then a public one by a sociological research organization. By making it clear both that ETS was a highly reputable organization and that it was nevertheless being carefully monitored by the Carnegie Corporation, these had a reassuring effect on educators. Gardner also decided to undertake a book-length defense of the idea of using America's colleges and universities to select a national elite. And if you had to have a public critic, you couldn't do much better than Banesh Hoffmann.

The more serious challenge to ETS was E. F. Lindquist's ACT operation in Iowa. Unlike any of the other competitors or critics, Lindquist was an acknowledged giant in testing, and he had a lifetime of contacts in just the area where ETS was weak and needed to improve its position, public education. ETS was poised to broaden its reach into the state universities, and if it succeeded its tests would be truly the national standard. Now here was ACT competing with it for the same schools.

"Up to the present year the (College) Board has enjoyed what amounts practically to a monopoly in college admissions testing," said a confidential

ETS internal report on the ACT situation written in 1958. From the ETS point of view, this was not only convenient and gratifying but good for America: "To put it bluntly, there needs to be one national admission test program." Heretofore ETS had been colonizing higher education from the top down. Now ACT was attacking from the bottom up. ETS's base was the East, ACT's the Midwest. The tests of ETS, whose roots were in IQ testing, primarily measured aptitude; those of ACT, whose roots were in public-school skills tests, achievement. ETS's primary mission was selection of the few; ACT's, guidance and placement of the many. As the ETS report put it: "The emphasis in the ACT literature is on screening out the impossibles and providing a basis for placing the possibles at course levels best fitted to their needs." ETS, on the other hand, emphasized its skill at finding those who scored highest in academic aptitude, singling them out for education at the best universities, and politely guiding the rest to lower their aspirations.

Conceivably, the two organizations could coexist on the theory that, as the ETS report put it: "We [ACT] will deal with the great unwashed and the [College Board] will deal with the rest." In practice, however, they were competing for the same university clients, so the real question was which organization would persuade more schools to require applicants to take its test.

Inside ETS, the reaction toward ACT was the usual one when another testing organization appeared: a surge of indignation over its temerity in coming into the world, followed by all-out competition. It was assumed that ETS was the morally superior organization. ACT had some admissions directors at state universities serving as its local coordinators (which, to ETS's mind, was completely different from having admissions directors be members of the College Board). ACT had a "high-pressure" and "aggressive" national sales force (which was different from ETS having field representatives). ACT made "harsh misrepresentations" of ETS's tests (while ETS merely laid out the facts about ACT's). ACT was "commercially, rather than educationally, motivated" (look at its early arrangement with the hated Science Research Associates).

So ETS had little choice but to fan out across the country, taking the battle to the enemy, state university by state university. In the fall of 1959, for example, after the Associated Press put a story on the wire saying that ACT was "the first real challenge to the long-established but often criticized College Entrance Examination Board," ETS drafted a form letter of protest that College Board members could fill in with their name and institution and mail. "I believe it to be ungentlemanly, if not unethical, to make a vague reference to public criticism of one product in support of another product," the letter said.

Each side had its victories. ETS felt it had Texas, Michigan, Georgia, and Colorado sewed up. ACT had Illinois and Ohio. But the real prize, the crucial piece of territory, was California. California's population had increased by more than 50 percent between 1940 and 1950, and was increasing that much again between 1950 and 1960. It was obviously on its way to first place among the states. It was out of the regional ambit of both ETS and ACT, so for either organization its conquest would represent truly becoming national. More important, it was enormously committed to public education—compared with the East, it hardly had any private educational establishments.

California was America's America, the place heaviest in possibility and lightest in restrictive existing arrangements. Whatever utopian possibilities Henry Chauncey's ancestors may have perceived in New England were nothing compared with the possibilities of California, which was bigger, richer, and more unformed. And among the utopian thinkers attracted to California were not just the familiar cast of socialists, personal liberationists, and tableau presenters, but utopian bureaucrats, who dreamed of big perfect systems such as the world had never seen: water systems, highway systems, park systems, court systems, and—the main one, really—educational systems. California was potentially the leading practitioner of scientifically assessing, sorting, and routing people through schools.

ACT, typically, concentrated its efforts in California on the low-prestige, high-body-count part of higher education, the state's colleges and junior colleges. ETS, also typically, concentrated on the crown jewel, the University of California. The university's original and leading campus was in Berkeley, on San Francisco Bay; there was another full-scale campus in Los Angeles, and several smaller operations around the state, such as an oceanographic institute outside San Diego and a school of agriculture in Davis, which were being upgraded. Plans were afoot to establish a system of campuses everywhere in California. The University of California was obviously going to become the country's largest state university system.

Even before the negotiations to create ETS had been successfully completed, Henry Chauncey had persuaded the College Board to open its first branch office in Berkeley. The University of California then became the first public university member of the College Board. Ordinarily, to be admitted to membership in the College Board, a university had to promise to use the SAT as an admissions requirement. It was inconceivable, however, in 1947, when the office opened, that the University of California would do that. It would be out of character, and extremely unpopular, to begin excluding California citizens from admission to UC on the basis of their scores on a mental test.

Instead, like most state universities, Berkeley overadmitted and got rid of students who were out of their depth by flunking them out during freshman year.

So the College Board bent the rules: the University of California wouldn't have to require the SAT, but would have merely to promise to use it experimentally, as the Eastern schools had done back in the 1920s and 1930s, to conduct validity studies and assess out-of-state applicants. But if Chauncey had believed that this was all the SAT would ever amount to in California, he would not have opened the Berkeley office. Instead, he had in mind waging a lengthy campaign that if successful would produce an immense reward. Should the day ever arrive when the University of California required all its applicants to take ETS tests, then ETS would have its biggest single customer, and would have established itself as the national organization Chauncey wanted it to be. If the SAT was like the railroad standard gauge, bringing in the University of California would be the equivalent of driving the golden spike. It would complete the system.

The head of the ETS office in California was A. Glenwood Walker. Like many people who gravitated to ETS, Walker was someone for whom education had been the dramatically determining factor in his life, and he had a total belief in its power to do good. He had grown up poor on a small farm in western Pennsylvania and gone on to graduate from Teachers College at Columbia University, the best graduate school of education in the country. A good-looking, well-dressed, talkative man, Walker was a natural salesman, and it was a good thing he was. During the 1950s he roamed the unorganized educational wilderness like a forward scout, assigned to begin imposing some uniform structure in the form of ETS tests. It was tough, demanding work, trying to put in place a new procedure that people didn't realize they needed.

Walker spent much of his time on lengthy road trips through lonesome rinky-dink cities in the West, staying in drummers' hotels and proselytizing for testing. He believed that he could win people over, that his magnetism could help make something big and important and progressive happen in a new part of America. Once Walker and another man from ETS were in Socorro, New Mexico, calling on the New Mexico School of Mines. They decided to spend the night in a local motel, and after dinner, in the bar, the other man from ETS politely rebuffed an advance from a middle-aged woman who was there. Afterward Walker was furious: Why hadn't she tried to pick *him* up? It wasn't that he would have been interested; what bothered him was that she hadn't sensed that *he*, not his friend, was the key man.

Walker often used whatever spare moments he could find in his incessant traveling to grouse to the home office. "For over a week I haven't been home until after midnight and haven't had a free weekend since you called me back to St. Louis in February," he wrote from a hotel room on Palm Sunday, 1952. "I'm working harder than in my own business & I'm not certain it's appreciated." A few months later, on the stationery of the Albuquerque Hilton, he wrote to Chauncey: "I have just about had 'it' on this trip—working conventions 8 a.m.–10 p.m., visiting state depts, colleges, and school systems till 3–4 p.m. then driving 300–400 mi. to next city—I guess I'm getting old." Amid all the complaining, he let it be known that he was entertaining an offer from SRA, which seemed to appreciate him more than ETS did.

In 1953 it was decided that Walker should stop representing the College Board tests, get off the road, and instead spend his time selling elementary- and secondary-school achievement tests to school systems in the Los Angeles area. This news provoked another outburst, issued from the Hotel Utah in Salt Lake City: "I've stayed with ETS because of a 'cause' or 'crusade' for what I believe is right. Situations such as this one disillusion me on the 'cause.' In fact, it appears that the more I do out here . . . the more my base of operations is restricted. Frankly, it looks hopeless."

Once he calmed down, Walker reacted to his setback by bringing all his uncontrolled intensity to bear on his new assignment, which, it turned out, wasn't any easier than his old one. The benignity, the calm Puritan order, the new scientific sheen that Chauncey and ETS saw as shimmering radiantly off the surface of its tests—none of this came across in wide-open California. A constant thorn in ETS's side, for example, was the organized right wing, one of the many social formations in California riding its boom. The best-known organization was the John Birch Society, founded in 1958, headquartered in Massachusetts, but most popular and influential in southern California. Members of the Birch Society and similar groups, if they became aware of ETS, tended to see it as part of a cozy, clubby, liberal, Eastern way of doing things that, if it were permitted to spread, would choke off all the freedom and vitality that had drawn them to the West. In Bakersfield a rumor circulated that one ETS test asked the question "Would you rather spit on the Bible or the American flag?" (It didn't, but the rumor started because someone in the education department at Berkeley had devised a test with that question and did administer it to a few students.) For years ETS had to go around denying that the question was on one of its tests. In San Diego a Bircher radio personality railed on the air against the tests. In Palos Verdes the school district, under intense pressure from a retired Michigan congressman (and member of the House Un-American Activities Committee) who had recently moved to the area, wouldn't use the ETS tests because one of the reading comprehension passages used a text of someone criticizing the government.

Glenn Walker's biggest specific problem was competing with a small company called the California Test Bureau, which, through a series of cozy arrangements, had the testing business of the Los Angeles school system locked up. "If a copy of the list of [California Test Bureau's] stockholders should get into the hands of one of the local Los Angeles newspapers 'by accident,' " he wrote to Chauncey, "all we would need to do would be to stand by and pick up the pieces of CTB." Later he arranged to have a California Test Bureau stockholder offer to sell Chauncey a few shares on the quiet, so that he would have access to inside information, such as the amounts of the supposedly regal salaries its executives were paid. Chauncey immediately declined. Still, Walker was getting signals from people one level down on the ETS organization chart that he should fight hard against the California Test Bureau. One of Walker's superiors in Princeton wrote to him: "A list of CTB stockholders comes under the heading of incidental and interesting, but not essential, intelligence. It would be interesting if you stumble across it but not worth much going out of the road to obtain." (This same executive, upon hearing that a psychologist who did some work for ETS was writing a test for the California Test Bureau, wrote to the man: "Just as a friend, and *entirely* unofficially, I want to recognize that some future situation might develop in which it would be better for your own professional future if your skein of relationships with two organizations that are as different as ETS and CTB were not a tangled one.")

The combination of Walker's overzealousness, his unhealthy preoccupation with the competition with the California Test Bureau, and the deep disappointment he felt over ETS's relative lack of success in California despite all his efforts led people in Princeton to worry about him. "For heaven's sake, don't kill yourself on this promotional trip," a superior wrote to him in 1953. "It just isn't worth it. I know that even if you take it easy on such a jaunt, you will still be covering twice as much ground as the ordinary person." The wording turned out to be unfortunate. In 1955 Walker had "problems" that necessitated the appointment of an acting director of the West Coast office. An unstable man miscast in and ground down by playing the brutally tough role of a colonist in the open, unorganized, populist American West working on behalf of the new order represented by ETS, in 1956 Walker committed suicide.

It looked as if California would not submit to ETS and the order it represented, preferring instead to have opportunity without a structure and public education as an open conveyance. Actually, though, things were moving in ETS's direction much more than they appeared to be. The main reason was that in 1958 Clark Kerr, a small, neat, bald, bespectacled labor economist, was named president of the University of California. Kerr had become chancellor of the Berkeley campus in 1952 when he was only forty-one, and Henry Chauncey had quickly spotted him as a comer. He gave Kerr a seat on the ETS board of trustees. That gave Kerr a chance to get a close look at the impressive ETS operation in Princeton, and it gave Chauncey a chance to establish a warm relationship with Kerr. In November 1953, Chauncey wrote to his deputy, William Turnbull: "Clark Kerr spoke to me twice at the Trustees' meeting about a matter in which he was very much concerned, namely, the caliber of students at Berkeley and their educational growth while they are undergraduates." So Kerr was an ally—someone who might find attractive the idea of linking access to the University of California to performance on ETS's tests.

9 In the System

This is how things looked from the vantage point of the ETS campus in Princeton. Establishing ETS's reach nationally got a little rough at times—wasn't it always that way with ambitious projects? But the jostling and rivalry occurred out of public view. The men who ran universities, foundations, and the test industry knew about it; the millions of people who would be affected by the spread of testing didn't have a clue, and ETS presumed that to them the system would appear entirely smooth and benign.

Every so often young people would be asked to take a little time off to sit down and take a test. No studying or preparation was required—all you had to do was fill in a multiple-choice answer sheet. Then, a few weeks later, a sympathetic adult would call you in, glance over a sheet of paper that you couldn't see, and tell you that such and such was the next move in life for which you were best suited. You'd be grateful to have this advice and you'd follow it, happy in the knowledge that you and the college or school to which you were headed would be spared the unpleasantness of a bad match.

Why did people at ETS believe this? They were social scientists, so it was their job to find ways of seeing more order in humanity than is apparent. They lived at a comfortable remove from the students who actually took their tests. The tenor of American society in ETS's early years was one of admiration and deference toward large organizations and authority figures. In Henry Chauncey's case, the Grotonian ethos was so deeply imbued that he couldn't imagine ETS's tests being perceived by the great mass of test-takers through the lens of personal ambition.

But of course they were. If tests are introduced—mysteriously, from above, and with an aura of great consequence—into a clamorous, class-less, opportunity-obsessed nation, then it's inconceivable that people will react to them in the passive, accepting way that ETS imagined. Conant had wanted to turn higher education into the modern equivalent of the frontier as Frederick Jackson Turner had imagined it—as the locus of opportunity in America. And now it was happening. Well, the frontier had not been placid. How could one expect higher education to be, given the expectations that were being placed on it?

Tests, the obvious hurdles to be crossed on the way to higher education, looked to those who had to take them like a way of determining how big a share of America's goodies they'd get. People whose scores consigned them to a place that was less than what they wanted did not, as envisioned, simply accept this. And the fortunate few whose scores were high enough to qualify them for membership in the natural aristocracy that got educated at Amer-ica's best schools quite often used the chance that testing had given them to get ahead in the world, rather than to use the education to train themselves to become Platonic guardians of the state. Testing, as soon as it was in place and began to function as the all-powerful bringer of individual destiny in the United States, generated a whole culture, a set of folkways, that its fathers had never dreamed of.

The earliest symbol of nonacquiescence in the test-taking world was an unprepossessing, perpetually smiling little man, Stanley H. Kaplan of Brooklyn, New York. The son of a plumber and a secretary, who relentlessly pushed him to get good grades in school, Kaplan obliged. He graduated from the public, free-admission City College of New York at the age of sev-enteen, having finished in three years and gotten the second-highest grades in his class. Then he applied to five medical schools, all of which turned him down. He wondered whether his being Jewish could have had anything to do with it—or maybe it was that the medical schools didn't feel that a degree from CCNY had any real weight. (The Medical College Admissions Test was more than a decade off in the future, and therefore there was no way to compare Kaplan with a boy from a private college.) Like a lot of other billets in those days, places in medical school were given out in a lim-ited contest; lower-middle-class, Jewish, public-school-educated Stanley Kaplan was far outside the limits.

From earliest childhood Kaplan had been such a good student that his friends would ask for his help with their schoolwork. By the time he was in high school this avocation had evolved into a small tutoring business, at twenty-five cents an hour; and when Kaplan finished college, during the

Depression, with his medical-school rejections and no job prospects, he decided to go back to tutoring. His office was his parents' basement and his territory was a long swath of Brooklyn running from Prospect Park through the Flatbush and Midwood neighborhoods down to Sheepshead Bay: this was aspiring Jewish America, running the class gamut from blue-collar to lower-middle up to middle-middle. Kaplan's students, typically, were grandchildren of the kind of immigrants from Eastern Europe whom the young Carl Brigham had feared would swamp the country and pull down the national intelligence level. The second generation, the parents of Kaplan's students, had made the leap from the Lower East Side to Brooklyn and from unskilled manual labor to trades or small-business proprietorships. Now the third generation was poised to get all the way to the top, to the famous universities and the professions and the suburbs.

It was a big moment. Not to be too grand about it, full unimpeded opportunity to thrive in a large national society had been denied Jews for millennia. Now, finally, in Flatbush, it seemed to be presenting itself. And there was more good news. The Jewish reverence for study and scholarship, which dated back at least to the fall of the second temple in A.D. 70, and the reinvention of Judaism as a compendium of book learning carried in the heads of rabbis and scholars, had previously had had only a religious payoff (learn that Torah portion, boychick!). Now, by lucky accident, it had become a big advantage on the road to secular success. You would go to college, you would go to graduate school, and you would arrive—and if you needed a little help, Stanley Kaplan was there to provide it.

Like Max Weber's (and Henry Chauncey's) Puritan ethic, the Jewish preoccupation with success, if channeled through education, had an element of moral righteousness carried over from its religious origins. Making it through education wasn't just the crass pursuit of *gelt*, but also a way of doing good, of becoming a figure of learning, respect, leadership, wisdom; and, by the way, educational success was much more secure than business success—not a small issue when your people have had a long history of worldly positions being suddenly snatched away. A perfect example of this line of thinking can be found in one of the best-known works in the literature of postwar Brooklyn, Arthur Miller's *Death of a Salesman*. The official message of this perennially popular play is that the American preoccupation with individual success is soul-obliterating—but there is an exception, Bernard, the high-school classmate of the salesman Willy Loman's son Biff. In high school Bernard studies hard and everyone makes fun of him, whereas Biff is athletic and popular. It's obvious to Willy that Biff is going to be more successful in later life: "Bernard can get the best marks in school, y'understand, but when he gets out in the business world, y'understand, you are going to be five times ahead of him," he tells his son confidently.

Miller's message today seems so conventional, so exposing of a nice-Jewish-boy essence lurking a sixteenth of an inch beneath the facade of the angry left-wing social critic, as to be impossible to recapitulate with a straight face. Guess what? It's *Biff* who becomes a failure and *Bernard* who gets to be a big success! In one scene, Willy pathetically asks the grown-up Bernard why Biff never "caught on"; Bernard, who's in a hurry because he's on his way to Washington to argue a case before the Supreme Court, nevertheless takes a minute to explain patiently to Willy that the reason is that his family never forced Biff to complete the course that would have gotten him a college degree. Miller goes to the trouble to make clear that the grown-up Bernard moves in a moneyed world (Bernard comes onstage carrying a tennis racket under his arm—he's going to be staying with a friend who has his own private court), but, because he's a professional man, that somehow only adds to his moral luster. Willy, on the other hand, has the worst of both worlds: no money and, because he wants to make money in the lowly field of sales, no moral standing either.

In one scene in *Death of a Salesman*, Willy asks the young Bernard to give Biff the answers on the New York State Regents Exam. (Doing well on this test, Ben Wood's creation, was, in Brooklyn, the best route from public high school to a prestigious university in the days before the SAT caught on.) During just the same period when the play's action takes place, the young Stanley Kaplan was segueing from general academic tutoring to preparing kids specifically to take the Regents. In 1946 one of his students asked him to help prepare her for the SAT, which he had never heard of. He took a look at the information booklet the College Board gave out, liked what he saw, and said sure he could.

Through the 1950s Kaplan built up a nice little business in SAT tutoring. He set up a second-story office at Sixteenth Street and Kings Highway, in the heart of Flatbush, which was a Brooklyn landmark. Practically everybody, it seemed, took his course. Why would you not? Here was a somewhat strange test that, if you did very well on it, could magically transport you from Brooklyn to a faraway world of Gothic spires and green lawns. The word on the street was that Brooklyn kids tended to do a whole lot better on the SAT if they had studied with Stanley Kaplan than if they did not. So they did.

Inside ETS, it was a cherished assumption that the SAT was uncoachable. The whole idea of psychometrics was that mental tests are a measurement of a physical property of the brain, analogous to taking a blood sample. By definition, the test-taker could not affect the result. More particularly,

ETS's main point of pride about the SAT was its extremely high test-retest reliability, one of the best that any standardized test had ever achieved. The correlation between a person's scores on successive administrations was almost always over .9 on a scale of zero to one. (Validity was the SAT's weaker point, but nobody within the testing world questioned the test's reliability.) So confident of the SAT's reliability was ETS that the basic technique it developed for catching cheaters was simply to compare first and second scores, and to mount an investigation in the case of any very large increase. ETS was sure that substantially increasing one's score could be accomplished only by nefarious means.

By that logic, if someone claimed to be able to teach you to do better on the SAT, he must be doing one of two things: lying to his customers or stealing tests. For quite some time Stanley Kaplan flourished without ETS even knowing he existed. One day Abe Lass, the principal of Abraham Lincoln High School in Brooklyn, asked ETS's number-two man, Bill Turnbull, for an appointment. In Princeton, he laid out before Turnbull the story of Kaplan—which there was more to than just his tutoring business for the SAT. According to Lass, after every administration of the SAT, Kaplan gave a party for his young charges. Each student was instructed to remember one question from the test and to tell it to Kaplan at the party, then on to hot dogs and root beer. After a few of these parties, Kaplan had a pretty good set of actual SAT questions that he could go over with his students, many of which might turn up the next time the test was administered.

From Kaplan's perspective, the story was very different. Yes, sure, there were parties. Why not? Being done with the SAT was something to celebrate. And at the parties, did everybody talk about what was on the test? Of course. Who wouldn't? But it wasn't a tightly organized operation along the lines of Fagin and his flock of street urchins. What ETS never seemed to understand was that Stanley Kaplan loved the SAT. He thought it was great. It gave the little people a chance. He liked to call his test-prep course "the poor man's private school." He was helping hundreds of kids to go to fine colleges and enter professions that had been barred to them only a few years earlier, and he was proud of it. It wounded him that ETS treated him as a pariah—that every time he went to a conference of educators and stuck out his hand to a tester, he got a cold glare in return.

Following his meeting with Turnbull, Abe Lass was invited to become a trustee of the College Board, to provide the Board with a touch of big-city street wisdom—as he later put it: "We were a little rougher, I suppose, and we didn't have the same good manners or clean fingernails and shined shoes that the other boys had." He helped to launch an investigation of test preparation, which concluded that it did not raise scores. ETS and the College Board put test preparation into the category of organized cheating, and made inquiries with prosecutors in New York City and legislators in Albany about whether Kaplan could be put out of business. These inquiries were unsuccessful, so there wasn't much choice but to continue insisting, in calm, reassuring tones, that the SAT was uncoachable.

Once in 1961 an ETS executive wrote confidentially to Chauncey: "From time to time I have reacted with a tinge of skepticism to the statement that studies of coaching for scholastic aptitude tests have demonstrated that it is futile. . . . The skepticism has been reinforced by data from several studies in which students improved their test scores more with special coaching than without it." Chauncey asked him to prepare a memorandum on the subject—it wasn't as if he wanted to suppress evidence that coaching worked. But he was able to remain sincerely convinced that it didn't. If coaching did work, that would raise two possibilities that profoundly undercut Chauncey's, and ETS's, self-concept. It made the SAT look like a series of parlor tricks and word games, rather than a gleaming instrument of scientific measurement; and it presented the test as a pitiless determiner of individual worldly success or failure, rather than as a benign, helpful public service that would somehow make everyone's life a little better. It would have been uncharacteristic for a man of Chauncey's supreme moral certainty to dwell on these uncomfortable possibilities, and he did not.

10 Meritocracy

The United States was far ahead of the rest of the world in establishing universal public education. In Great Britain, only with the passage of the Education Act of 1944 did the idea of keeping everyone in school until the age of sixteen become a national goal, which by then it had been in the United States for half a century. In the years after the Second World War, when the United States was expanding higher education, Britain was creating high schools. Opportunity for all, the American creed, was only just beginning to penetrate through the thick mists of the British class system.

In both countries, though, an expansion of education coincided with the apogee of optimism about social science in general and mental tests in particular. Both countries used multiple-choice aptitude tests as a way of organizing the new, growing part of the educational system. Britain, much more than America, nakedly used IQ tests to sort students. (France, by contrast, though it was the birthplace of the IQ test, had a central education ministry that controlled the public-school curriculum and tested students on their mastery of it.) The leading academic expert on educational testing in Britain, Cyril Burt, was both a more open champion of IQ and more influential than the equivalent American figures. Anyway, the idea that most of the citizenry just wasn't intellectually up to snuff—"ineducable"—was much more a part of the mental equipment of the governing class there than in the United States.

So Britain established a national exam called the eleven-plus, given at the age when IQ was thought to stabilize permanently, and on the basis of the results it consigned to their lifelong social fates those eleven-year-olds whose parents didn't have the money for private education. New, free public schools were created in two varieties: grammar schools, where higher scorers on the eleven-plus would be educated for white-collar jobs and middle-class life; and secondary moderns, where the lower-scoring majority would get vocational-technical training. This represented not a restriction of opportunity in Britain but an expansion, because previously there had been hardly any way for ordinary people to advance at all.

The passage of the Education Act was a triumph for the British Labour Party; it looked like a fundamental advance toward Labour's goals of social-ism and human dignity. Just after its enactment, the job of chief thinker for the Labour Party—secretary of the policy committee and head of research—was given to a young intellectual named Michael Young, who, though pas-sionately committed to Labour, had a detached, curious, ironic quality as well.

Young began to doubt that the advent of educational opportunity in Britain (or, for that matter, of opportunity generally) would be such a good thing for the working class. Up to that point the strength of the Labour Party lay in the total unfairness of the class system: Britain had an elite that one could unreservedly hate, because its position was inherited rather than earned. Also, the lack of opportunity meant that there was plenty of bottled-up talent in the working class from which the Labour Party could draw its leaders.

But once the new system was in place, Britain would presumably have a new elite made up of those who had done well on the eleven-plus and then been well educated at government expense. Who could resent them, when they deserved their place? To Young's mind the good health of social justice as a cause depended upon the society's being unjust; as he put it years later, "You need a *fault* to have a good society." With equal opportunity for all, inequality would increase and the Labour Party would be powerless to do anything about it because its central argument, that British society was con-structed unfairly, had been taken away. Better, Young thought, for Labour to stop holding up equal opportunity as its goal.

Young left his post at the Labour Party to become a self-trained sociolo-gist. He set up an institute in East London from which he and his colleagues would go forth to study how the society around them worked. Richard Cross-man, a leading Labour intellectual-statesman, asked Young to contribute something on education policy to a volume called *New Fabian Essays,* which was modeled on the original *Fabian Essays* of 1904, edited by Beatrice and Sidney Webb, the founders of the Labour Party, with contributions by H. G. Wells and George Bernard Shaw among others. Young wrote up his idea about the danger to the Labour Party posed by the Education Act and opportunity. Crossman rejected it—angrily. He told Young that it was complete nonsense and could not be published in a book written by socialists.

When Young got over being upset he decided to work on his idea more until he got it into a form that somebody would be willing to publish. He decided to write a dystopian fantasy about the new social order, in the spirit of *Animal Farm* and *Brave New World*, which would be cast in the form of a mock Ph.D. thesis in sociology written in the year 2030. The immediate problem was what name to give to this system of, in his words, "rule not so much by the people as by the cleverest people." Aristocracy? In Greek it meant rule by the best, but all over the Western world in the 1950s it was understood to mean the opposite, rule by inheritors of wealth. So Young thought of a substitute: meritocracy.

Actually it was the same word, with the first syllable changed from Greek to Latin. Young tried "meritocracy" out on a friend of his, a philosopher named Prudence Smith, but she was horrified. To combine a Latin and a Greek root in the same word, she said, violated all the rules of good taste: it was an outrage. She was so dead set against that Young remembered the scene precisely for decades, the two of them standing outside the crematorium at Golders Green cemetery in London arguing about whether it would be an unpardonable breach for him to invent the word "meritocracy."

He could never think of a better word, so he stuck with "meritocracy." Nobody but Prudence Smith ever complained. "Meritocracy" entered the language.

Not easily, though. Young holed up in a rich friend's empty apartment for months and wrote *The Rise of the Meritocracy*, a secret agent living under the protection of the old upper class whose demise he was predicting. When he was done he sent it to eleven publishers, all of whom turned it down. Leonard Woolf of the Hogarth Press, who was the most encouraging, suggested that he rewrite the book as a novel instead of a Ph.D. thesis, but when Young handed it back, Woolf said he now realized that Young didn't have the ability to write a novel. So it was back to the Ph.D. thesis. Finally Young was able to prevail upon an old friend who ran Thames and Hudson, a publisher of art books, to put out *The Rise of the Meritocracy* on the cheap, with no advertising or publicity. It was published in 1958.

What is striking about the book forty years later is Young's casual, automatic assumption that IQ scores and merit are the same thing—in fact that universal IQ testing followed by educational sorting is the only possible way of organizing a society so as to provide fair opportunity to all. "Intelligence tests . . . were the very instrument of social justice," he writes. Young mentions effort as being important, too, but on the whole he treats IQ as being an exact measure of a person's future economic productivity. Therefore, in *The Rise of the Meritocracy*, the advent of the eleven-plus exam inexorably causes Britain to become the leading economic power of the world.

Of Young's predictions, the one that got almost all the attention was that the old landed aristocracy would become irrelevant and would be replaced by a new upper class made up of highly intelligent, well-educated people. This resonated deeply all over the world with readers who had not been born into the old elite but who qualified for the new one: their moment had arrived. Young's main point, however, is that this salutary-sounding development is devastating to the cause of social justice. The cream of the working class is discovered through testing, then educated and inducted into the new upper class. The Labour Party, deprived of both its leadership and an unfair class system to complain about, withers and dies. Highly intelligent people intermarry and pass on their brainy genes to their offspring, so that a meritocratic upper class begins to look like an aristocracy, more deserving of its place but also more arrogant than the previous elite based on inherited wealth.

At the end of the book "Michael Young," the fictitious twenty-first-century graduate student who is the supposed author, reports that the meritocratic elite has triumphed so completely that "the lower classes no longer have the power to make revolt effective"—and then a footnote informs us that he has been killed in a bloody uprising by the low-IQ masses. In Young's view, in other words, the great economic advantages of meritocracy would finally be overwhelmed by the even greater social disadvantages.

Young's idea had the force of originality; it made him, gratifyingly, a minor immortal, although people never seemed to understand that he had invented the word "meritocracy" for the purpose of damnation, not praise. It wasn't just the main point of *The Rise of the Meritocracy* that was arresting; a lot of the smaller ones were, too. Young correctly foresaw, for example, that the rise of testing would create a test-prep industry. But he was wrong about the way meritocracy would play out in British politics. Rather than disabling the opposition by co-opting its ablest members, the system of eleven-plus exams, grammar schools, and secondary moderns generated furious enmity on the left. As a result, it was well on its way to being dismantled within a decade of the publication of *The Rise of the Meritocracy*. More broadly, Young now seems naive for believing that commitment to meritocracy would sweep through society so totally that inheritance of wealth and position would be abolished, that government would fund education so abundantly that private schools would wither away, that scientists would rule the society, and that schoolteachers would be highly paid. (Conant, writing fifteen years earlier, in his "Wanted: American Radicals" article, made exactly the same confident and wrong predictions.)

Another mistake of Young's was that he misunderstood the United States. In *The Rise of the Meritocracy* he portrays it (as European onlookers often have) as a nation fanatically committed to social leveling and therefore incapable of setting up a meritocratic apparatus as England might. The American public schools, according to the book, have to "wrest nationhood from polyglot chaos"—and so can't possibly select and train an elite. A certain "Professor Conant," who appears to be the chief theoretician of American education, "is simply asking for the impossible" in his calls for putting the entire citizenry into common public schools, rather than having a dual system like Britain's. With such madmen in charge, the United States is bound to fall behind Britain in short order.

In the United States, the appearance of *The Rise of the Meritocracy* was duly noted by the key figures in education and testing, not so much with alarm over its dire predictions as with an appreciative chuckle over its wittiness. John Gardner of the Carnegie Foundation read it. Clark Kerr of the University of California read it. ETS's lawyer, Alexander Henderson of the New York law firm of Cravath, Swaine & Moore, sent Henry Chauncey a copy, and Chauncey read it. Finally Michael Young must have figured out that there was meritocracy in America, too, because in 1959 he wrote to Chauncey to request an interview for a documentary he was making for the BBC. (The interview never took place and the two never met.)

What all these American men believed was that they were building an American meritocracy that would be much more stable and sustainable than the one in Young's book—a meritocracy that couldn't be toppled in a revolt. In fact, they believed in the very idea that Young had written his book to make fun of, that a meritocracy, their meritocracy, could be a truly good and just society.

Michael Young's meritocracy in Britain was clear-cut, horrifying, and unstable. The American meritocracy was blurry but survivable. Young, an intellectual, was sharp and brilliant; the American meritocracy builders were administrators, duller and more politic in print but quite effective in action. Being absolutely clear about the inherent contradictions between principles (like equal opportunity and social justice) is a necessity only for people who comment on society. People who run it have to be sloppier in their thinking.

By 1960, an American child with a very high IQ would quite likely be spotted early and given special treatment, but Americans did not publicly announce that they were sorting their children on the basis of IQ tests. The reason that Young treated Conant as an anti-elitist, which he certainly was not, was that he had undertaken a large research project on high schools (with funding provided by John Gardner at the Carnegie Corporation and office space by Henry Chauncey at ETS) that had held up the comprehensive high school—large, new, suburban, open to young people of all races and classes—as an ideal. Within each school, however, Conant insisted upon two tracks, equivalent to Britain's grammar schools and secondary moderns. The dividing point was an IQ score of 115. Partly thanks to Conant's influence, tracking proliferated in large public high schools, with the result that Americans had the elite-selection features of the British system without the obvious social irritant that operating two separate public-school systems would have created.

"I tend to be a little wary of people who use the word meritocracy," Henry Chauncey wrote to one of his successors as president of ETS years later. The theory was too knowing, too neat, for his taste. He didn't believe that he and his colleagues had been explicit social engineers; they were simply trying to help the country. Young, as an Englishman, was protesting the provision of universal opportunity, which was a novelty in Britain that, because of an accident of timing, was tied to IQ testing. But to Americans the idea of universal opportunity was old news. In the United States the Democratic Party, representing liberal politics, was organized around opportunity, rather than, as with the British Labour Party, around class. The great new development here was the *systematizing* of opportunity through testing and education.

Men like Chauncey and Conant and Kerr were devoted educators operating during the heyday of reverence for large organizations. To them the choice between chaotic, frontier-style opportunity and organized opportunity could not have been clearer, especially if the organizing was to be done within schools. They presumed—so deeply that they did not even realize it was their presumption—that to reward educational performance was to reward merit itself. Back in the 1930s, in the Pennsylvania Study, Ben Wood and William Learned had expressed very well the true feeling of educators when they wrote: "The democracy of merit on the campus, though far from perfect, is finer than that of the street."

If there is an official American riposte to *The Rise of the Meritocracy*, it is a short book written by John Gardner and published in 1961. In *Excellence*, Gardner devotes several pages to Michael Young, concluding, in prose as bland and reassuring as Young's is witty and subversive: "The book is an amusing and effective sermon against a Utopia based upon rigorous and unimaginative application of the merit principle. It is not, however, a sermon which we particularly need. Our society has numerous and powerful defenses against excesses of that sort." And the pageant of American society Gardner presents in *Excellence* is one in which the new, highly educated, technical-professional elite occupies center stage. These people would have attended local public schools, comprehensive regional high schools where they would have been on the upper track, and finally elite universities.

Clark Kerr, the new president of the University of California, thought bigger. As a labor economist he was concerned with the great mass of working people and with industrial management as well as with the professions. During the late 1950s, Kerr got a grant from the Ford Foundation to set up a team of experts to perform a grand global inquiry into labor-management relations. If John Gardner was trying to refute Michael Young, Kerr was aiming at a higher target, Karl Marx. In 1960 he and his group finished a book called *Industrialism and Industrial Man*, which is a kind of *Management Manifesto*. They announced that the great age of conflict between labor and capital had drawn to a close; "the structuring of the labor force" was now the essential issue. One could run a modern industrial society in a number of ways, but the best, the ideal, was to have a "middle-class elite" in charge—people drawn from all segments of society without regard to caste or family background. They would be in charge of the very large organizations (the largest being the federal government) that advanced industrialism required. And who would create this middle-class elite? A greatly expanded educational system, of course. Inevitably, "education becomes one of the principal means of vertical social mobility in the technical world," and—notwithstanding Marx, or Michael Young—everybody benefits. Efficiency and justice, rather than being inconsistent, could be achieved simultaneously by means of education.

Clark Kerr's inauguration as president of the University of California in 1958, the year *The Rise of the Meritocracy* was published, was as elaborate as a medieval coronation—appropriately, for Kerr was taking charge of an empire. It lasted for seventeen days and encompassed formal dinners, academic processions, convocations all up and down the length of the state, even a review of the University of California oceanographic fleet. In his inaugural address, which he chose to deliver at the university's least prestigious campus, the one at Riverside, he proudly proclaimed that "universities today are at the vital center of society" and that "it is no exaggeration to say we are entering a new era in the history of mankind." At the top of the new technological, complex, highly organized society would sit a new, meritocratic American elite, minted by the universities:

. . . we must again concern ourselves with educating an elite—if I may use this word in its true sense, free of the unhappy connotations it has acquired. But this time we must train an elite of talent, rather than one of wealth or family. . . . [O]ur national welfare and even our survival may depend upon a body of highly trained talent, including both the unusually gifted pursuing their special interests and the more broadly oriented leaders of public and industrial life.

That was the theory; Kerr had to put it into practice.

It wasn't a completely remade world yet, though. Henry Chauncey's second son, Henry Jr., known as Sam, was sent to Groton like all the Chauncey boys. There he was, like his father, a decent student, one of the leaders of his class, and a devoted adherent to the Groton ideal of public service. As a small rebellion he went on to Yale instead of Harvard, and after graduation, again like his father, he became an assistant dean at his alma mater. He decided to take advantage of his new position by doing what every student wants to do but can't: he went to the Yale admissions office and dug out his application folder. In the place reserved for the office's assessment of the candidate, somebody had written these words: "Henry Chauncey's son."

book 2

THE MASTER
PLAN

11
Rah! Rah! Rah!

When Clark Kerr took it over, the University of California was still well short of a hundred years old. It was a new, raw Western state university, built on an entirely different model from the private universities of the East. UC was a land-grant school that had been brought to life by the Morrill Act of 1862. It aimed to keep itself open to anyone who had graduated from a California public high school with a good record, and that included women, who had been admitted on an equal basis from the very start. The professors were state employees without tenure, meant to be teachers more than scholars. An independent Board of Regents, appointed by the governor, offered some insulation from the whims of the state legislature, but its members' understanding of upper academe was hazy at best. The regents rubber-stamped faculty appointments but insisted on individually debating and approving the hiring of the head football, basketball, track, and baseball coaches.

Even within the realm of state universities, the leading institutions of the East and Midwest, some of them founded back in the eighteenth century, had a long head start on the University of California. Probably the two best-reputed state universities were Michigan and Wisconsin, both built up by towering late-nineteenth-century presidents (respectively, James Burrill Angell and Charles Kendall Adams) and enthusiastically supportive legislatures at a time when the University of California had only a few dozen students.

The dominant figure at the University of California from 1930 until the ascension of Kerr was Robert Gordon Sproul. If there was a type, in the central-casting sense, for head of a state university, Sproul was the type. A man with "a reverberating voice and a phenomenal memory" who had risen to the presidency of the university from the comptroller's office rather than the faculty, Sproul was an educator-politician who could slap backs with legislators and entertain rich, conservative regents at football games. He once seriously considered leaving his post to become head of a bank.

Still, there was an element of grandeur in the university. The city of Berkeley (just an empty stretch of ranchland until the university's founders decided to locate it there) was named after George Berkeley, the eighteenth-century cleric and metaphysician, in honor of one of his lesser accomplishments: writing that famous line of bad poetry, "Westward the course of empire takes its way."

Having been started by transplanted patrician Easterners, Berkeley had some feeling of being a stately outpost of New England, if only by virtue of its Brahmin street names: Channing, Allston, Shattuck, Dana, Dwight, Bowditch, Bancroft. And it also had an Aegean aspect, a *civitas*, owing to its physical setting at the foot of brushy hills with a view of San Francisco Bay and the sea; people in togas discussing philosophy would not look completely out of place in Berkeley. Finally there was a layer of 1930s social realist uplift, expressed in the campus's big, grand, plain big-government buildings (and giant-trunked eucalyptus trees). Sproul had helped Ernest Lawrence, the inventor of the cyclotron, to build a major laboratory in Berkeley with government and foundation funds, and this had made the university a center of science and an early outpost of the modern American research apparatus.

If you squinted and used your imagination, as Clark Kerr surely did, here is what you could see: the University of California as a new kind of institution, a great, elite research university run on the German model, by serious, formidable professors, which was at the same time a free, democratic school for the people. It would combine the best in the American tradition and the best in the European under one roof. It would be free of both the suffocating class snobbery of the Ivy League and of the mediocrity that, Kerr believed, was always threatening to infect the state universities. Nobody had ever thought of that before.

It wouldn't be possible to find a perfect twentieth-century embodiment of Thomas Jefferson's idea of the natural aristocrat—American society had become urban, industrial, complicated, and stratified beyond Jefferson's imagining—but Clark Kerr would be about as close as you could get. Although the United States never became the nation of farmer-intellectuals that Jefferson envisioned, Kerr's family were, in fact, farmer-intellectuals. His father held a master's degree from the University of Berlin and spoke five languages; one of his aunts was an official of the American Association of University Women in Washington; one of his uncles was Grenville Clark, a leading corporation lawyer in New York; and still, Clark Kerr grew up on an apple farm in Stony Creek, Pennsylvania, and got his elementary education in a rural one-room schoolhouse.

Were you looking, Mr. Jefferson, for agrarian self-sufficiency combined with reverence for learning and education? Too bad you couldn't have met Kerr's parents. Their courtship was long, to the point of strangeness, because his mother, a milliner with a sixth-grade education, insisted upon saving up enough money to pay for the college education of all her future offspring before the wedding could take place. This squirreling-away period lasted, as Kerr remembered it, "at least five and maybe even ten years, and Father resented it all his life." Kerr's mother died of cancer when he was twelve. His father then married a woman who didn't warm to his children, and the rest of Kerr's upbringing was studious, disciplined, and emotionally chilly.

In the mid-1920s at blue-collar Reading High School (memorialized in the novels of John O'Hara and John Updike), Clark Kerr was given some kind of standardized IQ test. When the results came back, he was told he had made the second-highest score in the school. This qualified him to become, in Jefferson's terms, one of the best geniuses to be raked from the rubbish. He was encouraged to apply to Swarthmore College, a private college outside Philadelphia, probably the most intensely academic liberal-arts college in the United States, which ordinarily did not recruit students from Reading High. Swarthmore changed his life. He converted to the religion with which it was affiliated, the Quakers, he joined in its tradition of liberal political activism, and he became a great believer in its policy of putting the more ambitious students (like him) into a special honors program to do scholarly work. He intended to become a lawyer, but a summer trip to California in a Quaker "peace caravan" after his graduation in 1932 convinced him to move West and study economics.

By today's standards the young Kerr looks like a student radical. He was active in the peace and labor movements, joined the left-wing Student League for Industrial Democracy, and visited the Soviet Union. He wanted to change the correlation of forces in the American economy, such that working people would get more power and then use it to wrest a more decent life from their employers. All that obscures the real point about him, however, which is that by the standards of that time and place he was not a radical, because he was not a socialist or a Communist. In 1933 he was involved in a cotton pickers' strike in the San Joaquin Valley—but as a mediator, not a fomenter of revolution. In 1934 his roommate, Dean McHenry, served as a precinct captain for Upton Sinclair, the socialist author (*The Jungle* and other exposés of the dark side of capitalism) and agitator who was running a serious campaign for governor of California; Kerr wouldn't support Sinclair. Kerr met his wife, Catherine Spaulding, when they were both trying to keep the Communists from taking over a political meeting. Kerr's mentor in economics at Berkeley, Paul Taylor, involved him in liberal government reform efforts from the early 1930s on. Their cause (and the subject of Kerr's 1,200-page dissertation) was self-help cooperatives for the unemployed, as an alternative to relief.

Clark Kerr became a labor economist and a professional mediator of disputes. As a Quaker, he believed in consensus seeking and dispute resolution as moral, almost divine causes. As an economist he was a supreme rationalist who believed that a system could always be devised to solve a problem, so long as it perfectly balanced all the interests at stake. Government ought to be the highest, biggest, and best system. Academic experts like him could help make it run properly. Kerr was bald before middle age, quiet, and expressionless, with clear blue eyes and rimless spectacles—literally an egghead. He was imperturbable. In the days when labor disputes were much rougher than they are now, he traveled up and down the West Coast taming them, his mind going click, click, click as he calculated the solution. Even Harry Bridges, the bare-knuckled boss of the San Francisco docks who was always under suspicion for being insufficiently anti-Communist, and Dave Beck, the tough-guy head of the Teamsters Union, were susceptible to mediation by Kerr. He became a professor at Berkeley in 1945. He served on government boards and commissions and in the university's academic senate. He started an institute to study industrial relations.

The event that redirected Kerr's trajectory came in 1949, when the University of California regents, intending to root out Communist faculty members, required that all university employees sign an oath of loyalty to the United States government. Kerr's opposition to the loyalty oath was, typically, not strident or quixotic. He signed it himself. His concern was that it represented an unwarranted intrusion by the regents into a matter the faculty ought to handle. Kerr's principled position was that a great university must be governed by its faculty—but this wasn't a principle that went against his own interest. After all, he was a member of the faculty that he believed should be in charge. Berkeley was on the way up, partly because California was and partly because it had established itself as a center of defense research and been much favored with government funds during the war. The idea of its becoming one of the world's leading universities, and one of the leading institutions in American society, shone brightly in Kerr's mind.

If the regents could claim the power to dismiss faculty members for their political views, it would embarrass Berkeley on the world stage.

Kerr joined a faculty committee that met one by one with the fifty-two professors who had refused to sign the loyalty oath. The committee would satisfy itself (or not) that these teachers were not Communists, in which case they would be permitted to stay on. After interviewing all of them, the committee recommended that forty-seven be kept on and five dismissed. On July 21, 1950, Kerr appeared before the regents and explained the situation to them in his customarily calm, crisp, rational fashion. The regents voted ten to nine not to fire the faculty members who hadn't signed the oath. After the meeting a vote changed and the nonsigners were, in fact, fired, only to be rehired later when a court ordered the university to do so. But the July 21 meeting had defused the crisis, and the thirty-nine-year-old Kerr became an overnight hero, the mediation genius who had won the trust of all parties and found a way out of a situation that might have destroyed the university. In 1952 he was made chancellor of the campus at Berkeley.

Sproul, as president of all the university's campuses and therefore Kerr's superior, saw himself as still in charge, with Kerr as a pallid, unimaginative administrator who would efficiently carry out his orders at Berkeley. Kerr could not make even minor moves such as assigning office space or hiring teaching assistants (let alone full professors) without first obtaining Sproul's approval. He found the situation humiliating—especially since Sproul had no discernible views on education and society and Kerr had elaborate ones. In 1956 Kerr threatened to resign as a way of forcing Sproul to give him a modicum of autonomy. But for a man whose hands were tied, Kerr accomplished a great deal as chancellor. He built up Berkeley in the social sciences to the kind of status it already had in the hard sciences—quite a feat against the impediments of Sproul and the bad odor left by the loyalty-oath controversy.

Kerr presided over his utopia from a Japanese-style house, plain but intricate, like him, that he and his wife had built in El Cerrito, on the eastern shore of San Francisco Bay. He often worked from home, going through stacks of memoranda and resolving whatever issues they raised by writing tiny, cryptic messages in the margins in green ink. He traveled regularly all over the world, a figure in an international community of modern scholar-administrators. In his spare time he would pick a period of artistic or literary history and master it.

Sproul finally retired in 1958 and Kerr was made president of the University of California, just at the time he was finishing the research for his book about the world's bright future under the management of a new, highly educated elite drawn from the middle class. As chancellor of UC Berkeley he installed Glenn Seaborg, a Nobel Prize-winning chemist, as if to underscore that an age of philosopher-kings had dawned at the University of California. In the same spirit he persuaded the regents, finally, to replace the university's system of year-by-year faculty contracts with a full-fledged academic tenure system. These moves did not, however, lay to rest what to Kerr's mind was the main threat to his precious university.

The state of California was growing by 500,000 people a year; the usual prediction in those days was that it would have a population of 50 million by the year 2000. (It actually has 32 million.) This in itself was not bad news for the university. The people coming to the state were taxpayers, there was plenty of money in the state treasury, and the legislature loved higher education, which was both prestigious and popular with voters. There was no question but that higher education was going to grow, enormously, along with the state. What troubled Kerr was the possibility that the growth would be haphazard, rather than orderly and rational.

Order was always preferable to Clark Kerr, but he saw a more particular peril. He had watched how universities in other states had slipped into the realm of pork-barrel politics. The schools in the districts of the legislatures' chairmen of the education and appropriations committees got the most money, regardless of need. For decades a series of reports had recommended that higher education in California grow according to some kind of plan, but the legislature had ignored them. In 1957, twenty-two separate bills to create new state colleges were introduced, of which four passed. The one that particularly galled Kerr created Turlock State College in a tiny town that was the self-proclaimed turkey capital of the United States—and, more to the point, in the district of a powerful member of each house of the California state legislature. The situation was out of control.

Kerr could see quite clearly what would happen absent some forceful intervention. Most of state-university education in the United States was in four tiers: universities, land-grant agricultural colleges, "normal schools" for the instruction of (mostly female) future public-school teachers, and two-year "junior colleges," which had been founded in the early twentieth century by Germanophile university presidents in the hope of eventually ridding their campuses of freshmen and sophomores. In California the situation was slightly different because the university was also the land-grant school, but that only underscored the secondary status of the state colleges, which had begun as normal schools.

Lately, though, the state colleges had developed higher ambitions. They were hiring faculty with doctorates, who resented the faculty members at the University of California with their higher pay, lighter teaching loads, tenure, and the glow of association with a research university. The state-college professors pressured their presidents to upgrade their status, and the presidents pressured the legislature. Historically the legislature had been dominated by graduates of the University of California who protected the university's budget; but if the state-college campuses were allowed to multiply, more of *their* graduates would be elected and the university's grip on the legislature would weaken. The figures at the center of the whole enterprise, the academic royalty on the Berkeley faculty, might go elsewhere.

Robert Sproul believed that the way to handle the threat from the state colleges was to identify the most ambitious and successful ones and approach them with the offer to become branches of the University of California. That was too seat-of-the-pants for Kerr. He wanted to create a plan for something that would solve the problem forever, and have it made law.

In the winter of 1959, during his first year as president, Kerr began to move. At first he thought he could simply send emissaries to work things out with Roy Simpson, who as State Superintendent of Public Instruction ran the state colleges. But, as Kerr's old graduate-school roommate, Dean McHenry, now a professor at UCLA, wrote afterward, Simpson "pulled the double cross and came out with no elaborate statement of state college expansion. Kerr was furious." Simpson wanted seven new state college campuses on top of the four he had gotten in 1957.

McHenry wrote Kerr a long, salty confidential memo sizing up the situation. "We cannot allow any other State-supported institution to use the name of 'University,' " he wrote. "Never, ever! . . . We need to: 1. Define our vital interests, re name, degrees, functions, etc. 2. Protect them by whatever means we find necessary."

Kerr got the message and focused his mediator's mind with great precision. He set up a series of committees to study the future of higher education, with the membership subtly loaded to favor the university's interests over the state colleges'. By the end of the summer of 1959 there was a rough plan. The essential point was that the state colleges would be banned from ever granting the Ph.D. degree. This meant that any money the legislature (or federal government) ever appropriated for academic research would have to go to the University of California, since the state colleges' faculty were being paid only to teach undergraduates. One simple, minor-sounding rule, and the university's position would be safe and protected forever.

A second feature was that the university would tighten up its admissions requirements so as to move toward having a student body made up only of outstanding high-school graduates, rather than, as was traditional, any reasonably studious high-school graduate. Kerr, the labor economist, calculated that one-third of California's workforce needed to be made up of people with administrative or technical training, and one-eighth of people with graduate or professional training; hence, the state colleges should begin admitting only the top third of high-school graduates and the university only the top eighth. In truth Kerr would have preferred to limit the university to the top tenth, but he thought there would be too much of an outcry.

The plan was naked in its surgical disabling of the state colleges' ambitions. It mandated a secondary status for them that extended even to such matters as the average square footage of a dormitory room. And it proposed enshrining this new system in an amendment to the California state constitution, which would make it all but impossible to change. In November 1959, the sociologist Seymour Martin Lipset, one of the bright stars Kerr had attracted to the Berkeley faculty, warned Kerr that he was overreaching: "The American norms of equality operate against setting up a system which includes first- and second-class citizens. . . . I have strong doubts that the current objectives of the University are realistic." Even Herman Spindt, the Berkeley admissions director, an enthusiastic believer in selective admissions who had been put in charge of reporting on admissions under the new plan, thought Kerr wanted to tighten access too much. "Within the bounds of polite language, I cannot find words that will strongly enough express my opposition to the . . . formula!" he wrote Kerr. Kerr replied, calmly, icily, with a rebuke to Spindt for having been too soft, too inclined to open the university gates widely: "As you say, I had hoped for a stronger set of recommendations."

What made Kerr think he could win so total and crushing a victory over the state colleges? Long experience as a mediator had taught him how to read people and learn to identify the one key factor that would move them to assent. He had carefully assessed all the elements, personalities, and institutional interests, and he believed he had the state colleges checkmated. Glenn Dumke, the state colleges' representative, was a young man. He wouldn't fight so fiercely as to risk sacrificing his long-range career. The governor, Pat Brown, was a University of California graduate. His chief of staff, Frederick Dutton, was a state college sympathizer, but Brown's other essential aide, Warren Christopher, the future Secretary of State, was firmly in Kerr's camp, and so was Brown's big financial backer, Edwin Pauley. California's junior colleges would be supportive because they got a bigger budget. The private universities got a new state-funded scholarship program. The state colleges got a new governing board. Click, click, click.

It became clear later that Kerr could be ill served by his own strategic brilliance. He was capable of forgetting that there is a limit to the Swiss-watchness of human affairs, that precision engineering can't eliminate all of life's messiness. In this case the state college presidents, egged on by their faculties, were more upset than Kerr had expected them to be, and came out against the plan.

Kerr had prepared a script for this contingency, which he carried out through the autumn of 1959. He arranged a secret meeting with the presidents of the four best and most ambitious state colleges—San Francisco State, San Jose State, San Diego State, and Fresno State—and asked them what their reaction would be if he were to offer to upgrade their institutions into branches of the University of California. To Kerr's surprise, they said they weren't interested. They were going to get university status on their own without being under his control; Governor Brown had promised it to them. Kerr, as he remembered it later, said to them very coolly and without rancor, just reporting the facts, "You don't have a chance."

The state college presidents picked up the gauntlet Kerr had thrown down. They got in a car, drove to San Francisco, picked up Glenn Dumke, and took him to Sacramento and back—a four-hour excursion. By the end of "the long auto ride of Glenn Dumke," as Kerr called it, Dumke had gone from being a supporter of the plan to an opponent, and therefore it looked dead.

Kerr quickly called a summit meeting of all the key players and offered a compromise: the state colleges could offer Ph.D. degrees jointly with the University of California. This amounted to very little—hardly anybody has ever gotten one of these joint Ph.D.s—but it gave the state colleges a way to save face. Kerr made it clear to Dumke in particular that those who had supported the plan would have a brighter future in California higher education than those who had not. Dumke got back on board. Soon he was named president of the California state-college system, a position he held for twenty years.

On December 18, 1959, the University of California regents and the state board of education held a ceremonial joint meeting in Berkeley, with Governor Brown in attendance, where they unanimously approved all sixty-three recommendations made by Clark Kerr's committee. All three levels of California's higher-education system would grow significantly, but henceforth they would be fitted into a firm structure. The university would get three new campuses to add to the five it already had, two of which would be built from scratch. For California residents, education at every level would be tuition-free. And, to aid in figuring out who could go to which place in this newly rigid educational class system, the plan mandated the use of standardized admissions tests, which, despite more than a decade of the best efforts of ETS, were being used only for out-of-state applicants.

Now the legislature had to be won over. There was only the barest hint of opposition on principle, from liberals upset about the end of free and easy access to the higher-education system. "It is tragic that our educators urge a smaller percentage of our total population should have the advantages and development of higher education," one of Governor Brown's aides wrote to him. Another complained:

> . . . the top students (top insofar as high school records, etc., are really valid) shall be entitled to go to larger campuses, with better buildings, better and more expensive facilities, and, presumably, study under better faculty members. . . . The next level of students, as predetermined by high school records, etc., will study in second-level institutions, in the same communities, on small campuses, more austere buildings, and lower faculty. . . . Log-rolling is not unknown in the rarefied atmosphere of higher education.

But Kerr had read the situation pretty well. Many parties had been cut in on the action, and, on the merits, the Master Plan was being received as good for California, so supporting it would reflect well on politicians from the governor on down. During the legislative debate Kerr lost only one thing he had wanted: the plan was downgraded from a constitutional amendment to a mere law. The legislature passed it with only one dissenting vote. On April 26, 1960, Brown signed the Master Plan.

California's Master Plan made Clark Kerr famous around the world.

In the ensuing avalanche of praise and publicity, the plan's aspect as a successful bureaucratic power play by the university against the state colleges was almost completely missed. For decades, California state college professors talked bitterly about "Clark Err" and his "Master Sham," and seethed as they watched their university brethren live out the whole Herr Doktor Professor fantasy of grants and graduate assistants and international conferences and light teaching loads—while nobody, it seemed, noticed or cared about them. Nor was attention paid to the plan's tightening of undergraduate admissions to both the university and the state colleges, and its distinct tilting of the university toward graduate education, so that its faculty could be freed from the burden that state-university professors had traditionally borne: teaching an enormous number of students who had been let in under open-admissions policies, many of whom they would have to flunk out.

No, what everyone noticed about the Master Plan was the new campuses, and the establishment of the principle that every high-school graduate had a legal right to higher education at public expense (usually in a junior college, if you read the fine print). The news was that Clark Kerr, the great democratizer, had invented free higher education for all and devised a legislated system to deliver it. He was both theorist and practitioner, the twentieth-century equivalent of Horace Mann, only greater, because his achievements were on so much larger a scale. *Time* magazine put Kerr on its cover in 1960 with the headline "Master Planner"—a great compliment at the time. *Life*'s headline was "Fever of a Mass Thrust for Knowledge." *McCall's* was "Rah! Rah! Rah! College for Everybody!" Official delegations visited Berkeley from Great Britain, Japan, Norway, Indonesia, and the newly independent Ivory Coast. Other states and other nations, inspired by the Master Plan, began to arrange to bring higher education to the masses. In the White House, where President Kennedy had just arrived and was rumored to be considering Kerr for a top job, a note was placed in the personnel file that said, "In short, a remarkable man. He is a man of quiet force, wins arguments without ever raising his voice, and leaves all who know him with a belief in his complete integrity. He is of cabinet stature."

Time ran a second cover story on the Master Plan in 1962, this time focusing on the new University of California campus at Irvine and its glamorous architect, William Pereira. Kerr had persuaded the Irvine family of Orange County, owners of the second-largest ranch in the United States, to deed a thousand acres of their holdings to the University of California and to sell another five hundred acres at the bargain price of $500 an acre for another UC campus. He also acquired a large tract of beautiful redwood forest in the hills above the Pacific for the construction of UC Santa Cruz, headed by his old friend Dean McHenry, which would be northern California's new campus. It was simply unheard of to undertake to build a nationally prominent university on empty land, in just a few years, but Kerr was doing just that—twice!

Kerr's public image was not misleading, exactly. He did believe in mass, or at least expanded, higher education. Anyway, if he had gone before the legislature and merely asked for a magnificent level of funding and protection for an upper professoriate with few official duties, who were supposed to work freely at whatever they were interested in and give wise guidance to the society, he wouldn't have had a chance. On the other hand, a system that gave everybody a free education, teaching Californians and affording them skills of real economic value, would win their firm allegiance, especially if they did not pay close attention to how the system sorted everyone into quasi-permanent categories at the age of eighteen. You had to cut the public in on the deal.

Clark Kerr was a realist. He did not subscribe to the gooier liberal notions about mass higher education making everybody into a somebody. Having analyzed the labor market, he believed about half of the state's young people could benefit economically from education beyond high school; the junior colleges were there to give a few people a second chance, to remedy the inadequacies of high school, to siphon off students who might otherwise pressure the university to let them in, and, mainly, to send the signal that the Master Plan gave everyone a chance to get more education if they wanted it.

He did believe, then, that the Master Plan would at least create a fair opportunity for anyone to join the elite, which was a historic development, and that a big, orderly educational system would bring at least California as close to the Jeffersonian social ideal as it was possible to come. Once, many years later, Kerr came across a book arguing that mass ownership of common stock represented the true fulfillment of Jefferson's dreams for America. This notion aroused an open display of emotion in Kerr, a great rarity; he so much disagreed with the idea that he could not speak about it without shaking with anger. "I thought that was *phony*," he said. "A travesty. It's more nearly Jeffersonian if there's equal opportunity through education. You really controlled your *life*, not just a share of stock." The educational system was better, fairer, purer, more apt to reward true merit and moral worth, than the great grubby unorganized marketplace.

Kerr was certain that the public shared his view, that it wasn't just a professorial attitude. Once in the late 1950s a friend of his came out to Berkeley to give a lecture and stopped by to see Kerr. Kerr laid out the whole glowing picture of the Master Plan: if Berkeley was impressive, imagine eight Berkeleys by the year 2000! His friend asked him how such a vast enterprise was going to be funded. With his usual complete calm assurance, Kerr said that would not be a problem. California would keep growing, and the people would always support the Master Plan because they would realize it was good for everybody.

Like potentates who conclude a peace and then pay state visits to each other's courts, the two leading visionaries of the American meritocracy, after the system was completed, traveled across the country to give reciprocal series of lectures. First, in 1960, James Bryant Conant came to Berkeley to give the annual Jefferson Memorial Lectures; then, in 1963, Clark Kerr went to Harvard to give the annual Godkin Lectures. Each series was then published as a book. Together they represented the completion of a powerful alliance between the country's leading private university and its leading public one, and the unveiling for the world of the new social vision that Conant and Kerr shared and that, evidently, they had persuaded the United States to adopt.

Conant's lectures at Berkeley proposed a political program in the guise of discussing Thomas Jefferson's views on education. In preparation he had read deeply, but selectively, in the great man's writings, looking for support for his own views. Conant found this chiefly in the "natural aristocracy" letter to John Adams and in the description of Jefferson's failed education bill in *Notes on the State of Virginia*. Jefferson's central belief on this matter, as Conant read him, was that one should select a small number of outstanding students, regardless of their background, to educate at universities at public expense; these would go on to become the leaders of American society. (Jefferson himself, by the way, maintained that if forced to choose between primary education for all and university education for this natural aristocracy, he would choose the former.) Now, Conant believed, this excellent idea was being threatened by democratizers who wanted to educate everyone equally, without selection. "Over the past twenty-five years," he wrote, by way of recounting his quixotic opposition to the GI Bill, "I must admit I have frequently encountered something less than enthusiasm for my plea for a renewal of Jefferson's concern with 'raking geniuses from the rubbish.' "

He had to acknowledge that in the past the United States' lack of a university-educated governing elite had been considered one of its strengths, because it meant that society was much more fluid and democratic than in Western Europe, where publicly funded universities turned out an officialdom in a way that generated "something approaching a caste system." But times had changed, mainly because of the advent of the atomic bomb: "What the nation today requires for its welfare—indeed, for its survival in freedom—is the identification of the most promising of the next generation and their education at public expense."

Kerr's lectures at Harvard were more expansive and sunny. That he had been invited to deliver the Godkin Lectures, a venerable endowed series that was usually given by a leading social or political thinker, was a remarkable tribute in itself. No state university president had ever been a Godkin lecturer before, or ever would again. It was a sign of Kerr's prestige at the time that in addition to being the administrator of the biggest educational system in the world and the recent winner of a signal political victory, he was also considered an intellectual giant.

At the lecture podium in Cambridge, Kerr delivered a dazzling *tour d'horizon* encompassing the entire history of higher education—Athens,

Oxford, Bologna, Berlin, Johns Hopkins, Chicago—and coming to rest at its culmination, its apotheosis, the California Master Plan (not, however, mentioning the part about the state colleges). Previously the academy had been a rarefied, protected realm, set apart from the rest of society, a sanctuary for a small number of scholars, scholars-in-training, and children of the rich preparing to enter the professions. Now it had moved to the center. What grandiose, commanding language Kerr used, for a quiet, bald, bespectacled Quaker! The new university was "an institution unique in world history," "a prime instrument of national purpose," "the focal point for national growth," "an imperative rather than a reasoned choice among elegant alternatives." The University of California, Kerr reminded his audience, was bigger than IBM, a far-flung academic empire with 40,000 employees. Knowledge had become the essential product of postwar industrial society; therefore universities would become the essential organizations. Governments would fund them more and more generously, to the point that the distinction between public and private universities would become meaningless. They would all be part of a finely calibrated nexus of large organizations that would run America.

When the Godkin lectures were published in book form under the title *The Uses of the University* (an echo of John Henry Cardinal Newman's *The Idea of a University* with a practical modern twist), one reviewer remarked, unkindly but not inaccurately, *"The Uses of the University* is the work of a deeply satisfied man." In Kerr's scheme the university would meet every need, social, political, intellectual, and economic. To underscore the point he gave it a new name, the "multiversity." Nothing could go wrong because every actor in society would benefit in some way from the new regime of knowledge. Kerr brought up possible problems for the multiversity only to demonstrate that he was aware of them and to explain why they would not be serious. (For example, as federal money flowed into universities to fund research that tied up the faculty's time, "the resultant student sense of neglect may bring a minor counterrevolt." The emphasis was on "minor.")

Kerr meant the multiversity to be not a gigantic vocational-technical training operation, but a true university, run by scholars. Everybody in American society would now be related to the university system, but at its center would still be a pure priesthood of the mind—purer, in fact, than ever before, in addition to being much more influential. One could see that the rule of the few would require the consent of the many; this was on the list of issues that Kerr contemplated from a comfortable position under his large umbrella of optimism:

The great university is of necessity elitist—the elite of merit—but it operates in an environment dedicated to an egalitarian philosophy. How may the contribution of the elite be made clear to the egalitarians, and how may an aristocracy of intellect justify itself to all men?

Good question.

12 Chauncey at Yale

Conant and Kerr both proclaimed that in the new America, with its brainy elite and its great educational personnel system, the distinction between private and public schools would fade away. Lesser private schools would become insignificant and better ones would get so much government money that they would become de facto public institutions. The main point was that education would be available purely on the basis of ability, not money.

This didn't happen.

During the 1950s Henry Chauncey's old friend Wilbur J. Bender became dean of admissions at Harvard. After a few years he announced that Harvard was moving toward a policy of "need-blind" admissions, in which every person let in would be guaranteed enough scholarship money to attend. Over time most of the Ivy League universities adopted the need-blind principle (though in recent years several have dropped it), but the connection between family money and higher education was never truly severed. The level of government support for private universities never rose high enough to allow them to stop needing alumni contributions. Instead they had to improvise a hybrid system. The new idea of an educational meritocracy was sweeping across the country with an immense force that no school could deny, but if it were adopted wholesale, there would be no way to pay the bills. What really occurred was a pronounced, even wrenching transition ending distinctly short of the original idea.

As Sam Chauncey moved through his formative institutions, which were elite private schools, the basic machinery of the American meritocracy was in place, but from his corner of the system you wouldn't have noticed.

At Groton, he was, by his own reckoning, the poorest member of his class and one of the few boys whose family was not so rich that adult employment for its members was strictly optional. During his student days there, Groton admitted students whom Sam understood were its first-ever Jew and first-ever Negro. Sam's own class was all high-Protestant Anglo-Saxon. Like making a career choice, getting admitted to college brought with it no element of insecurity or nervousness; the boy and his family simply decided where he wanted to go and that was that. Every member of the class got into his first-choice college except one, who was thought to be brain-damaged. The students took the SAT and other standardized tests but were not told their scores. Once a group of daring boys in Sam's class—not including Sam, who was not daring—went rummaging through teachers' desks at night until they found everyone's test scores, and read them, receiving the illicit thrill that comes from forbidden information.

At Yale, the students came mainly from private schools along the Eastern seaboard. The biggest New England boarding schools, Andover and Exeter, sent as many as fifty boys on to Yale every year. Smaller schools like Groton, St. Paul's, Hotchkiss, and Taft each sent dozens. These boarding-school graduates, nearly all of whom were Protestant and most likely Episcopalian, whose families lived in dignified splendor, set the tone of undergraduate life. Sam was intensely conscious of being a scholarship student. Yale men wore crew cuts and button-down shirts and thin striped ties and tweed jackets, perhaps a little frayed. They studied, but not to excess. A certain kind of offhanded but secretly very intense male camaraderie, which ran along a spectrum with hedonism at one end and heroism at the other, dominated the ethos of Yale College. One of Sam's classmates, Calvin Trillin, who as a Jewish public-school graduate from the Midwest was quite atypical, in later life, as a writer, invented the name Baxter Thatcher Hatcher to denote his typical classmates. That was a good Yale joke: genial, but with a distinct, bracing, competitive male edge.

Merely to say that Yale College had a boarding-school cast does not fully communicate what the tone was like. To say that Yale, as an institution, was like a very big boarding school gets closer to the essence of it. Yale in the 1950s was not a major international research university. Its president, A. Whitney Griswold, was the opposite of a higher-ed tycoon sitting atop a multiversity. His schedule customarily consisted of one appointment every morning and one appointment every afternoon. (If he had an evening appointment, he would cancel the afternoon appointment.) The senior fellow of the Yale Corporation—the group of men who functioned as Griswold's boss—was Wilmarth S. Lewis, a gentleman-scholar who lived at a country estate in Farmington, Connecticut, surrounded by butlers and cooks, and who suspected Whitney Griswold of being too modern. One year the Connecticut legislature got the idea of forbidding universities to ask for information about the religion of applicants. Griswold persuaded the student editor of *The Yale Daily News*, William F. Buckley, Jr., to go up to Hartford and testify against the bill; Griswold told him such information would be indispensable for the Yale Archives (though Buckley, an opponent of government regulation, didn't need to be persuaded very hard). A few days later, when Buckley told Yale's Catholic chaplain about his political mission, the chaplain broke the news to him that Yale maintained a ceiling of 13 percent on Catholics and on Jews and that was why they needed to ask the question.

Yale had an engineering school and a medical school, but in the pure sciences it was barely in the game. Its best academic departments were English and history; even in these the leading professors were themselves graduates of boarding schools and Yale (rather than members of the world academic royalty like the professors Clark Kerr had brought to Berkeley), who had intense, familial, character-molding relations with the undergraduates. Triple-named Episcopalians set the tone of the faculty: Chauncey Brewster Tinker, William Lyon Phelps, Samuel Flagg Bemis, Norman Holmes Pearson. English professors wrote about their own literature (high Anglo-American), history professors wrote about their own history (English and American, with an emphasis on the leadership class), economics professors championed their kind of economy (free-market capitalism) and tried to resist the vogue for John Maynard Keynes.

There was no office at Yale devoted to career counseling or job placement for undergraduates. It was assumed that every Yale man had a job waiting upon graduation, either with his father's company, or with his mother's father's, or with one of his uncles', or at one of the many Yale-dominated banking or finance firms. The view of men like Kerr and Conant that an elite college education ought to be a prelude to graduate school did not have much currency at Yale. In the spring, Yale men who worked at the leading New York banks would drift up to New Haven, drop by their old fraternities and senior societies, and casually extend job offers to the current members. It was a given that you could go from Yale to being comfortably prosperous and well situated; for the more ambitious, a big-time world of money and power was also within the Yale orbit. Without too much trouble a well-presented Yale man could obtain an introduction at such Yale-tinged institutions as the CIA or Time Incorporated or J. H. Whitney and Company, the venture-capital firm.

And yet, to say that Yale in the 1950s was just like Harvard in the 1930s as Conant had perceived it—an institution dominated by a self-conscious hereditary aristocracy—doesn't capture the tone of the place either. The rising idea of meritocracy would have been offensive to much of Yale, because it elevated what the Episcopacy considered a minor quality, academic ability, to supreme status. Still, Yale men believed themselves to be wholly devoted to the principle of constant, open, fair competition in which those who were staunch and stalwart would always triumph over those who were a little "wet." (Remember, the fierce term "social Darwinism" was invented by a Yale man—alumnus and faculty member—who was also an Episcopalian minister, William Graham Sumner.) The inheritor who lazily awaited his due was a scorned figure; the leaders, in a group obsessed with the idea of leadership, were those who had best survived the running of a long, tough gamut.

The best place to imbibe the code in pure, sustained, unembarrassed form, the *locus classicus*, is a work of boys' fiction published in 1911 that even now functions as a kind of sacred Yale text: *Stover at Yale*, a novel by Owen Johnson. The book follows the undergraduate career of one Dink Stover, a clean-limbed boarding-school lad. It never occurs to Stover or anybody else in the book to notice Yale's mono-ethnicity or to think of college as primarily an academic institution. The one character who studies a lot, "Wookey, the little freshman from a mountain village of Maine, the shadow of a grind, whom no one knew in his class, and who would never know any one," is presented as a nobody and a loser, sure never to get anywhere near the elite. In the course of four hundred pages of ceaseless undergraduate self-examination, the question of careers, the main preoccupation today, pretty much never comes up. On the other hand, the animating idea of the book *is* meritocracy—with merit decoupled from intelligence.

Upon his arrival at Yale, Dink is told, in reverent tones, "It's the one place where money makes no difference . . . where you stand for what you are." Then he and his classmates begin a lengthy process of proving themselves, which will culminate late in their junior year on Tap Day, when a lucky few are selected for membership in Yale's senior societies—the luckiest handful for the most prestigious one, Skull and Bones, election to which "stands as a reward of merit here." (Once tapped, inside the windowless senior society clubhouses they would undergo a pre-Freudian Episcopacy version of psychoanalysis, relentlessly revealing and analyzing each other's innermost secrets in order to buff themselves to an even higher competitive polish.) The definition of merit is "ambition and industry and character," as demonstrated on the football field and in campus politics; the beau ideal is the golden young man whom everyone naturally follows because of his athletic ability and his pure devotion to high ideals.

At first Dink accepts all this, but then he has a crisis of confidence when what has been thunderingly obvious to the contemporary reader finally dawns upon him: Yale is populated by rich boys, not self-made yeoman-heroes. He responds by shifting his social circle to include the college's handful of scholarship students and by taking a summer job on a construction crew. He and his friends commit themselves to the goal of creating a better Yale, a more national, inclusive institution. As Brockman, the book's student-philosopher, puts it:

> "I'm not satisfied with Yale as a magnificent factory on democratic business lines; I dream of something else, something visionary, a great institution not of boys, clean, lovable and honest, but of men of brains, of courage, of leadership, a great center of thought, to stir the country and bring it back to the understanding of what man creates with his imagination, and dares with his will. It's visionary—it will come."

In the end Dink is tapped for Skull and Bones, but it's the new, lofty, awakened Dink. His success is a morally elevated one. The point that *Stover* demonstrates about Yale is that, self-satisfiedly Baxter Thatcher Hatcher as it may have looked, residing in its soul was the idea of itself as a noble, heroic, open, and, yes, in its own fashion, meritocratic institution. Otherwise what happened later would not have happened.

In 1953, the year Sam Chauncey arrived at Yale as a freshman, Whitney Griswold gently eased out his dean of admissions, Edward Noyes, and replaced him with a younger man named Arthur Howe. Noyes was an old-fashioned gentleman, a former head of the College Board, who presided over an office that filled Yale substantially with the sons of alumni and did not aggressively canvass the country for talent in the manner envisioned in *Stover at Yale* (and put into practice in the 1930s at Harvard by Conant and Henry Chauncey). Although Noyes had conferred his blessing upon the formation of ETS, ETS's principal allies at Yale were the men who ran the scholarship office, Baldy Crawford and Paul Burnham, who believed to a far greater extent than Noyes did that the SAT was the best way of picking Yale students.

Arthur Howe, the new admissions dean, thought of himself as an aggressive liberal reformer whose mandate was to open up Yale's student body and nationalize it. As a second-generation Yale (and Hotchkiss) man and an Episcopalian, he wasn't an obvious applecart-turner, but he came from a family of educational crusaders. His great-great-grandfather commanded a black regiment in the Civil War and then founded Hampton College. His father had been president of Hampton. His brother, Harold, was a rising star in the world of public education, who eventually served as U.S. Commissioner of Education. Art Howe wanted to make a similar mark.

Ned Noyes had sat serenely in New Haven, but Howe hit the road. He set up an elaborate apparatus with America's leading high schools (well, okay, most of them were private schools in the East) which he called the ABC system. Figuring that the headmasters and guidance counselors knew their own boys better than a Yale admissions officer possibly could, he let the schools grade their Yale applicants with either an A, a B, or a C. The boys graded A were, essentially, automatic admits, and were told so immediately; later the admissions office evaluated the B and C boys. The ABC system did two things: it effectively reserved most of the places in each Yale class for the participating schools, and it allowed for admissions decisions to be made on the basis of the Episcopacy's idea of merit—that is, character and leadership, as judged by headmasters. Moreover, it was understood that if a boy's father had gone to Yale and he was capable of doing the work, Yale ought to admit him. Howe put quite a lot of work into setting up the ABC system, and he talked Harvard and Princeton into adopting it, too. He was proud of it.

The problem was that Whitney Griswold's campaign at Yale of gradual modernization (so gradual as to be on the point of being invisible to the outside world) was proceeding on more than one front. He was also bringing in new faculty members not of the traditional Yale mold, and these men were not satisfied with Art Howe and his ABC system. The professor who seemed to Howe to be the ringleader of this group was James Tobin, in the economics department. For much of his life Tobin had been walking point for the American meritocracy; you may recall that, as a boy in Champaign, Illinois, he was one of the early students selected by Henry Chauncey to be a Harvard National Scholar. When Tobin joined the Yale faculty in the early 1950s, the place felt to him the way Harvard had when he arrived there in the 1930s only more so. He and Howe began having regular arguments about admissions policy.

It was not so much that Tobin and Howe were enemies—they were always cordial—as that they profoundly didn't understand each other. Tobin was Clark Kerr's idea of a faculty member. Plucked from virtuous, studious obscurity and given the finest education, he was now a natural aristocrat on the national and world stage of scholarship, producing internationally recognized work, advising the American government, helping to operate the increasingly complicated machinery of modern society from the terrestrial location in New Haven that he happened to occupy. He was a key actor in prodding America toward using government to smooth out the severest disruptions of the market economy. Did he have freshmen from Taft and Hotchkiss over for brunch on Sundays, to make sure they were feeling at home at Yale? No, he did not. To Tobin the question of Yale admissions was a simple one. The world's great universities admitted students on the basis of their academic promise. That was what Yale should do.

Art Howe thought that Tobin, by so much emphasizing academic qualities, wanted to fill Yale with "what you'd now call nerds or wimps—high distinction but not communal," as opposed to the future leaders of society. In 1960 he grumbled to a reporter from *The New Yorker*:

> Sometimes I lie awake nights worrying about whether we've been kidding ourselves into taking a lot of brainy kids who are too egocentric ever to contribute much to society. Or have we been taking a lot of twirps who have read the how-to-get-into-college books, listened to their counselors, and learned to take tests and to give the right answers to interviewers—a bunch of conformists who will keep right on doing the smart thing for themselves? . . . How far should a university go in accepting candidates whose reasons for applying are based on such shallow values?

Howe's comment shows how little space there was in those days between harboring doubts about the new meritocratic order and simply longing for the *ancien régime*. He felt that compared to Tobin's way, it was far better to give fine, selfless men like Horace Taft of the Taft School, a dear friend of Howe's father, or Henry Chauncey's old football teammate William Saltonstall, who was now headmaster at Exeter, the opportunity to pick boys they knew to be devoted to the old ideals of public service. You had to see that; it couldn't be measured by any test.

A good example of a boy who wouldn't have been admitted to Yale by Tobin's criterion was Sam Chauncey. He was never an outstanding student, and he did not cut the same spectacular figure as his father. He was smaller, quieter, less commanding and exuberant. He had fine, tight, organized features that did not stand out. He was fit but not a star athlete. His virtue was, precisely, his good selfless character, along with an acute observational eye that his father lacked. Henry Chauncey unreflectively took up a leading position in society, while Sam Chauncey tended more to watch and to assess, from a spot further from the rostrum. Sam could see that the new world Jim Tobin represented had the stronger argument behind it, that it was more modern and democratic, more fair, even though it might hold a lesser place for him personally than the old world in which he had grown up. So, as his father had, but much more quietly, he allied himself with it.

When Sam was a senior, his senior society, Wolf's Head, admitted its first Jewish member. Since the senior societies' status as the psychic ground zero of Yale College—membership in them was the means of denoting who really mattered on campus (and who was anointed for the best future positions out in the adult world)—had hardly changed since Dink Stover's day, this was a big step, signaling Jews' release from second-class status. The Wolf's Head alumni, who had the power to approve new members, vetoed the boy. Sam and the other seniors threatened to resign, and the alumni backed down. On the day after he graduated in 1957, Sam went to work as an assistant dean at Yale. At a party the next fall for new employees, where everyone got thirty seconds in a receiving line with Whitney Griswold, Griswold asked Sam what he had done over the summer. Sam said he had worked at a camp (run by Groton) for the underprivileged. A few weeks later, the phone rang in Sam's rooms at eleven o'clock one night. It was Whitney Griswold. "Four Negro boys are throwing horse chestnuts at my house. What should I do?" he said. "Tell them to go away," Sam said. A few minutes later the phone rang again. "When I told them to go away, they threw horse chestnuts at me," Griswold said. "I'm going to form a committee on this."

So it was that Sam Chauncey was brought into the meeting room of the Yale Corporation, with its vast imposing oaken table and its carved chairs, and introduced by Griswold to the leaders of the city of New Haven (summoned by him for the occasion) as, in effect, Yale's expert on social unrest, diversity, and multiculturalism. Sam appreciated the irony of it, but, at the same time, he turned to the job with a Grotonian sense of Christian duty. He was a kind of spy: to outward appearances he was the perfect Yale man almost to the point of parody, an inside player with no expressed views, but he unobtrusively devoted himself to bringing Yale into better synch with the times.

In 1963 Whitney Griswold died of cancer and the Yale Corporation appointed his provost, Kingman Brewster, Jr., president of Yale. One morning when Sam got to work he was surprised to find Brewster sitting in his office waiting for him. Sam, by that point, had worked his way up to the position of dean of students, a job he liked a lot. Brewster asked him to come to work as his personal assistant. Sam hemmed and hawed, then, ever loyal, he took the job. It was a smart choice on Brewster's part. Sam could be counted on to execute orders quietly and efficiently; by virtue of his lineage and bearing he was profoundly reassuring to the forces of conservatism at

Yale, but he was on the side of change, and that was where Brewster wanted to be, too.

Like Sam, Brewster was a Puritan descendant. His family had come to America on the *Mayflower* to settle the Plymouth colony. This was a golden credential, and in addition he met his culture's high, if hard to measure, standards of character and leadership. Brewster's class at Yale (1941) was a strikingly homogeneous group—30 percent had been sons of alumni, 10 percent came from a single boarding school, Andover, and the top six boarding schools supplied more class members than all of America's public high schools put together—whose wholehearted admiration he won. He ran *The Yale Daily News*, and, going Dink Stover one better, he turned down Skull and Bones on Tap Day because he objected on principle to senior societies. In a way that would be difficult for non-Yale people to appreciate fully, this last was a magnificent act of heroism that resonated down through the decades and was still a leading item in Brewster's reputation at the time of his selection as president of the university.

Although Brewster was something of a rebel, at bottom he was very much a man of the Episcopacy. He was not at all like Kerr or Conant; he was not a technocrat or strategic thinker who received the world through a filter of formal, learned social and economic theory. What animated him were not the main ideas of the world intellectual community, like industrialism and modernization, but the old themes of his group, public service and nobility of spirit. His rebellion was played out not against big, outside institutions like Capital or The State, but against subcultural institutions like Skull and Bones—and, in fact, Yale. What he had been best known for before becoming president of Yale was being a student spokesman for the isolationist America First Committee in the period before the United States entered the Second World War; he testified in Congress while still an undergraduate. This wasn't an episode that stood up well, but at the time it was another Stoveresque valorous, character-displaying stand against prevailing opinion, so it did not undercut his standing. For all his life Brewster comfortably maintained the understated, graceful, rumpled, charming style of his group. He was a liberal Republican. He went to Martha's Vineyard in the summers. He referred to people as good eggs and bad eggs.

As Whitney Griswold had eased out Ned Noyes as dean of admissions, so Brewster eased out Art Howe. He asked Sam Chauncey to help him find a successor, and he settled on one of Sam's Yale classmates, R. Inslee Clark, Jr.: a clever choice. At a cursory glance Clark would have been reassuring to Old Yale. He had a Yale-sounding name (and a Yale-sounding nickname, Inky). As an undergraduate he had been a popular campus leader, president of the intrafraternity council. After graduation he had spent three years teaching at a boarding school. He looked like a Yale man—tall, with a crew cut, forthright, ruddy, with a physique of the former athlete getting just ever so slightly chubby. In fact, Clark was a subversive. He had been educated in public schools on Long Island, his father had not even gone to college, and at the time of his appointment he was an intemperate twenty-nine years old. Brewster, interviewing him for the job, asked, "Do you see yourself as an architect or an engineer?" "Architect!" Clark answered unhesitatingly.

In his first year as dean, 1964–65, Clark turned Yale admissions upside down. Twenty years earlier, when Conant and Chauncey wanted to change the admissions policy at Harvard, they moved cautiously, concentrating at first on just a handful of scholarship students and leaving the rest undisturbed. Clark, operating in a more conservative institution, waged a frontal assault. He began by replacing the entire staff of the admissions office.

Howe was intensely proud that he and his staff had visited five hundred high schools a year; Clark and his new staff visited a thousand, including Abe Lass's Abraham Lincoln High School in Brooklyn ("Where the hell have you guys been all these years?" Lass asked him), and schools in ghettos and barrios and on Indian reservations and in remote rural areas. Applications to Yale increased by 40 percent. Howe, with his long family history in Negro education, had carefully brought a handful of Negro students to Yale; Clark admitted dozens. Clark abolished Howe's ABC system and tried to talk Princeton and Harvard into abolishing it, too (Princeton did, Harvard didn't). He increased the public-school share of the Yale freshman class by 9 percent in a single year. And for the first time, Yale admitted without regard to financial need. The son of Yale's biggest donor, Paul Mellon, was rejected. The mean SAT verbal score (which educators thought is the best proxy for IQ) of Clark's first class of admittees was 683, nearly a hundred points higher than the mean for the class that had included Sam Chauncey and Clark himself.

The result was open warfare of a kind that had not gone on at the other Ivy League universities, which had moved toward meritocratic admissions more gradually. It was somehow very Yale that Yale had chosen the same course as everybody else but had organized the adoption of it around the figure of a brave, glorious, crusading, character-rich young man. Among the alumni a cult of Clark hatred quickly developed. Admissions is a zero-sum game; when new people come in, somebody has to be squeezed out, and the alumni knew who it was. The percentage of alumni sons dropped from 20 in Howe's last class to 12 in Clark's first. The number of admissions from Andover, Yale's number-one feeder school, was cut nearly in half.

An apocrypha of Clark horror stories sprang up. Clark had gone to a boarding school (St. Paul's or St. Mark's or Groton, depending on which version of the story you heard) and told the headmaster, "The last thing we need at Yale is another preppie!" He turned down a boy from Hotchkiss who was president of the student body, captain of the hockey team, and an alumnus son—the ideal applicant by the standards of just a year earlier. Clark had mused publicly before an alumni group that having a father who had been to Yale conferred so much advantage that the admissions office shouldn't use it any longer as a plus factor. William F. Buckley, Jr., ran for a position on the Yale Corporation (whose members were technically elected by the alumni, though except in rare cases like this one the election was merely the ratification of a slate proposed by the Corporation itself), on a platform of undoing the works of Inky Clark and establishing a policy under which any alumnus son judged capable of graduating would automatically be admitted. "The son of an alumnus, who goes to a private preparatory school, now has less chance of getting in than some boy from P.S. 109 somewhere," Buckley groused to a reporter from *The New York Times*. He didn't win, but his candidacy frightened Yale so much that it lined up no less than a future Secretary of State, Cyrus Vance, to be his opposition.

Finally Clark was hauled before the Corporation to explain himself. He made a presentation and then, as he remembered it, one Corporation member, a bank president, raised his hand and said, "Look around this room." He swept his hand to take in such figures as John Lindsay, mayor of New York, and William Scranton, governor of Pennsylvania, both liberal Republican, Episcopalian boarding-school graduates, either of whom at that point quite possibly might be the next President of the United States. "What you see is the leadership of this nation. What you see here in this room is not the class you just admitted to Yale."

From that point on, Brewster had to devote himself to modulating the impact of Inky Clark. He did this with shrewdness and a nice political touch.

Brewster appointed a faculty advisory board on admissions and instructed it to prepare a report and present it to him, privately, with no publicity. He had to know what the outcome would be: James Tobin was the chairman. The Tobin Report declared that admission to Yale should be based on the premise that "Yale is first and foremost an intellectual enterprise." It recommended stacking the admissions committee with a majority of faculty members and dropping entirely two favorite old criteria for college admissions, "personal qualities" and likelihood of successful performance on Yale's athletic teams. The report came about an inch away from stating outright the premise that gave the admissions debate its special ferocity, that Yale should accept more intelligent Jews from New York: "It is just as well to be candid. The Board suspects that in the past, at Yale and elsewhere, 'character' and 'leadership' have sometimes been rubrics under which favoritism has been shown to candidates of certain family, economic, religious, ethnic, and scholastic backgrounds."

The purpose of the Tobin Report was to give some official cover to Clark and his admissions policies. After it was completed, in the fall of 1966, Brewster set up a quiet dinner so that Tobin could present his findings to a few members of the Corporation. But while he was doing this with one hand, with the other Brewster was communicating to the alumni that he was going to rein Clark in.

Without Brewster's fingerprints being visibly on the deed, Clark appointed as his number-two man a deeply reassuring and moderate older gentleman from Canada named John Muyskens, who from then on tended to make the admissions office's public pronouncements. Also, the reliable and discreet Sam Chauncey was placed on the admissions committee to keep an eye on things. Then Brewster decided that he would write a long, musing private letter to Muyskens, copies of which, mysteriously, soon seemed to be in the hands of everybody who mattered at Yale.

The beauty of the letter to Muyskens was that it allowed Brewster to distance himself from Inky Clark's policies without appearing to be rebuking Clark—he was just welcoming Muyskens, whom Clark had appointed, into the Yale community, and he never imagined that anybody but Muyskens would read it (or so he said). The most important sentence was this: "The only preference by inheritance which seems to deserve recognition is the Yale son." The second most important sentence was: "We want Yale men to be leaders in their generation," which was code for, roughly: It isn't going to be all grinds from Stuyvesant High School who want to be professors when they grow up.

After the Muyskens letter, Brewster published an official report on admissions in Yale's alumni magazine in which he backpedaled even more openly ("we undoubtedly made some mistakes in the manner and style with which we approached some schools"), taking pains to say that character as well as brains still counted for something and that Yale would still train people to be "movers and doers," as well as scholars. Yale would still be in part the Episcopacy's idea of a meritocracy, not just the faculty's idea of one.

Brewster's retreat was strategic, though. He was giving up some ground in order to persuade the alumni to change their conception of what Yale was— to think of it henceforth as an institution where "the intellectual potential quite properly deserves more weight than any other." This had to be done not just through reassurance but by making a positive argument. Brewster knew exactly how to appeal to his constituency. You had to play the trump cards of public service and fair play and doing the decent right thing. And you had to make people understand that these virtuous factors, devoutly adhered to as they might be, were something of a cover for a less self-effacing quality, a strong drive for power and importance. William Brewster had not sailed to the New World, and whatever patriarch founded every other Old Yale family had not intended, to be part of a minor enterprise. They were not Amish. The idea of a faded, insignificant Yale—"a finishing school on Long Island Sound," as Brewster used to go around saying—was, he knew, profoundly unappealing to at least the key alumni, people like Paul Mellon and John Hay Whitney.

Brewster understood not only that making the threat of Yale's decline was decisive but also that it would not do to make the threat directly, to say to the alumni: You don't want Yaleness to become a second-order quality, do you? It had to be put in the more elevated terms that fit with their self-concept. So he wrote: "It seems to me that this ethic is not just important to Yale's selfish ambition or Yale's self-respect, but to the nation itself." To serve is to reign.

Inky Clark served as dean of admissions for five years. Toward the end of his tenure, the Yale Corporation agreed to admit women as students for the first time—another revolutionary change, but one that followed upon the first; it would have been impossible if the idea that Yale was primarily a college for the country's most outstanding students had not been put across. After Clark left, Brewster temporarily installed Sam Chauncey as John Muyskens' superior, with the odd title Director of University Admissions Policy, to manage the shift to coeducation and continue unruffling the feathers of the alumni (by, for example, sending a letter to all sixteen- and seventeen-year-old alumni children inviting them to apply). Sam then helped put into place a new dean of admissions, Worth David, who stayed in the job for many years.

To say that Brewster entirely weathered the storm begun by Inky Clark would not be right. He was never truly popular with the Yale alumni. In the spring of 1970 there were large demonstrations at Yale by students opposing the American invasion of Cambodia and protesting the trial in New Haven of a group of Black Panthers. Brewster's handling of the situation, in which, with his customary subtle touch, he artfully hinted at sympathy for the Panthers and the protesters, won the approval of most elements of Yale, even the Corporation (he had avoided a campus revolution, after all), but a group of conservative alumni were so angry that they started a protest group called Lux et Veritas, after Yale's Latin motto. They did battle with Brewster for years. In 1973, Brewster launched a large Yale fund-raising campaign by assuring alumni, in a way that must have been at least a little humiliating for him, that the Corporation had ordered the admissions office "to see to it that every effort be made to attract, to admit, and to gain the acceptance of every qualified alumni son and daughter." In 1977, when he left Yale to become ambassador to Great Britain, it was widely understood (Brewster himself joked about it) that the fund-raising campaign would finally be able to reach its goal because all his alumni enemies would now contribute to it.

Still, Yale had changed. It now conceived of the elite it was educating in essentially academic terms. It would choose its students mainly on the basis of their predicted grades (which is to say, their SAT scores would be very important), and after Yale their key asset would be learned expertise, rather than simply good character. Going to work for Father was not what a Yale degree led to anymore; another of Sam Chauncey's duties during this transition period was helping Yale to set up an office to place students in graduate schools and jobs. The effect of the change was neatly demonstrated a generation later, in 1993, when the White House was turned over from George and Barbara Bush, he Old Yale, from Greenwich, Connecticut, a Skull and Bones man, she a college dropout who had met him at a debutante ball, to Bill and Hillary Clinton, who, having been plucked out of public-high-school obscurity in the South and Midwest, had met in the library of Yale Law School in the late 1960s.

In 1988 Kingman Brewster died. By that time Sam Chauncey had left Yale, but somehow he was eternally Brewster's indispensable man, the person who understood best how quietly to manage the change from the old order to the new, being sure to save what was worth saving. Therefore it fell to him to figure out how Brewster should be buried. All presidents of Yale rest in the venerable Grove Street cemetery in New Haven. For Brewster, Sam designed a site that was more than just an ordinary person's grave but at the same time was simple, tasteful, and modest. A low, unadorned black marble wall surrounds the grave site.

After searching through all of Brewster's speeches and writings, Sam settled upon a passage to have chiseled into the wall, one which, he believed, captured what Brewster would have wanted people to remember him for. It seemed to combine the best of the Episcopacy, its moral purity and grandeur, with the best of the new meritocracy, its promise of opportunity for all regardless of origin:

> The presumption of innocence is not just a legal concept. In commonplace terms it rests on that generosity of spirit which assumes the best, not the worst, of the stranger.

13 The Negro Problem

Back in 1943, in his "Wanted: American Radicals" article in *The Atlantic Monthly*, James Bryant Conant had thrown in this cryptic sentence: "To be practical, we can't promise white-collar jobs to all the ex-soldiers. We could fix some quotas, perhaps, and see that they are fairly distributed." What kind of quotas was he thinking about? Geographical quotas would be a fair guess—to stave off complaining from the South when it got its perennial smallest share of whatever academic prize was being handed out. What Conant was displaying was some awareness that if you created an organized system to distribute opportunity, then there might be complaining about its unfairness, complaining of a kind that is impossible when there is no system at all.

Any institution that is seen as being in charge of individual opportunity in the United States will generate political turmoil. Opportunity is the great onrushing force in American society, the thing that every single person is supposed to have as a fundamental right and whose denial is morally unacceptable. Through most of the nineteenth century, when opportunity meant access to capital to start a small farm, a shop, or a business, banking, currency, and credit were inflammatory political issues. In the late twentieth century, when opportunity meant education, the same thing happened to schools.

That was the general situation. In particular, the politics of the American meritocracy turned on a problem its founders didn't foresee, race.

Standardized educational tests created a ranking of Americans, one by one from top to bottom on a single measure. If one analyzed the ranking by social or ethnic group, then at the bottom, always, were Negroes. Living mostly in the benighted, educationally inferior South, consigned to separate schools that operated only sporadically with ill-trained teachers, historically denied by law even the chance to learn to read and write and figure, disproportionately poor, ill-nourished, and broken-familied, Negroes as a group were in a uniquely bad position to perform well on tests designed to measure such school-bred skills as reading and vocabulary and mathematics fluency. So whenever goods were distributed on the basis of test scores, Negroes got a disproportionately low share of them.

The new system hadn't been set up with the intention of excluding Negroes. Its founders had in fact been more completely blind to the aspirations of women than to anybody else. The idea that women should devote themselves to housekeeping and child rearing and volunteer work, no matter how talented they were, was so deeply ingrained in the American leadership class in the mid-twentieth century that calls for greater opportunity for women are just about impossible to find—even though the air was thick with calls for greater opportunity generally. The rhetoric of a perfected America, though, made it difficult to deny the aspirations of either women or blacks as they arose, and of the two groups women had generally better access to good education and so were better positioned to move through the narrow gates of the American meritocracy. Race was the area that threw the contradiction between the idea of the system (that it would fully deliver on the promise of American democracy) and the reality of it (that it apportioned opportunity on the basis of a single, highly background-sensitive quality) into the starkest relief.

By the time of the passage of the landmark Civil Rights Act of 1964, which is now remembered as having been aimed simply at outlawing segregation and putting blacks and whites on a completely equal legal footing, the inherent tension between the emerging meritocratic system and the cause of Negro advancement was already apparent to anyone who was looking closely.

Years before the Civil Rights Act, the more liberal states had set up commissions rhetorically in charge of "fair employment" or "human relations," whose specific task it was to get better jobs and better housing for Negroes. Creating these commissions had been an important cause within the movement for Negro advancement at least since New Deal days, and the only reason they were part of state government rather than federal was that segregationist Democrats from the South had too much power in Congress for a law creating a strong national version of them ever to pass.

In 1963 a young black man in Chicago applied for a job at a Motorola television factory and was turned down on the basis of his score on an IQ test the company had given him. He filed a complaint with the Illinois Fair Employment Practices Commission, which ordered Motorola to hire him.

During all the time that ETS and other testing companies had been promoting the use of tests as a hiring instrument by American business, it never occurred to them that the results would be used to exclude Negroes or, for that matter, that there could be any bad side to the miracle of testing. But excluding Negroes was the effect. In the early 1960s, Negro leaders—even Whitney Young, Jr., of the Urban League, a man never seen dressed in anything but business attire—were starting to suggest the establishment of quota systems that would force businesses to hire more Negroes, even if that meant disregarding whatever the hiring criteria were. In the summer of 1963, after President Kennedy had proposed the Civil Rights Act, he was asked at a press conference for his position on quotas (he said he was against them), and Attorney General Robert Kennedy was accused in Senate hearings on the bill of being soft on quotas (he denied it).

So the Motorola incident, which occurred just as debate on the Civil Rights Act was beginning in the U.S. Senate, got a lot of attention. Southerners who opposed the Civil Rights Act made the argument that it would visit Motorola verdicts upon private businesses all across the country. Most of the Southern senators' complaint about the Motorola case was simply that government had no right to tell a private business whom to hire. But a handful of them—the better class of Southern senators, from an educational point of view—made a more specific defense of tests. Senator William Fulbright of Arkansas, Rhodes Scholar, former university president, and hero to liberals, who knew he'd lose his seat unless he found a reason to vote against the Civil Rights Act, warned that the Motorola case boded ill for the new testing programs spreading through colleges and universities. Senator Lister Hill of Alabama, whose authorship of the National Defense Education Act of 1958 made him the father of federal funding of higher education, said the Motorola case "threw merit and ability out the window."

The senator who most ardently took up the defense of testing was John Tower of Texas, the only Republican member from the old Confederacy and a college professor until he had been elected to the Senate. Tower was within range of the East's stereotype of a crude right-winger: provincial, Southern Baptist, educated at state schools. Perhaps because he sensed this, he got himself up as a cross between a London clubman and an Oxford don, with pinstripe suits, elevated tastes, and a reverence for the intellect. "I point out that college entrance examinations discriminate against deprived and disadvantaged persons," he said during the debate on the Civil Rights Act, which was perfectly true but was the sentiment that ETS would least have wanted voiced, because it expressed nakedly the elitism that ETS had learned to elide. Tower inserted an amendment into the Civil Rights Act specifically permitting the use of ability tests in employment. Thus did standardized testing become a part of a landmark law in American history.

Sensing that pressure from the civil-rights movement in the South might finally have made the time ripe to create a federal version of the state fair employment practices commissions, President Lyndon Johnson put a provision in the Civil Rights Act that would set up a new Equal Employment Opportunity Commission. But most Southern Democrats and many Northern Republicans were highly suspicious of it. In order to get the Civil Rights Act passed, the Democrats had to accede to the demand of the Senate Republican leader, Everett Dirksen of Illinois, that the commission be nearly powerless. It could investigate complaints and that was about it; it could not sue companies or issue the kind of order-to-hire that the Illinois Fair Employment Practices Commission had issued to Motorola.

The Civil Rights Act represented an enormous liberal victory. Its supporters were understandably much more focused on its having passed a Congress thought to be civil-rights-proof than on signs of conflict between two powerful new forces in American life, the meritocratic apparatus and the drive for Negro opportunity. And for any liberal who was worried about this, an answer was at hand. Another not much noticed provision of the Civil Rights Act directed the federal Office of Education to conduct a study of the progress of school desegregation. The study was so well funded that it could be the occasion for much more than a simple head count. Instead it could be a full-scale social-scientific analysis of the problem of poor Negro performance on standardized tests. An ambitious survey would be conducted and correlations established. Whatever was found to be the cause of low Negro test scores could then be fixed.

The backdrop to the study was that the Supreme Court's decision in 1954 in the case of *Brown* v. *Board of Education*, which declared school segregation unconstitutional, had had frustratingly little effect in the South. The combination of intransigence by school districts, the exodus of white students from public schools, and residential segregation meant that nearly all Negro students in the South still attended inferior all-black schools. So if they weren't performing well on educational tests, surely the reason would turn out to be that their schools' budgets were too low. The federal government was steadily expanding in size and scope. The civil-rights study would give evidence that would break the American prejudice against federal funding for public elementary and secondary schools.

In the spring of 1965, the Office of Education awarded the contract to conduct the civil-rights survey to the Educational Testing Service.

ETS's role in the civil-rights survey was not a secret, but it wasn't widely advertised either. The government hired as lead investigator James S. Coleman, a chemical engineer turned sociologist. In keeping with academic etiquette, Coleman, the full professor, stood alone in the spotlight, and the people who executed the survey and performed the calculations kept themselves offstage. The name of the chief ETS technical expert on the survey, Alfred Beaton, did not even appear on a roster of Coleman's assistants published in the report, probably the single best-known piece of quantitative social science in American history—the Coleman Report. Coleman himself became one of the best-known social scientists.

ETS was just as happy to stay out of sight in this case. The survey had to be done in a great rush—the deadline, summer 1966, was written into federal law—and school participation was strictly voluntary. Therefore it might be difficult to get a scientifically valid sample. It would be hard to bring off the civil-rights survey at the usual ETS standard of technical proficiency.

On the other hand, this was a very big contract, the biggest ETS had had since the draft-deferment test of 1951. Each project encapsulated the mood of the government and educational establishment at the time: the draft-deferment test was born of a panicky urge to train an elite to win the Cold War; the civil-rights survey expressed a preoccupation with lack of opportunity, especially for Negroes, as the country's leading problem. In his correspondence and his diaries, Henry Chauncey, whose thinking was always unselfconsciously at one with that of the Establishment, evinced increasing concern with these issues in the 1960s. It looked as if there would be a chance to win many government contracts concerning equal opportunity in the coming years, but Chauncey was not a cynical man. The situation of the Negro genuinely bothered him, now that he was more aware of it, though like most members of the leadership class he had not given it much thought during the years of the Depression and the war. He was certain that, like all problems, it could be solved by experts.

So the civil-rights survey was gladly taken on and handled with special care. Chauncey put one of his best young men, Robert Solomon, in charge of it. Coleman wanted to use an IQ test as part of the survey, but Solomon, well acquainted from his years at ETS with the troublesomeness of IQ tests for the testing industry, explained to Coleman that when the Negro children got low scores, people would say that it was because they were congenitally stupid. Instead Solomon found, he later recalled, "a test of skills that you couldn't connect in any way, shape, or form to IQ." Another problem was that many schools refused to participate, most notably the entire public-school system of the city of Chicago. ETS could do nothing about that, but it meant that the response rate was only 65 percent, which is now considered unacceptably low for a government survey.

Coleman was actually living in Germany, on sabbatical, during the 1965–66 school year, when the survey was conducted, but ETS administered the tests, scored them, and prepared the data with its usual efficiency. When the preliminary data analysis was done Coleman came home to look it over and found, to his astonishment, that the differences in Negro and white achievement levels did not correlate much with the funding of the students' schools. Before the survey, Coleman had been going around saying publicly that he was sure it would show that low Negro test scores were the fault of poor schools. For example, "we really thought that the Northeastern Negro would score higher than the Southern whites," says Alfred Beaton, the ETS statistician on the survey. "The magnitude of the black-white difference and the uniformity over the country was mind-boggling. I can say it was a total surprise to me and to Jim too."

Coleman, who prided himself on his intellectual integrity, did not try to prize out of the data a case for pouring resources into Negro schools. Instead he moved strongly to nearly the opposite position: that student performance was much more heavily influenced by family than by school. "Differences between schools account for only a small fraction of differences in pupil achievement," the report said.

Within ETS, the feeling was that Coleman, because of some combination of convert's zeal, haste, and flaws in the data collection and analysis, had wound up understating the effect of schools on student achievement. Even before the report came out, an ETS executive named Henry Dyer was writing lacerating memos about it to Bob Solomon. "Most of the single variable comparisons, as they stand, strike me as terribly misleading," he wrote. After the report was published, Dyer wrote another, even stronger memo saying that the report's "bias would probably have the effect of reducing the evidence of educational disadvantage of minorities." Another ETS statistician thought that Coleman's use of the data "tends to depress the effect of school differences." Alfred Beaton produced an internal technical report for ETS two years later saying that if the data were manipulated differently, they would produce precisely the opposite of Coleman's conclusion: school factors were correlated more with student achievement than with family background.

But the public effect of the Coleman Report was to deal a crippling blow to the view that pouring resources into Negro schools would increase Negro test scores. The report came out in the summer of 1966; only a year earlier, Congress had passed the first-ever program to provide direct federal funding to poor local schools. The expectation was that the Coleman Report's findings would justify a substantial increase in this new federal commitment. Now, instead, better-informed liberals either adopted an attitude of quiet fatalism about the problem or looked for a solution other than the obvious one that Coleman had apparently discredited.

Nobody did more to promote the idea that reformers ought to abandon their hope of improving all-black public schools, which two-thirds of America's Negro students attended, than Daniel Patrick Moynihan, then a Harvard professor and soon to be a U.S. senator from New York. Moynihan secured funds (from the Ford Foundation) and sponsorship (from the Harvard Graduate School of Education) for a yearlong series of seminars on the policy implications of the Coleman Report, which itself had made no recommendations. The seminars wound up focusing on the finding that Negro students who attended integrated schools scored higher than those who went to all-black schools—a finding that ETS had not made much of, because the likelihood was that Negroes in integrated schools were a self-selected group, the children of parents who had moved to better school districts precisely to help their children. Moynihan's seminars were crucial in creating the view that the Coleman Report showed that by far the best way to improve Negro achievement would be not to upgrade Negro schools but to integrate large school systems, assigning and transporting children to schools outside their all-white or all-black neighborhoods if need be. Busing therefore attracted liberals' main energy for the next ten years. That was the chief effect of the Coleman Report.

Henry Dyer of ETS, reviewing the same data, came to precisely the opposite conclusion:

> The most important contribution of the survey, based on analyses reported to date, clearly lies in the documentation of gross inequities in educational opportunities and in the evidence that, without major intervention, such inequities will almost certainly continue far into the future.

Besides the Coleman Report, another aftereffect of the Civil Rights Act was the birth of affirmative action—a signal development that nobody noticed as it was taking place. The official act that began affirmative action was the issuing of Executive Order 11246 by President Lyndon Johnson on September 24, 1965. Executive Order 11246 was published in the *Federal Register*, but otherwise it got no attention. *The New York Times* didn't bother to mention it until nearly a month later, far down in an article about something else.

The birth of the term "affirmative action" itself dates from a few years earlier, under equally obscure circumstances. On the evening of John F. Kennedy's inauguration as President in 1961, a young Negro lawyer named Hobart Taylor, Jr., dropped by an inaugural ball for Texans in Washington. Taylor's father was a businessman in Houston and an ally of Lyndon Johnson's; this was the ball where Johnson got to reign, and Taylor was there to pay his respects to the new Vice President. As he got to the head of the receiving line, Johnson pulled him aside and whispered that he needed to see Taylor about something the next day.

When Taylor came around, Johnson handed him a draft of Executive Order 10925, which established a body called the President's Committee on Equal Employment Opportunity. Taylor read it and said he didn't like it. Johnson rented him a room at the Willard Hotel and told him to go there and rewrite the executive order. While Taylor was working, two lawyers (and future Supreme Court justices) dispatched by Johnson, Abe Fortas and Arthur Goldberg, showed up to help him. After they had finished a draft, the three of them walked over to Fortas' law office to have it typed up. It was there that Taylor, as an afterthought, inserted the words "affirmative action." "I was searching for something that would give a sense of positiveness to performance under that Executive Order," Taylor later told an interviewer, "and I was torn between the words 'positive action' and the words 'affirmative action.' . . . And I took 'affirmative' because it was alliterative." From this humble origin sprang one of the resounding phrases in contemporary American life.

The executive order was part of the old story of the federal government trying to set up the kind of fair employment practices commission that liberal states had. President Franklin Roosevelt had set up a Committee on Fair Employment Practice, with no power, in 1941. President Harry Truman had created a Committee on Civil Rights, with no power, in 1946, and an anti-discrimination Government Contract Compliance Committee, with no power, in 1951. President Dwight Eisenhower created a Government Contract Committee, with no power, in 1953; Vice President Richard Nixon chaired it. Kennedy now kept up the tradition by creating a President's Committee on Equal Employment Opportunity, chaired by Vice President Johnson, with no power: that was what Executive Order 10925 did.

Johnson would call in big federal contractors and lobby them—not just to abjure discrimination but to take "affirmative action" by coming up with concrete "Plans for Progress" to increase their Negro employment. This was strictly voluntary; in fact, to the extent that the committee generated criticism, it was for being too soft. The committee met twelve times. The best-known of the meetings around Washington was the one at which Robert Kennedy showed up late and delivered a lacerating, humiliating critique of Johnson for letting the contractors off too easily.

When Johnson became President in 1963 after John Kennedy's assassination, he followed custom and put his Vice President, Hubert Humphrey, in charge of the committee. Then Congress passed the Civil Rights Act, creating the Equal Employment Opportunity Commission, also with no power; there was no longer any need for the President's Committee on Equal Employment Opportunity. A new executive order—the now famous Executive Order 11246—was drawn up to abolish it. The import of Executive Order 11246 was thought to be that President Johnson was clipping the wings of Hubert Humphrey, who had a long record as an ardent supporter of civil rights. The headline on *The New York Times*'s story noting its signing (three weeks later) was: "Rights Groups Fear Easing of U.S. Enforcement Role."

That obscured the real import of the executive order. As a sop to liberals who didn't trust the new Equal Employment Opportunity Commission, the function of all those good-hearted ineffectual White House committees charged with nudging federal contractors to hire more Negroes was moved to the Labor Department. Unlike the White House committees and unlike the Equal Employment Opportunity Commission, the Labor Department could launch investigations, require contractors to submit written hiring plans, and even revoke the contracts of companies that were recalcitrant. So now a permanent bureaucracy existed, shielded from political pressure, with a legal charter that would allow it to force, if it were so inclined, a significant portion of the private economy to hire more Negroes.

The climate of the country was changing in the summer of 1965. Three months before issuing Executive Order 11246, President Johnson gave a commencement address at Howard, the country's premier Negro university, in which he proclaimed, in words scripted by Daniel Patrick Moynihan: "We seek . . . not just equality as a right and a theory, but equality as a fact and equality as a result." That was a strong signal, coming right from the top, that the new laws outlawing discrimination against Negroes were not going to be the end of the story; for the struggle to be successfully completed Negroes had to get good jobs. Rather than Johnson's call for equality of result being unpopular, as it surely would be today, it fell comfortably within the national consensus at the time. The White House didn't get a single protest about it. Thousands of private institutions all over the United States, including virtually every private university and big corporation, set out to increase their Negro representation—not merely to stop discriminating but to get more Negroes. They weren't doing this because the federal government was making them.

At the Labor Department, the new Office of Federal Contract Compliance began pushing federal contractors to establish specific numerical "goals and timetables" showing how many Negroes they would hire, for which jobs, and when. These were not exactly the same as the quotas that had been such a concern during the debate over the Civil Rights Act, but they were also a far cry from a simple enforced ban on racial discrimination in hiring. Edward Sylvester, the first head of the Office of Contract Compliance, says, "The average business guy wants to know what to do. You've got to give him numbers. . . . They'd say, tell me what you want and when you want it. And then we'd get into the quota thing." The same kind of racial number-keeping began all across the federal government, in state and local governments, and in universities and businesses. The Civil Service Commission quietly okayed as an official policy what had long been done informally, maintaining statistics on the race of government employees. In 1967 another executive order put women, who hadn't been mentioned in Executive Order 11246, under the purview of affirmative action.

The net effect was that, in technology- and organization-worshipping mid-century America, two conflicting sets of numbers had been generated: the first was everyone's scores on standardized tests; the second was a record of the share of good jobs and educational billets held by Negroes. The first set of numbers consistently gave Negro advancement low priority, but the purpose of the second set was to give it high priority. Two widely held national goals, equal opportunity for all and a better deal for Negroes, were now, thanks to the completion of the national testing and statistics-keeping apparatus, explicitly, openly contradictory.

Both affirmative action and a meritocratic system based on standardized testing began without any public debate or vote (indeed, without the public's even noticing). The inherent contradiction between them was an all-absorbing national conflict waiting to happen. Affirmative action evolved as a low-cost patch solution to the enormous problem of improving the lot of American Negroes, who had an ongoing, long-standing tradition of deeply inferior education; at the same time American society was changing so as to make educational performance the basis for individual advancement.

The dilemma, once it became apparent, could be resolved by entirely remaking American education, but that was a dauntingly large project that the Coleman Report seemed to indicate would not produce the desired result anyway. One could take away from education the job of choosing an elite and have it stick to its old job of simply teaching its students, but that would vitiate the whole project of setting up a meritocratic elite. Or, easier, one could simply bend the rules of the meritocracy for Negroes, so that they'd get a little more than they'd be entitled to strictly on the basis of test scores. This would help them advance and help to integrate the new elite, thus making it better equipped to manage racial conflict in American society.

Affirmative action was not a profound betrayal of the idea of meritocracy but a quick (and, its inventors assumed, temporary) fix for one of its obvious shortcomings. The new meritocractic elite didn't resist affirmative action at all—in fact it voluntarily established affirmative action in every institution under its control. Affirmative action's potential for generating conflict was not clear in the muddled circumstances of its birth. So the new educational structure that was supposed to rationalize one American preoccupation, opportunity, was firmly attached in a logically contradictory, not very workable way to another American preoccupation, race. They were stuck with each other.

14. The Fall of Clark Kerr

Even in shiny-clean California, where slavery and segregation may have seemed like part of the ancient history of some entirely other country, the race issue kept intertwining itself with the new American meritocracy. The California Fair Employment Practices Commission, an active one like Illinois', was putting pressure on Clark Kerr to hire more Negroes as early as 1962. Kerr took the position that the University of California was not under the Fair Employment Practices Commission's legal authority and that it would handle the race issue on its own—in the same liberal spirit. In 1964 the Berkeley campus created an Education Opportunity Program to bring in more students who were members of disadvantaged minority groups.

Although the meritocracy had been created with no racial intent whatsoever, except maybe to cut down on discrimination against Jews, the connection had a genuine logic. Men like Conant and Kerr had promised that the system would generate social justice, that a rational, efficient structure would give opportunity to all Americans and prevent the development of castes or classes. Once this expectation had been created, it was a natural next step for anybody concerned about America's shortcomings, of which racial inequality was the most obvious in the early 1960s, to come knocking on the meritocracy's door in search of redress. An institution like the University of California, in return for its grand new role and its generous public funding, was taking on quite a heavy burden of implied responsibility for solving the ills of society.

In the spring of 1964, with the civil-rights movement at its peak and the Civil Rights Act moving forward in Congress, the San Francisco chapter of the Congress of Racial Equality began holding sit-ins to protest the paucity of black employees in prominent local businesses, such as the Sheraton-Palace Hotel and the city's leading Cadillac dealer. It was the same cause that the state Fair Employment Practices Commission had been pursuing, with the blessing of Governor Brown, though the means were different. Several Berkeley students were arrested for taking part in the sit-ins. Conservative state legislators demanded that Kerr stop his students from taking part in illegal political activities; Kerr responded in a typically measured way, on the one hand defending the right of students to engage in political activity, on the other condemning law-breaking.

Over the summer, many Berkeley students went to the South to participate in the civil-rights activities of Freedom Summer, and they returned in a state of heightened moral agitation and tactical wisdom. Kerr warned his administrators to be ready for student protests in the 1964–65 school year. He considered himself a product of the era of *real* student protest, the 1930s, and so he tended to underrate the seriousness of student protests now. This time around the United States was not in an economic crisis and socialists, let alone Communists, were a spent force. Whatever was coming was bound to be small. He understood the situation of the students at Berkeley as a matter of labor economics. Of all the interest groups in the multiversity, the most favored was the tenured faculty. That was no accident—it was Kerr's design. He could see that the students, on the receiving end of the reduced faculty teaching obligations he had fought for, were likely to become upset. He expected the target of their ire to be the professors. But he was wrong.

Before the start of the school year, Kerr, whose reputation as the world's leading visionary in higher education was continually rising, embarked upon a lengthy tour of the Far East. There he would open new University of California study centers in Tokyo and Hong Kong and confer with key figures. Kerr made a point of trusting the chancellors of the various University of California campuses, rather than breathing down their necks as Robert Sproul had breathed down his when he was chancellor at Berkeley. So he left the Berkeley chancellor, Edward Strong, another modern liberal educator, if a little more mulish and less good at mediation than he, fully in charge while he was away.

On a small patch of pavement outside the main gate to the Berkeley campus, politically minded students liked to set up tables to hand out leaflets. This annoyed the regents of the university, prominent citizens appointed by the governor. Kerr had placated them by announcing he would deed the land to the city of Berkeley. The students could continue their political activities simply by getting permits from the city, and Kerr would rid himself of the regents' nagging about the left-wing students on the patch of pavement. It looked like another successful Clark Kerr mediation. But somehow the deeding over of the land never took place.

In September 1964, students representing the Congress of Racial Equality and other groups got their permits from the city and set up their tables on the pavement. Somebody informed Ed Strong that the land was still the university's, and he responded by ordering the students to clear out.

The main offstage presence in this drama was William Knowland. Publisher of the leading local daily newspaper (*The Oakland Tribune*), former United States senator, leader of California's conservative political movement, and University of California regent, Knowland, to the minds of Kerr and Strong, was the single leading threat to the greatness of the University of California, far more threatening than a few student protesters. If Strong let the students stay, Knowland might become enraged, and given his political and press clout, the consequences would be truly disastrous.

Kerr would surely have dealt with the incipient problem through a negotiation rather than a mandate, since that was what he always did, but by the time he got back from Asia it was too late; to countermand Strong would be to humiliate him publicly. The battle—university administrators versus the Free Speech Movement—had been joined, and it dominated the life of the University of California for the entire autumn. On September 30, the students staged a sit-in at Sproul Hall, the main administration building. On October 1, with Kerr over in San Francisco at a meeting of the American Council on Education, Ed Strong had the campus police arrest a student who was operating a CORE table in front of Sproul Hall; other students surrounded the police car and kept it immobilized for thirty-two hours.

Kerr rushed back across the Bay Bridge to take over. But the mediation process he set up did not have the customary healing effect. On December 2, students took over Sproul Hall, and Governor Brown called in the California Highway Patrol to remove them by force. Once again Kerr tried to mediate. On December 7, at an open meeting attended by 16,000 people, he made a moving plea for calm and the greater good of the university and got a standing ovation. It was a moment of Quaker triumph—immediately shattered when Mario Savio, leader of the Free Speech Movement, rose to respond to Kerr and was restrained by police. The meeting descended into chaos.

The crisis finally ended in January when, at Kerr's request, the regents dismissed Ed Strong. Things had turned out terribly for Kerr. His relationship with Strong, which he had worked so hard on, had become one of bitter enmity. And just as Kerr had finally undermined Strong's authority by taking over management of the crisis, Governor Brown had undermined Kerr's by calling in the Highway Patrol. It was a signal to the world that Kerr was unable to control his domain. The students had won an almost total victory on the major point, their right to political activity on campus, but they continued to feel aggrieved. The faculty, whom Kerr had recruited and pampered and worked hard to protect from the regents and the legislature, whose privileges he suspected would be the root cause of the student unrest, to his utter surprise and great distress mainly sided with the students and against him.

Aside from the most obvious irony, that the master mediator had allowed a conflict in his own painstakingly designed institution to spin out of control, there were others. Mario Savio was a true child of the Master Plan, the kind of brilliant (as assessed by SAT scores) out-of-state student (he was from New York) whom Kerr had gone out of his way to make room for at Berkeley, so as to make it a national institution. Now Savio and people like him, rather than being grateful, rather than appreciating just how difficult it had been to get them to Berkeley, rather than savoring their bright technocratic futures, were turning on their institutional father.

The Free Speech Movement singled out Clark Kerr as its villain: not Ed Strong or William Knowland or Pat Brown, but Clark Kerr. Its leaders went around quoting derisively from *The Uses of the University*. They disastrously missed the point, which was that Kerr wanted to elevate liberal intellectuals to a higher social position than they had ever occupied in the history of the world. Instead they perceived him merely as a drab little man who wanted to devise big soulless structures in order to quench the human spirit. Kerr's writing over the preceding five years had consistently predicted that the 1960s would be a time of mediated solutions, not conflict. So he had been shown up not just as a university president but as a thinker.

Kerr at least felt that with Strong gone, the sit-ins over, and a new group of committees in place to ponder the future, the Free Speech Movement chapter of his life was closed. But he was wrong about that, too. During the time of the Free Speech Movement, Barry Goldwater, the Republican Party's challenger to Lyndon Johnson, had been staging one of the most spectacularly unsuccessful presidential campaigns in American history. This was taken by consensus-oriented liberals like Kerr as a demonstration that the American right wing was now dead. Instead, in California, Goldwater's campaign gave birth to the political career of Ronald Reagan, who had made sensationally popular speeches on Goldwater's behalf in which he explicitly attacked the "intellectual elite." In the next election cycle, Reagan ran for governor against Pat Brown. One of his main targets was the mess in Berkeley. He promised to crack down forcefully on radical students, as he claimed

Brown and Kerr had not. Once he even called on the California legislature to impose a "code of conduct" on the Berkeley faculty.

After Reagan won the election, a Republican on the Board of Regents, H. R. Haldeman (later White House chief of staff under Richard Nixon), gave a small dinner at his house in Los Angeles to introduce him to the other regents and to Clark Kerr. Not much ice melted there. Reagan and Kerr stayed at opposite ends of the party, and a couple of regents took the occasion to pull Kerr aside and suggest that he think about resigning.

Kerr had reason to believe that he could continue to serve successfully under Reagan, however. California had a tradition of respect for its university—as a source of civic pride and business prosperity more than as a pristine intellectual glade, but still. The regents included some of the most powerful people in the state, serving sixteen-year terms, and they were perfectly capable of standing up to hostile politicians; governors tended to leave university presidents alone. At just the time that Reagan was elected, a national survey ranked UC Berkeley as the number-one research university in the country, which was extremely gratifying to Kerr as a ratification of his hard work over a decade and a half. Surely that would count for something with the regents.

More specifically, Kerr had, as usual, carefully analyzed the power balance of the situation, and believed it was favorable toward him. Out of twenty-two regents, eight were reliably liberal, and Kerr had taken special pains to build good relations with four others: Edwin Pauley, a rich Democratic oilman; Edward Carter, of the Carter-Hawley-Hale department stores; and the doyennes of the two great newspaper-owning families of California, Catherine Hearst of the *San Francisco Chronicle* Hearsts and Dorothy Chandler of the *Los Angeles Times* Chandlers. Their papers represented the two major print media in the state, they both got along well with Kerr, and they believed deeply in the university. So Kerr had twelve votes, a majority, and the press on his side.

Again he had overestimated. In California the entire budget of the university appears as one line item in the state budget, which the governor has the power to veto. A head-to-head struggle could therefore be extremely damaging, and Governor Reagan made it clear that a head-to-head struggle was what he had in mind. The regents, who had to think about the long-term welfare of the university, also had their own particular priorities. For example, Catherine Hearst, a devout Catholic, was horrified by the short-lived flowering in 1965 of a "Filthy Speech Movement" at Berkeley. Dorothy Chandler was busy building a big new cultural arts center in Los Angeles, which required that she maintain good relations across the political board.

In early January 1967, Governor Reagan proposed that the university's budget be cut by 30 percent—an unthinkable figure. Kerr, who was off on another trip to Asia, immediately flew home. He was let know that the governor wanted him to resign; he refused. On January 20, the regents had their first formal meeting under Reagan's governorship. By a vote of fourteen to eight, Clark Kerr was fired as president of the University of California. Edwin Pauley voted against him. Edward Carter voted against him. Catherine Hearst voted against him. Dorothy Chandler voted against him. At the age of fifty-five, just four years after his triumphant delivery, from a position grander than anyone in American higher education had ever occupied, of the lectures that became *The Uses of the University*, Clark Kerr was through.

Right away, Kerr received an attractive offer from the Carnegie Corporation, which he accepted, to oversee a series of studies on the future of American higher education. These generally promoted his idea that universities should function as the nation's personnel department, rank-ordering, sorting, and routing people to their proper socioeconomic roles. Kerr never left Berkeley. After a few years had passed he could walk across the campus unrecognized. The Master Plan itself became, over the years, oddly obscure, too. Kerr's reputation was as the guy who had been standing in the way when the 1960s came roaring through California, foil first to the Free Speech Movement and then to Ronald Reagan.

After the Carnegie project ended, in 1980, Kerr moved into an unpretentious office at the Institute of Industrial Relations, which he had founded back in the 1930s. He was working there all through the 1990s, when he was in his eighties. People who didn't know him evinced surprise when told that he was still alive and well in Berkeley.

The same year that Kerr was fired, the University of California began requiring that all applicants take the SAT: a requirement that still stands. This was sweet news for ETS. The University of California became and still is today by far its biggest customer.

Two decades had passed between ETS's opening its first branch office in Berkeley and the University of California's requiring the SAT. The reason the campaign had taken so long—despite ETS's having, in Clark Kerr, a staunch friend and board member at the helm of the university—was that the university's basic function had to change before it could succeed.

The university that Kerr had taken over had operated as if it were an extension of California's public-school system. It was supposed to be open to anybody who had compiled a good school record in California. This meant that it overadmitted, and the freshman year was a kind of open audition at the end of which many students would either flunk out or leave. Also, the university operated an accreditation system for California high schools: a set of requirements and standards which, if a high school met them, would automatically give its students who graduated with a B average admission to the university. In this way the university was making itself responsible not just for its own affairs but for the quality of California's high schools, too. As a government agency it got public funds, and in return was supposed to look after the education of as many Californians as possible.

Kerr's idea of what the university should be was different. The public and the press, entranced by his guarantee of free higher education for all, didn't notice how profoundly he wanted to shift the University of California toward being more selective and less local. Most of the beneficiaries of California's universal higher education would be going to its community colleges; access to the university, and particularly Berkeley, was limited to a coterie of especially gifted students, and they were drawn from all over the United States and even abroad. The more success Kerr had in attracting academic stars to the Berkeley faculty, the less interest the faculty was likely to have in doing the grunt work of high-school accreditation and teaching swollen classes of not especially academic freshmen. In the struggle between the old university and the new, both sides rightly saw standardized tests as a means of abandoning the old and embracing the new.

The battle seesawed back and forth. In 1958, as a way of seeding the ground, ETS began offering the SAT at no cost to University of California applicants. In 1959, the university required that all out-of-state applicants take it. Then, in 1962, it dropped the SAT entirely, which was terrible news for ETS. As one of ETS's men in California wrote to the high command in Princeton, "The University of California is the largest university in the world and an extremely important institution. If they drop the SAT we will lose a great deal more than the revenue; we will suffer a damaging blow to our prestige." He proposed an all-encompassing "Operation Golden Bear," in which every possible connection, starting with Chauncey's with Clark Kerr, would be exploited to get the decision reversed. "Let us attack!" the memo ended.

Two factors set the stage for ETS's victory. The Master Plan legally restricted admission to the university to only the top eighth of high-school graduates. Even so, with the state growing as rapidly as it was and grade inflation taking hold in high schools, the old policy of letting in all eligible applicants produced more university students than the law allowed. Then, in 1963, the university decided to stop accrediting high schools. Afterward its confidence in a student's high-school transcripts inevitably dropped and it needed some other way of evaluating applicants, and also a way of becoming more selective so as to comply with the Master Plan. ETS provided a handy, no-cost solution to both problems. So, beginning in the 1968–69 school year, all university applicants had to take the SAT.

One obvious result of the new policy was going to be a reduction in the number of black and Mexican-American students at the university, just at the moment when America's main concerns were the welfare of minority groups and the Vietnam War, and when liberal institutions were at pains to demonstrate their social conscience. To compensate, the university doubled, from 2 percent to 4 percent, the share of admissions reserved for students who did not meet the ordinary requirements but "whose ethnic or economic background had disadvantaged them." This was becoming a familiar pattern. Previously the university had been a relatively open institution. Now, when it had decided it was an elite institution and would not burden itself with policing high schools anymore, it was softening the harsh edge of these changes through affirmative action.

California's was the biggest and most influential state system of public higher education. From a free public conveyance, like California's freeways, meant to give everyone who was interested the means to a white-collar livelihood, it was turning itself into a restricted institution that selected and sorted, conferring its most munificent benefits on a deserving few. In that sense, even with Clark Kerr gone, it was increasingly his university—indeed, his state.

15 The Invention of
the Asian-American

At the same time that Ronald Reagan was toppling Pat Brown and Clark Kerr, two national liberal icons, a less obvious drama (unnoticed by anyone but the participants, in fact, but still distinctly dramatic) was unfolding in California. Men of the Old Yale were visiting public high schools, looking for promising boys who could be made into men of the New Yale, the Yale of Kingman Brewster and Inky Clark. In the Bay Area they ventured forth from misty, lofty-named Pacific Heights and Hillsborough into the high schools of ordinary, flat Richmond and Oakland; in the Southland they left their landscaped estates in Hancock Park and Beverly Hills and went to Watts and East Los Angeles.

It was as part of this effort that, in the fall of 1966, David Toy, Yale 1958, a prosperous lawyer on the West Side of Los Angeles, met Don Nakanishi, a senior at Roosevelt High School in the dry, plain, blue-collar Boyle Heights section of East Los Angeles. Don was the exemplary new man of the American meritocracy—or anyway he would be once Yale got through with him. To begin with the obvious point, he was a Buddhist Japanese-American whose family had no money, who had no connection to the established institutions of the East Coast, who had been educated in local public schools. He was not tall and blond, but rather short and wide. Instead of being casual and offhanded in the Yale style of the day, he was bubbly with naive eagerness and enthusiasm.

Beyond all that, there was a redemptive aspect to Don's being taken into the elite—redemptive not of Don but of America. For someone not black, Don had been ancestrally mistreated by the United States about as badly as was possible. His parents, like most Japanese-Americans living in the West, had been interned in relocation camps during the Second World War. They had been sent first to the Poston camp in Arizona, and then, because they refused to sign an oath disavowing loyalty to Emperor Hirohito and promising to fight abroad against Japan if called, they were sent to the Tule Lake camp in northern California, home to Japanese-Americans who caused trouble. Don's grandparents, who lived in Hiroshima, were killed when the United States dropped the first atomic bomb there.

Nonetheless, Don was a cheerful young man, a budding politician and a joiner. His parents, after being released from Tule Lake, had slowly made their way back to Los Angeles by working as migratory agricultural laborers. They had settled in a neighborhood of narrow faded-white one-story houses that was rapidly changing from being Jewish to being largely Mexican-American. His father worked as a produce clerk in a supermarket, his mother as a seamstress in a garment factory in downtown Los Angeles. As a high-school student, Don joined the Key Club, the junior division of the Kiwanis, which put him into a whirlwind of future-leader activity. In 1965 he was named Boy Mayor of Los Angeles and got his name in the newspaper. That brought him to the attention of the Yale Club of Los Angeles. He took the SATs, made mediocre scores, crammed (though cramming, according to ETS, didn't work), took them again, and did much better. The Los Angeles Key Club gave a scholarship every year to pay for a student selected by the mayor's office to go to Yale; Don won it, and this, in addition to Yale's having paid much more attention to him than any other college had, made his decision to go there an easy one.

In the spring of 1967, there was a party for all the boys from Los Angeles who had been admitted to the Yale class of 1971. You couldn't have staged a more dramatic demonstration that Don was about to enter an unfamiliar world of money, ease, and power. The party was held in a Yale man's house in Bel Air, the fanciest, most columned-mansioned, most specimen-treed, most winding-drivewayed section of the fancy West Side, a world away from the jammed-together houses of Boyle Heights. Somebody told Don that his host either was married to or had once been married to Zsa Zsa Gabor. Who knew, maybe she was upstairs primping or trying on furs. There was an open bar, and Don, to commemorate the explosion of his horizons from the perilous lower edge of the working class to somewhere in the vicinity of a purring movie star, got gloriously drunk.

But when he got to Yale, Don found that he was not actually a member of the charmed circle. For all the blaring of trumpets about the arrival of the New Yale, to a blue-collar Japanese-American kid from East LA Yale still seemed pretty Old. It was still all-male. Graduates of private schools were vastly more represented in the Yale student body than in the population at large. In 1814, Thomas Jefferson wrote to a young cousin whom he was instructing in the ways of the world: "The learned class may still be subdivided into two sections: 1, Those who are destined for the learned professions, as means of livelihood; and, 2, The wealthy, who, possessing independent fortunes, may aspire to share in conducting the affairs of the nation, or to live with usefulness and respect in the private ranks of life." The distinction still applied at Yale in the fall of 1967. People like Don, whose parents expected them to use Yale as the avenue to a respected and, above all, secure livelihood, went into demanding, practical fields of study. Don was initially a biology major, planning to go to medical school. But the center of the Yale student body was still held by boarding-school boys who studied history and English (much more casually than people like Don), who seemed graceful and comfortable in addition to being intelligent, who didn't seem especially concerned about launching their careers, and whose chief Yale ambition was to be tapped for a senior society. This Yale, which still presented itself as the true Yale, looked to Don like an entirely different institution from the one that he attended, impossibly distant and inaccessible.

Japanese-Americans of Don's generation lived in dread of December 7, Pearl Harbor Day—a day that never seemed to pass without somebody making a remark about murderous Japs. On the night of December 7, 1967, Don was studying in his room, with the door closed, when he heard a commotion outside. He opened the door and confronted an assemblage of riotous blond Yale boys, who pelted him with water balloons and shouted, "Bomb Pearl Harbor! Bomb Pearl Harbor!" A boy from Yale's debating society stood out from the crowd and recited from memory Franklin Roosevelt's speech declaring war, the one with the phrase "a date which will live in infamy." Everyone laughed and laughed and then went off to bed.

Don decided it was time to stop being a meek little premed. Some of the Yale preoccupation with leadership, which had been designed for boys from much more favored backgrounds than Don, had worked its way into his psyche, although his idea was to use it to fight injustice rather than to rule. He switched majors, first to sociology, then to psychology, finally to political science. He joined the closest available ethnic student association, the one for Mexican-Americans, since he considered himself an honorary member by virtue of being from East LA. He began to read up on the experiences of Japanese in the United States, particularly the internment, which in those days Don's parents and other people who had lived through it never mentioned, as if it were a big suppurating blemish on the face of the United States, where they expected their children would thrive, so disturbing one had to pretend it wasn't there. Finally, in his junior year, having personally become more self-consciously ethnic and more politically confrontational, and having been influenced by the rising note of protest on the campus, Don led a small group that founded the Asian-American Student Association of Yale.

The notion of an Asian-American was a bold and new one. It also was a completely artificial construct, but Caucasians didn't have to know that. They seemed to be willing to accept the notion of a monolithic, on-the-march, slant-eyed juggernaut, so why not use it? At that point Asian-Americans at Yale were an amalgam mainly of two groups, Chinese-Americans and Japanese-Americans, which spoke different languages, lived back home in different ethnic enclaves, and had been taught by their war-generation parents to think of each other as the enemy.

Japanese-Americans had come to the United States mainly as agricultural laborers, and had moved up from there. In Los Angeles in the 1950s and 1960s, a Japanese-American lower-middle-class paradise had taken form in the town of Gardena, which is south of downtown and close to black neighborhoods like Watts, Compton, and South Central. As the name connotes, Gardena was home to many nurseries; for Japanese-Americans, a logical next step from picking fruits and vegetables was professional gardening. To the extent that anything distinguished Gardena from the endless procession of suburbs in the Southland, it was known in white Los Angeles as the home of poker parlors, where gambling was legal. But to the Japanese-Americans who lived there, it was a whole world of judo schools, and Saturday-morning lessons in the mother tongue, and fathers driving their pickup trucks up to Beverly Hills and Bel Air to groom rich people's estates. In the library at Gardena High School, there was a copy of *Stover at Yale* that every so often a studious boy would read, and then he could begin to envision himself in a picture with a backdrop of Gothic towers so tall their spires disappeared into the clouds.

Don Nakanishi was the rare southern California Japanese-American at Yale who wasn't from Gardena, but that was an advantage as far as the Asian-American Student Association of Yale was concerned, because it made it easier for him to broker between the different groups. He had grown up nearer to the Chinese-American parts of Los Angeles than the Japanese-American ones.

Chinese-Americans had entered California at the rock bottom layer of society, as unskilled, brutally treated workers who took on jobs that the native-born didn't want, notably the dangerous work of building the railroads through the Western mountains. One layer up from that were hand laundries and Chinese restaurants. In Los Angeles, Chinese-Americans were just beginning to create their equivalent of Gardena in Monterey Park, the first town you would get to if you proceeded east from the shabby fringe of downtown, where Chinatown was located, through East LA and over a mountain pass into the San Gabriel Valley. Like Gardena, Monterey Park did not register high on the white Los Angeles awareness scale—it was just another lower-middle-class suburb of one-story tract houses—but from the Chinese-American perspective, it was a suburb with the one great desired thing, a good public-school system, as well as a location near other, better suburbs where one could dream about one's children or grandchildren someday living: Alhambra, South Pasadena, and, what the hell, even Pasadena and San Marino.

By the time Don was at Yale, the combination of the Chinese revolution, in 1949, and the liberalization of American immigration laws, in 1965, meant that better-educated Chinese, such as government mandarins and export-import entrepreneurs, were turning up in the United States, and the children of a lucky handful of them were turning up at Yale. One of these was the only female member of the founding group of the Asian-American Student Association of Yale, Alice Young, who had transferred to Yale as soon as women were admitted, in the 1969–70 school year.

The golden lads from Greenwich, Connecticut, and Andover, who stood before their intimates on Wednesday nights in the senior society buildings and confessed their secret problems—Father's coldness, Mother's tippling—were probably better off not knowing about family histories like Don's and Alice's, lest they be shamed into embarrassed silence because of the paltriness of their difficulties. Alice's father, John Young, had led a fantastic life of Scarlett O'Hara–like high drama against a storm-tossed backdrop of war and revolution. Born Yang Chuen Yung in China in 1920, he was descended from a line of test-acing elite civil servants. When he was past seventy, he visited his ancestral village and confirmed as true the family legend that in the official registry book there were recorded not only births and deaths and marriages but every male's score on the imperial examinations that were the route to government jobs. His father was an outstanding student—John Young checked his record—who became a diplomat. John himself grew up substantially in Japan, away from his family; his father had the idea of John's becoming the one man in China who best understood the archenemy, through long inside experience. "Study and learn in what way they may fail," was the father's parting instruction to the son.

John Young was perpetually at the top of in his class ("because I wanted to be *better* than the Japanese and *compete* with them"). He graduated from the extremely selective Tokyo Imperial University, then returned to China and became a junior diplomat and, at the same time, a wartime courier and translator for the Americans (which is when he Americanized his name), with the ambition of becoming Chinese ambassador to Japan. In 1946 he was posted to Washington. Then came the revolution. Young and his wife, who came from another family of studious, high-test-scoring civil servants, were the kind of people who could expect the worst under Communism. The exiled Chinese government assigned him to its embassy in Korea but would not let him bring his family, so he decided to stay in Washington, unemployed. Soon his parents and his two brothers fled China and arrived on his doorstep, needing to be taken care of, and then three children arrived: Alice in 1950, Peter in 1952, and Nancy in 1954.

The one thing that never occurred to John Young during this period, with his career as a diplomat over, was that he might go into business and make money. He believed that all callings except scholarship and government service were unthinkably low. Desperately poor, with six people to support, he enrolled in graduate school so that he could get his Ph.D. in Chinese history. He translated documents at a penny a word and taught Japanese, his wife taught Chinese, his father worked at the Library of Congress, and his mother worked as a nurse. It was a terrible time. There was no money: the coming due of the rent every month induced stark fear. The Youngs moved a lot. They sold off family heirlooms to buy food. Many of their relatives were incommunicado in China, in who knew what circumstances. In the United States, the basic assumption, in those highest days of the Cold War, was that every Chinese was a Communist, so even the Youngs were constantly subjected to nervous, sidling-away treatment.

The severe strain in the Youngs' situation took its toll on Young's wife, who was cut off from her family in China. In 1957 she died, and John sent his children away. Alice and Peter spent two and a half years living as paying boarders with a family in the Virginia suburbs of Washington, seeing their father and sister, who was boarding elsewhere, only on weekends. In a few years the situation eased—thanks to education, of course. John Young finished his dissertation and got an assistant professorship at Georgetown; he was far from prosperous but at least no longer destitute. One day a young woman from a prominent Korean family showed up at his office to complain about his having given her a B, not an A. They got to talking, he told her his story, she offered to help, and soon they were married. He reunited his family and moved to McLean, Virginia, a suburb he chose for its outstanding schools.

In 1964 he was made chairman of the Asian languages department at the University of Hawaii, which finally enabled him, at the age of forty-four, to settle down to a stable, middle-class life. All three Young children were driven, fabulously good students. That was a long-standing family tradition, as their father constantly reminded them, and now it was invested with a specially fierce intensity because school was the island of calm and order in their chaotic childhoods, and the only route they could see that led from poverty to prosperity. Alice, under the demanding gaze of her father, was perpetually the best student in her school. She went to public schools in Hawaii, then to the University of Hawaii, then on scholarship to Georgetown. Finally, as soon as Yale announced that it would accept a few female transfer students, she applied and got a scholarship there. Peter and Nancy went to Punahou, a private school in Honolulu, and also to Yale.

Alice Young was so small and innocently pretty that she looked like a junior-high-school student who had wandered into Yale by mistake, but she had the forward thrust of a Saturn V booster rocket. No bashful transfer student, no hesitant first-cohort Yale woman she: within a few months of her arrival, she was helping to run the Asian-American Student Association at Yale.

Other people, Don had to work on for a while before they would agree to join. One of these was Bill Lann Lee, another member of the class of 1971, who came from the opposite end of the Chinese-American world from Alice. His father, Lee Wei-lim, was the youngest son in a family from a poor fishing village in China, a place plagued by murderous bandits; his parents sent him away as a child to be raised with relatives in Canada because they wanted to be sure that one of their offspring would survive to adulthood. When he grew up he returned to China, married, went back to North America, and drifted to New York City during the Depression. He Americanized his name to William Lee and opened a laundry.

For someone who spoke no English and had no access to capital, a Chinese hand laundry was a good way to make a bare-bones but fairly secure livelihood. An immigrant's whole family could work around the clock in a laundry, and, if necessary, live there, too; it was one step up from washing dishes in a Chinese restaurant (there was no boss to answer to, and laundries went out of business much less frequently), but many steps down from owning a business in Chinatown, which required connections, or entering a profession, which required higher education. William Lee volunteered for Army service during the Second World War, partly out of love of his adopted country and partly out of hatred for Japan. When he came home he settled on the Upper West Side of Manhattan and operated Lee's Hand Laundry at several locations, mainly 124th Street and Broadway, at the edge of Harlem, where the rent was low.

Although William Lee came from a background nowhere near the mandarin class in China, he was still the product of a society in which education was the highest value and considered the best way to get ahead. William Lee believed in hard work, not culture—reading a book for pleasure, or attending a concert or a play, was to him unthinkably frivolous. Still, he constantly pushed his son Bill to study, without knowing what it was that Bill was studying. Bill and his younger brother Ernest spent their free time working in the laundry.

It was the family's good luck that they happened to live in the American city with the most advanced apparatus for selecting a meritocratic elite through the school system. From elementary school onward Bill took standardized mental tests and, on the basis of his scores, he was put onto a separate gifted-student track—with the result that during his childhood, he studied at small, nearly all-white virtual schools contained within the big, mostly black public schools. The New York City public-school system had (and still has) a handful of high schools that admit students from all over the city by competitive examination. It was assumed in the Lee family that Bill would go to one of these. Bill's own preference was the High School of Music and Art; he put a good deal of time into assembling a portfolio of drawings for the admissions committee. For his parents, though the High School of Music and Art was out of the question—it would lead only to careers that were terrifyingly insecure and unstable. Instead he went to the Bronx High School of Science, where children and grandchildren of immigrants, lacking any connections or social polish, speaking in nonmellifluous city accents, could hurl themselves into demanding school subjects and technical course work and wind up with real, solid, quantifiable academic accomplishments, of the kind that would always be a good meal ticket, no matter how personally awkward you were.

At Bronx Science, then mostly Jewish, now mostly Chinese- and Korean-American, nobody bothered to conceal beneath a veneer of uplifting rhetoric the connection between grinding away for good grades and escaping from the lower middle class. The student newspaper published everyone's academic averages, as if to keep at bay any ambient urges toward well-roundedness that might be at large in the student body. So when Bill got to Yale (on scholarship, of course, and thanks to Inky Clark's being more kindly disposed toward Bronx Science boys than previous Yale admissions deans had been), it struck him as a hotbed not of meritocracy but of easy inherited wealth. As he was leaving home to start his freshman year, his father dropped his usual brusqueness for just an instant and ceremoniously handed him a letter saying how proud he was. The family mythology had it that William Lee was an educated man; during the war he served as a Cyrano for his Southern hillbilly buddies, drafting the letters to their sweethearts back home that they couldn't write. But when Bill read his father's letter, he saw at once that the true situation was nowhere near that. My God, he thought, my father is functionally illiterate—he's just a very short step from a coolie on a nineteenth-century railroad gang. It's nearly a miracle that he got the family from where it was to where I am in one generation.

Bill was not an easy convert for Don Nakanishi and the Asian-American Student Association because, first, he thought of himself as quiet, apolitical, and studious, not as a leaper to the barricades, and, second, he had been raised to despise Japanese-Americans. Ambling along Yale's pathways in his jeans and short-sleeved shirts, he was the kind of undergraduate nobody much noticed, and he didn't mind. The idea of joining a confrontational pan-Asian organization seemed all wrong to him. He was at Yale to work hard so he could get a good job.

The way to hook Bill Lee, it turned out, was to use the race issue. The one thing Bill saw at first hand that was obviously wrong with miraculous America was that black people were consigned to a lower rung than everybody else. Bill grew up and had gone to school on a racial dividing line. If you moved from Lee's Hand Laundry northward into Harlem, everybody was black. If you moved south, in the direction of nicer housing, everybody was white. In school it was the same story with the educational tracks. It was hard for Bill to believe that the position of black people was the result of a fair process. The very optimism and faith about the United States that his father had drilled into him made the racial situation bother him even more. At Yale he encountered a similar soaring sense of the nobility of the country, along with a new feeling that if something was awry, one had the influence to do something about it.

In the spring of 1970, when New Haven was alive with incipient protest because the Black Panther trial was about to take place there, Don Nakanishi came to Bill and asked him to draft an Asian-American Student Association statement of solidarity with the defendants. Bill, who'd been resisting Don's entreaties, agreed, and then he joined the organization. Asian consciousness began to seep into him. He wrote his undergraduate honors thesis on Yung Wing, who had gone to Yale in the late nineteenth century and become the first Chinese-American graduate of an American college. An adapted version was published in the inaugural issue of *Amerasia Journal*, which Don started in 1971.

Don looked as straightforwardly enthusiastic when a radical student leader at Yale as he had been in his days as Boy Mayor of Los Angeles. Actually his political touch was subtle: selling the idea of Asian-Americans to

Asian-Americans, he knew, was going to be quite difficult. Who had to know that, though? Once he'd gotten everyone to join, he figured that the outside world would accept the idea readily—and indeed it did. He also knew there was a less than complete commonality of interest between the Asian-American Student Association and the other new minority organizations at Yale. The Asians were nearly all children of families obsessed with studying, so they usually did well academically, especially in culture-free fields like science and mathematics. Many other minority students at Yale had not been so well buffed up by family and school for life at a big-time university, and they struggled. Better for the Asians, though, to stress the similarities (that outsider feeling) and not the differences.

The Asian-American Student Association therefore always supported left-wing campus crusades, such as solidarity with the Panthers, and it emulated the black and Latino student groups in demanding ethnic studies courses. But more than the other new ethnic student groups the Asians made admissions work their main activity, their baseline. They pushed Yale to establish the kind of warm relations with public high schools in places like Gardena and Monterey Park that it had with the fine old schools of the Northeast. Don's overriding goal was to increase the number of Asian-Americans in the student body. He and his cadre got themselves sent out on recruiting trips, they flushed out good applicants, and the Asian presence at Yale steadily rose. The class that included Don, Alice, and Bill had nine Asian-Americans; the class admitted the year they formed the Asian-American Student Association had thirty-five; today, Asian-Americans, though of course not a single ethnic group, probably account for more of the Yale student body than white Anglo-Saxon Protestants.

One of the jobs of a Yale administrator during the late 1960s was to meet with the insistent new ethnic groups of students. Sam Chauncey, as a manager of the transition from Old Yale to New, developed this as a specialty. Angry undergraduates would march into his office and shout at him, he would be firm but understanding, and a hard-won mutual respect would form. This was, in fact, an ancient ritual of the Episcopacy in new student-revolution guise: the trial by fire leading to bonding and socialization. Many years later, in 1990, the Mexican-American Student Association, which Don Nakanishi had joined as a freshman, had a reunion in San Francisco, and they invited Sam to come as a guest. The members even chipped in and bought him a plane ticket. That meant a lot to him.

The Asian-American Student Association eventually had a meeting with Kingman Brewster himself. On the way to that the Asian students met with a succession of lesser figures, including Sam. They went through their usual drill of working up a list of demands and an attitude of fierceness to go along with it, and agreeing to let the most aggressive members of the group, Don and Alice, do the talking.

What they didn't know, as they sat in Sam's office glowering, was that he was really thinking: These Asian kids are so *polite*!

16 Mandarins

After graduation Alice Young severely disappointed her father by going to the Harvard Law School.

John Young had hoped—more than hoped, presumed—that his three children would all go on from Yale to graduate school. He wanted them to be the modern version of mandarins, or Platonic guardians, or natural aristocrats: scholars, selected on merit, elaborately trained, indifferent to material things, who would move easily back and forth between the university and government, occupying the highest position in society. But Alice, though she applied to study history in graduate school, went to law school; Peter went to business school; and Nancy, the last hope, after actually getting her master's degree at Yale under Jonathan Spence, the distinguished scholar of Chinese history, went to law school, too.

John Young hadn't presented his children with a very pretty picture of the scholar's life while they were growing up, but they were also engaging in what was becoming standard behavior for the new American meritocrats. The more perfectly one fit the ideal of outstanding student from an obscure background given a first-rate university education on scholarship, the more likely, it seemed, that one would choose a career as a well-paid, securely positioned provider of expert advice: corporate lawyer, investment banker, management consultant, high-end specialized doctor. Members of the meritocratic elite in France and Britain and Japan very often went into lifetime government service; in the United States, never. (The American domestic civil service was not for the elite.) Even academic scholarship was a distinctly second choice.

Why was this? Some countries had meritocracies that were pretty purely based on the Platonic idea of selecting a few deserving people to become statesmen. The American meritocracy, set up as a system for everybody and fueled by powerful rhetoric about equal opportunity, blended into this idea the distinctive national obsession with success. The result was that the meritocracy began to look more and more like a means of handing out economic rewards to a fortunate few. Rather than being about public service for the elite and expanded opportunity for the mass, it was about opportunity to join a prosperous elite. Arguments about American education concerned how fairly it distributed the goodies, not how wisely the new elite it created was guiding the nation. The drama of the lives of those chosen had a large complement of that old, simple American theme, making it.

So. You're an adolescent, the men from the palace knock on your door, you try on the glass slipper—and it fits! What do you do next? If you're a person without money, connections, or an easy sense of privilege, you try to lock in the immense advantage you've been given by converting it into the hard currency of a professional credential. Upper meritocrats who'd done extremely well thus far had excelled as students. They weren't natural risk-takers, misfits, or nonconformists. Compared with a handful of professions, nearly every other possible course in life seemed to present terrible disadvantages, being either ill-paying (like the arts) or insecure (like starting a business) or something that put you back into the great undifferentiated pool of aspirants (like being a junior employee of a big company). Whereas, in the early 1970s, if you went to Harvard Law School, it looked to you, at the age of twenty-one, as if you were assuring yourself of a prestigious, secure livelihood with a six-figure income.

That was the practical side of becoming a new-style meritocrat. The psychological side was important, too. It was a powerful experience—being constantly evaluated as you grew up and then being admitted into a special group. One's impulse was to go through life repeating the fundamental cycle of gratification: selective admission, followed by membership in a tight, reassuring (though rivalrous) cadre of similarly chosen people. The best way to do that was to get into a professional school. At the same time, the idea that you might be a national leader was still alive. You wanted assured success and security, yes, but not just that. The most popular professions were not dentistry or certified public accountancy. You also wanted to matter, to be admired, to take a part in shaping American society. So if you went to law school, you went with a sense that you were keeping your options open—putting yourself in the way of prosperity and also of influence. You had a cause you wanted to pursue. Alice Young wanted to help promote Asian-

American understanding. Bill Lee, who also went from Yale to law school, at Columbia, wanted to devote himself to civil rights.

What wasn't clear to Alice or Bill at the time was that for their dream of a life balanced between career and cause to come true, the whole country had to accept the idea that this new meritocratic elite would run things. Performing their hoped-for function required a complex, regulated American society with big, publicly funded institutions, which they would operate as their way of doing good. If the public didn't support and accept this vision, then the foundation of government money and laws on which your plans depended wouldn't be there.

By the 1970s there were already signs that the meritocratic order was not going to be so popular in American society as its founders had anticipated. Federal funding for the expansion of universities was beginning to tail off, and the academic job market had crashed—that was one reason why Alice Young decided to go to law school instead of graduate school. (Don Nakanishi bravely enrolled in the same history Ph.D. program at Harvard that Alice turned down.) The people selected for the elite were starting to look less like wise, selfless leaders. They were on their way to making a lot of money, they took advantage of the tradition of draft exemptions for the brainy to get out of serving in the armed forces during the Vietnam War, they held themselves apart. And what had they done, really, to earn such privilege or authority other than to get high test scores and good grades? The astonishing rise of Ronald Reagan demonstrated that political careers were being built by people who were exploiting public resentment of this new elite.

The consequent social tensions were much more complex than the ones imagined by Michael Young. Rather than there being a simple rivalry between a new elite and everyone else, several elites were competing for power and for public allegiance. Each considered itself to be more truly meritocratic than the others.

These different elites can be labeled according to the routes they used to get ahead. Mandarins, let us call them, were the products of the new formal educational system: they went to outstanding colleges and then on to professional schools, and they hoped they were furthering the liberal idea of helping the United States to become highly regulated and organized, as a modern society needed to be, with a group of experts at the helm. Lifers, a second group, were people whose college education was more routine and who went on to beginner jobs in large organizations—industrial corporations; the armed forces; city, state, and federal governments—and tried to rise to the top. The qualities they valued most were loyalty, steadfastness, leadership, and managerial skill. And then there were the harder-to-type Talents, uncredentialed but lively people who tried to get ahead in some disorganized entrepreneurial field like small business or entertainment. Their virtues were aggressive drive, imagination, persistence, and the ability to perform.

For the rest of the twentieth century, these three types, Mandarins, Lifers, and Talents, would duke it out, each controlling certain economic, geographic, and cultural territory within American society, their alliances shifting, their fortunes rising and falling. Alice Young, Bill Lee, and Don Nakanishi, and fellow Mandarins they met along with way, never enjoyed the feeling of a serene assumption of power and position. Instead they experienced the struggle of a well-defined, coherent, laboratory-created group trying to attain the high place in American life that they had been encouraged to believe would be theirs, and that they longed to occupy.

Alice Young's was the first class in the history of the Harvard Law School that was more than 10 percent female. Larger colleges and universities, a standardized way of measuring student candidates that didn't grossly favor men, and the glorification of equal opportunity as the noblest cause in American society all combined to increase the chances for women to have careers. The women in Alice's class were participating in a great, exhilarating (and scary) breakthrough: many of them were going to go through life being the first woman ever to do whatever it was they did. Even a conventional legal career would be unconventional, and it had an aura of progress that it did not have for the men in their class.

In the past, any woman at the Harvard Law School stood out as a rarity. In the class of 1974, women as a group stood out, and when individual women stood out it was for a more elaborate reason than the simple fact of their gender. One of these was certainly Alice Young, who was unusual in being a Chinese-American, in being intensely focused to an extent rare even at the Harvard Law School, and in looking, by now, as if she were maybe in high school. But probably the woman who stood out most, at least in the minds of the men in the class, was Molly Munger, from Pasadena, California. As *Where They Are Now*, a book about the women in that law school class by Jill Abramson and Barbara Franklin, put it: "Molly, with her shiny blond hair and perfect features, was the one almost all the men in the class fantasized about. She was so beautiful that her looks were distracting."

Well, fine, but that wasn't what Molly thought she was about. Like Alice, like most of her classmates, Molly was highly conscious of being a new American type, a carefully groomed member of a rising elite who was also a champion of democracy, devoted to making the country better for ordinary people

and to eliminating social and economic class privilege. A moralist, an opti-
mist, and an enthusiast, at least as self-dramatizing as she was dramatic in
appearance, she embodied all the aspirations and contradictions of the new
Mandarins. She wanted her own triumphs to be triumphs of social progress
as well. Was that possible?

Molly's father, Charles T. Munger, had been an early beneficiary of standardized testing. Charlie Munger had grown up in Omaha, Nebraska, in, as
he put it, "the upper ranks of the professional bourgeoisie." His father was a
lawyer. After high school he enrolled in the University of Michigan to study
physics. Then, when the Second World War began, Charlie enlisted in the
Air Force (then a part of the Army), so he became one of the ten million takers of the Army General Classification Test. A score of 120 was enough to get
you the special treatment reserved for the brainy; Charlie's score was 149.
(He wasn't supposed to know that, but he snuck into the office and looked it
up.) He was ordered to transfer to the California Institute of Technology and
study meteorology.

Caltech, a private university in Pasadena, California, was descended
from an astronomical observatory but had developed close ties to, and was
getting generous funding from, the research divisions of the armed forces. It
fit precisely into the ideas of men like James Bryant Conant about how the
United States could train an elite technocratic class. Charlie was thrown in
among brilliant young physicists and liked to think of himself as one of
them, but he did not want to live out the prescribed life course: professorship, government consultancies, and, later, administration of some part of
the machinery. What made the strongest impression on him during his time
at Caltech was not life within the technocracy, but the luster of southern
California.

Charlie had been brought up in an atmosphere with a lot of the nineteenth century in it. Nebraska's pioneer days were well within the collective
memory. The story people told themselves about their society was that they
had come with no money to a flat empty prairie and, through sheer patience
and determination and self-denial—in short, through virtue!—had built
there a world of lasting value. When he was a boy his grandfather, following
a family tradition, read *Robinson Crusoe* to Charlie. This he received as a
story not of adventure upon the bounding main, but of improvement. Crusoe
lands on the island, makes out a list of all the things he has to be grateful for
despite the misfortune of being shipwrecked, and gets to work, continually
planting, chopping, building, harvesting, storing, and making precise nota-
tions of the exact quantity of everything he has—not because he loves pos-

sessions but because they represent capital he can build on. Although Crusoe believes that God is watching over him, he is not passively waiting for His providence to be delivered, but rather exhibits what Max Weber was later to describe as the Protestant ethic. Religion inculcates a certain supreme confidence that enables him to figure things out for himself and prosper by applying his rationality to the world around him.

Another book that imprinted itself upon Charlie during his boyhood was *Poor Richard's Almanack*, with its endlessly cheerful aphorisms linking good behavior to material betterment. In fact, Benjamin Franklin—the man whom Max Weber held up as Exhibit A of the Protestant ethic—became Charlie's lifelong hero. (In later years, visitors to Charlie's office would be confronted by two heads of equal size, Charlie's and Franklin's, in bronze, on Charlie's desk.) As soon as he got to Caltech, Charlie saw that southern California was a big, open field—the possibilities were strikingly greater than in Omaha. It was a Crusoe's island, a Franklin's Philadelphia, for a mid-twentieth-century American, only enormous.

Charlie got married during his Caltech period. His sister had come to California to study at Scripps College, thirty miles inland from Caltech, and she introduced him to her roommate, a girl from Pasadena named Nancy Huggins. Because she had grown up there, and because she was quiet and still by nature, very much unlike restless energetic cocksure Charlie, Nancy didn't see her hometown in the same light that Charlie did. Pasadena had started out as a small agricultural town and in the late nineteenth century it became a winter resort for rich people from "back East" (meaning, mostly, the Midwest) who liked its January sunshine. Nancy's grandparents, who were from back East but not rich, had moved to Pasadena in the 1880s. They met as fellow clerks in a shoe store and then started a shoe store of their own, catering to the society women in town.

Over the years Pasadena grew into a small city with a few five- and six-story buildings downtown. The first freeway built in California connected it to downtown Los Angeles, and it became an early commuter suburb, too. It was probably the one place in southern California with the most Eastern, traditional, rooted flavor, and it also harbored a small community of artists, actors, craftspeople, architects, and social reformers, but to note this is to run the risk of misleading. At its core Pasadena was a transplanted Midwestern town, only with better weather, more opportunity, and fewer strict social arrangements. It was quiet, conservative, and Republican. People thought of themselves as small-town, not urban. They pronounced "Los Angeles" with a sharp-cornered, unmellifluous hard *g*. Glamour, showbiz, and fast living went on somewhere twenty miles west, across a mountain pass, and none of their tremors registered in Pasadena. The big city, to the extent that Pasadenans thought about it, was a place where oil was extracted and airplanes built. Mr. Huggins pedaled his bicycle slowly down Oak Knoll Avenue to bring shoe samples to ladies settled in for long stays at the grand old Huntington Hotel.

After Charlie and Nancy were married and the war was over, Charlie decided he would go to Harvard Law School, his father's alma mater. He presented himself to the dean of admissions, who pointed out that Charlie had not graduated from college and told him to go back and finish, then apply to law school. Fortunately for Charlie, the way such things worked was just then in transition between the old system, based on family connections and personal assessments of a young man's character, and the new one of credentials and test scores. (The first administration of the Law School Aptitude Test was still a couple of years off in the future.) It just so happened that the retired dean of Harvard Law School, Roscoe Pound, was a native Nebraskan and a friend of the Munger family. Charlie called upon Pound and pleaded his case, and Pound called the new dean of the law school and got Charlie admitted.

Charlie took to law school immediately and was an outstandingly good student, to the point of being somewhat arrogant about it, but he had mixed feelings about actually being a lawyer. The standard course for a Harvard Law School graduate to follow was to join a big-city law firm as an associate and laboriously compete for the tenured position of partner. Like the law school, the law firms into which it fed were in the early 1950s still institutions of the Episcopacy, just beginning a transition to the new Mandarin regime. Therefore, although they mostly served big business, they were still heavily invested in the notion of gentlemanliness, of their belonging to an ancient and honorable profession rather than to the unlettered commercial world. As if to demonstrate the point, law firms didn't pay their associates very much. Many of these young men came from rich families who could help them along until they became partners. But Charlie didn't, and anyway, would Ben Franklin or Robinson Crusoe have spent a lifetime at Cravath, Swaine & Moore, for example, taking the commuter train from Greenwich, Connecticut, settling into a position just below the very top of the comfortable established system? Serving clients, instead of being his own master? Not likely. It didn't fit Charlie's idea of himself as a self-reliant character.

On the other hand, Charlie was not entirely devoid of the tendencies of the emerging Mandarin class. He liked having been identified as intelligent, cut from the herd, and put in the exclusive company of other intelligent people. He recognized that his Harvard law degree was a valuable credential that ensured him a life substantially protected from the risk of falling below a certain pretty high level. Not to use the credential once it was in hand seemed foolish. Even Ben Franklin had been prudently risk-averse, starting each new venture from the protection of a position in an older one. So Charlie compromised. He joined an established law firm as an associate, but it was in Los Angeles, where many other possibilities were available, rather than New York or Boston or San Francisco, where the law firm would have been the whole story. He and Nancy moved to Pasadena and had two daughters, Molly and Wendy.

Even as a relatively impecunious junior associate with a family to support, Charlie practiced the primary Franklin virtue, thrift, and he began to invest the money he saved. In 1953, he and Nancy got divorced. Both of them remarried, happily, within a couple of years. Nancy stayed in Pasadena, Charlie moved to Los Angeles, and Molly and Wendy saw him every Sunday and during the summers. For Charlie the divorce only intensified his eagerness to move on from the practice of law. His new wife, also named Nancy, had two children from her first marriage, and together they had four more children. Even though Charlie became a partner at his law firm, raising eight children on his earnings was a struggle. He stepped up the pace of his investing. He bought shares of common stock here, a stake in an electronics firm there, apartment houses in Pasadena and the surrounding towns. He bought a house near the Wilshire Country Club, tore it down, sold half the lot, and used the proceeds to build himself a new house on the other half.

By 1962 he had accumulated $300,000. Along with a few colleagues he started his own law firm, Munger, Tolles & Olson—something you could do in Los Angeles much more easily than in an older city—but for Charlie the impetus was not so much to control a legal institution as to create a berth for himself from which he could invest more actively and aggressively than before, when he had superiors to please. He was using Munger, Tolles as a halfway house on the way out of the Mandarin class into the ranks of the Talents.

Nancy Huggins Munger's second husband was Robert Freeman, a radiologist in Pasadena and the son of a prominent local Presbyterian minister. Her two girls grew up in a somewhat complicated position. They had regular strong tastes of Charlie's bright, aggressive optimism, but only a taste, because their mother did not share it. Their stepfather was anything but a rebel—he was a man who played the accordion once a week at the Kiwanis Club—but he had been involved in reformist causes around Pasadena for years and was an elected member of the Pasadena school board. At dinner he would rail against the intransigence of the other board members about integrating the elementary schools in town. This put him in contrast to practical-minded Charlie Munger, who believed in charity as Franklin had but was proud to call himself (maybe a little teasingly) a right-winger.

In the extended Huggins clan in Pasadena, there was also a note of social ambition. Nancy and Bob Freeman sent Molly and Wendy to the Westridge School for Girls, which had a finishing-school feeling about it (assemblies were conducted in French), with the expectation that they would one day join the local upper class. As a final complication the girls grew up with the sense of being different because they were the children of divorced parents, when that was still rare. So Molly had a lot of options, sociologically speaking: her mother's secluded old-Pasadena world, her stepfather's liberal improving one, her father's old identity as a lawyer and new one as a free-booting investor.

When Molly was in the eighth grade, she announced that she wanted to go to McKinley Junior High School, which was known in Molly's part of Pasadena as the Negro junior high school. After one year there she went on to John Muir High School, which had the same reputation.

If you had gone to look at John Muir High School, what you would have seen was a typically magnificent California high school of the 1960s, a little like a college campus, with a series of linked dun-colored buildings, beautifully planted and maintained grounds, and the San Gabriel Mountains looming in the near distance. The student body was 80 percent white, but that was less white than the student body at Pasadena High School on the other side of town; John Muir was the alma mater of Pasadena's most famous African-American, Jackie Robinson.

To travel to John Muir High from the part of town where Molly lived was to cross a distinct boundary. Home was on the south side of town, where the houses ranged from enormous mansions built by rich Midwesterners down to pleasant respectable bungalows. School was on the north side, in a section where the small frame houses had originally been built for servants and gardeners; it had a dusty feeling, because the people who lived there didn't have enough money to landscape their small patches of the terrain out of all semblance to its natural aridity.

Part of Molly's going to John Muir was her acting out the principles she heard around the house from her Democratic mother and stepfather. Another part (at least in her mother's view) was ambition. Molly did not want to grow up to be a lady in Pasadena who went to teas, which was where the Westridge School for Girls seemed to be pointing her. She wanted to be in a bigger sphere where things of consequence were done—to be somebody important, to help fix the problems of society. John Muir was the immediately available step toward it.

After John Muir, Molly went to Radcliffe College—nominally the women's college at Harvard, actually an institution that admitted students and housed them but that sent them to classes at Harvard—thinking that because it did not have fraternities or sororities like Stanford it would be a democratic institution devoid of consciousness of social rank. Actually, Harvard in the fall of 1966, when Molly arrived there, was, three full decades after Conant and Chauncey began meritocratizing it, still very strikingly a class-bound institution, at least to the eyes of someone newly arrived from California. It was like moving from the United States to England. Molly received a particularly strong dose of indoctrination into the intricacies of East Coast snobbery because her freshman roommate was Alice Ballard, from Philadelphia.

Alice was a direct descendant of the first child born in Philadelphia, Edward Drinker. The man who invented the very terms "White Anglo-Saxon Protestant" (WASP) and "Protestant Establishment," the sociologist E. Digby Baltzell, was a childhood friend of her father's. The Ballards lived in Chestnut Hill, an enclosed, cozy upper-class enclave of fieldstone houses on the north side of Philadelphia, the kind of place where everybody had lived forever and seemed to be somehow related to everybody else. Alice's parents were both the offspring of families that ran prominent old-line Philadelphia law firms: Drinker, Biddle & Reath, which represented banks, in the case of her mother's family; Ballard, Spahr, Andrews & Ingersoll, which represented the old traction companies that predated public transportation authorities, in the case of her father's. Frederick Ballard and Ernesta Drinker Ballard met at a debutante ball. He went to work at Ballard, Spahr, and she became a legendary doer of good works, who built the annual Philadelphia Flower Show into a national event. The Ballards were patrician, reformist liberals— Ernesta later served on the boards of the National Organization for Women and the National Abortion Rights Action League. They lived in a large, comfortable (but not showy!) turreted stone house with lovely gardens and two grand pianos in the living room.

The Ballards had been brought up in an environment so tight and serene that men would go fox hunting in the mornings in Chestnut Hill and arrive at work a little late but invigorated; where there was always room for another son in the family firm; where money was never, ever discussed in the home (partly because there was never an insufficiency of it). To rebel against the insularity of the Philadelphia elite—a group so provincial that its awareness of universities other than Penn was a little hazy—they sent their children to Harvard, where the four Ballard progeny accumulated seven degrees among them. Alice, at the time that Molly met her, was an unrepentant Philadelphia debutante who in addition to her social credentials was very proud of having gotten an 800 on the verbal portion of the SAT.

From Alice and her circle of private-school and boarding-school friends, Molly, who thought she had encountered social snobbery at its very apex in the snootier members of her class at the Westridge School for Girls in Pasadena, was given instruction in the game at a level she hadn't even imagined. Newly arrived in Cambridge, they would pore over a small yearbook of the freshman class and clue Molly in: New Canaan is a better hometown than Darien, but Greenwich is better than New Canaan. Girls from Milton Academy are arty and girls from Foxcroft are horsey. Philadelphia debutantes outrank New York debutantes. Don't say commence, dear, it's Jewish for begin. Molly took all this in with an unavoidable fascination mixed with horror—she had thought she was escaping the clutches of the Theta house at Stanford, only to find that Radcliffe contained everything she thought she was avoiding, only with an added measure of competitive nastiness.

Cambridge and Pasadena shared the quality of being supposedly open, free, ideal locales where if you poked around a little you found that things weren't quite so utopian as they seemed. What Molly did when she realized this was perhaps contradictory, but it was typical for her generation of rising Mandarins. She wanted very badly to make it, to earn her way to a berth in the American elite, but at the same time she wanted to fix the country's flaws, which burned her up. The ideal was to occupy a top position in a fair system. Thus far Molly had encountered a system that didn't deserve the self-celebration that encased it. But maybe someday it could and would. Like Conant, like Kerr, like Chauncey, she became inexorably attached to the idea of a perfected American social order.

Alice Ballard changed. In the course of four years at Harvard—four years that coincided with the peak of the student-revolution period there—she metamorphosed from debutante to plainspoken feminist and social reformer. She went around in wire-rimmed glasses and blue jeans and long straight hair and did not join the small but distinct boarding-school group at Harvard. Did Molly change? In her view, no. She arrived as a culturally conservative but politically liberal, optimistic, candid, idealistic, enthusiastic Westerner, and left that way, too, giving radical politics a wide berth. She majored in economics and, after the assassination of Robert F. Kennedy, supported the Democratic candidate, Vice President Hubert Humphrey, for

President in 1968, which made her almost bizarrely middle-of-the-road by the standards of Harvard students, who were for either Eugene McCarthy or nobody. In the court of undergraduate opinion, her reputation was set by her looks: the unlikely California blonde at Harvard, who appeared in a highly atypical (for Cambridge) dazzling explosion of white-pinkness, with a cloud-burst of pale-pale hair, glowing skin, deep blue eyes, and a strong triangular face with wide-set cheeks and forward-minded chin.

But it is true that Molly wound up socially in the very group that horrified her when she first encountered it, and that Alice left, the substantial remnant of the Episcopacy. These people, though, were themselves changing. They were still a presence at Harvard, but it was clear that the tide was running out; and internally, the Harvard students from the Episcopacy began adopting meritocratic values, so that being very intelligent, which had meant nothing back in the A. Lawrence Lowell days, was now crucially important even within their own subculture. As they told each other their life stories, the shadings were new. The rich fathers and Puritan origins and debutante dances were played down, and whatever hint of difficulty or obscurity might be found in the background was played up: it was better to have achieved status than ascribed status. And even if you were to the manner born, you had to show that you could cut it in the new meritocratic world. Thus Molly's major Cambridge boyfriend, William Weld, future governor of Massachusetts, was rich, insouciant, boarding-school-educated, athletic, and devoted to public service (though not earnestly so!)—the whole traditional package—but also, the key point, he was academically outstanding.

After college Alice Ballard and Molly Munger both went to the Harvard Law School. Both of them came from legal families but they had their own reasons for making this decision. Alice went to law school to learn how to help the poor and powerless to get justice. Her reputation was as the leading feminist in the class and as one of the most unrepentant sixties-politics people. After law school she moved back to Philadelphia and became perhaps the leading people's lawyer in town, the first person you'd call if you wanted to sue for discrimination.

Molly went to law school for less clear, therefore more typical, reasons. She didn't know exactly what she wanted to do, but she wanted it to be something significant, something with scope. Molly liked economics, but she didn't think she could master higher mathematics to the point where she could become a professor at a leading university. She had some interest in journalism, a quasi-Talent field with considerable appeal to Mandarins, but when she tried out for *The Harvard Crimson* and didn't make it, she took the failure as a sign.

For somebody like Molly who was able, ambitious, accomplished, but not obsessively focused on one goal, law school tended then to rise automatically to the top of the pile of options. She called it the S & H Green Stamp phenomenon, after those stamps that one could get at grocery stores, paste into a book, and then redeem for prizes. You asked yourself what was the highest-value thing you were eligible for as possessor of a Harvard degree but no one unusual skill, what prize your stamps would buy you, and the answer was law school. With a Harvard law degree you would have your pick of high-paying job offers. You could live in any city in America. You had a good shot, at least, at becoming a partner in a law firm, which was a completely secure, highly prestigious job. You were on a well-defined, structured path that would feel familiar and comfortable if you had spent your early life becoming a Mandarin.

Going to law school certainly wasn't daring, but as a woman lawyer in the 1970s you had automatic trailblazer status. If Molly had a career in a law firm (even though that would represent the cautious path for a man) she would be participating in a movement, a social advance that felt vitally important to her. Molly saw the world as a site for improvement. She wanted being a lawyer to be about more than just getting ahead; she wanted it also to be about making the world better. It could be both, couldn't it?

17 The Weak Spot

During her first year at law school, Alice Young got a summer job, which she continued part-time through her second year, with the Boston office of the federal Office of Civil Rights. Her assignment was to research the state of racial integration in the Boston school system, to generate backup for the lawsuit that would soon lead to busing in Boston. The experience left Alice shocked at the state of the Boston schools. Lucky circumstances, mainly her and her father's unstoppable drive to excel in school, had made education a clear route to unlimited advancement for her. But for people in Boston who were less extraordinary and who didn't have the money to get themselves to the suburbs, where the schools were good, the United States was hardly a land of opportunity: public schools in Boston were racially segregated almost to the level of the Jim Crow South, with the white schools pretty bad and the black schools much worse. At the same time, the research left Alice exhilarated by the possibilities for lawyers to right social wrongs. She didn't like law school much—it seemed too impersonal and unintellectual—but she liked the idea that, as a lawyer, she would possess tools for changing things.

Bill Lee, at Columbia, didn't like law school either—too much like the grade-mad Bronx High School of Science. He went to see one of the deans and complained that he felt unfulfilled. Was there any way he could get involved in civil-rights issues? The dean sent him to the two professors at Columbia most involved with those issues, Drew Days and Jack Greenberg. Bill wound up working as a research assistant to Greenberg for the rest of his time in law school.

Bill was being inducted into a family with a blood-bond and a shared history: the family of civil-rights litigators connected to the NAACP Legal Defense and Education Fund, Inc. Jack Greenberg had been one of a small circle of assistants to Thurgood Marshall, the Fund's founding head and since 1967 the first black Supreme Court justice; he had been at Marshall's side during the crowning triumph of his career, his argument of the *Brown* v. *Board of Education* case before the Supreme Court. Drew Days, a younger member of the Legal Defense Fund family, represented the next generation of civil-rights litigators, and law students like Bill could plausibly feel they represented the generation after that. Bill now had a direct, and not very distant, link to the whole tradition.

For any reform-minded law student of Bill's age, Thurgood Marshall stood out as the model of the public-interest lawyer. For more than two decades, with a small staff and no money, often under conditions of physical peril, Marshall had painstakingly filed lawsuit after lawsuit, each building on the last, and in so doing had dealt the crucial, fatal wound to the Jim Crow system in the South. It would be hard to think of any solo performer in American history who had been so politically consequential, and in so unquestionably a noble cause.

Marshall's was a particularly Mandarin achievement. His staff included the very brightest graduates of the very best law schools; a job at the Legal Defense Fund had pure-gold credential value. The Fund effected social change in the manner of Plato's guardians, by using its lawyers' superior training to make brilliant courtroom arguments rather than by appealing to popular sentiment through politics. What other choice was there? African-Americans couldn't vote in the South, so it was inconceivable that the state legislatures there would undertake the overthrow of segregation; and in Washington, segregationist Southerners held the balance of power in both Congress and the Democratic Party, which explains why even Franklin Roosevelt hadn't dared touch the Jim Crow system. Reform via judicial decree was the only option. And the aspect of American society that Marshall and his staff were trying to reform was the one Mandarins cared about most, the educational system as a guarantor of individual opportunity. Marshall embodied the Mandarin dream of an educated elite getting enough power to create a good society for all.

Alice Young was emotionally involved less in the civil-rights movement than in being a first-generation Chinese-American and woman in the law. After law school she thought about moving back to Hawaii and running for political office, but instead she made the more standard choice to join a big law firm, one based in New York but with a substantial practice in Asia. But

Bill Lee, after law school, went right to work for the NAACP Legal Defense Fund. In so doing he was forgoing a lot of money that he could have made in a law firm, but he was not forgoing being a Mandarin.

By the 1970s, the grandeur of the original idea of the American meritocracy was subtly ratcheting down, even as the system itself was becoming pervasive and entrenched. Nobody had ever picked up Conant's call back in the 1940s for 100 percent inheritance taxes and the end of private education. Even the popular idea of a continually growing higher-education system was passing out of vogue. Affirmative action, though, as a way of correcting the country's (and the meritocracy's) most obvious form of unfairness—that, at least, was a moral principle woven permanently, it seemed, into the social fabric of the American system. It was just and it was cheap and it had been accepted by thousands upon thousands of American institutions, hadn't it? But even this small reformist aspect of the meritocracy soon proved hard to sustain.

When Richard Nixon became President in 1969, the main home of affirmative action in the federal government was the Labor Department's Office of Federal Contract Compliance, the obscure bureaucracy that Lyndon Johnson had created with his Executive Order 11246 in 1965. At the end of Johnson's term, the head of the office, Edward Sylvester, took a big aggressive step by imposing requirements to hire minorities on recalcitrant building-trades unions in Cleveland and Philadelphia. But the plans were ruled illegal because they mandated hiring by race.

With Nixon's accession, out went Edward Sylvester and in came Arthur Fletcher. Nixon thought of Fletcher as the embodiment of his favored solution to the race problem, "black capitalism." Fletcher was a black man and a Republican who had run a manpower-training program in the state of Washington that had fought with the local Democratic interests—so he had to be a black capitalist, right? Actually the only reason Fletcher was a Republican was that he came from a part of Kansas where the black political structure had never left the party of Reconstruction. He was a lifelong government employee whose views were not very different from those of black Democrats. By self-description he had been "a mad son of a bitch" ever since 1960, when he lost a job in the Berkeley, California, public-school system because he had a reputation as a racial troublemaker, which caused his family to be plunged into poverty, which caused his wife to commit suicide by jumping off the Bay Bridge, which caused him to have to raise five children single-handedly in dire financial straits until the manpower-training job came along. Nonetheless, Nixon liked the idea of this big, handsome man, who had briefly played professional football with the Los Angeles Rams, as the symbol of black capitalism, so Fletcher had clout in the Nixon administration.

Fletcher decided to revive the "Philadelphia Plan," with its minority hiring requirements. The situation he was trying to rectify was genuinely horrifying. The building-trades unions, unlike the big industrial unions, had a long history of excluding blacks. They were built on ethnicity as well as class; the typical building-trades union local functioned as a cozy, informal, neighborhood-based hiring club for members of particular immigrant groups and their children; all outsiders, particularly blacks, were relentlessly excluded and regarded with suspicion and hostility. If you were black, it would be about as easy to crack one of the Philadelphia building-trades locals as it would be to buy a row house in white-ethnic South Philadelphia, move in, and be warmly welcomed by the neighbors. Nixon once entertained a group of his aides with the story that George Meany, the building-trades man who was head of the AFL-CIO, had told Secretary of Labor George Shultz: "When I was a plumber, it never occoid to me to have niggers in the union!" According to Fletcher's statistics, the Philadelphia chapter of the ironworkers' union was 98.4 percent white, the steamfitters were 99.35 percent white, the sheet-metal workers were 99 percent white, the electricians were 98.24 percent white, the elevator workers were 99.46 percent white, and the plumbers and pipe fitters were 99.49 percent white.

But there was more to the situation than just the numbers. Fletcher had picked Philadelphia from among the various moribund causes of his predecessor because it had an especially active NAACP chapter that he thought would generate support for him, and because it was a heavily Democratic city that he wouldn't get in trouble with his superiors for alienating. At a higher level of the administration than Fletcher had access to, there was positive delight over what he was doing. Ever since the 1964 Civil Rights Act the Republican Party had been making heavy inroads in the once completely Democratic South. With its Southern base eroding, the Democratic Party had to rely more heavily than ever before on both blacks and unions, and the Philadelphia Plan neatly brought tensions between them to the fore. "A wedge has been driven into the liberal Democratic ranks and should be exploited for the confusion it puts them in," one aide in the White House wrote. Another wrote: "The key issue is that we have laid bare the split between the Blacks and the trade union movement. . . . The Justice Department, working with the Labor Department, should draft some follow-up legislation, which, together with moving the Plan into additional cities, should serve to keep the pot stirred."

Congress passed the Philadelphia Plan just before Christmas 1969, and sure enough, George Meany was soon attacking it. It would be too facile to say that it split up the Democratic coalition in exactly the way that the Nixon White House planned. The split occurred, but it would have occurred without the Philadelphia Plan, as an inevitable consequence of blacks being a rising group and contesting for white-held turf. The greater import of the Philadelphia Plan was that it pushed the government's enforcement of affirmative action to a newly aggressive level. With the Philadelphia Plan the federal government established itself as, if necessary, the unbidden imposer of numerical goals. That was a big step, and because it was taken by a Republican President it appeared to represent the new reasonable middle position on affirmative action. Thus the Philadelphia Plan sent a signal to thousands of state and local governments and private organizations practicing affirmative action on their own that more toughness was now in order.

And yet, by the time he was running for reelection in 1972, less than three years after ramming the Philadelphia Plan through a recalcitrant Congress, Nixon was changing on affirmative action. Arthur Fletcher, once such a presidential favorite that Nixon had thought he should run for the United States Senate, was given a new appointment at the United Nations so as to get him out of the Office of Federal Contract Compliance. "Fletcher's basic problem with the building trades was that he had a limited understanding of labor relations," Fred Malek, a White House staff member, wrote his boss, John Ehrlichman. What that really meant was that the Philadelphia Plan had so successfully alienated the labor movement from the Democratic Party that the AFL-CIO was now a potential Nixon ally in the 1972 campaign and had to be appeased by sacrificing Fletcher. Fletcher says the Nixon administration had pamphlets printed boasting of the success of the Philadelphia Plan to hand out at the 1972 Republican National Convention, then destroyed them before anybody had seen them when polling data showed that white union members might vote Republican if handled properly. Both Nixon and his Democratic opponent, George McGovern, spent the fall campaign season strenuously denouncing quota hiring.

Affirmative action was also beginning to generate serious opposition elsewhere in American society. For the Mandarins it was one thing when affirmative action was about manning tables for pipe fitters—one could view it purely as an abstract public-policy matter—and quite another when it occurred on their own home ground of higher education. There it was deeply personal and set off the strongest possible emotions. The number of billets in the best universities was limited, and if affirmative action gave some of them to blacks, then it was, inescapably, taking them away from whites who had higher test scores. Race, if one was white, was standing in the way of joining the Mandarin class.

In the late 1960s and early 1970s a psychology professor at Berkeley, Arthur Jensen, began writing articles in which he asserted that intelligence tests were not biased against minorities and that programs aimed at improving their performance in school were likely to fail. In 1971 Richard Herrnstein, a psychology professor at Harvard, wrote an article published in *The Atlantic Monthly* saying that the United States was rapidly becoming a Michael Young–style meritocracy: intelligence was now the key quality in society; it was substantially inherited; and therefore standardized testing and selective higher education, by gathering up all the most intelligent people and depositing them in one place so they were likely to intermarry, would soon produce a distinct, quasi-hereditary upper class made up of people with high IQs.

Jensen and Herrnstein were conservatives staunchly opposed to affirmative action, but their views were not entirely out of synch with those of the liberal founders of the American meritocracy, like Conant and Kerr. The aspect of the meritocratic system that their inspirational rhetoric about democracy obscured—namely, if you made high scores on IQ tests your opportunities would be distinctly brighter than most people's—Jensen and Herrnstein put under a harsh spotlight. Many angry protests and demonstrations showed how potentially explosive these underlying assumptions were.

Affirmative action was stirring up dispute that was not on public display, too. In the archives of the Nixon White House, for example, there is a lengthy memo submitted by six Jewish organizations just before the 1972 Republican convention protesting against thirty-three examples of universities giving preferential treatment to blacks (and therefore harming whites).

The advent of meritocracy was supposed to have put an end to the informal but strict Jewish quotas that Ivy League universities, and many of the employers who hired from them, had maintained since the 1920s. But now, with everything in place for a great Jewish meritocratic advance, quotas seemed to be coming back in the guise of helping black people. It seemed a short step from a university's putting a bottom limit on its percentage of black students to its putting an upper limit on its percentage of Jewish students. If the proportional representation of every group were the goal, where would that leave Jews, who were 3 percent of the American population and far above that in the Ivy League even in the heyday of quotas? Admissions is a zero-sum game; it was not hard for the Jewish organizations to surmise that the more places in higher education which were handed out not strictly on the basis of test scores and grades but reserved for blacks and Latinos, the fewer places would be left for Jews.

Item 25 on the list of thirty-three was Yale's asking applicants to indicate their race. Items 26, 27, and 28 were complaints about ETS asking takers of the SAT, the LSAT, and the MCAT the same question. Items 5, 8, 9, 16, 18, 19, and 31 were complaints about attempts to identify, hire, and admit minorities in one or another outpost of the vast California public-higher-education empire built by Clark Kerr. Item 1, the longest and most detailed, concerned a young man in the state of Washington named Marco DeFunis, Jr., who had recently sued the University of Washington Law School for rejecting him. DeFunis had found out that of the thirty-one black applicants to the law school accepted in his year, thirty had lower grades and LSAT scores than he did. The Washington Superior Court ruled that he had been a victim of racial discrimination and ordered him admitted. The university appealed to the state's supreme court and won. DeFunis, still enrolled in law school thanks to the order of the lower court, appealed to the United States Supreme Court, which agreed to hear the case.

For several years the issue of racial inequality in whatever was being handed out on the basis of standardized test scores had been bubbling up to the level of consideration by the Supreme Court. The most important early case was *Griggs* v. *Duke Power*, in 1971, a replay of the old Motorola case in Illinois. A group of black employees challenged the use of an intelligence test by the Duke Power Company, because even if the test hadn't been designed to exclude blacks, it had that effect. The Supreme Court came down unanimously on the pro-black, anti-testing side, ruling that a business could not use standardized tests in hiring or promotion unless the tests measured specific skill at a task, not general intelligence, and could be proved to be a "business necessity."

The DeFunis case may have been legally similar, but for the lawyers in the case it was psychologically quite different. The Griggs case involved the somewhat distant matter of job opportunities for blue-collar workers. The DeFunis case was much closer to home. Every member of the Supreme Court had done brilliantly well in law school. The idea of legal meritocracy—law school as a completely open contest in which academically outstanding students could put themselves on the road to great success—animated the story of each of their lives. The justices' clerks had all been fabulously good students, too. So the argument that law schools shouldn't choose among applicants on the basis of their transcripts and test scores because doing so would disadvantage blacks and wasn't a "business necessity" was not an easy one to make at the Supreme Court.

On the other hand, the Supreme Court was also the emblem of the idea that Mandarins in power could be relied on to bring social justice to the nation. It was these nine appointed brainy guys who had ended school segregation—not the elected officials in the other two branches of the federal government. For nearly twenty years the Court had handed down a string of thunderous unanimous decisions forcing the United States to do right by the descendants of slaves. This was not a tradition to be given up lightly.

Did the Supreme Court, confronted with this direct, long-building, historic conflict between black progress and meritocracy-by-testing, find its way to an intellectual breakthrough that would resolve the conflict? It did not. The justices may have been intelligent, but they weren't, perhaps, wise enough to accomplish that. Instead they became confused. The perfect example of Mandarin ambivalence about affirmative action in higher education was the bizarre reaction to the DeFunis case of the Court's longest-serving and most self-consciously crusading member, William O. Douglas, which surely must qualify as the leading documented example of judicial indecision (and by an unusually decisive judge) in American history.

Douglas had grown up in the state of Washington, where he had risen from rustic poverty on the strength of his performance in school—he was a perfect self-made man of the American meritocracy. He also had a carefully maintained reputation as a champion of the dispossessed, with only one blot on it: he had written the Court's decision during the Second World War that ratified the internment of Japanese-Americans like Don Nakanishi's parents. Now, seventy-five years old and close to the end of his career, Douglas did not want to finish on a note that had him abandoning the cause of minorities.

Inside the Supreme Court building Douglas was known, *pace* his public image, as a cold, remote man who when confronted with a new case made up his mind almost instantly and dashed off an opinion that was often a rehash of one of his previous opinions. Other justices' law clerks drafted decisions for and formed close relationships with their bosses; Douglas' law clerks spent their time on minor paper-shuffling and almost never saw him. On the DeFunis case, though, Douglas asked one of his clerks, Ira Ellman, to draft a memo on the case, without telling him what position to take. Ellman had not met Douglas before, though he had been on the job for several months, and the justice had certainly never asked him even indirectly what he thought about something. He got the distinct impression that Douglas was having trouble figuring out where he stood.

It was the fall of 1973. DeFunis had just started his third year in law school. Ellman, himself a meritocratic son of middle-class Queens, New York, and a graduate of Stuyvesant High School, a public school where admission was gained by exam scores, went to work. He produced a memo urging Douglas to decide in favor of DeFunis, because "there really was some kind of quota here." Then the Court recessed for the winter.

On February 26, 1974, the Supreme Court heard oral arguments in the DeFunis case. It was a big show, generating crowds on the Supreme Court steps and the sense of moment that comes when the justices are deliberating on a great question of national life. Afterward the justices held their first conference about the case, during which it quickly became clear that they were nowhere near a consensus. When informally polled as to which way they were leaning, Douglas came down on DeFunis' side.

After the conference, Ira Ellman hesitantly approached Douglas and offered to try his hand at a draft opinion—something Douglas ordinarily did not allow his clerks to do. To Ellman's amazement, Douglas readily agreed, but he told Ellman to suspend the usual procedure of circulating draft opinions to the other justices and just keep what he wrote between the two of them. By way of direction, Douglas told Ellman, "I don't know about these tests," and gave him a few passages he had dashed off, which said that the LSAT was "by no means objective" and might contain "hidden bias." Douglas was suspicious of technology; perhaps the conflict between meritocracy and black progress could be gotten around by finding that the real problem was in the standardized tests themselves.

Ellman called ETS. To arrive at the position Douglas was hinting at, he would have needed data showing that even though blacks got lower LSAT scores than whites, they got the same grades in law school. What he got instead was data showing that the LSAT predicted blacks' law-school grades just as well as whites'. Nonetheless, he put a little of Douglas' anti-LSAT rhetoric in his draft opinion. The main thrust, though, was a Jeffersonian defense of meritocracy: "The democratic ideal as I read the Constitution and the Bill of Rights presupposes an aristocracy of talent; and all races must be permitted to compete for a position in the hierarchy." How, then, should a law school admit students? It should first admit "those clearly qualified" purely on academic merit (how to determine that, the opinion didn't say), then fill the remaining places by lottery.

On March 11 the justices decided to declare the case moot, on the grounds that DeFunis was by this time only a few weeks away from graduating. What they were really indicating was that they couldn't find a position. Douglas decided he would write a dissent to this decision that would address the merits of the case, something none of the other justices were evidently moved to do. He saw himself as being in a special situation; as he told Ellman: "I might not be around next time this issue comes up."

Douglas spent the next three weeks ordering up draft after draft of his opinion as he went through in sequence every possible idea one can have about affirmative action; his papers contain eleven draft opinions in all. The DeFunis case seemed to have the capacity to blow out his usually hardy intellectual circuitry.

One draft dropped the idea of a lottery and suggested that we might "allow racial groups into graduate schools on a pro rata basis." In other words, Douglas was reversing field and endorsing quotas, although, oddly, he ended by ordering DeFunis admitted to law school.

The next draft argued that admission preferences for people from disadvantaged backgrounds were constitutional, but "racial classifications cannot be used." This was just the opposite of the position in the preceding draft.

The next draft angrily opposed admission by race, because "the essence of the policy here—the assumption that is unmistakably communicated—is that Blacks or Browns cannot make it on their individual merit. That is a stamp of inferiority I would never place on any lawyer."

The next draft returned to the idea of a race-neutral lottery to fill "say the last twenty seats" in a law-school class as "the only fair solution," and cut the thunderous condemnation of racial preferences.

The next draft quoted at length from Chief Seattle of the Muckleshoot Tribe, as a segue into an attack on the LSAT. Douglas wrote that "insofar as the LSAT tests are based by the creators of them on the dimensions and orientation of the Organization Man they do a disservice to minorities." This line of thinking led him to reverse field again and endorse the race-conscious admissions that had so recently drawn his disapproval: "the presence of an LSAT test is sufficient warrant for a school to separate minorities into a class in order better to probe their capacities and potentials."

With this version, unlike the preceding drafts, Douglas was sufficiently content that he ordered Ellman to circulate it to the other Supreme Court justices. Ellman did so one afternoon, and the following morning Douglas called him in and said there had been a mistake, he hadn't wanted it circulated, please go and retrieve all the copies. Douglas said that from now on he wouldn't require Ellman's help with the case, he would just work on his own as usual. He wasn't exactly reproaching Ellman, but he seemed to be saying that Ellman had botched the job in some hard-to-define way. "The opinion you wrote had a homogenized vision," he said, somewhat cryptically. "America would be like a big milk-shake machine: all mixed up."

Douglas' next and final draft returned to a stern condemnation of allowing race to be considered in admissions: "The purpose of the University of Washington cannot be to produce black lawyers for blacks, Polish lawyers for Poles, Jewish lawyers for Jews, Irish lawyers for Irish. It should be to produce good lawyers for Americans and not to place First Amendment barriers against anyone." At the same time Douglas went at the LSAT with renewed fury. It was racially biased, he wrote; its bias justified reverse bias by the law school; in fact the LSAT should be abolished entirely. Then, bizarrely, having ended every previous draft by ordering the law school to admit DeFunis, Douglas now said that the university hadn't violated his constitutional rights and could reject him. When the Supreme Court printer delivered the opinion to Ira Ellman he said, with a quizzical look, "He changed the bottom line."

A year later Justice Douglas had a stroke and retired from the Supreme Court. With affirmative action still almost universally practiced in university admissions and standardized tests almost universally required, minority applicants continued to be admitted over white applicants with higher test scores. Absent a clear signal from the Court, it was inevitable that one of these rejected whites would sue.

One complaint in the Jewish groups' memorandum to the Nixon administration about affirmative action was that the new medical school of the University of California at Davis had reserved an unspecified but large number of places in each class for members of minority groups. It was this issue that produced the case of *Bakke* v. *Regents of the University of California*, which, finally, generated a Supreme Court decision on affirmative action in university admissions as the DeFunis case had not. The medical school at Davis admitted one hundred students a year. The admissions office had set aside sixteen of the hundred places for minorities only. Allan Bakke, the plaintiff, a thirty-eight-year-old engineer, had been rejected even though he had done better on the Medical College Aptitude Test than all sixteen of the minority applicants who had been admitted. Bakke, unlike DeFunis, had not been ordered by a lower court into the medical school, so the escape route that the Supreme Court took in the DeFunis case was not available this time.

The DeFunis case had put the American meritocratic system on notice. The contradictory blend of testing and affirmative action that had evolved as the universities' preferred admissions policy was at legal risk. A great deal in American education and American society was at stake. Fuzzy ententes do not often survive judicial review. Affirmative action might go, which would mean a great reduction in the minority presence in the Mandarin elite, and thus also a reduction in the Mandarins' plausibility, to themselves and to the country at large, as America's natural leaders. Or—the possibility raised by Justice Douglas' published dissent—testing could go, which would mean an end to the mechanism by which the American meritocracy had organized itself.

Everyone mobilized. Harvard filed a friend-of-the-court brief. The deans of the law schools in the University of California system filed a brief, and so did the NAACP Legal Defense and Education Fund. Clark Kerr, a highly interested party since he was one of the fathers of the Davis medical school, of ETS testing as an admissions requirement at the University of California, and of special handling for the university's minority applicants, used his position at the Carnegie Corporation to commission a young research scientist at ETS named Winton Manning to produce a paper for the Court about standardized testing and admission.

One of the people put to work on the Legal Defense Fund's brief was Bill Lee. It was a thrilling assignment for Bill. Here he was only a couple of years out of law school, at a time of life when his classmates who had gone to work for big firms would be performing tedious state-by-state checks of securities laws, and he was helping to settle a major issue in American life. His name (seventh in a billing of eight authors, to be sure) would be on a brief that would be read by Thurgood Marshall himself.

Bill's assignment from Jack Greenberg was to prepare an appendix about the history of public education in California. One part concerned admissions. Bill was supposed to show how the Master Plan had set aside 2 percent of the places at the University of California for special cases, and how that had evolved into the Equal Opportunity Program and finally into the current affirmative-action program—to find, in other words, justification in Clark Kerr's original grand design for the rejection of Allan Bakke by the medical school.

What engaged him more deeply was the other part of the appendix, which was about public elementary and secondary education. Bill wanted to demonstrate that the public schools of California—California, the farthest thing from the old Confederacy—had been so deeply segregated by race for so long, and had allowed schools of such unequal quality, that the University of California's affirmative-action programs were merely a mild corrective for the deep flaws lower down in the system. California's big cities, Bill learned, had maintained legally separate school systems for blacks, "Mongolians," and Indians between 1860 and 1880, and after that most local school systems remained segregated by custom and by the artful drawing of district lines. So many school districts had lost lawsuits accusing them of maintaining this segregation that fully three-fifths of all black students in California went to school in districts that had been found in violation of the Fourteenth

Amendment. Forty percent of black students in California attended all-black public schools. Seventy-five percent attended black-majority schools. As he compiled all this information, Bill dreamed the dream of every writer of a brief to the Supreme Court: that the justices would pluck his argument out of Appendix B of the Legal Defense Fund's brief and make it the centerpiece of their opinion, mandating a sweeping improvement of minority education from kindergarden on.

For ETS *Bakke* was of the utmost importance. It presented both a risk, because of the frightening possibility of a ruling that limited the use of tests, and an opportunity, to explain that it had never been intended that tests be used to keep blacks out of higher education. Winton Manning's report laid out a careful justification for keeping both testing and affirmative action in place. Strict racial quotas such as the Davis medical school's were a bad idea, and so was strict reliance on test scores as a sole admissions device. Instead, tests should be used only as a guide, a way of identifying students who might do brilliantly in school and of those who might have difficulty keeping up. For the large middle, the school should look at a number of criteria (including test scores, of course) and make its own judgments. It would be all right for race to be one criterion, because that was a way of giving special help to applicants from disadvantaged backgrounds and of making student bodies more diverse.

On June 28, 1978, the Supreme Court handed down its decision in the *Bakke* case. On the issue of whether it was constitutional for the Davis medical school to have a racial quota, the court split 5–4, ruling against quotas. On the other issue, whether the school could consider the race of an applicant in making admissions decisions, the court also split 5–4, this time saying that considering race was okay.

Justice Lewis Powell, a gentlemanly former corporate lawyer from Richmond, Virginia, the one justice who voted conservatively on the first issue and liberally on the second, was the author of the opinion. Naturally everyone read it very closely to see who had influenced him. The Harvard brief seemed to have provided the structure and wording for Powell's argument that seeking racial diversity in admissions, without a strict quota system, was constitutional. At ETS there was great joy over the decision because in footnotes Powell twice cited the ETS-Carnegie study. And Bill Lee was just a little disappointed when he read Powell's decision because it said nothing about public-school segregation.

It looked as if the line had held. ETS retained its unusual position as a private company that was all but essential to the operation of public institutions, and yet was exempt from regulation or legal strictures. Affirmative action in university admissions was safe. The specter of admission solely by test scores and grades, which would mean nearly all-white classes at the leading law schools and medical schools, had been banished. Higher education could continue to operate as it pleased so long as it avoided quota systems like Davis'.

Actually, affirmative action was in a far more precarious position than it appeared. The *Bakke* decision was not a clarion call to the nation, a firm inarguable resolution of a question that had heretofore seemed fuzzy but henceforth would seem clear. The Court was practically coming out and saying that this was no *Brown* decision, that this was a tough one. It had taken five years and two cases before the justices were able to reach even this most hesitant, finely grained, close-vote decision. The admissions policy that Powell had endorsed was much easier for a rich private school like Harvard, with its lavishly staffed admissions office, to put into effect than for a public school. Schools that couldn't afford admissions staffs big enough to read a detailed folder of information about each applicant were under the constant temptation to do what was now illegal, admit by the numbers and avoid excluding minorities by creating a separate admissions pool for them. Over time quite a few yielded to the temptation. To people who didn't like affirmative action, the real message of the *Bakke* decision seemed to be that quotas were still okay, you just had to be a little more subtle about them from now on.

The conflict between testing and black progress hadn't gone away. Decisions like *Bakke* only heightened it, by making it clear that the structure of opportunity was now the supreme question in contemporary American life. Politicians, including Presidents, talked about it more and more. It had been a central concern of the Supreme Court since the *Brown* decision, and would continue to be in the years to come. The most important American work of social philosophy of the 1970s, *A Theory of Justice* by John Rawls (James Bryant Conant University Professor, Harvard University), was centrally concerned with trying to reconcile equal opportunity for individuals with justice for all (just what Michael Young thought couldn't be done). The issue couldn't be put back out of sight—but it hadn't been settled either. Rawls devised an elegant solution, which he called the difference principle: special advantages, like getting into an elite school, should be allotted in a way that serves the larger cause of social justice, not simply to ensure that only the deserving are put on the road to personal success. But by now most people understood the meritocracy simply as a reward system. Allan Bakke's individual opportunity had (in a way that could be numerically proved) been trimmed for a political purpose, and that kind of thing wasn't supposed to happen in America.

18
Working

The two big questions for women lawyers coming out into the world in the 1970s were whether they would make partner and whether they would be able to have children at the same time. To become a partner in a big law firm was to arrive at the place to which all the years of academic overachieving had pointed. First came several years of grinding hard work and competition as an associate (but Mandarins were used to that), then a final winnowing, and then a job with guaranteed high pay (not wealth, but Mandarins didn't need to be rich, only prosperous), tenure, and respectable prestige. It wasn't the nature of the work involved that was the key to the appeal of a law partnership—indeed, the work wasn't always very alluring—but the unassailable position it represented, one that women had only rarely occupied before. Women had worked through much of American history, but they had never routinely held positions at the level of partners in law firms.

The years when the race for partnership is on for any lawyer—with a key standard being the sheer number of hours one puts in at the office, including in the evenings and on weekends—are also the years when childbearing happens, or it might not happen at all: late twenties, early thirties. It had been eternally accepted that men were permitted not to worry about this and more or less to drop out of family life during those years. Could women?

After law school Alice Young went to work for the law firm of Coudert Brothers, headquartered in New York but with an office in Hong Kong. She was back and forth a lot between the two cities. She told herself that by becoming a corporate lawyer with a transpacific practice she was fulfilling her father's wishes in content, if not in form: she would be promoting Asian-American understanding and cooperation, which was just what John Young thought of as his life's work. She married a man named Glenn Lau-Kee, a Yale classmate who was the son of a pioneer lawyer in New York's Chinatown, but that didn't work out.

In 1981 Alice left Coudert Brothers to start a New York office for a California firm, Graham & James, a job change that bumped her up from associate to partner. She still went back and forth to Asia constantly. In 1984 she married Thomas Shortall, Yale 1972 and an investment banker. They were a good match of different temperaments, he relaxed and unruffled, she driving and meliorist. The day after they returned from their honeymoon, she left on a business trip to Asia. When their first child was born—a daughter, Amanda, in 1985—Alice, as head of her office, not only couldn't take a full maternity leave but billed more hours than anyone else in the office during the first few postpartum weeks. Then, when she became pregnant again in 1987, Alice left Graham & James for a partnership at a bigger, more established firm in which she didn't have to run an office and could lead a slightly calmer life—if running a transpacific legal practice counts as a slightly calmer life.

Molly Munger decided to move back to Los Angeles after law school, partly because she was so worried about child rearing. If she went home, there would be two parents, two stepparents, seven siblings, and many collateral relatives around to help out. Besides, her years in Boston had led her to revise upward her opinion of southern California. When she was growing up, she thought of Pasadena as marred by stuffiness and social snobbery— that was its assignment among the communities of the Los Angeles basin. But compared to the East Coast, obsessed as it was with the finest gradations of status and rank, Los Angeles, including Pasadena, seemed remarkable for its openness and its optimism. It was still possible there, in the 1970s, to hold firmly in one's mind an all-inclusive vision of a good, classless society, in a way that seemed impossible to Molly in the East.

In coming home, Molly found herself in an exquisite dilemma, the modern equivalent of the complicated pickles involving marriage that confront the heroines in nineteenth-century novels. The law firm her father had founded in 1962, Munger, Tolles & Olson, had prospered. At an exclusive preserve like Harvard Law School everyone was closely aware of which firms were deemed Okay (not so much because they served a certain kind of client or practiced a certain kind of law as because they offered an exclusively high-Mandarin peer group) and which were Not Okay. The three most Okay firms in Los Angeles in the mid-1970s were Gibson, Dunn & Crutcher and O'Melveny & Myers, the biggest corporate firms—and Munger, Tolles, the comer, which was the most Okay of all because it was small, the legal equivalent of an elite unit in the Army.

The first rule of meritocratic life is: No nepotism. So everybody in Cambridge thought Molly was barred, alas, from working at the one place in Los Angeles where a Harvard Law School graduate would most want to work. But Charlie Munger had actually left Munger, Tolles in 1965, only three years after he started it—partly because he got into an insoluble quarrel with one of his partners, mostly because his plan all along had been to get out as soon as his investing career was successful enough to make practicing law unnecessary. Molly, in her aspirations, was a Mandarin through and through; Charlie was a Talent trying to burst out of the Mandarin carapace. He didn't like serving clients, he didn't like having partners, and he didn't like being upper-middle-class. He wanted to be rich so he could be completely independent, like Crusoe on his island, and not have to do what anybody else said. Charlie's investments in apartment houses, in a decade when a thousand new people a week were moving to the Los Angeles basin, had begun to pay off handsomely, and he had also started an investment fund and persuaded a few people to pay him to play the stock market for them. Charlie got a ratty little office in the Pacific Stock Exchange building on the edge of downtown LA, with a sign on the door that said BLUE CHIP STAMPS, which was the name of the company he used as a business base. The scene didn't scan at all from a Mandarin point of view, but Charlie's change of careers meant that Molly was not banned from Munger, Tolles.

Molly went to see the leading female corporate lawyer in Los Angeles, Carla Hills, who was a friend of her father's (and soon became U.S. Trade Representative). The meeting was upsetting. What Molly wanted was exactly what Charlie didn't want, to spend her life as a partner in a prestigious, established law firm. That would be a breakthrough achievement for a woman in a way that it wasn't for a man, and Molly had a different personality from Charlie anyway, less obstreperous, less impatient with other people, more drawn to structure. Had she been elected to the *Harvard Law Review*? Carla Hills asked her. No. Well, then, Hills said, we're going to have to be a little creative here. She couldn't work at Munger, Tolles, or at Gibson, Dunn & Crutcher, or at O'Melveny & Myers. Los Angeles had come up in the world, it wasn't a provincial Western outpost anymore, and these firms were now filling their ranks with only the very best graduates of the very best law schools. Molly, who to outside appearances occupied the most rarefied possible niche in the American meritocracy, didn't make the cut. That hurt. Molly, Hills told her helpfully, life is tough and competitive.

Now Molly had an additional ambition motivating her in life. She had to demonstrate that she wasn't a notch below really first-rate. Her experiences thus far had put her into a certain peer group. Like anybody else, she judged herself by peer-group standards, in addition to her own larger and more abstract notion of what was good and valuable. Within her peer group— intelligent, rivalrous, conditioned to excel—distinctions that might be invisible to outsiders, like the distinction between a first-tier corporate law firm and a just-below-first-tier one, were vitally important. You couldn't not think about them. People are complicated, and life goes on at many levels at once, but still, when one aspect enlarges, others tend to shrink. It's inevitable. So as Molly's attention turned toward professional redemption, it turned away from the state of the wider world. This was ironic. What had propelled her into the meritocracy in the first place was a dissatisfaction with the smallness of white-glove women's Pasadena, its lack of a large democratic cause. Now she found herself preoccupied with the narrow inside concerns of her new milieu, and the concerns that had drawn her out of the Westridge School for Girls ten years earlier receded into the background.

Molly went to work for a small new firm called Agnew, Miller & Carlson, founded by lawyers who had left established firms (including O'Melveny & Myers) to start it. Its clients were corporations and bond companies, just like the clients at the big firms. The partners had gone to Harvard Law School, and they liked to hire from Harvard Law School. So Agnew, Miller, & Carlson was Okay: there was the security of meritocratic validation. Molly was the first woman to work there.

Having gone to law school without much focused enthusiasm, having disliked it, having half expected to be bored and frustrated by the practice of law because it involved hard long detailed work on recondite business disputes with no clear right or wrong, Molly was pleasantly surprised to find that she loved being a lawyer and was very good at it. She became a litigator, the toughest, most time-consuming, most confrontational and aggressive, most traditionally male of all the specialties within a typical corporate law practice. What attracted her to litigation was a love not so much of court battles as of big all-absorbing cases, and of breaking gender barriers. Her main case was a lawsuit being brought by a company that was trying to break into the tight but substantial (in those pre-video days) market for film reels and cans. Traveling, reading through cases, taking depositions, learning about the film-reel industry, all in search of the small decisive advantage—it was fun.

And at Agnew, Miller & Carlson, Molly fell in love. The lucky fellow was another young associate at the firm, Stephen English. Steve was also a Harvard Law School graduate. In fact they had overlapped there, but Molly hadn't known him, and he hadn't known her except in the sense that every male Harvard Law student knew who Molly Munger was. Love, or at least love leading to marriage, is often (one might even say, ideally) an unlikely mix of conventional surface social compatibility and the deepest inner longings of the soul. On the first of those dimensions, Molly and Steve were both lawyers, both children of southern California who had gone to Harvard. They were a good Mandarin fit, and that mattered to Molly.

It also meant a lot to Molly, though, that Steve wasn't just a standard-issue Mandarin. He had more depth, more humor; he saw life from an angle. Steve was the son of a career Navy officer who had grown up mostly in brand-new Los Angeles suburbs, not gracious suburbs like Pasadena but the kind where you were the first person ever to live in your house and there were no trees, where farmland butted up against the edge of the subdivision, where the people had moved out to California from some small cold place and felt themselves to have been transported to paradise. Steve wasn't much of a student. After high school he bounced around a little and worked odd jobs—lemon picker, encyclopedia salesman, fire-department brush clearer, collector and tabulator of response cards at a place where movies were test-marketed—and then wound up at Los Angeles Valley College in Van Nuys, in the San Fernando Valley. Educationally, Steve was a child of Clark Kerr and the Master Plan. Valley College was one of the two-year community colleges that Kerr had incorporated into the university system in order to be able to guarantee every high-school graduate a free higher education, and Steve was one of the tiny handful of community-college students who did well enough to qualify for a second-chance escape route from his original Master Plan destiny: he transferred to UCLA.

So Steve was atypical to begin with. At UCLA he did something that made him even more atypical, which was that he refused to take advantage of the great Mandarin perquisite of the Vietnam years, the student deferment from the draft, because he thought it was wrong. Instead he left school and applied for conscientious-objector status. That way he felt he could protest the war from a cleaner position than if he had made no personal commitment to accompany his views. As a conscientious objector, he got a part-time job washing test tubes in a hospital in East LA and slowly progressed through UCLA a few courses at a time. When he finally graduated he applied to Harvard Law School.

It wasn't that Steve was a typical 1960s protester. Molly's law-school friend Douglas Hallett, who was famous for being practically the only Republican at Harvard (and a minor White House aide during Watergate days), was also a friend of Steve's and a promoter of the courtship. It was that Steve was not the typical self-satisfied product of the new American meritocracy. His plain background, his easy, modest manner, his refusal to take himself too seriously, and his capacity for taking a moral stand were all at the core of his appeal to Molly. He wasn't like most of the men she had known in Cambridge, even though he had been validation-stamped. He didn't even look like a golden boy, being slight and dark-haired and understated in his handsomeness. He represented the system at its best, its most democratic and least cozy and arrogant. Molly felt a suffusing love and gratitude. She was so lucky! She had threaded some kind of needle. Having felt that she might never quite fit in—Pasadena was too stuffy, Harvard too snobbish, the political movements of the day too angry—she believed that in marriage to Steve she had found a spot that offered the blend of belief and betterment she had been looking for all her life.

Molly and Steve got engaged and left Agnew, Miller & Carlson. He went to a bigger firm where he could litigate major cases. She went to the U.S. Attorney's office. All over the country, the offices of the U.S. Attorneys— appointed federal prosecutors—provide safe harbor for people seeking temporary respite from the world of big law firms. You gave up some money to work in a U.S. Attorney's office, but in return you got litigation experience, the comfort of being in the company of a critical mass of other Mandarins (U.S. Attorneys' staffs were a blend of street-smart criminal lawyers and Ivy Leaguers), a chance to battle injustice rather than just one's client's business enemies, and, most important to Molly at that point, a significantly shorter workday than one had at a law firm. You could leave at six instead of nine. Molly was entering her thirties and she wanted to start a family. In the early 1980s she and Steve had two sons, nineteen months apart, Nick and Alfred, and bought a house in Pasadena.

19 The Fall of William Turnbull

Something that's terrible is coming.
I hear it in the depths of a forest. . . .
Steady, remorseless, slow-moving now, but slightly louder
And I know it is coming—
I know I can't escape it—
Know it will advance to where I stand, looking on all
  sides,
Knowing it will come steadily to me wherever I go.
And when it rises it seems to challenge me from far off.
To tell me it is coming, marching slow and steady,
And when it dies it seems to whisper, to mock me,
To say, "My power is irresistible, though I hush my voice."

Poor William Turnbull. In 1970, Henry Chauncey turned sixty-five and retired as president of ETS in a blaze of triumph. ETS had grown constantly, amazingly, during his time in charge of it. The SAT had just passed 2 million takers a year for the first time. Enrollment in American higher education was more than 8 million. Chauncey had successfully dodged every one of the many bullets that had been aimed at his organization over a quarter-century. He was silver-haired, still thickly black-eyebrowed, tall, and vigorous. The campus he had acquired and built for ETS and where he lived with his young wife and four daughters was mature now, a refuge from the world for psychometricians, with landscaped nature paths and a flock of geese swimming in the pond next to the entrance. At Chauncey's retirement dinner, which was held at the Pierre Hotel in New York City, one speaker said, grandly, "I think it's not too much to say that the standardized test has been a major factor in building an American society based upon individual merit and performance, and has helped us to avoid an aristocracy of wealth and family status." So Chauncey had fulfilled his original charge from James Bryant Conant.

Henry Chauncey did not write the poetry quoted above. For one thing he did not write poetry, and for another he did not fall prey to doubt or depression. Even William Turnbull, his successor as president of ETS, who did write the poem, would have seemed incapable of such bleak thoughts at the time he took over. But then things changed.

Bill Turnbull had grown up in St. Thomas, Ontario, Canada, where his father ran a department store. The youngest of three sons, he was a brilliant student; after graduating from the University of Western Ontario, he was awarded a scholarship to Princeton. There he completed his Ph.D. in psychology (his dissertation was on auditory function) in the shortest time ever recorded, eighteen months. And he met Henry Chauncey, who was working across the street from the Princeton campus at the College Board testing office. During his first months of graduate school, Turnbull began working part-time for the College Board, helping with the Army-Navy tests. Toward the end he moved into the Chaunceys' home in Princeton. Immediately upon getting his Princeton degree Turnbull went to work full-time for the College Board office rather than pursue an academic career. A few months later he married his high-school sweetheart and moved into his own place. Many years later he told an interviewer that ETS appealed to him because he wanted to find a way to avoid spending his life in a laboratory, but still to maintain "a rather orderly, quantifiable approach to phenomena of human characteristics."

By the time he became president of ETS, Turnbull had been Chauncey's number-two man for twenty-six years and had never worked anywhere else in his life. They made a good team. Turnbull, fifteen years younger, handled the administrative details and Chauncey dealt with the outside world. Chauncey, enthusiastic and commanding, made speeches, took trips to meet other leadership figures, and performed the innumerable ceremonial duties required of the head of ETS, toasting retirees and welcoming advanced-placement exam graders and so on. Turnbull, an indoorsy man with horn-rimmed glasses and fine, sharp features (thin lips, pointed nose, hair swept back from a widow's peak), was much more generously endowed than Chauncey with the quality that ETS measured, whatever you called it—scholastic aptitude, developed ability, intelligence. He was truly versed in psychometrics in a way that Chauncey was not. The professional staff adored him because he understood their work and protected them from Chauncey's amateur's enthusiasms, like the Census of Abilities. Chauncey depended on Turnbull because he was absolutely efficient and trustworthy.

An aging and somewhat crotchety Ben Wood wrote Turnbull a congratulatory letter when he became president, predicting that Chauncey and Turnbull together would one day be acknowledged as the "Educational Statesmen of the Century." Even to the less grandiloquent, Turnbull's succession to the top job looked like a sign that ETS had come of age and was being put in the hands of the expert class it had helped to create. The personnel department of the Mandarinate now had a leader who was himself a certified Mandarin.

Turnbull was prepared to deal with the conflict between the spread of standardized testing and the rising aspirations of minority groups, especially blacks. It had been building for years, and Turnbull had given it a great deal of thought, though he hadn't been able to find a dramatic solution—like most people at ETS, he strongly believed in the rightness of both sides of it, testing and black progress. What Turnbull was not prepared for at all was the possibility that the prime beneficiaries of the rise of ETS—extremely bright and ambitious young people who were good in school and hadn't been born into privilege—did not have warm, grateful feelings toward the organization.

Why was this? Was this bastion of psychologists who had stiffly resisted incorporating Freud and Jung into their work now being punished with some kind of Oedipal conflict or clash of archetypes? Whatever the reason, ETS, which had up to now been both admired and not very well known, was now famous and resented. The creation of a national educational market open to all, along with the unusual size of the young-adult generation in the 1970s, had made admission to the best colleges and graduate schools intensely competitive. Slots in elite higher education seemed like a resource that was both much scarcer and much more precious than ever before. And to get a slot required taking an ETS test. From there it was a short step to the idea that ETS was a "gatekeeper" that actually decided who went through the door and who was kept out.

The ETS style, that smoother-than-would-seem-possible blend of Grotonian paternalism and technological superefficiency, did not play well in the 1970s. From the outside ETS looked rich (that campus!) even though it was officially nonprofit, and also powerful, unaccountable, and secretive. As important as its tests were, it refused to give out much information about them, and it insisted that those who did, like Stanley Kaplan the test-prep king, were charlatans. The test-takers, who after all were paying for ETS with their fees, had no protection against a scoring error; they received their scores in the mail but were not allowed to see the graded tests they had taken. You had no option but to put yourself in ETS's hands, not ask questions, accept your scores trustingly—and, by extension, accept the fate to which your scores consigned you.

ETS's critics during Chauncey's regime had been either professional competitors in the testing business, or right-wingers, or bemused, recalcitrant members of the Episcopacy, or eccentric professors like Banesh Hoffmann. Now, in the Turnbull years, new critics appeared: left-wing academics reviving the war against IQ testing, black organizations, and, mostly, students. For aggressive young journalists, going after ETS was in the 1970s what questioning the official line of the American embassy in Saigon had been in the 1960s: a demonstration of the power of independent inquiry to discomfit entrenched power. Among the well-known figures who wrote populist attacks on ETS early in their careers were Steven Brill, founder of *The American Lawyer*, Court TV, and *Brill's Content*; the author James Fallows; Steven Levy of *Newsweek*; and David Owen of *The New Yorker*.

In 1971, at the annual convention of the American Psychological Association, a group of black psychologists formed a group that began criticizing ETS, previously a serenely accepted part of the APA world. In 1972, ETS's director of minority affairs, a former journalist named Chuck Stone, quit and began appearing on national television to say that ETS tests were biased against minorities. Steven Brill's article, the first of the new journalistic salvos against ETS, appeared in *New York* magazine in 1974, when Brill was still a student at Yale Law School. For the first time ETS was being talked about, and not reverently, outside the world of educational administration. The talk reached and affected many people—the single most troublesome of whom, as far as ETS was concerned, was Ralph Nader.

Nader was the kind of person who would have been favorably commented upon if his name had come up during lunchtime at the ETS cafeteria. He was himself a product of the American meritocracy, the son of a small-town Lebanese-American shopkeeper who had been able to attend Princeton and Harvard Law School thanks to his superior academic ability (as demonstrated, no doubt, by his test scores). When Nader became famous in the 1960s for his crusades against automobile companies and federal agencies for their parlous inattention to public safety, he was doing just the kind of thing that people at ETS thought they were doing: building a better world by trying to replace shoddy, corrupt practices with clean, good, modern ones. As he went from solo reformer to head of a series of organizations (nonprofit, just like ETS), he surrounded himself with assistants who were idealistic young people with the very finest Mandarin credentials, just like the people who had worked for Henry Chauncey in the early days of ETS.

In the early 1970s Nader happened upon a copy of Banesh Hoffmann's book *The Tyranny of Testing*, and read it with consuming interest. Nader spent a great deal of time speaking on college campuses. After his lectures were over, he liked to sit around with students and talk into the night. In these sessions he began hearing complaints about ETS as the General Motors of the education world, an arrogant, unaccountable monopoly. Nader worked criticisms of ETS into his campus lectures. One fateful evening in the spring of 1974 Nader spoke at a community college in New Jersey, and afterward one of the people who came up to talk to him, a high-school senior named Allan Nairn, proposed that the two of them team up and mount a full-scale investigation of ETS. Nader said: Sure.

As a student at a public high school in New Jersey, Nairn had been horrified by the gravity with which SAT scores were treated by his teachers, his fellow students, and their parents. There was a whole culture of obsession with them, the creepiness of which never fully registered within ETS. Students who got low scores would go around looking deflated, believing they had been scientifically adjudged stupid and sure never to amount to anything. Kids with rich parents would take Stanley Kaplan's course and their scores would go up, despite ETS's insistence that that was impossible; kids with poor or apathetic parents had to settle for whatever scores they got. Nairn wrote a letter to the Federal Trade Commission demanding that ETS be investigated for profiteering; he got a reply saying that ETS couldn't be guilty of that because it was nonprofit.

During the period of the Nader-Nairn investigation, Nairn was an undergraduate student at Princeton—not exactly the kind of person ETS would have thought qualified to evaluate its performance. How would Henry Chauncey have handled Nader and Nairn? Invited them for a tour of the campus followed by dinner with Laurie and the girls, and then perhaps an invitation to join one or another of ETS's advisory committees so that their provocative ideas could be given full consideration? Bill Turnbull's reaction was clenched and maladroit. He was both more open than Chauncey would have been (he met with Nairn three times, spoke several times with Nader on the phone, and gave instructions that other ETS officials speak to Nairn) and less open. Turnbull proposed to Nader that he add trained psychometricians to his team, have all the interviews professionally transcribed, and then submit the report to ETS before publication so that it could be reviewed for accuracy. He saw these suggestions as a welcoming of Nader and Nairn into the standard practices of academic peer review. They saw them as stonewalling and censorship. Even before Nairn's research had gotten under way, Nader and ETS were publicly feuding.

Nader was then at the height of his influence. His decision to investigate ETS had reverberations far beyond just Allan Nairn's writing a report. The Federal Trade Commission, an earlier target of a Nader inquiry, had reformed itself and become quite friendly to him. Its Boston office launched an investigation of the test-prep industry, and it found that coaching did raise scores. This was the next thing to a federal investigation of ETS, since the point was to undercut ETS's insistence that its tests were uncoachable. Several liberal congressmen who were sympathetic to Nader—Benjamin Rosenthal and Ted Weiss of New York, Michael Harrington of Massachusetts—let ETS know they were thinking of holding hearings about it, like the old sensational congressional hearings into the misdeeds of the banks and trusts and monopolies. Nader had founded state "Public Interest Research Groups" all over the country to encourage student political activity; the one in New York, followed by many others, began pushing for "truth in testing" legislation under which ETS would have to allow students to see their graded tests, and would publicly release old tests. At one point in the late 1970s there were bills to regulate ETS pending in thirty-seven state legislatures. By now Turnbull had trouble getting Nader to return his calls. For Nader the ETS project was merely one of 150 he was overseeing, and not the nearest to his heart. But Turnbull's whole life, it seemed, was devoted to fending off Ralph Nader and his allies.

What Turnbull did not do was become a public defender of ETS and testing. Instead he retreated into his office. For every argument made against ETS, he developed a response, which he would write down in his tiny, precise handwriting and not tell anybody. When a politician demanded the presence of an ETS official at a hearing, he would send one of the vice presidents rather than go himself. He had ETS, for the first time in its history, hire professional lobbyists to help take care of its problems in the state legislatures.

In 1978 the California legislature passed its truth-in-testing bill, but ETS's lobbyists in Sacramento and its many friends in California higher education had succeeded in watering it down so much that it had no effect on ETS. The next year, the battle shifted to New York, where the forces behind the truth-in-testing legislation were much more intransigent.

Donald Ross, head of the New York Public Interest Research Group, somehow got the head of the state senate education committee in Albany, Kenneth LaValle, to sponsor a bill. Usually it was Democratic and minority legislators who pushed truth in testing. LaValle was a white Republican from the Long Island suburbs, but he represented a district of middle-class people preoccupied with education above all else; he was himself a former public-school teacher; and a big public university, the Stony Brook campus of the State University of New York, was in his district. He heard endless complaints from his constituents and friends about the arbitrariness and exaggerated importance of standardized test scores. Although ETS always maintained that universities used test scores just as one piece of useful information, the word on Long Island was that the SUNY system had absolute minimum SAT cutoff scores below which they would not admit anyone. LaValle was personally annoyed at standardized testing because his daughter worked hard and got mediocre scores, and his son goofed off and did fabulously well on tests. It bothered him that the system favored his son over his daughter.

In 1977 and 1978 LaValle had introduced the truth-in-testing bill and nothing happened—it didn't even get on the legislative calendar. In 1979, though, political momentum, that mystical force, was somehow on his side. Allan Nairn arrived in Albany, accompanied by a crew of college-kid volunteer assistants, and moved into LaValle's office to lobby and to generate research materials. Everything about ETS's effort to fight the bill—its hiring of fancy Albany lobbyists, its marshaling of haughty opposition from the education establishment, its insistence that only trained testing professionals could possibly understand the issues involved—made it look like a high-handed cartoon villain, and that spurred on the gang in LaValle's office to stay up late more nights, fueled by more Big Macs, and write more rebutting memos and make more pleading phone calls.

Albany's legislative session ended in June. As late as early May, ETS was confident that the truth-in-testing bill would never come to a vote. On May 9, LaValle put on a long hearing on the bill, featuring a murderer's row of ETS critics ("ETS is one of the most extravagantly administered institutions in American education. Iran's Shah would feel right at home," Chuck Stone testified). Then ETS booked its highest-ranking black executive, E. Belvin Williams, onto the *Today* show to defend the cause. Williams was introduced as an opponent of test disclosure, but when Bill Turnbull turned on his television that morning, he was astonished to hear Williams correct the host: No, no, he wasn't against test disclosure, he thought it was a good idea.

LaValle's Democratic co-sponsor was a state senator from Brooklyn named Donald Halperin, who way back in the 1950s in Flatbush had been one of the striving Jewish boys tutored for the SAT by Stanley Kaplan. At the hearing, Halperin came out with Kaplan's little secret (the one ETS had known about for decades but kept quiet), which was that he encouraged his students to memorize test questions and then taught new students from the lists he had compiled. When Halperin took the SAT he recognized many of the questions and already knew the answers to them. Wasn't it unfair, Halperin said, that he should have had this immense advantage over the average SAT-takers who couldn't get hold of test questions?

The hearing frightened ETS and it began pushing much harder against the bill. Letters and calls from prominent people poured into the legislature. Columbia and New York University, the leading private universities in New York City, opposed the truth-in-testing bill. The American Council on Education and ETS's archrival, the American College Testing program, were against it. The state education department and the State University of New York and the state civil service commission were against it. The medical schools and the law schools and the business schools and the graduate schools were against it.

The main specific objection to the bill had to do with a process called equating, which is the art of making sure that scores on different administrations of a test are comparable even though exactly the same questions aren't used. On every SAT there was an "equating section" that, unbeknownst to the test-taker, didn't go toward determining the score. Instead it was made up of questions being tried out for use in future tests. ETS would cross-tabulate people's scores on the trial questions with their scores on the questions that counted, so as to be sure that after the old questions had been retired, the new ones were introduced in a mix that kept the test's overall degree of difficulty precisely the same. ETS's argument was that if it made old tests public, people would be getting an advance peek at questions that were likely still to be in use—that is, the questions in the equating section. The security of the test would be ruined.

The truth-in-testing forces faked out ETS by resisting and resisting and then, at the last minute, agreeing to exempt the equating questions from disclosure. That robbed ETS of its strongest argument.

The session was set to end on June 17. The Senate debated the truth-in-testing bill on June 14 and passed it by a vote of 38–17. The Assembly scheduled its vote for June 16, the last full day of the session.

For a legislative body to hold a last-minute debate on a vital matter without anyone knowing how the vote will turn out is the equivalent of the murderer confessing to the crime under cross-examination: it happens in the movies, not in real life. This was a case where the movie version actually happened. The debate went back and forth for a while, and then a big, bluff Republican ex-cop named John Flanagan (no liberal change-the-worlder, in other words, but a normal guy) stood up and gave an extemporaneous speech that palpably turned the mood of the chamber in favor of the bill:

> I only wish that all of you could take a little field trip to the Educational Testing Service laboratories and the big operation they are running in Princeton, New Jersey . . . and see how much money is being spent, not only in preparing the exams, but in preparing the people who prepare the exams for the kinds of life they want to lead, giving them the proper kinds of accoutrements.

That was just the warm-up. The knockout punch was Flanagan's expertly playing to the collective hatred of a chamber dominated by the grandchildren of immigrants toward the heartless plutocrat class of the early twentieth century. ETS, Flanagan explained, was, beneath its technocratic exterior, the same kind of folks that had caused New York's most notorious industrial accident, the Triangle Shirtwaist Factory fire of 1911, which killed 146 Jewish women who had been locked into a room with their sewing machines:

> Now, you know this State was the first State to put those little boxes on the doors with the bulbs in them that say "Exit," and that the Triangle Shirt Factory fire started that, and we know that was debated on the floor here and Al Smith was the fellow who was the big pusher for that particular bill. That was the guy saying, "It's going to hurt business. It's a little extra expense, we don't need it." They didn't say it after the fire.

The Assembly broke out in applause. So much for the natural aristocracy commanding the devotion of the people and their tribunes! The vote began at eight o'clock in the evening. The members were exhausted. When the clerk began to call the roll, name by name, it still wasn't clear how it would turn out. Both sides were still lobbying ferociously even after the voting had begun. The Assembly had 150 members. They voted alphabetically. Finally, at Strelzin, the seventy-sixth vote for the bill came in.

Governor Hugh Carey had to sign the bill within a month or it would become null and void. Carey was a lawyer. The deans of all the law schools in New York State went to see him and pressed him not to sign it. He began to waver. The truth-in-testing forces struck back with one final trick, which was inducing one of Carey's many college-age children, none of whom was a high scorer on standardized tests, to put a bit of direct family pressure on him. On July 13, three days before the deadline, Carey signed.

In the fall of 1979 Kenneth LaValle was finally invited to come down to Princeton for the traditional critic-disarming tour of ETS. It was conducted by a vice president, not Bill Turnbull.

The people who celebrated the truth-in-testing law as a great victory were the ones who had pushed it through, LaValle and Nairn and their motley crew. The person with the most reason to be overjoyed, though, was probably Stanley Kaplan. For more than thirty years one thing had eaten away at Kaplan. As successful as his test-prep business became, he could not get ETS to regard him as anything but a disreputable character who either stole test materials or made false promises to students about the possibility of raising their scores, or both. Kaplan revered education in general and ETS in particular. He didn't have a trace of Nader and Nairn's cynical attitude toward ETS; rather, he craved the approval of the fine, university-educated men at the Princeton campus.

Kaplan now had an opening, finally, to make peace with ETS. He became a spirited public defender of ETS against Nader. Once he participated in a public debate with Ralph Nader, he taking ETS's side. Tendrils of direct contact began to curl out from ETS toward Kaplan. In addition, the passage of the truth-in-testing law opened the way for the test-prep business to become respectable at last.

ETS decided to treat the New York truth-in-testing law as if it were federal legislation, since it would be too difficult to make up one set of tests for New Yorkers that would be made public later and another set for everyone else that wouldn't. So old tests were now published nationally. If the old tests were in the public record and Kaplan's instructors taught from them, there would be no question where they had gotten them. The claim that test prep was a waste of time was laid to rest, too. The Federal Trade Commission, an agency of the United States government, after all, had declared that it worked.

A few years later, Stanley Kaplan, the Brooklyn boy who hadn't been able to find a job after college, sold his test-prep business to the Washington Post Company for $50 million.

Allan Nairn's report on ETS was published in 1980. It accused ETS of just about everything it could plausibly be accused of, from being rich to having grown out of the eugenics movement to ignoring the rights of test-takers to being biased against minorities. Nairn's central premise was that ETS, under a veneer of science, functioned as the opposite of a meritocratic force in American society. It provided an official way for people with money to pass on their status to their children. Even the title of the report, *The*

Reign of ETS, was an insult, turning on its head as it did the old Groton motto, "To serve is to reign." ETS in the hands of Nairn was nakedly interested in the second half of the equation and not at all in the first.

"It's unrelievedly bad. Nader report is to reporting as caricature is to portraiture. What a contrast to his promise of an objective report that tells all, good and bad," Bill Turnbull wrote, in his neat, tiny hand, in the notes he made after reading the report, echoing unconsciously (or maybe not) the analogies section of the SAT-verbal. Nairn was not adept enough in his handling of the technical aspects of testing to have much impact in the world of psychometrics, but it did look as if he had started a movement. He was substantially responsible for the truth-in-testing law. He impelled ETS to launch a blizzard of research reports and special committees to look into charges he had made. Just after the report was published a student at Princeton, John Katzman, started a test-prep company called the Princeton Review, which competed with Kaplan and publicly struck a Nairn-like pose of contempt for ETS and testing, in contrast to Kaplan's reverence.

Katzman and Kaplan couldn't have been more different. Kaplan, no matter how much money he made, was eternally lower-middle-class, with his reverence for authority, his unnaturally neat coiffure, and his stiff unstylish suits. Katzman was young, rich, blond, tall, and handsome in a tousled, informal way. Kaplan's world was public schools in Brooklyn, Katzman's private schools in Manhattan. The emotional reservoir Kaplan drew upon was the dream of maybe, possibly making it, by getting into the right college or professional school; for Katzman it was the fear of downward mobility, of being cast out of the Mandarin compound and consigned to dreary Liferdom because of low test scores.

Like Allan Nairn, Katzman had grown up in a subculture that seemed to revolve around ETS tests and college admissions. Nothing would have tormented James Bryant Conant more than seeing at first hand this particular corner of the system he created. The very privileged denizens of Park Avenue he'd thought he was stripping of advantage were now trying like mad to manipulate testing and admissions on behalf of their children, and having quite a good deal of success. They were hiring SAT tutors at prices running up to hundreds of dollars an hour—if not "advisors" who'd "help" kids write their personal, deeply felt applications essays for fees in the thousands. They were relentlessly pressuring the expensive private schools where they sent their children to improve their Ivy League admissions results, by whatever means necessary. They were having doctors certify their children as learning-disabled, because that way ETS would let them take untimed SATs. They were making strategic donations to their alma maters, knowing that would hugely improve their children's chances. And the reason they wanted their offspring to be selected for the natural aristocracy was not so that they could be selfless public servants, but to put them on the track to prestigious jobs that paid a lot of money.

Within the private schools, everybody knew everybody else's SAT scores. Whoever got a high score was forever adjudged smart (including internally), and whoever got a low score, dumb. Everyone treated you differently once they knew your scores—teachers, other kids, even your own family. Katzman himself felt he had to score higher than his older brother, or . . . what? Well, it would be unthinkable. He did ten points better.

In this atmosphere of overwhelming anxiety, the Kaplan course, with its big, earnest classes, didn't fit the bill. As Katzman put it: "It had the sheen of being for losers," and no Manhattan private-school kid wanted to be identified as having taken a Kaplan course. But a course that accomplished the same goal of raising scores, maybe even more effectively, while at the same time taking the position that SATs were pernicious, meaningless bullshit foisted upon America's youth by a greedy corporation—that was what Katzman's constituency was looking for.

In the early days Katzman obtained his prep materials by doing exactly what Kaplan had done in his early days. As he put it: "We'd send people in to take tests, and send ourselves in. I'd take ten, fifteen kids and say: I'll buy you Chinese food if you tell me as many questions as you can remember." That technique, along with Katzman's pronouncements about testing, made ETS feel about him about the way it had once felt about Kaplan. Once Katzman let a few real SAT questions slip into one of his published booklets (Just an accident! Sorry!) and ETS sued him. But over the years Princeton Review, like Kaplan, became a respectable business, thanks in part to the publication of old tests under the truth-in-testing law. As much as Katzman opposed ETS tests, his activities didn't serve to make them any less important—if anything, the opposite. Test prep became one of the stations of the cross for upper-middle-class American adolescents. In a smaller way, teaching Princeton Review courses was a widely shared experience among young Mandarins who were out of college and in need of a little extra cash—the modern equivalent of what being a tennis instructor at a country club had been back in the heyday of the Episcopacy.

Even Ralph Nader, who had no pecuniary interest in testing, did not wind up whittling down its place in American society. Bill Turnbull came to believe that Nader's real goal wasn't the reform of ETS but, as he put it to an interviewer, "the substantial weakening, if not the destruction, of testing itself." But this was a misreading of Nader, born of self-pity.

It was true that Nader would probably have been happy to see the SAT abolished. The quality he valued most highly was "bulldog commitment," rather than scholastic aptitude. It bothered him that ETS anointed conventionally bright, studious, and obedient students, and weeded out tough, gritty underdogs who might shake things up. Nader once suggested to Turnbull's horror that perhaps colleges and professional schools should select their students on the basis of the likelihood of their becoming social activists, rather than their predicted grade-point averages.

Still, Nader believed in rules and systems, as long as they had been reformed. The idea of replacing the ETS tests with other, better, and possibly even more numerous tests appealed to him. A movement was beginning in psychometrics to replace IQ-descended tests like the SAT, which sought to understand the mind on the single dimension of intelligence, with tests for specific skills and a more complex set of mental traits, like creativity and practicality. That made sense to Nader. "Let's say the country desperately needs community organizers," he said. "How do you test for it?" He, like most other liberal critics of the SAT, was instinctively drawn to something akin to Henry Chauncey's Census of Abilities—an idealized, perfected, and even more comprehensive testing regime. The net result of the truth-in-testing movement was more anxiety about testing among students, more test prep, and, at least at the level of discussion, more tests. So much for the destruction of testing itself.

What was destroyed was Bill Turnbull. Turnbull felt more and more under attack, and helpless to do anything about it. All his lifelong assumptions about testing, education, and society had been turned on their head, and he had unwittingly led the institution he loved into a danger against which he was powerless to defend it. He brooded, he wrote tormented notes to himself, he shut himself up in his office, and, more and more, he drank. In the early years of his presidency colleagues who went on road trips with him were surprised to see how heavily he drank when he was away from ETS. Then as time went on he began to drink more in Princeton—even alone in his office. Once at a party at his house on the campus he passed out and had to be taken to the hospital. Another time he missed a dinner with the board of trustees because he was too drunk.

After the truth-in-testing law passed, Henry Chauncey happened to be in Princeton one evening before a board meeting. He stopped by Turnbull's office to ask him how things were going, and Turnbull said, "We've got troubles." What are the troubles? Chauncey asked him. "Me," Turnbull said.

That board meeting was the one where Turnbull was asked to resign as president of ETS. He didn't leave—he never left. He was appointed a senior research scientist. He made some notes toward a book that would defend testing against its attackers, but he never wrote it. In 1983, after being arrested for driving while intoxicated, he checked himself into a rehabilitation center for alcoholics. In 1986, while undergoing heart-bypass surgery, he died on the operating table.

As successor to Turnbull, the ETS board picked an outsider, Gregory Anrig, commissioner of education for Massachusetts—Horace Mann's old job. Anrig was like Chauncey and Turnbull in being a true believer in education, with a totality that only the unconscious and conscious minds working as a team can produce. His father had died, in the middle of the Depression, when he was only three, and his mother found that to get a job, she had to pretend to be single. So Anrig spent his childhood as a paying boarder in other people's homes, feeling exquisitely self-conscious and unwanted. The only thing good in his life was school. He was the first member of his family to graduate from college, and then he became a teacher, working his way up through the public-education system.

The difference between Anrig and his predecessors was that he had no particular commitment to protecting testing from outside interference. A beefy, hearty, extroverted, red-faced man, he was a natural politician who had only a hazy familiarity with psychometrics. Indeed, his passion was for public-school skills tests like the National Assessment of Educational Progress, not the mental tests for admission that were ETS's main business. Occasionally he would cause mild embarrassment at ETS by using a testing term like "reliability" in public in a way that showed he didn't quite understand what it meant. For a time he decreed that the SAT questions on which there was the highest black–white difference in the number of correct answers simply be dropped so that the racial gap in scores would shrink; an outcry from psychometricians made him drop the idea.

Anrig was almost unimaginably better than Turnbull at dealing with the world beyond the gates of the ETS campus. When he was in government in Massachusetts he had testified in the state legislature in favor of the truth-in-testing law, and at ETS he quickly established warm personal relations with Ken LaValle of the New York State Senate. He gave Stanley Kaplan the greatest thrill of his life by first arranging for him to be invited to speak at a College Board conference, and then inviting him to the ETS campus, from which he had long been barred, for a private chat in the president's office. (John Katzman wasn't invited.) He brought to ETS all the country's leading critics of testing, except for Nader and Nairn. He patched things up with the country's biggest teachers' union, the National Education Association, which had severed relations with ETS during the truth-in-testing battle. Turnbull had banned the use of the word "marketing" from all ETS materials (too vulgarly commercial); Anrig established a marketing department.

ETS had won. By shifting from resistance to accommodation—a shift symbolized by the switch from Turnbull to Anrig—it had been able to protect its unusual position as a private organization that conducts an important, and elsewhere public, job substantially free from public control. The United States remained the most extensively aptitude-tested nation in the world. All ETS had lost, really, besides the vote in Albany, was something so intangible and deeply buried that nobody outside the organization would have even noticed that it was gone: the conviction that testing was not an interest, but a cause.

book 3

THE
GUARDIANS

20
Behind the Curtain

Molly Munger and Steve English settled into a life in Pasadena, a life in which they had the feeling of exploring new social territory. When Molly was growing up, her father had a job and her mother didn't. That was the situation in every family she knew. Though her parents' personalities—her mother's shyness and doubt, her attunement to the world's injustices, her father's exuberant, almost arrogant confidence—weren't the products of this arrangement, they could have been. Now she and Steve were going to live differently, both carrying on important careers while raising their two sons. That meant they (which meant, especially, Molly) had to figure it out as they went along. What did you do? You worked. You tried to reduce your office hours, as Molly had done in switching from private practice to the U.S. Attorney's office, but still you worked, a lot. You were too busy to fix up your house to a level that would win the approval of your parents. And you got someone to help take care of the children.

Here is what *Where They Are Now*, the book about the women in the Harvard Law School class of 1974, had to say about Molly as a relatively new mother:

> Molly Munger . . . is determined not to let her two children slow her down and finds she needs an outward focus to her life. She returned to work as a litigator within five weeks after the births of each of her two sons. She had intended to take three months off after her first son was born but ended up calling her boss and begging to return earlier. "All babies do is eat and sleep," she says. "It was uninteresting to be around them. Their needs were easily met by others." Munger and her

husband, also a lawyer, now employ two au pairs to care for their children in their Pasadena home. During the week Munger spends two hours each morning with the children. When she and her husband arrive home from work in Los Angeles their children are already asleep.

These were the early days of the working professional mother. A mutually reinforcing fierceness, of determination to pull it off on the mothers' part and doubt that they could on their employers' part, gave the whole business a sharp edge. Alice Young, like Molly, obtained a three-month maternity leave after her first child was born, but she cut it short to get back to work. Alice's sister Nancy, also a corporate lawyer, took no maternity leave at all after the births of her two children; the morning after her younger child was born, a client called and said, demandingly, cluelessly, "I called you three times yesterday and you didn't call back! Where were you?"

Molly was working out something else at the same time. As a proud graduate-by-choice of the Pasadena public-school system and stepdaughter of a school-board member, she was wondering whether it was going to be okay to send her sons to public school. During the eight years she had been away, a successful civil-rights lawsuit against the Pasadena school system had been followed by a desegregation plan, which was followed by white parents pulling their children out of the system en masse. When Molly went looking for supplemental child care, she did it by posting a notice at Blair High School, which was heavily black, not the conventional place for a white Pasadena lawyer to look for babysitters. But she wanted to get a feeling for what went on in the Pasadena schools before she and Steve decided where to educate their boys.

So it was that Molly met two teenage sisters named Nina and Lisa Edwards, who changed her life.

Nina and Lisa first of all illustrated the peculiarity of race in America. Their father was a black man raised in the United States, their mother a Persian raised in India; he had served in Vietnam with the Agency for International Development, and they had met in Bangkok. After they married, they moved back to the United States and settled in Montclair, New Jersey, a suburb of New York City that prides itself on being racially integrated and tolerant—Alice Young and her husband, as an Asian-Caucasian couple, settled in Montclair for just that reason. Even in Montclair, though, the black families lived mainly on the poorer side of town, and the white families lived mainly in the other, richer section. The Edwards family lived at first on the black side and then bought a house in the least affluent part of the white side of Montclair. Still, by American customs of three centuries' standing, under which any detectable portion of African ancestry puts a person on the black side of the racial line, Nina and Lisa grew up thinking of themselves, and being thought of by others, as black.

Nina and Lisa's parents got divorced. Their father essentially disappeared, and their mother, suddenly poor, decided to move to Pasadena, where her former mother-in-law, practically the only person she knew well in the United States, lived. She was absolutely opposed to going on welfare or even getting food stamps or unemployment insurance; instead she got a minimum-wage job at a Bullock's department store, moonlighted by selling subscriptions to the *Los Angeles Times* door to door with her children in tow and getting herself licensed as a real-estate agent, and scrounged. The family was what sociologists would call working poor. They bought their food at a store that sold damaged groceries at low prices, and their household goods at a store that sold discontinued products, and their clothes at a store that sold factory rejects. They never went hungry, but they could never eat whatever they wanted either. They had no health insurance and couldn't go to a doctor except in an emergency. Happy family times, quiet evenings spent going over homework, long supportive talks, vacations—all that was lost in the press of an all-consuming struggle just to get by.

Through her real-estate contacts Nina and Lisa's mother found a great deal on a house in Pasadena only a few blocks from where Molly and Steve lived. In general the richer people in Pasadena lived on the south side and the poorer people on the north side; Molly and Steve, though, lived in a lovely little neighborhood on the north side, tucked into the parkland behind the Rose Bowl. Less than a mile away, directly east, was the center of Pasadena's black ghetto; and halfway there was a small middle-class black enclave where the Edwards family lived. Molly would often drive through this area and think: Here is the good news in American race relations, the growth of the black middle class. And meeting Nina and Lisa, who were warm, talented, intelligent, and attractive, only underscored the impression.

The situation looked quite different from Nina and Lisa's perspective. They were like characters in a stock drama about the vagaries of a rigid caste system. Although their connection to the African-American ethno-cultural experience was tenuous—they never saw their black father, their mother was not black, they practiced the Baha'i faith, and in appearance they were unidentifiably omni-ethnic, with olive skin and wavy black hair and unaccented speech—they had been assigned, or consigned, to live as black people. What did that mean, in post-civil-rights America, under the palm trees and the blue sky of Pasadena, California? It meant everything, actually. Black people's lives and white people's lives still differed profoundly.

If you were Nina and Lisa, being black meant that your ordinary range of social contacts extended east from your middle-class enclave into the ghetto, rather than west into the fancier white neighborhood where Molly lived. You went to a nearly all-black school: in the case of Nina and Lisa, initially, Washington Alternative School, a formerly wonderful place in the heart of the ghetto.

In 1978 California's voters passed Proposition 13, a citizen initiative that froze state property tax revenues and thereby choked off public education's money supply. Prop 13 was a big event not just in California but nationally. Proposed by a couple of men whom most politicians considered to be aging cranks, it was wildly, unexpectedly popular, and it ushered in a long period in which tax cutting was the dominant cause in American politics. Prop 13 spelled doom for the founders' idea of the American meritocracy, an ever growing government run by natural aristocrats for the good of all. More immediately, for Nina and Lisa, it brought budget cuts for Washington Alternative School of such magnitude that the school had to shut down part of its building. Lisa left and went to Wilson Junior High. If you were black at Wilson and approached the white kids in school, wanting to be friends, they treated you in a nervous manner and edged away, and you felt they would never be more than cordial, would never really stand up for you in a pinch.

Being black meant that there was no plausible link between your world and any social destination you'd enthusiastically want to reach. It meant that in your social milieu, the basic male-female bond for some reason wasn't working. Most fathers were gone; most mothers were depressed, struggling, preoccupied, and emotionally unavailable, like Nina and Lisa's mother; most boys seemed to be setting off down a road that would end with their being disappeared fathers one day, too, and most girls were having babies in high school. They wanted to! The appeal of it was the possibility of getting the kind of unconditional love you desperately wanted but didn't have in your own life—a love that was under your control rather than always tormenting you by moving out of reach. Lisa thought her friends were also feeling an unexpected, deep, strong impulse just to reproduce the race, to generate another black soul, a replacement for one of the myriad people who had died or drifted away.

It meant that drugs and violence—the threat of violence, the fear of violence, the loss of friends to violence—were part of your daily life as they weren't for people who lived on the other side of the color line. Lisa had a close friend named Jill. Jill's best friend, Theresa, was a student at Elliott Junior High. Thuggish older boys would hang around the margins of the public schools in Pasadena, selling drugs and trying to pick up girls. Theresa became involved with one of them, a guy who was working part-time as a security guard.

One day he murdered her, hacked her body to pieces, put the pieces in a box, and left the box outside the schoolyard.

Lisa went into shock. She decided not to tell her mother about the murder because that would just lead to a lecture about hanging around with the wrong people. So she locked it up inside of her and went around like a thirteen-year-old zombie, not thinking about schoolwork or anything else, not connecting to other people. That was the state she was in when she and Nina answered the ad Molly posted at Blair High School.

Lisa and Nina started working for Molly every Saturday. Had they gotten weekend jobs at Disneyland instead, the feeling of entering a fantasy world would have been no stronger. Molly's house was just a short walk away from their home, but traveling that tiny distance was like going to another planet—the planet of white people, of the rare white people who welcomed you—where all the rules and all the assumptions about life were different. People weren't strapped all the time; money was not a constant subject. An unlimited, ongoing review of what one might want to do in life (anything!) was part of the fabric of conversation. Nobody ever thought about physical danger. Women had husbands.

Nina gravitated to Nick English and Lisa to the baby, Alfred. Having Alfred in her life, she always thought, answered some deep need that otherwise she might have answered by having her own baby. And Molly, who may have been flummoxed by babies but was fabulous with teenage girls, became Lisa's second, much more generous and understanding, mother. Before long it wasn't just Nina and Lisa at Molly's house every weekend but most of their friends, too. Molly would talk to them about their lives, and she made the assumption, entirely strange to them, that they could play whatever role had the greatest appeal to them.

Underneath the bonhomie, Molly found her new relationship with Nina and Lisa and their friends—well, in truth, disturbing. She had had some contact with the black side of Pasadena in school in the 1960s. Now things seemed much worse—worse than she had let herself imagine. It was amazing to her that the color line was still so powerful. Molly's whole life since junior high school had been built around the general idea, which she truly believed in, of America as a meritocracy, and the particular idea, which seemed to fit with it quite naturally, of better opportunity for blacks. It was the governing principle in her own life, and she presumed it was in everybody else's, too. But she couldn't honestly make herself believe that the lives Nina and Lisa led were those of low-on-merit proletarians occupying their earned place in society. For example, the girls were bright and verbally adept, but Molly began to notice, without saying anything about it, that they couldn't read very well. Why was that? Why hadn't anybody noticed? And what about all the violence in their neighborhood? That wasn't supposed to be part of the package of life on the lower-middle rung of a fair society.

Molly and Steve decided not to send their sons to public school. Instead they enrolled Nick and Alfred in a new, experimental private school called Sequoia, started by 1960s people who wanted to instill a reformist spirit in their students.

That was only the beginning of the effect of knowing Nina and Lisa. It was as if Molly had been given a horrifying peek behind a curtain that for most people like her was firmly drawn shut. She was still focused, ferociously so, on the goal of becoming a first-generation important woman lawyer—of winning her own place in the new meritocratic elite. But encountering Nina and Lisa introduced another element into her thinking, a doubt about the goodness of the system overall, which went along with, and rubbed up against, her determination to succeed in it personally. Molly wanted the American meritocracy to be good for her, and also good. So even as she attended to her rise in the world, the upsetting new information that Nina and Lisa had presented to her began to fill up more and more space in her mind.

21

Berkeley Squeezed

B ill Lee and Don Nakanishi were not close friends, but their lives seemed to move in a time-delayed tandem fashion. The bolder and more confrontational Don would arrive at a position that struck shy, cautious Bill as excessive—but within a few years Bill would find that he'd wound up in the same place. Back in their undergraduate days at Yale, Bill had been much more resistant to political protest than Don, only to become, as an adult, a professional political reformer in the employ of the NAACP Legal Defense Fund. Don's idea of Asian-Americans as an ethno-cultural-political group had initially struck Bill as ridiculous: Chinese-Americans like him and Japanese-Americans like Don not only had nothing in common but were historic enemies. When Don, after graduate school, moved back home to Los Angeles and began teaching at UCLA and stirring up Asian-American political activity, Bill stayed in New York and involved himself in racial issues. But Bill found himself feeling the pull of California in the early 1980s, at around the time of the birth of his first child, substantially because he thought the pan-Asian atmosphere there would be good for his daughter. Bill decided to leave the Legal Defense Fund, which had offices only on the East Coast, move to Los Angeles, and take a job with the Center for Law in the Public Interest.

Something palpable was happening in California—maybe not the formation of a smoothly blended new ethnic group, but certainly a dramatic rise in the number and visibility and status of Asians of all nationalities. A series of changes in the immigration laws, beginning with those in the Immigration Act of 1965, had lifted a long-standing, nearly total ban on Asian emigrants. (Before the 1965 law, only 2,990 people a year from the entire continent of

Asia were allowed to immigrate to the United States.) The end of the Vietnam War set off a flood of refugees from the war itself, who were afraid the victors would kill them; and the new laws also allowed in Koreans, Filipinos, and Taiwanese, whose opportunities back home were severely limited. The Asian-American population grew from 1.5 million in 1970, to 3 million in 1980, to 7 million in 1990.

Los Angeles was the capital city of Asian America. Gone were the days of there being two Asian enclaves in the whole Southland, the old downtown Chinatown for Chinese-Americans and Gardena for Japanese-Americans. Now there was a big, booming Koreatown just west of downtown; the country's main concentration of Indochinese immigrants in lower-middle-class towns in northern Orange County, like Westminster and Garden Grove; an industrial heartland of transpacific import-export firms in the South Bay near the Los Angeles airport; and a newly Asian Canaan in the middle-class and upper-middle-class suburbs of the San Gabriel Valley, east of downtown. Monterey Park had become mainly Asian, and on its heels were Alhambra and South Pasadena and even the fancy enclave of San Marino, just next door.

What struck the eye in the Asian sections of LA were the foreign-alphabet signs and the ethnic restaurants and the two-story beige mini-malls full of shops selling incense and chop-socky videos. But the important underlying motif was a fantastic attention paid to education. Many Asian immigrants had gotten their visas because they had special academic skills or had come here to study at American universities (access to higher education in places like Taiwan and Korea was incredibly limited, beyond an American's wildest imaginings).

At ETS, the fastest-growing test by far was TOEFL, the Test of English as a Foreign Language, which many graduate schools required that foreign applicants take. TOEFL was administered worldwide, but the plurality of the market was in Asia, where it came to function like the modern equivalent of Ellis Island, the narrow point through which people who wanted to get to the United States had to pass. For that reason it was the most cheated-on test. Impersonation schemes were so common that ETS had to start printing photographs of the test-taker on TOEFL score reports. Time-zone scams were another thorn in TOEFL's side: questions would be spirited out of a test center in Taiwan and faxed to LA, where by the time dawn broke somebody would have produced answer sheets that could be sold to the day's test-takers. One guy figured out a way to print the answers on the actual pencils you'd use to take the test; another, when the authorities got on his trail and he realized he might be exposed and bring dishonor to his family, killed himself.

Every possible arena of academic opportunity in the United States felt the effects of Asian immigration, but none more dramatically than the University of California. One of the new campuses Clark Kerr had built from scratch, UC Irvine, in Orange County, became the only institution of higher education in the continental United States with a majority-Asian student body. The campus at Irvine had been designed to resemble the face of a clock, with the library at twelve o'clock, the humanities at two o'clock, and so on; but over the years the clock became lopsided, with more and more science and math and engineering buildings to serve the interests of the students.

Berkeley and UCLA, the university's two flagship schools, which unlike Irvine were places where the established upper middle class of California was accustomed to educating its children, became much more Asian in the late 1970s and early 1980s. Kerr's Master Plan had conceptually reserved the University of California in general and Berkeley in particular for the academic few, but for years the change was more theoretical than real. Think of *The Graduate* to get the immediate post–Master Plan feeling of Berkeley admissions: the heroine, Elaine Robinson, is a Berkeley student who is presented as an ordinary nice person attending State U, not a member of a rarefied intellectual elite. The rise in Asian applications—Berkeley had 8,000 applicants in toto in 1970, and 7,000 Asian-American applicants alone in 1980—was largely responsible for Berkeley's and UCLA's drifting away from the old tradition of quasi-open admissions. Until 1973, Berkeley and UCLA accepted any applicant who had finished in the top eighth of a high-school class in California; until 1979, they accepted two-thirds of all applicants who had passed that hurdle. There was another surge in applications in the early 1980s—Berkeley's applications rose by nearly 40 percent just from 1981 to 1984; and then, when the university began allowing students to file the same application at as many of the nine campuses as they wanted, Berkeley's applicant pool grew by another 70 percent in 1985 and 1986. Suddenly undergraduate places at Berkeley and UCLA had become scarce, precious public resources of the kind that people squabble over.

Don Nakanishi, after returning to Los Angeles in the late 1970s, became, of all things, an active member of the Yale Club. Before long he was the head of alumni recruiting in the area—the person whom younger versions of himself would meet (in a bungalow in the San Gabriel Valley, not a Beverly Hills mansion) as the adult representative of the enchanted Gothic-spired principality in New Haven. Don worked especially hard to generate Asian-

American applications to Yale, which, in turn, because his region was home to more Asian-Americans than any other, had a lot to do with Yale's becoming much more Asian in the early 1980s. As a faculty member at UCLA, he appointed himself Mr. Asian-American Crusader and Troublemaker there. It was a safe bet that in whatever was happening at the contact point between Asian-Americans and higher education, Don Nakanishi was involved somehow; at the very least he had good inside information.

Rumors reached Don's ears that all the elite universities were quietly placing ceilings on the admission of Asian-Americans. Every Ivy League school seemed to have a 10 percent Asian student body, just as, in the old days, they had had 10 percent Jewish student bodies. Was that coincidence? Berkeley and UCLA, as increasingly Asian as they were becoming, would, Don heard, be even more Asian if they admitted strictly on the basis of high-school grades and SAT scores.

Since the American meritocracy had been set up as a large unified system, everything in it was now connected to everything else in a delicate ecological balance that was easily upset. The University of California (particularly the Berkeley chancellor, Ira Michael Heymann) had presumed that the Supreme Court's *Bakke* decision in 1978, based on a UC case, was a signal from on high that it should very definitely take race into account in making admissions decisions. Conversely, the decision had an energizing effect on the just-stirring presidential campaign of Ronald Reagan, who had thus far done well by demonizing the Mandarins of the University of California. Here was a liberal indignity of the kind that a President Reagan would have the power to combat. So, as the University of California, especially the Berkeley campus, wrestled with the surge in Asian applicants and the concomitant need to ration admissions severely for the first time, it was being closely watched. Reagan was elected President; his White House was watching. Don Nakanishi and other politically active Asian-Americans were watching. The NAACP Legal Defense Fund was watching. Politicians in the California legislature and the U.S. Congress were watching. Doubtless the Supreme Court was watching, too.

In 1984, the admissions office at Berkeley announced that Asian-Americans, now more than a quarter of every entering class, were no longer an underrepresented group and so would not be eligible for any of Berkeley's special programs to help minorities. Taken literally, the point was inarguable—Asian-Americans, 5 percent of the California population, weren't underrepresented. But to Don Nakanishi, it looked like the most open and flagrant attempt yet to limit the Asian presence at Berkeley. An admissions office memo fell into Don's hands that said henceforth nobody with a verbal

SAT score below 400 would be accepted at Berkeley. That seemed to Don to be another explicitly anti-Asian measure, since most of the people academically outstanding enough to be eligible but unable to do better than a 400 on the SAT-verbal would be Asian immigrants with limited English-language skills. In one year, the Asian portion of the freshman class dropped from more than a quarter to less than a fifth. It would seem that Chicanos would also be hurt by the SAT-verbal cutoff, but evidently the people in charge of admissions had it in mind to limit Asians only; in the year that Asian admissions dropped, the number of places given to blacks and Latinos significantly increased.

That got the issue of Asian-American admissions out of the realm of concerned whispering and into the realm of public controversy. The legislature held hearings and the newspapers published articles. The state of California undertook an official audit of Berkeley admissions. Don and his Asian-American political comrades began lobbying ETS and the College Board on such causes as establishing Asian-language achievement tests and keeping an essay out of the verbal portion of the SAT. Chancellor Heymann publicly apologized for his insensitivity to Asian-Americans. Eventually the federal Office of Civil Rights launched investigations of Berkeley, UCLA, and Harvard for discrimination against Asian-Americans. It was getting to the point where the admissions issue was posing a threat to Clark Kerr's idea of a Berkeley that was the greatest university in the world and run by its tenured faculty, not politicians and interest groups. In 1988, hoping to get the situation under control, Berkeley's academic senate commissioned a report on undergraduate admissions. The lead author, and new head of the academic senate's committee on admissions (the senate having ousted the old one for perceived insensitivity to Asians), was a sociologist named Jerome Karabel.

Jerry Karabel was new to the Berkeley faculty to be given such a sensitive assignment—he had arrived only in 1984—but, on the other hand, it was right up his alley. His whole life up to that moment could be seen as having been an elaborate course of preparation for figuring out how to solve the devilish difficulties involved in making a meritocratic society a fair and good one, too.

Jerry grew up in Vineland, New Jersey, a town that sits alone in the middle of farm country in the southern part of the state. Oddly, given Jerry's later career, Vineland is an important historic site in the intelligence testing movement. In 1906, Henry H. Goddard, a pioneer tester, established a laboratory for the study of mental deficiency at the Training School for Feeble-Minded Boys and Girls in Vineland. Goddard formulated the concept of "morons" (thereby unwittingly launching a million schoolyard jokes) and invented the famous feeble-minded families the Jukes and the Kallikaks at Vineland; later, planning for the First World War Army intelligence tests was done there. Jerry grew up within sight of the school, but as a child he registered Vineland only as a dreary place to grow up.

It was his mother's hometown, and her father had a life story that sounded like the setup to a joke—Russian-Jewish immigrant moves to the countryside and becomes an American dairy farmer—but he did this for a reason, which was there was a left-wing agricultural community in Vineland. Jerry's father was the product of a more standard Russian-Jewish family saga: from Ellis Island to the Lower East Side to Brooklyn. He went to Brooklyn College and made a career as an inspector for the Newark branch office of the wage and hour division of the U.S. Department of Labor, back in the days when that was a fiery, reformist new agency whose staff were passionate New Dealers rather than government bureaucrats merely going through the motions. He spent his time traveling through New Jersey making sure that people worked in decent conditions. It was on a visit to inspect a business in Vineland that he met Jerry's mother.

In 1952, during the McCarthy period, Jerry's father was "laid off" by the Labor Department. Since career civil servants don't ordinarily get laid off, he was sure he was being purged for being a left-wing Jew, the kind of person who might become the target of an investigation (though they wouldn't have found anything) and cause the Department trouble. In 1953 he was fired. He opened up a shoe store in Vineland, and Jerry grew up in an atmosphere of lower-middle-class disappointment and unbelief in all the platitudes about the fairness of American society. Still, whether out of habit or because he hoped for some outcome from it, Jerry's father pushed him hard to do well in school. Once Jerry went rooting around in boxes in the basement until he found a cache of his father's old report cards, hoping to find evidence that even the old man hadn't gotten an A in every single course every single year. That was the case, all right, but it wasn't the news that came out of Jerry's exploration of the family archives. His father's name on the report cards was Karabelnick. Jerry asked him why. Well, his father said, when your grandfather came to America in 1924, he decided he wanted a real American name, so he changed his from Karabelnikoff to Karabelnick. And then, when I grew up, I realized that he had the right goal even if he was too green to achieve it, so I changed my name to Karabel.

Thus equipped with a new, improved (if not perfected) version of his family's quest for a real American name, Jerry went to Vineland public schools with the feeling that he had been assigned to membership in a group that was destined to pull the hard load for America. People from Vineland usually didn't go to college and, if they did, rarely to a fancy one. On the other hand, they did go to Vietnam to fight and die. The purpose of the Vineland public schools, so far as Jerry could tell, was to impart the basic three R's and make sure you understood the supporting part you were supposed to play in the national tableau.

By the time he was in high school Jerry, bookish and "different," had become a troublemaker. He organized a protest of the school dress code. He organized a critical study of the school itself. He organized protests against the Vietnam War. One day in 1967, sitting in the math room before class began, he delivered an impromptu lecture to his fellow students about the evils of the war. Vineland High was encouraging boys to volunteer and go to Vietnam, he said, when it ought to be encouraging them to refuse to go, and instead preparing them for the kind of good careers that upper-middle-class boys, with their informal military exemption, were allowed to pursue while Vineland boys (including, just a few months earlier, a friend of Jerry's named Joe Hayes) were dying. Therefore Vineland High was part of the war machine.

Jerry's math teacher, Miss Fiamingo, walked in and glared at him. Later that day, Jerry heard, Miss Fiamingo went into a tirade about him in front of another class. In the very seat where Jerry Karabel had been mouthing off a few minutes ago, she said, had once sat a boy who had gone off and fought and died in Vietnam. How dare Jerry desecrate the memory of a courageous Vineland hero by talking that way about the school and the war? Some of the kids in the class found Jerry and told him he'd better apologize to Miss Fiamingo. He refused.

Not long afterward Jerry was summoned to the principal's office and told that if he stayed at Vineland High School, he could be sure that when he applied to colleges he would get the kind of recommendations that would keep him from being admitted to any good ones. That was hitting him where he lived: he was an outstanding student, and he and his family had a sense that his school transcript—leading to a college transcript—was his only possible ticket out of Vineland.

Jerry had a cousin who had recently become the first person from rural Salem County, New Jersey, ever to go to Yale College. Jerry asked him for advice. His cousin said: Leave Vineland High and apply to a private prep school. Jerry said his family couldn't afford it, and anyway, prep schools don't admit Jews. His cousin told him times had changed: now they did admit Jews, and not only that, they gave them scholarships. He told Jerry that the best prep schools were Exeter and Andover and they were sort of like the Bronx High School of Science but for the whole country.

Jerry spent his senior year of high school at Exeter on a generous scholarship: he had been rescued by the meritocratic apparatus. The just-retired headmaster was Henry Chauncey's college football teammate William Saltonstall, who like Chauncey had undertaken as his life's mission making the institutions of the Episcopacy more academic, more national, and more open to all comers—not less elite, but elite in a different way. Fifty-four members of Jerry's graduating class (including him, on scholarship) went on to Harvard. Every year the valedictorian at Vineland High School applied to Harvard and was turned down. That would have been him.

At Harvard, Jerry was one year behind Molly Munger. They didn't know each other. They had something in common—descent from a shoe-store owner—but their places in the large Harvard landscape were so utterly different that they'd never have encountered each other for long enough to find that out. Jerry was—what? Let's be careful not to resort to a stereotype that didn't really apply. Just as Molly was not the boarding-school debutante she appeared to be, Jerry was not a typical student radical, though that's what he looked like, with his long hair and steel-rimmed spectacles. He was not a member of Students for a Democratic Society. He was not one of those who occupied the administration building during the Harvard strike in the spring of 1969. He thought of himself as a critic of the excesses of the student movement—someone who, as the relatively rare Harvard student who had sprung from the white lower middle class, was better attuned than most to the student movement's tone-deafness on class issues, especially the unfairness of the Mandarins' not having to serve in Vietnam. Still, Jerry was most definitely a man of the left. A Communist? No. A democratic socialist? Yes. A Marxist? Probably. He liked to call himself "a fellow traveler of the student movement."

Jerry and his friends at Harvard, who seemed to the old-timers like incomprehensible weirdos, were actually throwbacks to the original days of the institution, when the likes of Charles Chauncy busied themselves with the imagined coming of the perfect society, in which mankind's nobler instincts would predominate and baser ones fade. Jerry and his friends read, they studied, they talked and talked and talked about how the world should be, only with Gramsci and Bourdieu taking the place of antinomianism and the Halfway Covenant. Owlish Jerry, with his big unblinking eyes, seemed to have read everything there was to read. Theories and citations tumbled forth from him endlessly as if flowing from an inexhaustible clear mountain spring. He was proud, though, of having not abandoned working-class culture in the way that he thought many academics of older generations had. Rather than cloaking himself in a protective haze of big words and a refined accent, Jerry was determinedly plainspoken. "I'm thinkin' that Marx meant this," he'd say, in his Jersey basso profundo, or "That's not what Habermas was really sayin'."

Jerry's main interest was meritocracy, though he would never have used the word in a straightforward, unironic way. He read Michael Young's book with fascination. Harvard was not only itself substantially organized around the idea of meritocracy, thanks to Conant, but also was the center of academic debate about it. Jerry's teachers at Harvard included Nathan Glazer and Seymour Martin Lipset, leading experts on the structure of American society who had been at Clark Kerr's side in Berkeley during the great days of the Master Plan, before the Free Speech Movement ruined Kerr and drove them away. Christopher Jencks, another leading sociologist (and like Jerry a product of Exeter and Harvard), was conducting, with many assistants and generous funding, a long, ambitious statistical study of opportunity and inequality in America. Samuel Bowles and Herbert Gintis, Marxist economists, were developing a critique of public education; they saw it as a means of perpetuating the American class system—not, as Conant had hoped, of destroying it.

Jerry went on to graduate studies in sociology at Harvard, specializing in the question of the educational system's function in creating an elite and providing opportunity to the mass. He was in training to be a professor of meritocracy. He would be the scholar who could see the good in the system (who had benefited from it more bounteously than he?) without blinding himself to the bad. He would not strike either the too cynical note of Michael Young or the too triumphant one of Conant and Kerr. His first published work was an argument in favor of open admissions in universities, a position that was anathema to the uninflected meritocratic mind. Jerry didn't want to be a critic of the system who hypocritically took full advantage of it personally—so the idea of joining the tenured research professoriate made him uncomfortable. If what he really wanted was to do scholarly research, then he shouldn't get on some university's payroll on the fiction that he was going to be a teacher. Instead he should be an independent intellectual.

There was an opening for an assistant professorship at Harvard. Jerry, despite receiving signals that it was his for the asking, didn't apply for it. He decided instead to undertake a research project called "Politics and Inequality in American Higher Education." He had the good luck to get a substantial grant from an obscure federal agency that gave research grants to scholars, the National Institute of Education, and off he went. He rented an office upstairs from a café in Cambridge and spent a few pleasant years working on the project, in an atmosphere of intense comradeship with other young political scholars who felt that maybe, like the Puritans, like the fathers of testing, they were at the founding stage of something important that would change America. Jerry's plan was to take on meritocracy on two fronts: he would write one book about community colleges, the opportunity end of the system, and another about admissions at Harvard, Yale, and Princeton, the elite end.

The irony was that for all his intellectual distance from it, the educational system Jerry Karabel questioned was by now so completely up and running, so pervasive, that his own life was completely bound up in it. Even as an independent scholar he was still a Mandarin and therefore he required public support. When the Mandarin-hating Ronald Reagan assumed the presidency, the budgets of Mandarin-funding government agencies began to be cut. The National Institute of Education was abolished. Jerry got a smaller grant from the Ford Foundation instead, but his hoped-for life outside of academe was beginning to look like an impossible struggle. Finally, in 1984, at a low moment after he had slipped and fallen on the Cambridge ice and cracked a rib, he accepted a temporary appointment at the University of California, San Diego. There he fell in love with a sociologist named Kristin Luker.

Jerry and Krista were both in their mid-thirties by then, and they thought of themselves as the kind of people who would never marry—marriage was too traditional, entailing too large a sacrifice of independence. On their first date Krista won Jerry over by saying she had read an article he had written, which posited that the percentage of blacks on professional basketball teams correlated with the racial composition of the cities where they were located. It isn't often that you go out with somebody who subscribes to *In These Times*! Still, it surprised them, it made them a little sheepish, when they realized they were falling in love. Their romance moved forward pretty quickly. They were married in 1984. Jerry took a job at Berkeley, and in 1986 they achieved the late-twentieth-century academic version of the American Dream, husband-and-wife tenure-track jobs at a great university. They bought a comfortable old California bungalow in Berkeley, near the border with Oakland.

Krista, a military brat who had grown up all over the place, shared with Jerry a certain pride in being what she thought of as a rare bird: a left-wing academic who had sprung from white Middle America. Her work, on issues like abortion and teenage motherhood, showed her to be a feminist who understood real life, who didn't try to force the people she studied into conformation with neat seminar-room theories. In their own lives Jerry and Krista were, in effect, the Ma and Pa Kettle of Berkeley, almost outlandishly homey by the transgressive standards of the town. When they had people over to dinner

Krista would make chicken and dumplings, while their big shaggy golden retriever wandered around the house, the phone rang incessantly, and Jerry fished through the stacks of journals piled on every conceivable surface looking for whatever it was that he wanted to bring to his guests' attention.

Having resisted becoming a professor, Jerry took his duties seriously now that he was one. He spent time with his students. He served on committees. When he became head of the academic senate's admissions committee he was, like Jack Burden in *All the King's Men*, moving "out of History into history": he had to set aside his book on elite university admissions in order to straighten out admissions at the elite university where he worked. What he found was that over the past few years the dials of the admissions machine had moved quite dramatically in the black-Latino direction, much more than people realized. The faculty was supposed to set admissions policy, but in this case it hadn't; instead, a couple of minor-sounding administrative adjustments, some signaling by the chancellor and by the state legislature, and perhaps a bit of quiet zealotry in the admissions staff had added up to a big change.

In 1979 the regents had authorized an increase in "Special Action" admission to 6 percent of the total. This category of applicants who fell below the ordinary academic standard had been invented for athletes and then expanded for students from racial minorities. In 1985, when the advent of the common application caused applications to Berkeley to increase by 70 percent in a single year, admissions became much more obviously a matter of allocating a very scarce resource. Maintaining the custom of accepting all eligible black and Latino applicants—and, under Special Action, some who were not eligible as well—created this result: the white percentage of the freshman class dropped from 56 to 37 between 1984 and 1988, while the black share rose by four percentage points and the Hispanic share by four and a half in the single year of 1986–87. The percentage of blacks at Berkeley was actually much higher than the percentage of blacks in California. The academic performance of these minorities at Berkeley was significantly lower than that of white and Asian students: only about a third of the Special Action admissions were graduating within five years.

It would be easy to portray this state of affairs as the result of politically correct madmen having taken over Berkeley admissions. Indeed, articles in conservative magazines portrayed it in just that way. The truth was more nuanced. The average SAT scores of the Berkeley freshman class rose every year throughout the 1980s; graduation rates, which at Berkeley had always been closer to the level of a state university (under two-thirds) than the level of an Ivy League college (nearly 100 percent), were far higher than they had ever been before. Nonetheless, it was obvious to Jerry that Berkeley admissions had drifted into a position that was extremely vulnerable to political attack. He thought it was imperative to ratchet back affirmative action to a more defensible point. He wrote a report recommending that half of each entering class at Berkeley be chosen on academic criteria alone (as assessed by grades and scores on ETS tests), that Special Action be cut back from 6 percent to 5, that Berkeley drop the policy of admitting all eligible blacks and Latinos, and that a new form of affirmative action be created to favor people from disadvantaged backgrounds regardless of their race.

Jerry's faculty committee on admissions had nine members. He tirelessly jawboned the others until he was able to obtain a unanimous endorsement for the Karabel Report. He had the Supreme Court's decision in *Brown* v. *Board of Education* in mind: without the force of unanimity behind them, the recommendations would be ignored. The Karabel Report, published in 1989, did, in fact, change the direction of Berkeley admissions.

Jerry and Krista were skilled practitioners, as intellectuals usually are, of the art of noting the ironies in a situation with wry downturned smiles. In this case the ironies weren't very subtle and it didn't take much skill. Left-wing Jerry Karabel had moved Berkeley admissions policy a distinct step to the right. Jerry the critic of meritocracy had strengthened, or even rescued, the meritocratic order at Berkeley. Jerry the would-be independent scholar had become a model tenured faculty member, helping to preserve his university's tradition of solving its own problems free of outside political control.

And Jerry the critic of Clark Kerr's Master Plan (in his book on community colleges) was now befriended by the retired Clark Kerr. Kerr believed that the Karabel Report was a step in the right direction, though perhaps too small a step, and he greatly approved of Jerry. One thing that Kerr didn't like about the Berkeley he had helped to create, besides affirmative action's having been taken too far, was that so many members of the tenured faculty took unfair advantage of their privileged position, ignoring the university so that they could run their own writing and consulting businesses. Jerry Karabel, however, pulled his weight.

The year afer the Karabel Report was published, Berkeley got its first Asian-American chancellor, an engineer named Chang-Lin Tien.

Don Nakanishi turned his combative energies from Asian-American admissions to his own career. In 1987, when he was denied tenure at UCLA, he characteristically decided to fight the decision. Surrounding himself with a cadre of strategic advisors, including Bill Lee, Don mapped out a long, detailed, relentless campaign that included lobbying, a candlelight vigil, rallies, marches, and hearings in Sacramento. The Republican governor of California and the entire Asian-American caucus of the United States Congress issued public statements of support for Assistant Professor Don Nakanishi getting tenure at UCLA! Finally, after two years of this, at about the time that the California state senate held up a $60 million appropriation for a new UCLA business school pending resolution of the Nakanishi tenure controversy, the chancellor of UCLA threw in the towel. Today Don is a tenured professor and head of a new UCLA Asian-American Studies Center.

You'd think that by this time some tension would have developed between Asian-Americans, who were having such good luck in the meritocracy, and African-Americans, who were either getting special help or being shut out. Wouldn't Asians oppose affirmative action and minority politics? But at least in the case of the many activities of Don Nakanishi, the minority coalition seemed improbably cohesive. Don was able to get all the black and Latino groups at UCLA to back him in his tenure fight; in the California legislature, it was Democrats, still the party of integration, who consistently took up the cudgels to fight discrimination against Asians in university admissions; and while Asian opinion was split on affirmative action, mostly it was in favor. People would ask Don why he didn't take a stand for strict test-score meritocracy: wouldn't that be better for Asians? Don would answer, a bit elliptically, with an example. He would say: Let's compare Berkeley and Yale—Berkeley where the minority-loving left has supposedly turned meritocracy on its head, and Yale where meritocracy is the unchallenged reigning principle. Which has more Asians? Berkeley, of course. It isn't even close: 10 or 15 percent of Yale, versus 40 percent in California. So the alliances we have forged have served our interests well.

Not every upwardly mobile Asian-American was a Don Nakanishi type, to put it mildly, but Don's experience at UCLA did strike a chord. Asian-Americans who had done well at college and moved on had usually felt a little something, a subtle chill that played across the mind as discrimination. It didn't happen in school; it happened after you had left and gone to work in some Mandarin institution. Usually these institutions prided themselves on having extirpated every hint of old elite prejudice and become thoroughly meritocratic, but for Asians that attitude looked more like self-congratulation than realism. What would happen was this: You would be taken aside one day and told that you were too passive, too cautious, too nonconfrontational, not aggressive enough. "You need to get some lead in your pencil," a senior partner at the law firm he had just joined told Larry Ng, a Chinese-American from Monterey Park, one of Don's young Yale protégés. When meetings were held with important clients that mixed business and pleasure, you were somehow left off the roster. They couldn't relax around you, you were too stiff and formal and quiet, you lacked "finish." You didn't bring in business. You weren't an advocate. How about being our vice president for technical affairs?

All over the San Gabriel Valley on Saturdays, rising Asian-American guys would load their children into cars, drop them off at the supplemental weekend tutoring program so that they'd be sure to be at the very top of their class, and then go take golf lessons. That must be it! That would make the atmosphere change! But meanwhile, being Asian didn't feel so very different from being black or Latino, except that the members of those groups got appointed vice president for human resources or community relations. It was comforting to have affirmative action around, just as an official acknowledgment that the game hadn't yet become completely open and fair and beyond the need for rules.

At around the time that Jerry Karabel was writing the Karabel Report and Don Nakanishi was getting tenure, Bill Lee made a change in his life. The NAACP Legal Defense Fund, his employer for most of his career, decided to open a new Western Regional Office in Los Angeles, and in the fall of 1988 Bill left the Center for Law in the Public Interest to become head of it. He moved into a small suite of offices in a savings and loan building on the scruffy southern edge of downtown Los Angeles.

The opening of the office was momentous for the Legal Defense Fund, and not just because it was expanding its geographical reach. Bill was supposed to begin exploring what the Fund should do next. Its main activity ever since its founding in the 1930s had been to wage legal battle against school segregation, especially in the Deep South. Now what? Was it always necessary to operate by filing lawsuits, or could negotiation accomplish the same goals better? Could blacks, the traditional constituency of the Fund, make common cause with other minority groups, who were far more numerous in the West? Were there other issues besides school integration that would serve the overall goal of better opportunities for blacks?

In a sense Bill and Jerry Karabel had been given the two central problems of the American meritocracy to solve: Jerry, the problem of selecting the elite; Bill, the problem of providing opportunity for as many people as possible. The system had been set up to find people like Jerry and Bill, than whom nobody could have come from greater obscurity, to train them, and to prepare them for leadership. Now here they were, first-generation products of the new American meritocracy, finally middle-aged and in positions of real responsibility, with California, the capital of opportunity, as their laboratory.

22
Molly's Crisis

C harlie Munger, Molly's father, got rich.
 Back in 1965, when Charlie left Munger, Tolles & Olson, the law firm he had founded, to be a full-time independent capitalist, Molly had been in high school. Her understanding of what he was up to was that, in those days, partners in law firms didn't make all that much money, and Charlie had eight children whom he wanted to educate expensively, so he had to figure out a way to make more money. He had set up a company called Wheeler, Munger & Co. that invested for people, and he also owned real estate and shares in small businesses. He worked out of a shabby office in the Pacific Stock Exchange building. He continued to live in the same fairly modest house in Los Angeles. He usually drove a midsize American car that was a few years old.

Charlie's career wasn't a big motif in his conversations with Molly during the years when she was in school in the East. In those days Mandarins had an amazingly low awareness of business, money, and entrepreneurship; professional security and social reform were their preoccupations. So Molly didn't ask her father much about his work, and Charlie preferred to talk less about his real career and more about his political views (conservative), his previous career (as a lawyer), and his fantasy career (as a physicist).

Charlie's own version of his life would have been somewhat different from Molly's version of it. What he wanted was to get to the point where he no longer had to dispense professional services and could live solely by investing his own capital. That would mean he had achieved a state of complete self-sufficiency and reliance on his own wits, like Robinson Crusoe on the island, or like his idol, Ben

Franklin, who, as most people (but not Charlie!) didn't realize, had been a highly successful investor in addition to everything else.

In 1975, at just about the time that Molly was coming home to Los Angeles to practice law, Charlie achieved his long-cherished goal: he dissolved Wheeler, Munger and got out of the business of investing other people's money for a fee. His official job now was as head of two companies that nobody had ever heard of, Blue Chip Stamps and Diversified Holdings, catch basins for his motley holdings. Molly thought of him as a gruff affectionate Successful Business Dad, in the same category as hundreds and hundreds of others who had started their own companies and ridden the updrafts of the postwar boom in southern California: Charles T. Munger, president, Blue Chip Stamps, offices in the Pacific Stock Exchange.

But it became harder to think of Molly's father in this way after 1979, when he sold his companies and became second-in-command of Berkshire Hathaway, the company run by the most successful investor in American history, Warren Buffett.

Charlie Munger and Warren Buffett had actually been in business together for years. In 1959, when Charlie's father died, he moved back to Omaha for a few weeks to close up the old man's law practice. During that visit he met Buffett, who had grown up in the same neighborhood in Omaha and was also interested in investing. They hit it off, and began buying into each other's companies and talking on the phone a lot. Soon after they formally threw in their lots together, as the number-one and number-two men at Berkshire Hathaway, Buffett became a celebrity. His story was irresistible: the billionaire who lived and worked unpretentiously in Omaha, who made his fortune just by investing in the common stocks like you and me, looking for good old-fashioned fundamental value and holding on to it when he found it. What the frontier was to Frederick Jackson Turner, what public education was to James Bryant Conant, the stock market was to Buffett, an open arena of opportunity where the deserving could count on being rewarded.

Buffett wove Charlie into his legend. His annual reports for Berkshire Hathaway, whose cracker-barrel informality made his admirers swoon, were full of Charlie says this and Charlie thinks that. At the Berkshire Hathaway annual meeting in Omaha, Buffett and Charlie sat together on the dais facing a worshipful throng of little-old-lady investors. Each played a prescribed role. Buffett was the rumpled, folksy one and Charlie was the tough, brainy one. Buffett looked like the kindly, shopworn principal of your high school; Charlie, with his slicked-down white hair, his Buddy Holly glasses, and his tight thin-lipped smile, like the eccentric, intimidating professor who'd make you happy for the rest of your life if you could get him to give you an A. Buffett, according to the script, invested on the basis of liking the cut of the jib of a company's president; Charlie invested on the basis of having run every possible financial report through his Caltech mind. Buffett was the nice one, Charlie was the tough one.

Charlie had nowhere near as much money as Buffett, but today he has, according to *Forbes* magazine, $1.2 billion, which makes him one of the couple of hundred richest people in the United States. By the standards of rich people living on the west side of Los Angeles, he was a Gandhian ascetic. He never moved into a big house and he worked in a modest room set aside for him at Munger, Tolles. Local publications that printed articles on the richest Angelenos usually had to throw up their hands when they got to Charlie and call him "little-known" or "publicity-shy." He wasn't actually self-abnegating, though—just a very rich man who continued to comport himself like a bourgeois, partly out of habit and partly because he thought that was what had made him rich. He wasn't shy or ambivalent about being rich. He liked it, a lot, because it put him in the position of total self-reliance he had always dreamed of. He knew everybody in the Los Angeles Establishment, he made big donations to schools and hospitals, and, unlike Buffett, he believed in inheritance. He exerted a force field, the boundaries of which definitely encompassed Molly.

Molly had gone to work at the U.S. Attorney's office in search of a shorter workday, so she could spend more time with her children. That happened, up to a point—she didn't put in thirteen-hour days as she had at Agnew, Miller & Carlson. But the main point was that the longer she was a lawyer, the more intensely she wanted to get ahead in the profession. The lawyers in U.S. Attorneys' offices have not at all lessened their intense interest in the tokens of professional accomplishment and respect: they want to do good, but they also want to *be* good, good at the work.

Just after Nick, her first son, was born the head of the office asked Molly to take over a case that nobody else wanted, involving a complicated tax-fraud scheme. As Molly thought about it, she began to see an opportunity: she could establish herself as someone who could function as lead litigator on a big case. Besides, the two defendants in the case deserved to be brought to justice; it offended Molly's moral sense that they might be let off just because their case was difficult to prosecute. She proposed a deal to her boss. She would take on the case if he would allow her also to be lead prosecutor on smaller cases that came up, so that she could build up a courtroom record.

So for most of her time at the U.S. Attorney's office, Molly was involved—more and more all-consumingly involved—in that one enormous case. The two men she was prosecuting were promoters who had set up dummy partnerships in which people would make fake investments in order to take tax deductions. It was a difficult case to win because it was so complicated.

The case finally came to trial in 1983. The judge didn't want to clear his docket completely, so he made Molly try it in pieces between other, simpler cases. It took nine months in all, with the jury constantly coming in and out of focus. Finally Molly finished and the jury went out. It deliberated for a week. At the end of that time the foreman told the judge that it was hopelessly deadlocked with no hope of resolution.

Molly felt like throwing up. She had gone to the U.S. Attorney's office intending to stay three years and she had stayed five, all for this case. Now there had to be a retrial. How long would that take? One of Molly's lawyer friends, seeing how devastated she was, took her aside and gave her a little lecture. "Molly, it's worth a bottle of scotch and one bad night," he said. "If you're paying more than that, you're paying too much." She decided that was good advice. Her co-counsel wanted to retry the case as lead prosecutor—that way he'd get the same career benefit from it that Molly had gotten. Molly decided it was time to leave the U.S. Attorney's office.

The legal profession had an intricately calibrated career path that people were expected to follow, and Molly had already slightly screwed it up. At thirty-three, she wasn't senior enough to be made partner in a big-time law firm, but, by staying at the U.S. Attorney's office for longer than rising stars usually did, she had gotten too old to go into a firm as an associate without its being slightly embarrassing. The solution she devised was to set up her own small law firm with two other women who also were leaving the U.S. Attorney's office: Baird, Munger & Myers, Los Angeles' only all-female corporate law firm. No matter what happened to the firm, Molly was a name partner and she probably wouldn't ever have to be an associate again.

The tax fraud case was finally retried in 1985. Once again the jury went out for a week and came back with a note for the judge saying it was hung, this time with eleven jurors on one side and one on the other. The jurors wanted to keep deliberating, but one juror had to leave in order to take the LSAT. The judge asked the two sides if they'd allow the jury to keep deliberating without the one aspiring lawyer. The defendants agreed because they thought anybody smart enough to go to law school was probably smart enough to have figured out what they were up to and was a vote to convict. But it turned out that the juror who left had been the one holdout for acquittal. At last the U.S. Attorney's office won its conviction and the two defendants went off to jail.

By the time Molly got this news she was already deep into another monster case. A man had started a plate-glass business, built it up into a success, sold it, invested most of the proceeds in an oil deal, and lost everything. He came to Molly because he suspected that he had been gulled. All that work at the U.S. Attorney's office was paying off: she was now a recognized expert at untangling complicated investment scams. Molly and the plate-glass man agreed that she would take on the case and bring in all the other investors in the oil deal as co-plaintiffs; he would cover her expenses, but, in lieu of full fees, he would share the damages with her if she won.

Molly rented a separate small office and hired an assistant just to sort out the papers and put them into chronological order so she could figure out what had happened. She finally got to the bottom of it. All the bankers and lawyers and accountants involved in selling the oil deal to investors had gotten together, after they realized it was going sour, and arranged for another couple of deals, which they knew were no good but which gave them a pretext to collect money from the investors that could be used to pay their fees. So they had gotten out in one piece and the investors had gotten nothing. Once Molly made it clear to the defendants that she had them nailed they made a generous settlement offer. Having become familiar with the perils of jury trials in complicated financial fraud cases, she accepted. Because of her fee arrangement with her client she was rewarded with a sum well into six figures.

For years Charlie Munger had been grumbling good-naturedly to Molly and Steve about the way they lived. Their house in Pasadena was comfortably upper-middle-class on the outside and something of a student apartment on the inside, with two sofas and children's toys all over the place and that was about it. Molly and Steve were working all the time, too busy to fix it up. Charlie said that if they'd furnish the damn house he'd use a trust he controlled for Molly to pay for it.

That made everybody happy. Then, a few years later, Steve's mother, who was living in Pennsylvania, announced that it was time for her to move into a home for the elderly. That idea horrified Steve and Molly. They asked her to come out to Pasadena and live with them. She said she would do it only if there was some kind of separate apartment for her.

Molly and Steve were both making a lot of money by now. Molly had her big fee from the oil case. Charlie was hovering in the background, eager for an excuse to spend some of his fortune on his firstborn child. They needed a place for Steve's mother. So Molly started poking around in the Pasadena real-estate market. Pretty soon she came across a great possibility. An older couple whom she had known all her life, members of the Old Pasadena crowd, wanted to move to a smaller place. Molly proposed that they switch houses, with money changing hands, but less than if it were an ordinary purchase.

Thus Molly and Steve moved into a very grand old mansion perched on a cliff overlooking the Arroyo Seco and, beyond that, all of Pasadena and the San Gabriel Valley with the bare abrupt mountains looming behind. It looked like the kind of house you see in movies but not in real life. You drove in through a gate and down a driveway, passing beautiful gardens and a couple of outbuildings, one of which became Steve's mother's apartment. The house itself was in the California neo-Spanish style, with a stucco exterior and enormous rooms with tall windows and high beamed ceilings. Molly and Steve paid for the house, Charlie paid for fixing it up, and there they were, living like people in some fantastic advertisement for the bounties of American life, tastefully enjoyed. Every spring Molly and Steve would give the party for all the students from Los Angeles who had been admitted to Harvard, just as Don Nakanishi gave the party for all the students admitted to Yale. Nothing could have more dramatically represented to this group, which over the years was more and more made up of Asian-Americans from the San Gabriel Valley, where the road their academic achievements had put them on might lead.

By 1988 one of Molly's partners in Baird, Munger & Myer had been made a judge and the other told her she wanted to become a judge, too. Molly figured she'd better find a new job. She had been far too thoroughly socialized as a Mandarin to let her good fortune distract her from her career goals. All along she had been focused on a single prize, a partnership in a big corporate law firm. That, after all the elaborate winnowing and ranking of a lifetime in the meritocracy, was what stood at the end. It was the final award the system could confer, and only a handful of women had ever gotten it.

One night at a dinner party a partner in Fried, Frank, Harris & Shriver, a big East Coast firm with a medium-sized Los Angeles office, told Molly they had just lost their local litigation partner and were looking for a replacement. Could he take her out to dinner and talk about it? Tell you what, Molly said, let me take you out to dinner to talk about it. That was a signal that her interest was desultory. She thought of Fried, Frank as a securities firm whose litigation department in Los Angeles was distinctly minor. It would be rude to accept the firm's wining and dining if she knew it was likely to be pointless. But then at the dinner the man from Fried, Frank said one word that had an electric effect on Molly.

The word was "aerospace."

It must be understood that Molly did not inhabit the Los Angeles that exists in the imagination of people who don't live there—a Los Angeles of movie studios and beaches and body worship and strange ungovernable ambitions. The Los Angeles where Molly lived was a big, polyglot, conservative, prosperous, unsophisticated, provincial American city whose dominant cultural group was composed of transplanted Midwesterners who had moved there looking for a chance to prosper in pleasant surroundings. Molly's Los Angeles was not random and ramshackle with tires hissing across rain-slick nighttime pavement and dim streetlights peering through the smoky air. It was a clean, bright city stretched across a matrix of big, modern technical systems—freeways and corporations and military bases and school complexes and water districts. The essential institution, the bedrock on which Molly's Los Angeles rested, was the aerospace industry—and aerospace was also the LA subculture that would probably win the tough competition for being most inhospitable to women in positions of responsibility. To be a partner in a big firm with an aerospace practice sounded to Molly like everything she had always wanted.

She took the job at Fried, Frank.

Having finally got her fondest wish was not, strictly speaking, the kind of disappointment to Molly that it's supposed to be. She loved everything about being a lawyer, even serving on committees for the bar association. The long hours and constant travel were invigorating. One of the American meritocracy's founding missions was a great success: the United States did indeed have a system of selecting, training, and rewarding a small group of highly skilled experts who could deal with unusual, complicated situations. Molly was one of them now. And it was fun. Like a doctor on the staff of a big teaching hospital, or a full professor at a prestigious research university, a partner in a big American law firm was respected and in demand all over the world. Being able to feel that one's exalted position had been fairly earned rather than conferred as a birthright made it all the more gratifying. There are worse fates than fitting properly into a schema.

A couple of years after joining Fried, Frank, Molly was given another of the big, complicated cases that had characterized her career. Her client, a big defense contractor, had been sued in Santa Barbara by another big defense contractor for $88 million in damages. The two companies had thrown in together to build a device called a towed decoy, which is shot out of the backs of planes to attract enemy guided missiles away from the planes themselves. They quarreled over the division of work and money in the shared task, and Molly's client got sued. What it wanted was to be allowed to go on building the decoy all by itself without having to pay off the other company. The case was typical of high-end corporate litigation: a complicated dispute between two big businesses with no particular question of the public interest involved, since it was a given that the public would be paying for the towed decoy and the only question was which company would build it and on what terms.

After a preliminary hearing in Santa Barbara, which came a good two years after the initial filing of the case, the other company offered to settle under terms that would leave Molly's client free to build the decoy. Molly gladly accepted.

Molly left the hearing, which was on April 29, 1992, feeling that she had reached some kind of professional peak. She was a first-class corporate lawyer now, the kind big clients would turn to when a great deal was at stake. She went back to her hotel, and, feeling a little giddy, she strolled out to the beach and sat for a while looking at the ocean. She heard a kind of stir, a hum of excited talk, coming from behind her, in the direction of the hotel. What was that? She went back to her room and switched on the television. Los Angeles was burning.

In college Molly had philosophy-shopped, as students do. She found herself repelled by Marxism, existentialism, positivism—any system of thought that presumed people could solve the world's problems through the sheer application of reason. On the other hand, when one of her tutors taught her something about Catholicism, she was profoundly drawn to it. Molly had been raised as casually high Protestant but it hadn't sunk in. What she liked about Catholicism was its humility, its deference to God. She believed that the mysteries of existence were ultimately unknowable and that people should conceive of their own lives, humbly, merely as struggles toward the good. One had an obligation to try to make the world better, but one should never fall prey to the delusion that humans' plans could make the world perfect. So there was already some seed of doubt in her mind about the absolute midcentury faith in rationality in which the American meritocracy was born.

Molly and Steve had been married in a Unitarian church. They had "dedicated" Nick and Alfred in a Brethren church—a service of infant baptism—because that was the faith of Steve's family. But on the Easter Sunday after Nick was born, Molly suggested to Steve, for some reason, that they go to mass. A few years earlier a friend of Molly and Steve's in Pasadena, a man who worked as a volunteer counselor for parolees, had been brutally murdered, in his own house, in front of his family, by an intruder wearing a ski mask. The man was Catholic. At his funeral, the priest had asked the mourners to pray not only for the man and his family but also for the soul of his murderer. Molly and Steve had been so deeply moved by that depth of commitment to forgiveness that after Nick was born they began going to mass at that church, St. Bede's in Pasadena, every Sunday. They sent Nick and Alfred to the preschool there. Finally the priest called Molly and asked her why she and Steve had never registered as members of the church. She said they weren't Catholic; he said that's fine, but please get in touch if you want help on your faith journey. A year after that, Molly and Steve began taking instruction in Catholicism, and finally they converted.

That day on the beach in Santa Barbara, when Molly heard that the riots in Los Angeles had broken out, one thought that came to her mind was this: when she went to confession, the priest would ask her not just what she had done that was sinful, but what she had failed to do that was good.

Her city was going up in flames. The riot was an almost unimaginably horrible event, considering that it had happened in Los Angeles during a time of no crisis obvious enough to have reached the notice of most people Molly knew. The city simply went out of control and stayed there for five endless days during which fifty-four people were killed and two thousand wounded, thirteen thousand troops were required to restore order, and whole neighborhoods were destroyed. It was the worst domestic violence in the United States since the 1863 draft riots in New York City, worse than any of the terrible riots and disturbances that had marked the period of civil-rights struggles and opposition to the Vietnam War twenty years before. Los Angeles was as profoundly unwell, as sick at its soul, as it is possible for a community to be. What had Molly done or failed to do?

She had made Nina and Lisa Edwards into nearly members of her family. By that time Lisa had at times lived in Molly and Steve's house, when she wasn't getting along with her mother. Both sisters had acquired big ambitions that they seemed to be on the way to achieving: Nina was training as a singer at the Curtis Institute of Music in Philadelphia; Lisa was an undergraduate at Berkeley, with plans to become a lawyer, move back to Pasadena, and work at the Western Justice Center, which promoted the use of mediation as better than litigation in resolving disputes. It was unlikely that Nina and Lisa would be on these career courses if they had not met Molly and Steve.

So Molly had helped two individuals, a lot. What had she done that might bring to people whom she didn't know personally the benefits she had brought to Nina and Lisa? She had to be honest: not much. Molly's experience with Nina and Lisa had heightened her awareness that something was amiss in the world where she lived such a happy life. Through Nina and Lisa she had a piece of secret knowledge: how Pasadena, perfect Pasadena (except that you couldn't send your kids to the public schools and it was hard to park at the J. Crew on Colorado Avenue on a Saturday), looked if you were black. And once this had lodged in her mind, Molly hadn't been able to get it out. It was beyond the bounds of white presumptions. She began to feel that she had become different from most of the people around her, or that she didn't understand who she was anymore. She wasn't a cause person. She wasn't an extremist. She was a blond woman with nice clothes who lived in a big house and practiced corporate law. So why couldn't she stop thinking about this terrible situation in the United States that nobody else in her world seemed even to notice?

Molly began having what she thought of as "White Like Me" moments. She would go to parties on the south side of Pasadena, where, of course, everybody would be white. Molly herself, with her deep local roots and her appearance as a member in good standing of what she liked to call "the scarf and earrings set," did not come across as the kind of person you had to speak guardedly to at a party lest she turn out to be a crank. So, especially after the riots, she would hear things said by white people about black people that, because she felt herself to be someone who had black family, hurt her. What she heard was a complete unconcern about the parts of Los Angeles where blacks lived, unless the circumstances affected white people, in which case they should be fixed immediately, and harshly if need be.

Perhaps if the riots had come before Molly had achieved all her long and fiercely held career goals, they wouldn't have affected her in the same way. Or if she hadn't met Nina and Lisa Edwards. Or if she hadn't converted to Catholicism. Or if she had been struggling financially. But as it was, she had the strange sensation of finding the life for which she had worked so long and hard to be, once achieved, morally unfulfilling—interesting, challenging, but somehow hollow. In fact, her lifelong faith in the American meritocracy was flagging. Inarguably, something important had changed: elite institutions were no longer the preserve of white males from the Northeast. But the contest wasn't wide open, either. It was as if the deck had been shuffled only once. Now, the people who had wound up on top could (and did, madly: Molly saw it all around her) confer tremendous advantages on their children by buying them a better education than ordinary people got. And even if the contest were impeccably fair, it wouldn't mean that the society as a whole was suffused with moral valor.

Molly did not do things precipitously. The day on the beach in Santa Barbara had unsettled her, but she stayed at her law practice. She even served a term as president of the Federal Bar Association of Los Angeles. This new idea of the insufficiency of her life stayed on her mind, though;

and, now that it was, she found herself constantly being reminded of the wrongness of the society around her.

The immediate cause of the Los Angeles riots was the acquittal of police officers who had beaten a black man named Rodney King. Another cause, not well known outside Los Angeles, was the case of a Korean-American woman named Soon Ja Du.

Soon Ja Du was one of many Korean immigrants who operated small stores in the black ghetto of South Central Los Angeles. One morning in March 1991, a fifteen-year-old black girl named Latasha Harlins came into the store to buy orange juice. Soon Ja Du accused Harlins of intending to steal the juice, they got into a scuffle, Soon Ja Du pulled a gun, Harlins began walking out of the store, and Soon Ja Du shot her dead from behind. Aside from having punched Soon Ja Du during the scuffle, Harlins was as innocent a victim as it is possible to be. She was unarmed. She wasn't threatening Soon Ja Du when she was shot—her back was turned. She was holding the money to pay for the orange juice in her hand when she died.

Soon Ja Du was indicted for murder and found guilty of manslaughter. In November 1991 the judge in the case, Joyce Karlin, suspended Soon Ja Du's sentence and let her go free. Black Los Angeles was shocked. White Los Angeles barely noticed.

When the Los Angeles County Bar Association undertook its routine review of Judge Karlin's record in connection with her reelection campaign, Molly was appointed to run it. The inquiry was confidential—no public report was issued. But afterward, the bar association denied Judge Karlin its highest rating, so it isn't hard to guess where Molly had come out. It isn't hard, either, to imagine the emotional effect on her, given her years of involvement with black teenage girls, of watching the videotape from the store's security camera, over and over, of Latasha Harlins being gunned down and dying in a pool of blood.

In 1993, Molly worked as a volunteer tutor at her old high school in Pasadena, John Muir, partly because she wanted to do something productive with her reaction to the riots and partly because she and Steve were thinking of sending Nick and Alfred there. That was another heartbreaking experience. Muir was an almost unrecognizably different institution from what it had been when she was a student there. The school had gone from being 80 percent white to 10 percent white, and its prosperity had deteriorated terribly. The number of students was about half what it had been in Molly's day. The formerly verdant grounds had gone dry and dusty. (Proposition 13 had killed off California's public school landscaping departments.) Broken windows went unrepaired. The legendary John Muir drama department, which used to perform Shakespeare in Muir's magnificent auditorium, had been eliminated. The school newspaper had become a mimeographed sheet. The supplies in the art department consisted of crayons and construction paper. Classes had as many as thirty or thirty-five students, so individual instruction was out of the question.

Molly and Steve sent their sons to a boarding school north of LA.

In late 1993, Molly, like everybody else, found herself riveted by the Senate Judiciary Committee's confirmation hearing on the nomination of Zoë Baird to be President Clinton's Attorney General. Baird was forty, young for that job, a fast-rising lawyer who was the general counsel of a big insurance company, married to a professor at Yale Law School, an earnest, intense woman with a talent for making propitious associations. Her nomination got into trouble when it came out that she had failed to pay Social Security taxes for an employee, but like most all-consuming Washington controversies it bore a heavy psychological load of unstated content that was the true generator of its importance. Here America was getting an intimate look at a family of two high-end lawyers, an institution that Molly (and Zoë Baird, obviously) knew so well as to find unremarkable but that to outsiders came across as a contemporary version of the society swells caricatured in 1930s movies: the money, the well-scrubbed brightness, the round-the-clock servants, the unconnection to everyday life, the sense of possessing a special exemption from the ordinary obligations. In particular, a new figure in the American landscape, the super-successful working mother, was being put on trial, and found guilty of personal unadmirability.

Molly didn't disagree with the verdict. Watching the hearing became another moment burned into her memory. As she sat in front of the television, she found herself thinking: You are not a very appealing human being, Zoë Baird. You have a three-year-old child you never see. You pay your help peanuts. You have a chauffeured limousine driving you to work.

At that point Molly got up from the television and walked over to a mirror. She took a good long look at herself, and she thought: And you, Molly? What have you become? You're always on planes. You don't see your kids enough. You're working for weapons manufacturers.

And then Molly thought: Was this what the women's movement was all about? We broke the barriers, we chased our ideals, and we got ahead. Women had got ahead. African-Americans had not. The hard-won changes to the system had paid off unequally.

And Molly thought: To have women fight and fight and become a part of a system that isn't good constitutes an incomplete revolution. To live an extreme life where you stay at work till ten and never see your children is crazy.

Molly's nagging sense that something was wrong with the way the meritocracy worked, which was impinging more and more on her ability to enjoy her career success, combined with the feeling that feminist advance wouldn't cut it anymore as a moral justification for her life. She finally resolved that she had to make a change.

She called the head of the Los Angeles office of the NAACP Legal Defense Fund, Bill Lee, and suggested they have lunch.

Molly didn't really know Bill. She had done a little pro bono work for the Legal Defense Fund, and of course she knew the Fund's reputation. For somebody deeply concerned about race relations but not at all self-identified as a radical, a leftist, or a social critic, the Fund was a logical first call. It was part of her world. Its founder had become a Supreme Court justice, its staff was made up of graduates of the finest law schools, and it was committed to using the legal system to reform American society.

Still, Molly was thinking that she didn't know quite what she was going to say to Bill. This was a lunch outside the normal range of lunches for a partner in a big law firm. She decided she would just set off down the road of confession, tell him, a stranger, that she had unexpectedly become enveloped in a moral crisis and she didn't think her life was working anymore. If he didn't get it, then she would just change the subject to mutual acquaintances and children's schools, the old reliables, make it through the rest of the lunch, and go back to Fried, Frank feeling slightly embarrassed.

But Bill, in his quiet way, communicated that he understood exactly what she was going through. That jarring dissonance between how well America seemed to work for you and your friends and how poorly it seemed to work for people in the black ghettos, a dissonance that most people in Molly's circle of acquaintance did not notice, or noticed but didn't feel—Bill felt it. If you knew Bill's life story that would come as no surprise. Molly didn't, but she knew that Bill was the person she had been searching for over this last year and a half since the riots.

At the end of the lunch Bill encouraged Molly to apply for a job at the Legal Defense Fund. She did.

The Case of
Winton Manning

Public life, messy and chaotic as it often is, has the benefit of
having a running chronicle kept about it, season in and season
out. But most private organizations go about their affairs in a
directed, efficient way without an obbligato of contention or support constantly playing. The gain this produces in smoothness of
operation is offset by the loss of a sense of history.

In the 1990s, as ETS came within range of being half a century
old, its past had nearly disappeared. The original staff had all
retired or died. The events, the key figures, and the arguments surrounding its foundation were vanished information, even inside
ETS. Nobody knew that Carl Brigham, inventor of the SAT, had
been so adamantly opposed to the creation of ETS that it was necessary for him to die before the organization could be born. Nobody
knew that Henry Chauncey had wanted to mount a Census of Abilities—a grand project in which ETS would move beyond the SAT
and other aptitude tests and measure a wide range of human qualities, in order to steer the whole American population toward the
full use of its talents.

When a challenge to ETS arose, it usually represented a varia-
tion on one of the old themes: the inherent conflict between the
organization's two purposes as research center on testing and as
commercial promoter of its own tests; or the narrowness of the
quality most of ETS's admissions tests measured. These were
important matters, but because ETS was private they had never
really been debated and settled. People inside ETS now associated
the main criticisms of the organization with hostile amateurs like
Ralph Nader, not realizing that the essential figures in the founding
of ETS itself had been worried about them. And since just about

everybody who publicly raised what had always been ETS's weak points could be dismissed as an outsider, the question of what would happen if someone inside the organization raised them remained unanswered.

Then came the case of Winton Manning.

Win Manning was a psychometrician who had left academic life in his mid-thirties to go to work in the 1960s, first for the College Board and then for ETS. His career thrived under the presidency of Bill Turnbull, a research psychologist like himself. He was made a vice president in 1970. He ran the triumphantly successful ETS research project for Clark Kerr in connection with the *Bakke* case, and then he was made senior vice president for research and development, in charge of the technical aspects of all the ETS tests.

Manning was a Midwesterner with a goatee, a bit folksy in his appearance. Despite the Ph.D., he was more a Lifer than a Mandarin, having picked a relatively practical academic specialty and then pursued it in a company rather than as a professor. He was the equivalent of the head of an engineering division in a corporation, unimpeachably expert but not fully socialized into the folkways of influence and power.

After Turnbull's forced resignation and the appointment of Gregory Anrig as the new president of ETS, in 1982 Manning's career suffered a setback. One day Anrig, whom he barely knew, called him in, sat him down, and nervously read aloud from a brief typewritten statement, which he held in trembling hands. The statement said that ETS had decided to streamline its management by eliminating the position of senior vice president from the organization chart. There were four senior vice presidents. One of them would be promoted to executive vice president and the others would have to find new jobs.

The rumor at ETS was that Anrig had wanted to get rid of Belvin Williams, the organization's highest-ranking black official and the man who had surprised his superiors by publicly endorsing the New York truth-in-testing law on the *Today* show, when ETS had booked him on the show to do the opposite. To fire Williams would be impolitic; getting rid of all the senior vice presidents was a way of eliminating him indirectly.

Win Manning was quite hurt over being relieved of his administrative duties without any warning. He thought about leaving ETS, but he was well settled in Princeton. He decided instead to accept Anrig's offer to keep him on under the title of senior scholar. Turnbull had stayed on as senior research scientist, hadn't he? Manning would be a tenured member of the ETS research department, with the freedom to conduct whatever studies of testing he wanted. The handful of people who had these jobs were not central to ETS operations, but they were central to the justification for it. The fees paid by test-takers were supposed to finance top-quality pure research into test-ing. The research was the reason ETS had nonprofit tax status and a near-monopoly in some kinds of testing.

Manning took up his duties, enthusiastically though perhaps with some diminution of loyalty to ETS. He found himself returning to the subject he had explored in his *Bakke* report: how college admissions offices should han-dle the problem of minority students' low average test scores. Manning con-sidered the *Bakke* report to have been his, and ETS's, finest hour—but ETS had had no choice but to rise to that occasion. Now, without an incentive like a pending Supreme Court case that could lead to a ban on its tests, it wasn't clear how the ETS brass would feel about Manning poking around into fun-damental and inconvenient questions.

Once previously he had gotten a distressing glimpse of the organization's attitude toward self-criticsm. Back in the 1960s, the head of the College Board, Richard Pearson, an estranged protégé of Henry Chauncey's, had set up a Commission on Tests and put Manning in charge of it. At the outset, Manning later wrote, "I saw testing as a grand, rational system for applying scientific methods and statistical reasoning to the more effective utilization of human resources." By the end he and Pearson had come to the view that the SAT and other College Board tests were "inadequate." They took the position that tests should be used mainly for guidance, not selection, and should measure quali-ties beyond mere scholastic aptitude. They put together a book called *Criti-cisms of Testing: Background Papers*. After it had been printed, the entire press run was shredded—on whose orders, Manning never found out.

Early in Manning's time as senior scholar, he was invited to a conference at the University of Oklahoma to discuss minority admissions. Oklahoma, like a lot of other state universities, was having trouble complying with the *Bakke* decision. The decision had taken its model of how college admissions should work from Harvard's friend-of-the-court brief: race could be consid-ered as an unquantifiable plus factor. But Harvard had a large, expensive admissions staff who could read and discuss each application in detail. That was a luxury state schools couldn't afford. They fed the applicants' grades and test scores into a computer and produced a serial ranking, on which, invariably, very few students from minority groups were high enough to be admitted. To get the percentage of minority students at Oklahoma up above 1 percent, they would have to ignore the ranking in a way that was probably in violation of the *Bakke* decision. The purpose of the conference Manning went to was to figure out a less troublesome way of admitting minorities.

While he was in Oklahoma, Manning was struck by an inspiration.

For decades, ever since Walter Lippmann's attacks on IQ testing back in the 1920s, critics of aptitude tests had been pointing out that the scores, rather than radically ripping aside the veil of social class to reveal the pure individual merit that lay behind it, on the whole favored prosperous youths and penalized poor ones. The SAT correlates with parental income about as well as with college grades. Therefore these tests helped to replicate the class system from generation to generation, not to upend it. Allan Nairn had a chapter in his book on ETS called "Class in the Guise of Merit."

At ETS, this line of attack had never been taken very seriously. First of all, there was a possibility that the scores tracked class because people at the top of society were in fact more intelligent and their children inherited their brains. Second, in a more narrow, technical sense, when a critic like Nairn produced a chart showing that average scores were higher with each succeeding income group, it didn't cut much ice at ETS, where the basic analytic tool was correlation analysis, which shows the precise numerical effect of one factor upon another. Nairn and most of the other critics didn't have the expertise to produce r, the correlation coefficient, for social class and SAT scores, so psychometricians ignored them.

Win Manning knew that ETS had data on the class background of most students who took the SAT, because they filled out a form called the Student Descriptive Questionnaire, which was used in financial-aid calculations. So it would be possible for a professional like Manning to figure out the statistical relationship among class, scores, and grades for an individual test-taker, rather than having to work with averages as Nairn did. Manning's inspiration was this: You could derive the basic correlation between scores on the one hand and parental income and education on the other; and once you knew that, you could figure out what score you'd expect every test-taker to get, based on the family background. Then you could compare this, a class-predicted score, with the student's actual SAT score, and then you'd be able to identify (and admit to college) those students who had greatly outperformed their class background. If they'd done better than you'd expect thus far in life, then you might reasonably bet on their doing better in college. Like everyone who had ever been an ETS executive, Manning knew that state universities, with their short-staffed admissions offices and their meddlesome legislatures, hungered for the refuge of statistics that justified their admissions decisions; that was why they were ETS clients, never mind ETS's public insistence that its test scores should never be used to create rigid rankings of applicants. You needed to give the state schools a number. Manning proposed to create a new score, called the MAT, for Measure of Academic Talent, which would be an SAT score weighted and revised to account for background factors.

Everybody at the conference in Oklahoma loved the idea. When he returned to Princeton, Manning requested and got $40,000 from the ETS research budget to perform the data runs to see how the MAT would work. His memo outlining the idea eventually made its way to the desk of Gregory Anrig, who sent Manning a brief handwritten note of strong encouragement.

The more Manning worked with the statistics, the more excited he became. At ETS the real test of a test was its validity—that is, how well it predicted grades. The data he had did not allow him to correlate MAT scores with college grades, but the MAT did correlate just about as well as the SAT did with high-school grades. Manning's most amazing finding, though, was that the most stubborn, troublesome aspect of aptitude testing—the large difference among the scores of ethnic groups—was greatly reduced on the MAT. Manning originally calculated MAT scores separately for each group and then compared them, but then he calculated the scores without taking ethnicity into account and found that because blacks and Latinos were much more likely than whites to have low family incomes and parental education levels, which would enhance their final scores, the old racial gaps would decrease substantially. Manning's chart of MAT scores by ethnicity was a thing of beauty, every group's curve clicking along at exactly the same level. The MAT would enable state universities to get to a decent minority representation without violating the *Bakke* decision.

"He would use the powers of government to reorder the 'haves and have-nots' every generation to give flux to our social order," James Bryant Conant wrote in "Wanted: American Radicals"; indeed, the idea of factoring out parentally conferred advantage was a consistent theme in the writing of ETS's first chairman at the time of the organization's founding. Manning could, in devising the MAT, fairly be accused of proposing that ETS engage in social engineering, but it was social engineering of a kind that was consistent with the rhetoric that had accompanied ETS's birth. He was manipulating the scores to give the child of disadvantage a boost and the child of privilege a penalty, which meant that the test would, in fact, give flux to the social order much more than had ever been the case.

Manning wrote up his findings in a paper and began circulating it. He spoke with people from a number of Big Eight universities—Arkansas, Missouri, Oklahoma, Oklahoma State, Iowa State—about setting up a field trial of the MAT, which would determine how well it correlated with college grades and how honest students were in reporting their family backgrounds. He gave a well-received presentation about it at a conference on minority admissions in New Orleans.

On the other hand, the reaction in Princeton was distinctly chilly. Some of the objections Manning heard could be put into the category of legitimate concerns, he thought: the lack of a correlation with college grades, the explicit use of race in some of the figuring of scores, and the shaky trustworthiness of the Student Descriptive Questionnaire, the source of his data on class background. Also, the idea of the MAT raised a broader issue. The SAT score had never been a *raw* score (that is, a simple total of the number of questions answered correctly), but all the statistical manipulations that produced it—such as giving more weight in the score to difficult questions than easy ones—were done in the name of higher validity. To create a score from statistical manipulations done for sociological reasons would represent a real departure for ETS.

Then there was another objection that struck Manning as just a business one. Poor kids and kids whose parents hadn't been to college would score higher on the MAT than on an SAT, while the children of doctors and lawyers and professors would see their SAT scores adjusted downward to produce their MAT scores. The MAT scheme worked only because it refigured all scores. It would raise some and lower others—and the ones it lowered would be those of the children of the country's most influential people. Did Manning have any idea of what the reaction would be?

It was 1990. The SAT and the other ETS tests had worked their way deeply into the fabric not just of higher education but of the whole life of the American upper middle class, which was substantially oriented around trying to ensure that its children got high SAT scores and therefore berths in the better colleges. Stanley Kaplan and the Princeton Review and the other test-prep courses, which comprised a substantial industry, were only a part of it. Much of the curriculum in American elementary and secondary education had been reverse-engineered to raise SAT scores. Even first graders were being drilled in the art of answering multiple-choice reading comprehension questions. Average SAT scores were widely used as a measure of school quality, even though Conant had instituted the SAT on just the opposite theory, that as an admissions device it would negate school quality. Whenever SAT scores dropped nationally, there was a fiesta of hand-wringing about the decline of America's educational system. If they dropped in a particular community, real-estate values would fall.

So the SAT had become a powerful totem. To the taker it was a scientific, numeric assignment of worth which, no matter how skeptical one tried to be about testing, lodged itself firmly in the mind, never to be forgotten. It symbolized access to higher education at a time when higher education was becoming synonymous with opportunity, just as the founders of the American meritocracy had hoped it would. From the end of the Second

World War onward, Americans planned their lives and their children's around the idea that college was the key to getting ahead. For a surprisingly long time, this universal assumption was not confirmed by economic data; as late as 1976, a prominent labor economist wrote a book called *The Overeducated American*, scoffing at the idea that more education would produce more income later. But in the late 1970s, a pronounced and rapidly growing statistical gap began to open up between the earnings of those who had been to college and the earnings of those who hadn't. College versus noncollege was becoming the bright dividing line in American life; high-school graduates didn't seem to have a place in the economy any longer. And the SAT had gotten itself bound up in the eternal human impulse to cheat death a little by accumulating something and then finding a way to pass it on to one's offspring, since well-off parents believed that high SAT scores would guarantee their children the same prosperity and respect they enjoyed. The spread of test prep, the obsessing, the cheating, the fevered late-night freshman-year SAT-score-revelation sessions—all that was a tribute to the SAT's centrality.

ETS and the College Board, much as they officially disapproved of SAT madness, enormously benefited from the SAT's status as the cathected object of the professional classes. Test-takers, not colleges, paid the bills at ETS. The more important the SAT was taken to be, the more retaking of it there was and the more money came in. Imagine the hell that would break loose if the MAT were instituted and every lawyer's and doctor's kid in America got an envelope in the mail containing a score that had been adjusted downward to account for the parents' high socioeconomic status.

When he heard this argument, which he did whenever he tried to talk up the MAT in the corridors of ETS, Manning would respond with a kind of disingenuous childlike innocence: he affected to believe that he hadn't been aware until now of the quiet bargains that had made ETS's success possible. In a simple, almost singsong voice, the kind you'd use in talking to a child, he'd ask questions. We believe in meritocracy, right? he would say. Our organization was set up to remove parents and background from the valuation of an individual's worth, wasn't it? We've insisted for decades that the SAT measures "developed ability," not a supposedly inborn quality like IQ, haven't we? So! The MAT would accomplish everything that ETS has always said it wants to do. It knocks background out of the SAT score and measures, literally, the student's developed ability. All it shaves off of rich kids' scores is the advantage they've inherited—unless you believe that the SAT is really a measure of intelligence, but we don't believe that—do we? Well?

.   .   .

Win Manning's office as senior scholar was in the building at ETS where all the researchers worked, right next door to the office of Samuel Messick, ETS's most veteran and respected psychometrician. On September 24, 1990, Sam Messick's secretary stuck her head into Manning's office and asked him if he could come next door.

There he found Messick and the new executive vice president of ETS, Nancy Cole, who had strolled over from the administration building. Both of them had the intense emotional loyalty to the educational system in general and to ETS in particular that was typical of people in the upper reaches of the organization. Messick was a policeman's son from Philadelphia who had been able to go to the University of Pennsylvania, and from there to a distinguished career, solely thanks to his having scored outstandingly well on the SAT. He had been working at ETS since the age of twenty. Cole was the daughter of two schoolteachers in a tiny rural town in Texas and had spent her whole working life in and around testing, including a period at ACT, ETS's archrival, in Iowa.

Messick and Cole began peppering Manning with criticisms of the statistical work behind the MAT. Manning's way of handling these was to project an attitude that said: We're all technically adept people here, this is a complicated idea in its early stages, and I'd be happy to fix statistical problems as they are pointed out. But as the meeting went on, he got the feeling that this wasn't just about technical issues. Finally he said: What are you really driving at here?

Cole, stiffly, said that adjusting scores to account for factors outside the test itself was taking a step on a slippery slope. Once started, where would it end? Manning interrupted: Wasn't this not a research question at all, but a company policy question? Well, Cole said, that is a concern also. She went on to say that she would be very unhappy if Manning chose to continue this line of research.

The meeting broke up. Three days later, Manning received word from Cole's office that he would be given no more grants and no more travel funds in connection with the MAT. He had tenure and could pursue the research if he wanted, but it would be without ETS's institutional support or endorsement.

Manning was furious. He felt as if a sacred trust, ETS's commitment to disinterested research on testing, had been broken. "It was the most stark example of political pressure on a researcher to shut up that I ever observed," he later wrote. Rather than continue to work on the MAT without funding, he decided to bide his time until he would be eligible for early retirement. He became the figure every organization dreads, the professional pain in the ass. He wrote a memo to a senior researcher suggesting, with a showy denseness, that ETS hold a seminar on whether it would be more efficient to derive college applicants' inherited intelligence from DNA analysis of blood samples than to administer the SAT. "Or is it too politically sensitive? Perhaps this area of investigation is well in hand at ETS, and I am simply unaware of what is going on." He began spending time writing a long philosophical treatise on the shortcomings of testing. Picking up on a remark Bill Turnbull had once made, he described ETS's work using one of the old-standby metaphors of Greek mythology, the Procrustean bed. Procrustes, an Attic villain, would waylay passersby and contort them into conformance with his misshapen, uncomfortable bed. Now standardized testing was doing the same thing, by measuring people's abilities, and distributing society's opportunities, according to the single narrow criterion of academic aptitude during late adolescence.

Laboring endlessly over his paper, Manning read widely outside his own statistical field. He assimilated practically everything thought or said over a generation that could be marshaled against the use of the SAT as the key test in American society. Education, indeed American society as a whole, had been corrupted by the utilitarian values of the marketplace. Schools should confer knowledge of the broadest sort, not mere job skills. Tests should be used to help students learn more, not to help schools decide whom to put in line for remunerative jobs. Manning embraced most of the leading liberal-reformist ideas in the testing world, such as the idea that there are several types of intelligence, not just IQ, and the idea that tests should measure mastery of a variety of real-world skills rather than a single abstract ability.

What Manning didn't realize—not knowing, as nobody knew, the early history of ETS—was that some of his most subversive, most undermining ideas about testing had been in the air back in the early days. They wouldn't have struck Henry Chauncey in the 1940s as threatening or wrong. The best argument for setting up ETS in the first place, in fact, had been that it would work on and settle the thorniest questions about testing. But for ETS to become big and established, it had had to emphasize multiple-choice aptitude testing for use in selective admission to higher education. All the other potential uses for testing were more expensive, and nobody was willing to pay for them. Economic necessity and institutional ambition, rather than principle, had pushed ETS into being the Procrustes of contemporary America; but the result mattered more than the reason for it. The irony of the situation in the 1990s was that what were supposed to be ETS's home concerns had become, instead, threats.

Manning retired in 1993. In 1994, Gregory Anrig was stricken with brain cancer, resigned from the presidency of ETS, and died shortly afterward. The board of trustees appointed Nancy Cole as the new president.

As a veteran tester and educational administrator, Cole had, of course, dealt often with the difficult subject of racial disparities in test scores. She did not believe that the SATs were biased against minorities: "we have learned that there is not large-scale, consistent bias against minority groups in the technical validity sense on the major, widely used and widely studied tests," she had written in 1981. But she did not believe, either, that you should just admit students by their test scores and let the racial chips fall where they may. Instead, the solution was to leave the tests alone and explicitly take race into account in admissions decisions, "selecting equal proportions of those who would eventually qualify on the criterion in each group." That is, pick a certain percentage of the highest-scoring whites, the same percentage of the highest-scoring blacks, and so on.

This idea represented not just Nancy Cole's thinking but the standard practice in education. What it did was keep the locus of responsibility for handling the meritocracy's most difficult problem where it had been ever since the mid-1960s: with affirmative action. Testing and the educational system itself were off the hook, protected from having to make expensive, disruptive changes in their basic operations. But this meant that affirmative action, jerry-built and unlegislated, had to bear a very heavy load.

24 Surprise Attack

From the Mandarin point of view, which was Molly Munger's point of view, affirmative action looked secure and seemed well established.

A good example of the apparent solidarity of its position was provided in 1985, when in a small and mostly subterranean drama, a group within the executive branch of the federal government tried to persuade President Reagan to eliminate affirmative action using the same means by which President Johnson had created it, an executive order. Ronald Reagan did not accept the Mandarin view of how the world should work, and he did not care about the good opinion of Mandarins themselves. As governor of California he had fired Clark Kerr, as a presidential candidate he had full-throatedly attacked affirmative action, and now he was the most conservative President in modern American history. He of all people could be talked into abolishing affirmative action.

But Reagan didn't abolish affirmative action. The abolitionists—representing the conservative rather than the pragmatic wing of the Reagan administration—couldn't even advance their cause to the point where it would be brought to Reagan for a decision. Not only did they fail, but when Reagan nominated their leader, William Bradford Reynolds, Assistant Attorney General for Civil Rights, to be Associate Attorney General, the Senate wouldn't confirm him.

During the subsequent presidency of George Bush, two similar incidents occurred. A White House aide named Boyden Gray tried to get Bush to sign an executive order abolishing affirmative action in employment—in other words, to eliminate most of the function of the Labor Department's Office of Federal Contract Compliance, which has the power to review the hiring practices by race and gender of federal contractors, a category that includes nearly every sizable business in the United States. And an Assistant Secretary of Education named Michael Williams proposed abolishing government scholarships that were reserved for minority students. In both cases there was a public uproar, and Bush did nothing.

Then, for a while, affirmative action seemed to be in danger from the Supreme Court. Between 1968 and 1992 the Republican Party dominated presidential politics, not least because of its skill at painting a picture of an America ruled by a brainy, self-regarding new elite that cared only for the welfare of itself and of disadvantaged minorities. Control of the White House meant control of Supreme Court appointments, and by the late 1980s the days were long gone when the Court tried to be an institutional crusader about racial issues. In two cases decided in 1989, *City of Richmond* v. *J. A. Croson Co.* and *Wards Cove Packing* v. *Atonio*, the Court seemed to be signaling that it had reservations about affirmative action: in the first it struck down a requirement that 30 percent of the money spent on construction contracts by the Richmond municipal government be reserved for minority-owned firms; in the second it pulled back from the old *Griggs* v. *Duke Power* decision by saying that henceforth minority employees would have to prove that hiring standards were discriminatory in order to win lawsuits, rather than employers having to prove that they were not discriminatory.

But then the Supreme Court shifted back to approving of affirmative action. In 1990, in *Metro Broadcasting Inc.* v. *FCC*, it upheld the use of race as a factor in granting broadcast licenses. The same year, Congress, pushed hard by civil-rights organizations and liberal and minority representatives, passed a bill that would overturn the *Wards Cove* decision and restore the *Griggs* standard in employment: there could be no use of tests that had a disparate racial impact unless the employer could prove that they were a business necessity. Bush vetoed the bill. In 1991, Congress passed the same bill again, and this time Bush signed it into law.

The 1991 Civil Rights Act, as it was called, was far too technical to engender a public debate about race relations, but it seemed at least to show that affirmative action, after twenty-five years, was entrenched and popular enough for Congress finally to endorse it. This was quite a change from the situation in the early 1960s, when any hint of affirmative action had had to be extirpated from the Civil Rights Act of 1964 before it could be passed.

There was no visible organized political opposition to affirmative action. There was no chance that the divided Supreme Court would dramatically overturn it, sweeping away decades of law and custom overnight as it had swept away school segregation in the *Brown* decision. And most reassuringly of all, the White House after 1992 was occupied, for the first time ever, by products of the new meritocracy. The dream of a mature leadership class made up of people from ordinary backgrounds whom the glass slipper of ETS tests had fit and who then had been educated in America's best colleges and universities on scholarships and elaborately trained was, finally, a reality. Although President and Mrs. Clinton didn't talk publicly about affirmative action, probably because it wasn't politically astute to do so, one could safely assume that they believed in it and would protect it. He almost by birth and she by long residence were Southern liberals who had seen amazing progress made in race relations as a result of firm intervention by the federal government. And they knew from their own lives how much difference being given a special extra bit of opportunity could make to a person. Wouldn't they just naturally see affirmative action in that light?

When Molly Munger went to work at the NAACP Legal Defense Fund in the spring of 1994, Bill Lee put her to work on police brutality and other law-enforcement issues. That seemed natural in the aftermath of the Los Angeles riots—it was the main race-relations problem at hand.

The main point of the American meritocracy was to marry the primary goal of elite selection to the secondary one of mass opportunity. If you were a member of the meritocratic elite, you understood this instinctively; you knew that elite selection was the first principle, and things said and done in the name of mass opportunity would not be allowed to corrupt it. But if you were not a Mandarin and you viewed the system from a different perspective, it was much more difficult to tell what was really going on—to distinguish harmless signals and minor adjustments from real, fundamental attacks on the principle of rewarding those who deserved to be rewarded.

In 1988, for example, the California legislature's Joint Committee for Review of the Master Plan for Higher Education issued this recommendation: "Each segment of California higher education shall strive to approximate by the year 2000 the general ethnic, gender, economic, and regional composition of recent high school graduates, both in first-year classes and subsequent college and university graduating classes." A Mandarin like, say, Jerry Karabel knew not to take this too seriously. It was only a nonbinding resolution, a way for the legislators, who were passing the tax laws that paid for California's higher-education system, after all, to demonstrate concern for the welfare of their constituents. It wasn't law and it wasn't university policy; it was a symbolic gesture.

But what if you weren't a Mandarin? What if you were, say, Glynn Custred, a fifty-year-old professor of anthropology at California State University at Hayward, just over the hill from Berkeley? You'd have no reason not to take the recommendation at its word: proportional representation by ethnicity was going to be the official admissions policy of California's higher-education system. Not only that, but it no longer mattered to the legislature how students performed after they were admitted: the same proportions of men and women, of racial and ethnic groups, that had been admitted would have to graduate. The basic principle of grading students on the basis of their academic work was being sacrificed at the altar of ethnic balance.

You would become deeply alarmed.

It wouldn't improve your state of mind when, a little later, a couple of state legislators commissioned a report on California's future that repeated all the same recommendations about higher education—especially since one of the legislators was Tom Hayden, the famous student radical of the 1960s, now, evidently, as a state senator, the fox guarding the henhouse. Then the legislature passed an "educational equity bill," which was full of the same business about graduation rates having to reflect the ethnic composition of the state; this would have become law if Governor Pete Wilson hadn't vetoed it. Nor was it reassuring when the Cal State system adopted a faculty hiring program, "Targets of Opportunity," under which, as Glynn Custred read the advertisements, minority professors were promised jobs even if there didn't happen to be an opening in their field, just because of their race. The Cal State system, Custred's professional home, had been consigned forever by Clark Kerr's Master Plan to second-class status, and perhaps as a result affirmative action was carried out more crudely there than in the University of California system.

Custred joined the National Association of Scholars, an organization made up mostly of older academics who considered themselves liberals but were not happy with the turn academic life had taken. Often at National Association of Scholars gatherings the talk would turn, disapprovingly, to affirmative action, and Custred would observe that it could not be eliminated from within the universities because its supporters held the levers of power. The only way to get rid of it would be to outflank the Mandarins and appeal directly to the people who were paying for public higher education.

One day in 1991 the president of the California chapter of the National Association of Scholars, Aaron Wildavsky, a political scientist who had been one of the brilliant young liberal scholars brought to Berkeley during Clark Kerr's heyday and who, revolted by the Free Speech Movement, had begun a journey to the right, told Custred that he had gotten a letter from a fellow named Thomas Wood whom Custred ought to meet. Wood had the idea of a statewide ballot initiative to overturn affirmative action.

Tom Wood, like Custred, was a middle-aged man who occupied a place in the chilly Siberia of the Mandarin culture. He had a Ph.D. in philosophy from Berkeley, but, rather than lead the life of a tenured professor to which that credential was supposed to be the ticket, Wood had knocked around. He had taught a few years here and a few years there—SUNY–New Paltz and Duke, for example. At one point he worked as a word-processor operator. When he wrote the letter to Aaron Wildavsky, he was working at the San Francisco branch of the Federal Reserve Board.

One of Wood's employers a few years earlier had been a nonprofit organization that did mediation and arbitration for neighborhood groups. Wood decided that if he was going to be an arbitrator, he ought to teach himself how to go through the entire record of a legal case, so he went to the library of the law school at Berkeley. He searched his memory banks for a Supreme Court case to study. Two popped up: *Marbury* v. *Madison* (1803), the first great Supreme Court decision, which established the principle of judicial review; and *Bakke* v. *Regents of the University of California*. He picked the *Bakke* case.

Sitting in the law library, Wood methodically read through the case, from the earliest filings in district court up through all the friend-of-the-court briefs filed with the Supreme Court (the *Bakke* case drew the highest number in American history). As he watched the biggest guns in the American intellectual establishment, from Harvard and the University of California and ETS on down, firing away, Wood thought: They never really come up with an irrefutable reason why it should be permissible to make admissions decisions on the basis of race. Their strongest point, Wood thought, was that black and Latino doctors would be more likely to practice in places where members of their group live, which were underserved by medicine— but you could meet that need in other ways, for instance by favoring applicants who promised to practice medicine in the ghettos and barrios. There was no unerring chain of logic behind the standard admissions arrangement of test scores plus affirmative action, and of course there wasn't much public consensus behind it either, because it had been set up, like the use of testing itself, out of public view.

A couple of years after his law library experience, Wood flirted with the idea of returning to university life. He saw an advertisement for a job in the philosophy department at San Francisco State. Wood happened to meet someone who taught there, who told him over coffee, confidentially, that the job had been set aside for a "diversity hire," so a white male like him could never get it. Nonetheless, Wood applied and was interviewed. The interview was oddly strained and chilly. (Okay: the eccentric Wood mentioned that he'd like to offer a course in parapsychology, which didn't help him.) Then a black woman got the job.

Things like this happened all the time in the American meritocracy. You could never quite prove that it was on account of your race or gender that you hadn't gotten the job—but logically, if race were a factor in decisions, then some black people would get jobs who wouldn't have otherwise, and by the same inescapable logic, some white people wouldn't get jobs because of their race. Never mind that whites still got the vast majority of the jobs. Discrimination was discrimination.

This thought led Wood to his central insight: under the precise language of Title I of the 1964 Civil Rights Act, with its simple prohibition of race discrimination, affirmative action would be illegal. If that language could be put into a ballot initiative, and it passed, then that would be the end of affirmative action in California. It was so simple—why hadn't anybody ever thought of it before? The Civil Rights Act, controversial in 1964, historic holy writ thirty years later, conferred instant moral stature on the anti-affirmative-action cause, taking it from the realm of white aggrievement into the realm of principled opposition to all forms of racial discrimination.

Wood had read a couple of articles about the rise of "political correctness" at universities. One of them mentioned the National Association of Scholars as an organization opposed to p.c. Wood called its main office in Princeton and asked if there was a California chapter he could join. He was told to get in touch with Aaron Wildavsky.

Wood wrote a long letter to Wildavsky, suggesting, at the end, the idea of an initiative to overturn affirmative action. Not long after that he got a call from Glynn Custred. They met and decided to throw in together as partners.

The connection to the National Association of Scholars gave them access to the big leagues of the conservative intellectual world, in particular to law professors who could help them draft the initiative. Also, both of them had free time, a head of steam about the issue, and an imperturbable willingness to make whatever contact might prove useful. Custred, a loquacious man with a fringe of white hair and big searchlight blue eyes, was the outside guy, who could talk about the initiative to anybody for any length of time without wearying. Wood, quieter, brainier, more guarded, was the legal draftsman and strategist. They got in touch with people who had recently run successful conservative initiative campaigns in California. They talked to political consultants. They talked to Republicans in Washington. Before long they had an eight-line text which they called the California Civil Rights Initiative.

Nothing happened. Custred and Wood had joined the large ranks of Bay Area cause-pushers whom nobody paid attention to. They had been warmly received by everyone who already was a devoted opponent of affirmative action, but the rest of the world, notably the press, ignored them. It was as if an agreement had been made to treat affirmative action as if it were invisible, while to them it was sitting enormously in the middle of everything. Its merits could never be discussed.

One day Custred was driving along the freeway, feeling utterly frustrated and listening to a conservative talk show featuring William Rusher, former publisher of *National Review*. He decided that when he got home he'd just give Rusher a call and tell him about the Initiative. Rusher got excited and wrote a column about it. William F. Buckley, founding editor of *National Review* and for decades the best-known "movement conservative" in the United States, saw Rusher's column and wrote a column of his own about it. Pat Buchanan, another big name in the conservative world, a genial tough-guy television talk-show co-host and presidential candidate, saw Buckley's column and also wrote a column about it. This all happened in the summer and fall of 1993. Then Custred and Wood wrote every single elected state official in California a letter about the Initiative and got a few friendly replies from Republicans. Finally in the summer of 1994 a state assemblyman introduced their Initiative as proposed legislation. It didn't get out of committee, but there was a small flurry of press coverage. Still, at that point all the California Civil Rights Initiative amounted to was two people with a post-office box, an answering service, and no money.

The national elections in November 1994 changed everything. The Republican Party, running on an aggressively conservative program, surprised everyone by sweeping the country and getting control of the Senate and the House of Representatives in Washington. In California, which was in a sour mood because of a bad recession, another, different ballot initiative—the latest in the series of conservative-populist ballot initiatives that had begun with Proposition 13, this one taking away government services for illegal immigrants—was a big winner. Governor Wilson, who strongly endorsed the initiative, went from being far behind in the polls to being reelected so decisively that he began making plans to run for President in 1996. The following line of argument began appearing in the national press: The triumphant right needs a new issue; what about affirmative action? It has never had a firm base of public support, in fact is probably quite unpopular among whites. It can easily be cast as a nefarious liberal plot. California, the most important state, the one state that President Clinton absolutely has to carry if he wants to be reelected in 1996, has just passed one ballot initiative which had about it an aura of white resentment. Now there's this California Civil Rights Initiative. Why shouldn't it pass, too? Why shouldn't

Governor Wilson and the Republicans in Washington make as much of it as they possibly can? Why shouldn't it portend electoral doom for Clinton in California?

Custred and Wood became famous overnight. *The Chicago Tribune* published a front-page story about them. *The Washington Post* published a story, and its editorial-page editor flew to San Francisco to take them out to dinner. Television crews and photographers from magazines traveled to Berkeley to take their picture. The California Civil Rights Initiative, which was still just two guys with no money, took on the appearance of an unstoppable juggernaut.

During this period, in December 1994, Custred and Wood went to Los Angeles and acquired the rudiments of a political organization. It consisted of three people. The first, and least powerful, was Joe Gelman, their campaign manager. He was in his early thirties, a career political aide who had worked in the White House under Reagan and, more recently, had been a Los Angeles civil-service commissioner. In that position he had been horrified by the spectacle of good scores earned by white men on firefighters' and police sergeants' exams being ignored so that minorities and women could get the jobs. He began complaining about this so loudly that Mayor Richard Riordan, preoccupied with maintaining racial calm in the wake of the riot, fired him. The other two were middle-aged men, veterans of many years in the conservative movement, Larry Arnn and Arnold Steinberg.

Arnn ran a policy study center called the Claremont Institute, which was out in the flat, hot, dry expanse east of Los Angeles, many miles from the natural habitats of the Southland's liberals. He belonged to the "natural law" branch of the conservative movement, which believed that a set of embedded first principles, including religious faith, individual liberty, and limited government, should govern human society. The superiority of natural law was self-evident, and any superimposed government or legal structure that traduced its principles was illegitimate. The whole line of intellectual descent from Plato forward to the American meritocracy—the tradition of reverence for expertise and reason and centralized authority—Larry Arnn regarded with contempt.

Arnie Steinberg was a political strategist rather than an intellectual. He had been an active member of the conservative movement for a very long time—he was in attendance at the founding meeting of Young Americans for Freedom at William F. Buckley's house in Sharon, Connecticut, in 1962, which qualifies in the conservative world as having been present at the Creation. He had been a member of both Youth for Goldwater in 1964 and Youth for Reagan in 1966. He occupied a theatrical perch in a brand-new white stucco mansion protected by a security gate, which sat on a denuded hilltop in the Santa Monica Mountains northeast of Los Angeles; Steinberg had shaved the top off the hill, thereby getting himself in trouble with the California Coastal Commission, whose members, as far as he was concerned, were just a bunch of intrusive liberals. In his home-office command post, surrounded by a library of conservative classics and high-end computer equipment, Steinberg, a small, wiry man usually dressed in shorts and a T-shirt, spent his days talking in a low, confidential mumble on the telephone while gazing out a picture window eastward over the San Fernando Valley, past which, somewhere in the mists, was Molly Munger's much more proper mansion on a much lusher hilltop in Pasadena.

The child of uneducated Polish Jews who had come to the United States with nothing and worked their way up to operating a grocery store in South Central Los Angeles, back in the days when that kind of business was done by Jews rather than Koreans, Steinberg had not gone into a profession, as you might have expected (and therefore had not been properly socialized into the folkways of the meritocracy), because he was so involved in political activity. He had a deep antipathy to affirmative action; whenever he heard about a case of government's making a decision about someone on the basis of race, he immediately, instinctively thought of Nazi Germany, which had put most of his relatives to death as a result, he believed, of just that kind of thinking carried to an extreme point. The first time he bought a house, in the San Fernando Valley in 1977, the mortgage application had a little box on it where you checked your race. Most people hardly noticed it, but it sent an enduring chill through Arnie Steinberg.

Custred and Wood were the public faces of the California Civil Rights Initiative. At the heart of the Initiative's self-presentation was the idea of these two old-fashioned civil-rights liberals, political novices, spurred into action by watching the corruption of their dream of a color-blind society. While it was perfectly true that Custred and Wood were a pure example of citizen involvement in politics, right out of a Frank Capra movie, this official picture was a bit of a stretch: their main cause was the National Association of Scholars, not the civil-rights movement. But they were in much closer conformation to the Initiative's image than their colleagues in Los Angeles, all three of whom were lifelong, active members of the conservative wing of the Republican Party. Indeed, Arnn and Steinberg were just old enough to have opposed the 1964 Civil Rights Act that the California Civil Rights Initiative was supposedly dedicated to restoring. So their names never appeared in the very heavy national press coverage of the Initiative; meanwhile, though, they were busy doing all the contact-making, poll-taking, and money-searching that Custred and Wood, precisely because they were novices, were not equipped to do.

Toward the end of that same year, 1994, Bill Lee told Molly Munger he'd like her to set aside her police misconduct cases for the time being and devote full time to the California Civil Rights Initiative. It had gotten under the skin of the usually imperturbable Bill.

He was immensely suspicious of the official story of Custred and Wood as naifs motivated by simple outrage over any form of racial discrimination, unconnected to the Republican Party, unsullied by any wish to stir up prejudices that might be lurking under the surface of public life. "Willie Horton goes to college," was what he called the Initiative, after the television ads George Bush ran in the 1988 presidential campaign about a black convict who had gone on a murderous spree during a weekend furlough granted by the state government over which Bush's opponent, Michael Dukakis, presided at the time. The Initiative was about covert racial signaling. Although it was aimed at the whole vastness of California's state government operations, discussions of it seemed to come to rest on one small but emotionally loaded point, admissions preferences for black applicants to Berkeley. Berkeley was now only 4 percent black! And, thanks to the Karabel Report, the percentage was going down. Every freshman class at Berkeley had a hundred and twenty black kids. How much lower did they want the number to go? Fifty? Twenty? Why, in every article about the Initiative, was affirmative action defined in the same narrow way: blacks, blacks, blacks? The real goal of the Initiative, Bill suspected, was not to return to the spirit of the Civil Rights Act but to repeal its enforcement provisions.

Plus, it might pass.

That was why Bill and his superiors in the New York headquarters of the NAACP Legal Defense Fund decided to treat the California Civil Rights Initiative as a big problem. Not just Molly but also Bill's co-director, Constance Rice, was assigned to work on the Initiative—40 percent of the professional staff of the office, in other words.

Connie Rice, like Molly, was relatively new to the Legal Defense Fund (she had been a lawyer for UCLA before that), and, like Bill, she believed that the Fund had to get beyond its traditional business of filing desegregation suits against school districts. She had worked on UCLA's defense in the federal investigation for anti-Asian (and by implication pro-black and pro-Latino) bias in admissions, and had concluded that, as a solution to the problems of black America, affirmative action was a joke. Everybody was debating the size of the tiny sliver of black Los Angeles that would go to

UCLA, but the truth was that most black kids would be lucky to get into, let alone through, a community college. Connie had come to the Fund hoping to work on what she saw as the real issue: building up the basic educational skills of the mass of underperforming black students. She spent much of her first couple of years at the office on mediation, not litigation, with the Los Angeles Unified School District.

Connie was the most spectacular person in the office. An Air Force brat from a polyglot background, she had been, in accordance with the American custom for people of mixed race, raised as black. She had gone to Radcliffe and she came across as a Cambridge intellectual, with wire-rimmed glasses, a great wavy mane of graying hair, and a torrential, layered, allusive way of speaking. But she took some pride in being both a little more tough, because of her military background, and a little more street-wise, because of her being two generations away from black illiterate poverty, than most of her fellow Mandarins. For example, she had helped to negotiate a truce between Los Angeles' two leading gangs, the Bloods and the Crips. She and Molly, an unlikely-seeming pair, instantly bonded: before too long, Molly had persuaded the lady who owned the mansion across the street from her in Pasadena to rent one of her outbuildings to Connie, so they were neighbors.

However improbable its origins, a great battle had now been joined—the first open, pitched political conflict (and surely not the last) in the fifty-year history of the new American meritocratic order, putting at stake the meritocracy's way of choosing the elite, also its way of distributing opportunity (in the form of educational slots and jobs) to the mass, and finally, possibly, the presidency of the United States.

We have seen that the modern American meritocracy was set up privately, outside the purview of politics and open debate. Indeed, standardized testing for college and graduate-school admissions and its add-ons like affirmative action were probably the most consequential arrangements put in place without a public consensus behind them in late-twentieth-century America. Therefore it had never been clear exactly how much political support there was behind this new way of sorting people or what, indeed, the American people even thought meritocracy was.

To Molly and Connie and Bill, meritocracy was everything. They had lived their whole lives according to its precepts. Their concept of what it meant wasn't far from that of the founders of ETS: the idea was to have an elite, fairly chosen, of well-trained people who would run the complex institutions of a liberal society and enable all Americans to better themselves.

They were the first generation of this new elite, and they had built their lives around these goals. They were not the kind of wildly enthusiastic supporters of affirmative action that the other side imagined people like them to be, but they believed that eliminating it would be a step back down the road to a less liberal, less organized social order. So they went with true fervor at the defense of an idea about which they felt lukewarm.

The idea of an American meritocracy was no less important to Tom Wood and Glynn Custred, and their dedication to it was no less complete. They defined it differently, though: they thought the United States was committed to distributing opportunities, particularly prized educational opportunities, through an open and fair contest that did not take race or gender or ethnicity into account. By their lights, affirmative action wasn't part of the meritocratic order but a profound betrayal of it. You couldn't fairly accuse Wood and Custred of misreading the purpose of the American meritocracy, since there was no official source, no constitution, where one could ascertain what the purpose was.

What both sides agreed on was that nothing could be more important to Americans than settling the question of what this system of meritocracy really is and means. That the American meritocracy is not (not yet, at least) the all-encompassing social order it was supposed to be, and some people who have succeeded within it imagine it to be—this was a possibility that didn't occur to either side. Mostly, in 1994, the formal meritocracy was a subculture devoted to distributing a few prized slots in the Mandarinate and, in greater number, jobs in state, local, and federal government agencies. Most people didn't care about it nearly as much as the California Civil Rights Initiative combatants did. When they brought their argument about how an orderly, technical, contained system ought to work into contact with the big, unkempt world of politics and interest groups and money, they assumed it would be treated as vital, central—not as a minor dispute to be exploited cynically in playing a larger, more consequential game. They were in for a series of unhappy surprises.

Molly couldn't quite believe that Tom Wood and Glynn Custred had come up with the California Civil Rights Initiative all by themselves. She didn't think they were smart enough! Or, to put it more precisely, if they were as smart as you would have to be to write the Initiative, they would have gotten better positions than they had. Molly could see how somebody who came from the black ghetto in Pasadena might have great talents that had never been given a real opportunity to flourish—but middle-class white guys like Wood and Custred? To Molly it was much more plausible that people who had climbed to higher rungs of the meritocratic ladder than Custred and Wood were really responsible for the Initiative.

As she read up on affirmative action, it seemed to her that the most obvious candidates were two conservative law professors from the University of Chicago, Michael McConnell and Richard Epstein. McConnell was a man of the Christian right, and, she noted, the Initiative did not ban discrimination on the basis of religion. As for Epstein, he had written a book arguing that the courts had interpreted the Civil Rights Act's ban on sex discrimination much too strictly, and, sure enough, the Initiative had a clause that read: "Nothing in this section shall be interpreted as prohibiting bona fide qualifications based on sex which are reasonably necessary to the normal operation of public employment."

Molly's theory was partly right. Tom Wood had been in contact with Richard Epstein, who had put him in touch with Michael McConnell; both professors worked over the language of the Initiative. The author of the clause on sex discrimination, though, which Wood put in to ward off the accusation that the Initiative would lead to boys going out for girls' sports teams and male guards frisking female prisoners, was not Epstein but another conservative law professor, Lino Graglia of the University of Texas.

Molly had an intern at the Legal Defense Fund go get Epstein's book, *Forbidden Grounds*, for her. The intern burst into Molly's office and announced excitedly: It's not about blacks at all, it's about women! And, as she read, Molly could envision the passage of the Initiative as the first step California took down the road to undoing all the progress professional women had made, progress that had been the main cause in her life before she had joined the Legal Defense Fund. In the very early going of their work against the Initiative, she and Connie found that they got very strong, immediate, almost instinctive support from feminist groups, because they, too, found the idea of the precariousness of women's position a resonant one. And the majority of the California electorate was female.

The political foundation on which the campaign against the Initiative ought to rest, though, was not organized feminism but the Democratic Party. The California Civil Rights Initiative was quickly becoming a Republican cause. Already the Speaker of the House, Newt Gingrich, and all the leading Republican presidential aspirants for 1996 had endorsed it. The last important holdout, Senator Bob Dole, the front-runner, went on *Face the Nation* in January 1995 and announced that, despite having been a friend to affirmative action for many years, he, too, now supported the Initiative. He ordered up from the research staff at the Library of Congress a summary of all the affirmative-action programs operated by the federal government, so that he could review them. Surely the Democrats would see that the Initiative was going to be used to try to bring them down, and they would push back.

Molly was brought up short when, one day in February 1995, she got a call inviting her to go out to Palm Desert and participate in a debate on affirmative action at the annual convention of the executive committee of the California Democratic Party. The idea was that Molly and a state assemblywoman from Oakland, forming a black-white team, would go up against a black-white team from the other side, consisting of Tom Wood and a shoot-from-the-hip businessman–radio host–motivational writer named Erroll Smith. It seemed immensely fishy to Molly that the Democratic Party, instead of holding a strategy session on how to fight the Initiative, would be staging a debate about it. How many Republicans besides Tom Wood and Erroll Smith would be invited guests at the executive committee meeting of the state Democratic Party? Even worse, a crew from CBS News was supposed to tape the debate—not likely that the rest of the convention's deliberations would be taking place on-camera for national television.

Molly, still new to the issue, was being set up for an ambush. Her function was to serve as a matched set with Erroll Smith and demonstrate that the Initiative wasn't just a matter of angry white males versus righteous black people; a formerly poor black guy (Smith) was for it and a rich, blond white corporate lawyer who seemed the embodiment of every conceivable kind of privilege was against it. It didn't improve Molly's mood when, during a spare moment at the convention, she took Tom Wood aside and confronted him with her theory about Richard Epstein's being the real father of the Initiative. Wood was thinking: Who the hell is this woman and what right does she have to berate me? He did a little passive-aggressive hemming and hawing. So Molly thought: Bingo! Another suspicion confirmed.

In the debate, Molly played the passionate moralist, laying out the difficult position of black Americans, even those in the middle class, which was very recently and insecurely arrived, and thanks in large measure to affirmative action. One should not snatch away a policy that had done so much to move the United States toward being a more integrated and peaceful society, and black America toward a measure of prosperity, when the job was not yet finished. Erroll Smith's role was to get up and say that black people didn't need or want affirmative action—indeed, that as far as he was concerned, white people who favored it were patronizing them.

At the main luncheon of the convention, Don Fowler, head of the Democratic National Committee, a transplanted Alabaman who spoke in a deep, rolling Southern accent, introduced a parade of speakers, Democratic Party elders, who pointed out that the party's main goal over the next year and a half was to get President Clinton reelected, not to go down with the sinking ship of affirmative action.

Connie Rice, in the audience, got so angry as she listened to this that soon she was shaking in her chair, like somebody at a revival meeting getting a good jolt of the spirit of the Lord. Unlike Molly, eternally the sunny cheerful Pasadenan, Connie could twist the dials on her self-presentation and project herself in quite different ways, depending on what the situation was. Now she turned down the Ivy League lawyer dial and turned up the Negro dial; she stood up and said, with an artful hint of dialect: Mistuh Fowluh, looks to me like you're fixin' to sell us down the river.

Fowler knew how to play the other side of that scene. A pained expression of paternalistic regret and concern stole across his face, conveying that his intentions were the purest and he had put up with a great deal without ever complaining. As deeply as we all feel on this issue, he said, the public's just not *with* us.

25 No Retreat

What Molly and Connie had seen at the Democratic executive committee convention was, to a large extent, the handiwork of Arnie Steinberg. Although Steinberg's contacts were primarily in the conservative world, they were not limited to it. From his isolated mountaintop aerie, he had the ability to reach deep inside certain elements of the Democratic Party.

Steinberg's business was to purvey political advice and polling. One of his clients, probably the best-known at that moment, was Richard Riordan, mayor of Los Angeles. Riordan was a Republican, but his closest political advisor, and his partner in the investment business that had made him rich, was William Wardlaw, a Democrat—by his own account, a very, very conservative Democrat. Wardlaw, besides having been campaign chair for Riordan's two mayoral campaigns, had also been campaign chair for President Clinton in California. After 1992, when California went solidly Democratic, the grateful President had appointed Wardlaw's wife to a federal judgeship.

Steinberg and Wardlaw knew each other well. They could talk in a casual, assumptive, trusting way, keeping each other informed about matters of interest, implying requests and bargains that didn't have to be stated. Through his connection to Wardlaw, Steinberg had a line of communication directly into the White House. From an aide there who was sympathetic to the California Civil Rights Initiative, he had heard that it was not completely out of the question that the President might endorse it—certainly there were people urging him to do so. Hearing this kind of thing gave Steinberg every incentive to sluice as much information as possible about the political potency of the Califor-

294 The Big Test

nia Civil Rights Initiative into the Democratic Party. Maybe he could score a quick win by default.

Larry Arnn and Arnie Steinberg were able to extract a donation of $50,000 from Howard Ahmanson, an eccentric, extremely conservative man who was heir to a fortune his father had made building up Home Savings into southern California's leading mortgage company. Ahmanson's money, funneled from his foundation into Arnn's nonprofit Claremont Institute and thence into the hands of Steinberg, was used to conduct a quick poll during February 1995, just before the meeting of the state executive committee.

When the Initiative was read to people polled over the phone, it got a crushing level of support: 71.7 percent in favor, 21.6 percent opposed. More than half the people polled said they knew someone personally who had been hurt by affirmative action. Nearly three-fifths said they didn't know anyone who had been helped by it. From the point of view of the sympathetic Democrats in whose hands the poll's results very quickly wound up, those weren't even the most alarming data. Nearly half of blacks, 49.4 percent, and nearly three-fifths of Hispanics were in favor of the California Civil Rights Initiative. It swept all before it: Clinton voters, self-described liberals, avowed supporters of affirmative action. Even people who had voted for Jesse Jackson—the black two-time presidential candidate, avatar of a "rainbow coalition" of minorities and left-behind whites, and the closest thing the country had to a national politician of the left, in other words the informal representative of the people who would be directly hurt by the elimination of affirmative action—favored the Initiative. The Initiative polled better in swing districts than in Republican districts, better with high-school graduates than with college graduates, better in the blue-collar Central Valley than on the white-collar coast, and better in the Democrats' $15,000–$35,000-a-year economic heartland than in higher-income brackets. No wonder Molly and Connie got an unfriendly reception in Palm Desert.

Soon Molly had another taste of the strange attitude of the California Democratic Party toward the California Civil Rights Initiative. After the executive committee meeting, opponents of the Initiative asked the head of the Democratic Party in California, Bill Press, who had consistently treated them as if they were carriers of a major infectious disease, if they could meet with him and present their case. Press put them off for a while and then scheduled a dinner at an Italian restaurant in Beverly Hills.

As soon as Molly got to the dinner, she could see that Bill Press had turned it into another ambush. Out of twenty people there, only two were wholehearted opponents of the Initiative, Molly herself and Peg Yorkin, a small, dour, perilously frank woman who had acquired a fortune in a divorce settlement from a television producer and used it to start an organization called Feminist Majority. The rest were powerful Democrats—not politicians, but high-level backroom figures with money—whom Press had assembled, as far as Molly could tell, to demonstrate their lack of enthusiasm for opposing the Initiative.

The dinner went very badly. Molly began a presentation, but very quickly someone interrupted her and the whole tenor became one of grumbling about the prospect of fighting the Initiative. It's a loser, it's a black issue, it's welfare, it's crime, nobody cares, nobody wants to help those people—that was the kind of thing Molly heard. In preparation for the dinner, she and Connie had done a kind of rehearsal. Connie had told her that if she encountered hostility, she should point out that if people opposing the Initiative could not get a fair and friendly hearing in the Democratic Party, then African-Americans, the Democrats' loyal voting base, would simply leave the party. So that's what Molly said. She told the people at the restaurant that the only obvious explanation for the way they were talking was that they must not care about black people.

People don't say things like that to major political contributors. There was an uncomfortable silence. Then, mercifully, a black man named Gil Ray, a partner at a blue-chip Los Angeles corporate law firm (which is to say, Molly's kind of folks), said he didn't think the Democratic Party was handling the issue effectively. Molly took that as a cue that she should talk like a lawyer rather than a moralist. She drew herself up and said: I work for the leading civil-rights law firm in the country and we don't understand why nobody will even talk to us. She turned to Press and went on—getting, perhaps, a little swept away with this line of argument. I have to agree with Gil Ray, she said. This is not how things are done.

The minute those words got out of her mouth, Molly could see that she had made Press lose his temper. His pale skin flushed and his jaw tightened. Quickly she changed her tack and became conciliatory. She urged everyone to forget the bad feelings that had built up so far and move forward together. But Press was so angry he could hardly speak. Through clenched teeth, he muttered that that would probably be a good idea. Then, as the dinner was breaking up, he took Molly aside.

Press was a former Catholic seminarian and high-school teacher who had been working in politics for twenty-five years and, recently, supporting himself as a host of television and radio talk shows. To see this Molly Munger waltz into a meeting where everybody else had laboriously earned a position of respect and influence in the Democratic Party and now was desperate to find a way back from the humiliation of the November election, and to hear her accuse these people (Press in particular) of being (a) unprincipled and (b) unprofessional, was too much to bear. Molly lacked all the credentials that mattered to Bill Press, and of course, as Molly had made clear, the reverse was true, too. So, when it was just Molly and Press talking, he told her what he thought. You are nobody, he told her. You are not a major contributor to the party. You are not an elected official. I've never even seen you before. I don't have to talk to you. And he turned and walked away.

Molly's outstanding quality was unflagging enthusiasm. Once she got over her immediate shock from the dinner, she thought: Okay. I am now in a world where the rules I am accustomed to playing by do not apply. So I had better figure out how to play by whatever the political rules are.

On February 24, 1995, President Clinton held a press conference in Washington. A reporter asked him this question: "Mr. President, is it true that you have ordered a review of affirmative action programs? And does it mean that you are backing off from giving a leg up to those disadvantaged from past eras?"

Forthrightly, the President denied that he was backing off from anything. He admired all the good that affirmative action had done for the country. He did not want to let it be used now as a wedge to divide the American people. On the other hand, yes, it was true, he thought it was time to take a look at these programs and ask: "Do they work? Are they fair? Do they achieve the desired objectives?" So in that sense, he supposed, he had ordered a review.

To the White House staff members listening to the press conference, this came as a bit of a surprise. It was true that they were scared to death about the political situation in general and the California Civil Rights Initiative in particular. It was true that a couple of meetings had been held about how to respond to the Initiative. It was true that the Assistant Attorney General for Civil Rights, Deval Patrick, had been asked to produce an assessment of what the effect would be if President Clinton got out in front of the situation by endorsing the Initiative or even issuing a similarly worded executive order. Did that constitute a formal White House review of all affirmative-action programs? Well, if the President said there was a review, then that meant there was a review. A week later, at another press conference, he got another question about affirmative action and answered it even more strongly, saying clearly and without hesitation, "I have ordered a review of all the federal government's so-called affirmative action programs."

Glynn Custred and Tom Wood had gotten the attention of the President of the United States and induced him to reevaluate the fundamental merit of affirmative action—something that every President since Lyndon Johnson, even those Republicans who had campaigned against affirmative action, had declined to do.

The people the President put in charge of the review were George Stephanopoulos, the leading political aide in the White House, Christopher Edley, a professor on leave from the Harvard Law School, and William Galston, a political scientist affiliated with the conservative wing of the Democratic Party. That amounted to stacking the deck: Stephanopoulos was an expert at getting as liberal a result as possible without crossing over into politically perilous territory; Edley, son of the director of the United Negro College Fund, had spent his whole life in the civil-rights establishment and was a leading member of it now himself. They represented two enthusiastic votes for affirmative action against Galston's one against it. Stephanopoulos was skillful at manipulating the review without seeming to. For example, after an initial meeting that included Stanley Greenberg, one of the President's pollsters and an opponent of affirmative action, Stephanopoulos decreed that pollsters could spoil the purity of the review and Greenberg was not invited to any more meetings.

But the review was hardly going to determine the fate of affirmative action all by itself. In the early months of 1995 friends and enemies of the California Civil Rights Initiative were maneuvering energetically in presidential airspace. Jesse Jackson, who didn't see why there was any need at all to review affirmative action, let it be known that he would challenge the President in the Democratic presidential primaries if Clinton abandoned the party's commitment to affirmative action. On the other side, the President's political people in California, like Bill Wardlaw and Bill Press, were openly hostile to affirmative action and worried about Clinton's being politically hurt by the Initiative. In the heat of the 1994 campaign, only a few months earlier, the President, Senator Dianne Feinstein, and Kathleen Brown, Democratic candidate for governor, had all been persuaded to come out publicly against Proposition 187, the initiative that was intended to deny government benefits to illegal aliens, and they had done so on principle, because they believed it was the right thing to do. Brown, who at one point during the campaign was 30 points ahead of Governor Wilson in the polls, lost; Feinstein was barely reelected, in the most expensive Senate race in American history. Such were the dangers of standing in the way of conservative ballot initiatives in California.

Custred and Wood were occasionally invited to Washington to brief politicians on the Initiative. They met with Senator Dole; Custred had a brief, encouraging chat with Rupert Murdoch, the conservative media baron, in the office of his political magazine, *The Weekly Standard*. But it wasn't only Republicans who wanted to see them. They met with two Democratic congressmen from Los Angeles, Howard Berman and Robert Matsui. They met with Senator Feinstein, who gave them a polite but wary hearing. (Feinstein's chief fund-raiser, Duane Garrett, publicly endorsed the Initiative.) So the question of what President Clinton would do was, to say the least, unresolved.

On April 8, 1995, the California Democratic Party held its convention in Sacramento, with two thousand delegates in attendance and President Clinton as the featured speaker.

After Molly Munger's disastrous run-in with Bill Press, the opponents of the initiative had decided that they had better go up to the convention and take their case to the delegates. They had bold green-and-black buttons and signs printed up that said: "No Retreat! Stand Up for Affirmative Action." When they got to Sacramento they rented a hotel suite and did all the things that people do when they want to have political influence but can't get the party leaders to listen to them: they made themselves as visible and available as possible; they handed out lots of signs and buttons.

The warm-up speaker for the President was Barbara Boxer, the more liberal of California's two Democratic senators. Molly and her friends were in the audience. The President and his entourage, including Stephanopoulos, were backstage watching. When Senator Boxer came to defending affirmative action in her speech, Molly stood and held up her sign, and it was like magic: the whole room instantly became a sea of green-and-black "No Retreat!"s. Boxer, a small, vibrant woman, shouted back: "No retreat!" The delegates roared. This has to register on President Clinton, Molly thought. There was no way it could not have. The moment was too electric to ignore.

The President, tall, calm, confident, magnificent, took the stage. He thanked the many party dignitaries who were present. He wished Bill Press a happy birthday. Then he launched into a long, long speech about education, the economy, foreign affairs—everything but affirmative action. At the very end, when Molly was at the point of giving up hope, he said, "Let me close with a few words on this affirmative action issue." She stood up with her sign. Then everybody in the audience, it seemed, held up a sign. The whole place was alive with "No Retreat!" again.

The President talked for a long time. He talked about growing up in the Jim Crow South, about the economic difficulties that middle-aged white men were having, about black progress, about his White House review, about the importance of not letting Republicans use affirmative action to divide the Democratic Party. Then he said: "We don't have to retreat from these affirmative action programs that have done great things for the American people and haven't hurt other people. We don't. But we do have to ask ourselves, are they all working? Are they all fair? Has there been any kind of reverse discrimination?"

Molly, sitting in the audience, thought: We did it! He saw the signs and he used the words "don't retreat." Never mind Bill Press, we've brought him around to our side.

Bill Press, watching from the wings, thought: This is amazing! These hecklers have gotten to him and pushed him to make, extemporaneously, the strongest defense he has ever made of the integrity of the people opposing affirmative action.

And Stephanopoulos thought: Good, he stayed on script.

26
The Fundis and the Realos

If you read the text of President Clinton's electrifying speech, you would notice an omission that somehow hadn't been apparent while he was delivering it: he never actually said whether he was for or against the California Civil Rights Initiative.

After the convention, Bill Press set up a commission to decide what position the party would officially take on affirmative action. One of the first guests invited to address it was Jerry Karabel.

During this period, Jerry had been completing an essay called "Towards a Theory of Intellectuals and Politics," which was published in a journal named *Theory and Society*. Most of the essay was about Eastern Europe, but in it he also pointed out that in democratic societies like the United States, it is wrong to think of intellectuals as being opponents of the elite. Instead they are part of it, occupying a curiously limited position: they control cultural, not political or economic, affairs, which makes "their relationship with the powers-that-be a complex and ambivalent one." Quoting Zygmunt Baumann, a Polish sociologist who had been a refugee first from the Nazis and then from the Communists, Jerry described intellectuals' attitude toward politics this way: "suspicion and dissent constantly alternate with a powerful attraction—nay, fascination—with the power of the state."

Now it was time for Jerry Karabel to become a living demonstration of the aptness of his theory.

He may have realized, in a rational, analytic way, that Clark Kerr's idea from the 1950s that intellectuals could win the trifecta—that is, attain cultural, political, *and* economic power—had not come true. But, damn it, if you were a professor at Berkeley, it was an appealing idea. The political leadership of the Democratic

Party may not have ever come up with a clear position on affirmative action, but Jerry Karabel, chief author of the Karabel Report, certainly had. Who better than he to show the Democrats the way out of the fix Custred and Wood had put them in?

Although Jerry was officially unencumbered by illusions that people like him had political influence, it was also the case that at this particular moment he did not feel entirely unconnected to power. President Clinton was known to like consulting with intellectuals and academics, at least those who had practical-minded views on troubling current issues. Jerry's wife, Krista, author of books on abortion and teenage pregnancy, had actually been invited to dinner at the White House and been seated next to the President. She had gone full of resolve to be skeptical—he was a politician, after all—but she left as a believer: President Clinton seemed interested in her work, and he really listened to her. Jerry, for his part, was a contributor to a small but influential new political magazine called *The American Prospect*, which was aimed at promoting a revival of the left. Of the three founding editors, one, Robert Reich, was now a cabinet member, and another, Paul Starr, a professor at Princeton, had helped to formulate the Clinton administration's health-care reform plan. Through a fellow sociologist named Theda Skocpol, Jerry had met Stanley Greenberg, the President's pollster. He called Greenberg to offer his expertise on affirmative action, and Greenberg told him that if he wrote up a memorandum of strategic advice to George Stephanopoulos, he'd make sure it got into Stephanopoulos' hands.

Jerry did not know, of course, that Stephanopoulos had just barred Greenberg from the White House affirmative-action review. He wrote the memo. It was short (four pages), blunt, and practical-minded. The fear hovering behind the memo, though Jerry didn't state it directly, was that the President might endorse the Initiative unless he could be persuaded not to. To demonstrate his realism, Jerry opened by saying that the President was in maximal peril from the Initiative, which had the potential to be "a debacle for the Democratic Party" but couldn't be sidestepped, either. He laid out a crisp, clear, tough-minded position for the President to take: keep affirmative action but extend it to disadvantaged whites, and eliminate quotas and the hiring or admission of unqualified people. He ended by saying he was available to help the White House find a middle ground on affirmative action and devise a strategy for dealing with the Initiative.

Stephanopoulos never got back to him.

On the other hand, Jerry's talk to the California Democratic Party's task force, in which he acknowledged candidly that affirmative action was unpopular, went over so well that he was invited to join the task force himself. So he was directly involved in handling the Initiative in the state, and potentially involved at the national level, too. He had made the leap from theory to practice.

When Jerry met with the task force, it became clear to him that two camps were forming. He called them—privately, not in the task force, because he quickly realized that in the political world all professors were automatically suspected of being woolly, theoretical, and dilatory, so he'd better not throw around academic-sounding terminology—the Fundis and the Realos. The Fundis were people connected to Peg Yorkin's Feminist Majority organization in Los Angeles: Yorkin herself; the national director of Feminist Majority, Eleanor Smeal, a veteran warhorse of the left, short, sure, and feisty; the political director in California, Kathy Spillar, a thin, intense, driven woman who functioned as a surrogate daughter for Yorkin; and Lorraine Sheinberg, a beautiful blond actress who was married to an important Hollywood executive but, despite this good fortune, came across as deeply sad and wistful. Connie Rice and Molly Munger from the NAACP Legal Defense Fund appeared to be Fundis, too. The Realos, who included Jerry himself, were based in the Bay Area and thought of themselves as closely tied to practical-minded power centers like the California Democratic Party, the White House, and the labor movement—particularly two big California unions, the California Teachers Association and the Service Employees International Union.

The Fundis hired a pollster who told them that the Initiative could be beaten. The Realos hired a different pollster who told them that it couldn't be beaten. The Fundis wanted to mount a full-throated defense of affirmative action and attack the Initiative as an attempt by the far right to undo all the gains made by the civil-rights and feminist movements. The Realos wanted to acknowledge that affirmative action was prone to excesses but to preserve it in an improved form. The Fundis wanted to appeal primarily to women and minorities, the Realos to white male swing voters. The Fundis, livid over the backhanded treatment they had gotten so far from the Democratic Party, wanted the campaign against the Initiative to function as an independent political movement, with marches and sit-ins. The Realos wanted to work closely with the Democratic Party and campaign through traditional political activities.

Jerry and his fellow Realos finally concluded that the only way to beat the Initiative would be to get on the ballot a competing initiative about affirmative action. By California law, if two initiatives directed at the same subject attract enough signatures to qualify to be put on the ballot, they will both go before the voters: the one that gets more votes will go into effect and the other one will die. If the Realos could produce an initiative that banned quotas but endorsed affirmative action and it outpolled the California Civil Rights Initiative, that would be the end of the California Civil Rights Initiative.

They began to talk up this idea, and soon, quietly, out of public view, at high levels, it was being much discussed. There was interest. There was receptivity. Bill Press, for example, told Jerry he liked the idea. He had discussed it briefly with President Clinton himself backstage at the convention in Sacramento. Just before he gave his speech, the President had actually batted around possible wording for the counter-initiative—without committing himself, of course. It didn't seem unreasonable that a few million dollars would break loose somewhere in Washington and float downstream to the Realos in California for their campaign. In that case Jerry would have helped to accomplish in state and national politics what he had already done in admissions at Berkeley: to find the sustainable middle ground on affirmative action that would enable the American meritocracy to survive.

There was something Jerry hadn't worked into his calculations, though. Did his fellow Realos share his desire for the American meritocracy to survive, in better, fairer form? No, not exactly. What they wanted was to advance the interests of organized labor and the Democratic Party. And what about the Fundis? They didn't, either: feminism, not meritocracy, was their cause. Jerry had plunged into the well-populated world of politics, but he was actually much more alone than he realized.

Glynn Custred and Tom Wood had been hoping to wage a campaign for the California Civil Rights Initiative purely on the merits of the issue—one that transcended conventional politics. Everything about the campaign, at least its public side, had to do with playing against type. If the Initiative's natural supporters were supposed to be angry white males, then public speakers in favor of the Initiative would include a good complement of blacks and women. If it was seen as representing a rollback of victories won by the civil-rights movement, then it would have "civil rights" in its title and bill itself as a revival of the movement. The Initiative's Web site had a picture at the top of two clasped hands, one black and one white, and quoted Martin Luther King's "I Have a Dream" speech from 1963, even though King was a supporter of affirmative action. If people said, with some justice, that the Initiative would eliminate affirmative action, its authors said: No, it would eliminate "preferences" but leave affirmative action in place. (Polls were beginning to show that the words "affirmative action" were much more popular than the word "preferences.") And to anyone who accused the campaign of being a Republican plot to divide and conquer the Democratic Party, in the manner of President Nixon's Philadelphia Plan, its backers could truthfully say that they had no party affiliation and were actively soliciting the support of Democrats.

When Custred and Wood traveled to Washington, they called upon kindly disposed Democrats, such as the people at the Democratic Leadership Council, who represented the wing of the party most likely to be sympathetic to their cause. Arnie Steinberg was in constant contact with Bill Wardlaw and occasional contact with Bill Press. He spoke with Stanley Greenberg, the pollster who was Jerry Karabel's friend. He met with Duane Garrett, Senator Feinstein's fund-raiser, who at one point told him he had drafted an endorsement of the Initiative that she was going to deliver. He even met with Jesse Jackson!

None of this worked. Not one of the prominent Democrats who were supposed to be considering coming out for the Initiative did so. Then, out of the blue, Duane Garrett committed suicide, and Steinberg never heard anything more from Senator Feinstein. No Democratic checks arrived to help fund the petition campaign. Willie Brown, Democratic Speaker of California's Assembly, in a speech to a class at Glynn Custred's college, Cal State Hayward, said (while a student was running a tape recorder, unbeknownst to him), "Glynn Custred—all of you ought to take his class. By the end of the session he'll really need therapy. You ought to challenge him every day in class. He'll be a basket case by the end of the semester." Outside the gamut running from this kind of crude threat to sudden unexplained silence, there was no Democratic reaction at all.

The Republican Party was much more friendly. The party's chief operative in California was a ferociously quiet young man with a shaved head named Scott Taylor. He read about Custred and Wood in the newspaper, called them, and went to Berkeley to meet with them. His interest only intensified when Custred and Wood showed him Arnie Steinberg's poll. Taylor began to make propitious introductions for the California Civil Rights Initiative—for instance to Newt Gingrich, to Haley Barbour, head of the Republican National Committee, and to a donor or two.

But Taylor wasn't interested in the California Civil Rights Initiative for the reason that Custred and Wood would have wanted him to be, sincere and principled opposition to affirmative action. This was the way the situation looked to Taylor: The Initiative had the potential to create the kind of massive tactical advantage that will probably come only once, if it comes at all, in a political strategist's career. It could be what liberals called a "wedge issue" and Taylor preferred to think of as a "vote-determinative issue"—an issue whose presence on the ballot might induce people to switch their votes in other races from Democratic to Republican candidates. He could visualize seats in the state legislature and in Congress being won or lost because of the Initiative. He could even see its becoming, with a little luck, the next Proposition 13, a gambit that altered the correlation of forces in national politics to Republican advantage for a generation.

Just to get the Initiative on the ballot, never mind advertising it in the fall of 1996, would cost nearly a million dollars. That was money Custred and Wood didn't have. The Republicans did have it, or access to it, but if the Initiative wanted money from them, not just moral support, then the Republicans would ask some tough questions, the same questions you'd ask about any investment. To begin with, what would be the return? If the Initiative only barely won, with 52 or 53 percent of the vote, there'd be no return; if it won with 59 or 60 percent, and if California voters could be constantly reminded during the 1996 campaign season that all Republican Party candidates favored the Initiative and all Democratic candidates, starting with President Clinton, opposed it—then there might be a very nice return. California might even go Republican, and the Democrats couldn't win the White House without California. Conversely, if the campaign wanted Republican money—if it wanted the party to help the Initiative—then it would have to help the party. That was only fair.

The White House review of affirmative action was substantially complete by May 1995. The main uncertainty was not about its actual content—there would no doubt be a sober report offering moderate support for affirmative action, which not many people would read—but what President Clinton would say about it publicly, and where and when he would say it.

He might, for example, give a major address at one of the sacred sites of the civil-rights movement, such as Central High School in Little Rock, which, after long and total resistance, had finally opened its doors to black students when President Eisenhower sent federal troops to town and there was no other choice, or the Ebenezer Baptist Church in Atlanta, Martin Luther King's pulpit. That would send a powerful message of support for affirmative action. Or he could pick a more neutral location, and make more casual remarks, which would mute his endorsement. These questions hung in the air for week after indeterminate week—long enough to put the review itself in peril. Once President Clinton spoke on the issue, the report could be released to the public, and then it would represent an inviolable policy stance. Until then, the question of whether the administration was for or against affirmative action was an internal matter subject to argument.

During this nervous, uncertain period, the fax machines in the White

House began emitting memoranda from Dick Morris, the Democrat-turned-Republican political strategist whom the President had been consulting ever since the disastrous November election. Morris, who hadn't been involved in the affirmative-action review at all, believed that a presidential renunciation of affirmative action was politically imperative.

On June 12, while Stephanopoulos was attempting to hold Morris at bay, the Supreme Court issued a decision that ratcheted back affirmative action a bit. In a case called *Adarand Contractors* v. *State of Colorado*, the Court struck down a program that set aside a portion of highway construction contracts for minority firms. It did not declare all such programs to be unconstitutional, but it raised the bar of legal scrutiny they had to clear.

The *Adarand* decision gave the President cover. Here was a mostly Republican Supreme Court, offered the chance to do away with one form of affirmative action entirely, and declining. Surely that meant there was room for a Democratic President to endorse affirmative action without seeming to be a captive of the left. All the fog surrounding the scheduling of President Clinton's speech on affirmative action suddenly cleared, and a time and a place were put on the presidential schedule: July 19 at the National Archives in Washington, the place where the original copies of the Declaration of Independence and the Constitution were on display—a nonracial venue but one that connoted the statement of fundamental principles.

When July 19 dawned, the speech still wasn't finished. Christopher Edley arrived at the White House at eight o'clock in the morning, three hours before the President was due at the National Archives, to find a scene of controlled chaos in the Oval Office. The President was sitting in a wing chair in front of the fireplace, looking as if he hadn't slept much, with manuscript pages and scribbled-upon sheets torn out of a yellow legal pad strewn all over his lap. Kneeling at his feet was an aide holding up a tape recorder. The President would read out loud from some indeterminate mix taken from the prepared draft, the notes he had written on the legal pad, and his spur-of-the-moment thoughts. Sometimes one of the half dozen or so other aides who were constantly walking in and out of the room would object to something he said, and he would rephrase it. Time was passing—quite rapidly, Edley thought.

The aide with the tape recorder dashed out to a computer in the hallway to begin transcribing the beginning of the speech while the President and the other aides kept working on the end. The President of France called to discuss the war in Bosnia, and everyone had to leave the Oval Office for a few precious minutes. Somewhere during all this, Edley heard the President say into the tape recorder: "We should have a simple slogan: mend it, but don't end it." Where had that come from? Was it in the text prepared by the speech-writers, or on the legal pad, or had it just popped into the President's mind that second? Whichever it was, it was instantly clear that was going to be the line that summarized half a year's work and maneuvering and worry by hundreds of people in the executive branch of the United States government.

Only a little late, the transcribing was done and everyone piled into limousines to go to the National Archives. President Clinton came to the podium looking relaxed and thoughtful, as if he had contemplated affirmative action with the utmost gravity and deliberation and figured out just precisely which firm, unyielding patch of ground he occupied. The stately main rotunda of the Archives was packed with cabinet members, congressmen, civil-rights leaders, and other dignitaries. The President laid out the story of how affirmative action had been started to help overcome segregation and give opportunity to Americans of all races, but only if they were qualified and there were no quotas. He understood that some people did not believe in affirmative action, and that was all right, but he just felt people shouldn't unfairly blame their problems on affirmative action, and politicians shouldn't use it to divide the American people. He believed that perhaps some of the programs might be tightened up a little immediately, and that none of them should go on forever. "But let me be clear," he said. "Affirmative action has been good for America." And then he gave the audience his new slogan—mend it, don't end it—to huge and heartfelt applause.

Jesse Jackson decided not to run for President.

Jerry Karabel, watching the speech on television, thought: What the President is proposing is exactly what the Karabel Report proposed at Berkeley. He and the President thought alike. The course from this speech to the White House's helping to put an alternative to the California Civil Rights Initiative on the ballot was a short, sure one.

On July 20, the next day, Governor Pete Wilson and his leading black supporter, a Sacramento lobbyist and political fund-raiser named Ward Connerly, marched into a meeting of the University of California Board of Regents and proposed a resolution to abolish all the university's affirmative-action programs. It passed. In addition to taking the university's officials completely by surprise, the resolution positioned Wilson as the most determined Republican enemy of affirmative action in the country and Connerly as his indispensable partner.

On July 24, Bob Dole held a press conference in Washington to announce that he and a congressman from Florida had just proposed legislation to abolish all federal affirmative-action programs.

It was easy to get the impression that the whole political system had cued itself up for a national debate on affirmative action, which would run for more than a year and be decided in the presidential election; officeholding politicians, rather than sociologists, were now using terms like "merit" and "meritocracy" in their public addresses. But here was a sign that maybe the impression was wrong. The text of the President's speech hadn't said much about exactly how affirmative-action programs would be mended—Clinton didn't mention any affirmative-action programs specifically, just the general idea of them. He did not address the question of whether or not to adhere strictly to the results of standardized tests in handing out jobs and places in school, which was what the whole fight in California was about. In fact, the President never mentioned the California Civil Rights Initiative.

27

Changing Sides

D o you know how, when you start getting a little older, every time you get a medical checkup you imagine a scene at the end where the doctor calls you into the office and says you have a little growth that's probably nothing but it ought to be looked at? That happened to Molly Munger in the spring of 1995. She had exploratory surgery over the summer and it turned out really to be nothing, but in the meantime her mind was focused. She went to her twenty-fifth reunion at Harvard in June believing that her days were numbered. Quite a few of her old classmates were amazed to hear that Molly, the corporate lawyer to end all corporate lawyers, had quit and gone to work for the NAACP Legal Defense Fund, but for Molly the health scare made her realize how comfortable she was with her decision. She liked the idea that she was devoting her work to a cause.

The California Civil Rights Initiative had had the effect of bringing together all the strands in Molly's life. She had climbed the legal ladder as a feminist. She had gone to the Legal Defense Fund to fight racism. Now, in campaigning against the Initiative, which not only banned affirmative action on behalf of both minorities and women but permitted the use of "bona fide" sex discrimination, she was operating on both channels at once.

For some time Molly had been having unpleasant feelings about the racial situation in Los Angeles. To these she added unpleasant feelings about gender. Wouldn't it stand to reason that a lot of men might wish that things could just go back to the way they had been before, when mothers stayed home and raised the children and waited upon their fathers and deferred to them? Just as a lot of whites might quietly yearn for the days before the civil-rights revolution?

Molly knew Bill Wardlaw, the President's man in California, who lived not too far away in Pasadena and belonged to the same Catholic church. When she became involved in the campaign against the Initiative, she found an occasion to have a word with him about it. He looked her straight in the eye and said: Molly, I'm a fifty-something white guy, and I just don't feel this one. Exactly what she had guessed was running through the minds of people like Wardlaw! At least he was candid. His response showed how frighteningly little automatic resistance there would be to an undoing of all the gains won for women and for minorities over the past three decades. Molly also had known Larry Arnn, official chairman of the California Civil Rights Initiative—back in the Baird, Munger & Myers days, she had represented him in a lawsuit against a dead donor's recalcitrant family—and, ever friendly, she now drove out to Claremont and took him to lunch. They spent most of the meal just talking pleasantly, but at the end she turned the conversation to the Initiative. Did Arnn realize that its clause on sex discrimination would lower the standard of constitutional protection against discrimination against women? But, Molly, Arnn said, practically everything that's good to do is unconstitutional. So there was further confirmation of her suspicions.

Molly began to do research on the resurgent American conservative movement. She was especially taken by the work of a writer named Michael Lind, a former conservative who had left the movement and then spilled the beans on it. He confirmed what she had suspected about conservatives' racial views, and he explained that a few conservative philanthropists had decided to put their money into think tanks and books as a way of promoting the cause. Some of these people, such as Richard Mellon Scaife of Pittsburgh, had appeared on the list of contributors to the California Civil Rights Initiative. Before long a chart appeared on the wall of Molly's office, demonstrating the tight links among conservative money, conservative intellectuals, and conservative Republican politicians. These were the people she was fighting against—the people who wanted to turn back the clock, to a time before the establishment of the American meritocracy.

Another age-appropriate thing that happened to Molly was that she found herself becoming more interested in her family history. One of her great-great-grandfathers, on her mother's side, had been a Union soldier in the Civil War, stayed in Mississippi after the Confederate surrender, and became a county sheriff. With the end of Reconstruction in 1875, knowing that people like him were now going to be in harm's way, he bought his family bargain train tickets to California, which is how they had wound up in Pasadena. After the Harvard reunion Molly took her family to Aberdeen, Mississippi, to look for more information about her great-great-grandfather.

Now Molly was fighting the contemporary version of his battle, with the stakes just as high.

It was natural that Molly would gravitate toward the feminist end of the opposition to the Initiative—the Fundis, rather than the Realos. Peg Yorkin and Lorraine Sheinberg and Kathy Spillar were nearby in Los Angeles and were the opposition's main, practically only, source of funds so far. To go to a fund-raiser for the opposition, in those days, was to be in a roomful of professional women, listening to the exhortations of Connie and Molly and others about the right wing's plan to send women back to the kitchen.

Jerry Karabel watched the feminists' activities in Los Angeles in disbelief. These people thought the Initiative could be beaten straight up; he didn't. They talked as if the campaign could succeed solely with female votes and so didn't need to win men over, which was mathematically impossible. They wanted to wage the campaign mainly by staging confrontational public events, but Jerry was certain these would turn off swing voters. An anecdote that seemed to Jerry to sum it all up was that Dear Abby, the advice columnist, a priceless emblem of Midwestern common sense, had offered her services to the campaign and the Fundis had turned her down. They just didn't get it.

It was easy to caricature Jerry as a bearded left-wing professor from the 1960s, and people did. Ward Connerly, Governor Wilson's anti-affirmative-action ally on the Board of Regents, had seized upon a chart called "the Karabel matrix" as the symbol of all that was wrong with the way the University of California was run. The chart showed the precise ranges of SAT scores in which members of various ethnic groups would be admitted to Berkeley, with the ranges for blacks and Latinos falling well below those for whites and Asians. Jerry had actually had nothing to do with this chart—somebody at the admissions office had drawn it up as embodying, supposedly, the principle of the Karabel Report—but there's no justice in the world. Soon he was seeing himself referred to in the conservative press as "the quota king of California." His true role, or at least the role he yearned to play, couldn't have been more completely misconstrued. He was a practical-minded action intellectual who wanted to assist in the political rescue of affirmative action.

That was why Jerry was a member of the moderate camp within the campaign against the Initiative, which wanted to work closely with the White House and to sponsor a counter-initiative. At one meeting, Kathy Spillar, political director of Feminist Majority in California, got up and said confidently that she had talked to people in the White House and they didn't like the idea of a counter-initiative. But after the meeting Bill Press took Jerry aside and confidentially told him that Spillar was wrong, the White House actually did like the idea and wanted his group to move ahead with it. How could you tell who was right? "The White House," literally, was a complex of buildings in Washington where hundreds of people with all sorts of different political beliefs worked. Nobody knew definitively what President Clinton believed, about this at least. But Jerry thought it stood to reason that he was more likely to favor a counter-initiative than a direct fight.

Jerry and his allies moved forward. They tested the counter-initiative on focus groups. They maintained close communication with Bill Press, who gave them confident though slightly mysterious signals of encouragement—indications that he had been in talks he couldn't be too specific about with highly placed figures whom he couldn't name. They found lawyers to draw up precise wording for a counter-initiative. It was called the California Equal Opportunity and Non-Discrimination Initiative, and it required the state to ensure equal opportunity and prevent discrimination, but it also banned quotas and the selection of unqualified people.

A big meeting was scheduled in Los Angeles in October to discuss the counter-initiative. Jerry presented a briefing on the overall political situation that he hoped would cause opposition to the counter-initiative to soften. He went through figures from recent California elections and demonstrated that defeating the California Civil Rights Initiative would require getting 40 percent support among white male voters—a group that polls reported was 75 percent for the Initiative. That was why a counter-initiative was the only way for their side to win.

As Jerry was making his presentation, he could sense that it wasn't going over. The feminists' faces took on a hard set of displeasure as they listened, and soon they started to raise objections. He was conceding too much ground to the other side, granting it a moral victory at the outset by acknowledging that affirmative action needed to be fixed. The counter-initiative, if it won, would accomplish half of what the California Civil Rights Initiative was aimed to do. Jerry had expected this. What was supposed to happen next, though, was that his compadres from the unions and the Democratic Party would intervene strongly and carry the day. Instead they were weirdly silent—as if, by some prearrangement he wasn't privy to, they had decided to let the meeting dissolve into an unresolvable, bitter mess. And it did.

The aftermath couldn't have been worse. Jerry and his allies decided to proceed with the counter-initiative, knowing that to do so was a direct insult to the Feminist Majority people and an open indication that their movement was seriously split. Meanwhile, what had happened subtly at that October meeting in Los Angeles continued to happen more overtly throughout the fall of 1995: the White House, the Democratic Party, and the two big unions, for teachers and service employees, that had been so encouraging about the counter-initiative only a few months earlier, all took a powder. Phone calls stopped being returned. Insuperable scheduling difficulties prevented meetings from being held.

This was, of course, the symbolic manifestation of what was in fact *not* happening—namely, the counter-initiative's getting money. The feminists in Los Angeles had close ties to Hollywood, so there would be no Hollywood money for the counter-initiative, and evidently no party or union money either, no matter what the earlier expectations. So, after a few weeks, Jerry and the other people behind the counter-initiative quietly, sourly, dropped the idea. After that, opposition to the Initiative was like a married couple who have fought so bitterly and horribly that grimly limping along is about the best they can manage.

Jerry quite easily surmised what had happened. It was deeply naive to imagine, once President Clinton had come out for "mend it, don't end it," that he would naturally want to support an initiative in California that would precisely mend affirmative action. Jerry was beginning to learn not to be naive. Instead, he realized, the calculus worked this way: the President's speech in July had an almost magical calming effect, taking the issue of affirmative action off the boil, and this had changed how the White House saw the California counter-initiative. If it moved forward, the President would have to endorse it, which would make affirmative action a central issue in his reelection campaign, which was not in his political interest. Once the White House figured this out, somebody could whisper in the ears of the union presidents, who'd get the message and not fund the counter-initiative. The President's people didn't have to kill it in a heavy-handed way. It would die—it did die—on its own, from lack of money.

The situation was becoming surreal.

It appeared that President Clinton had made a firm, courageous stand in favor of affirmative action in July. Yet the President's people (did he know?) were pulling the plug on the one plausible way of preserving affirmative action in California.

It appeared that the California Civil Rights Initiative itself was a powerful juggernaut. Hadn't it already occasioned a tidal wave of press coverage, a national debate, a full-scale White House policy review, a major presidential address, the submission of a landmark piece of federal legislation by the

Republicans' leading presidential candidate, ringing endorsements by all the other Republican presidential candidates, and, possibly, a Supreme Court decision? Yet the truth was that it was about to fail to get on the ballot at all.

The rules for getting a California budget initiative on the ballot are pretty unforgiving. Once you officially file, you have 150 days to collect valid signatures, and there must be enough to represent 8 percent of the vote in the last gubernatorial election. In 1995, that meant 697, 230 signatures; to leave room for challenges and other problems, a safe number to shoot for would be a million. With a few rare exceptions, nobody but a for-hire signature-gathering firm can obtain a million signatures in 150 days, and the professionals charge anywhere from fifty cents to a dollar fifty a signature. So just to get the initiative on the ballot, never mind campaigning for it, could cost a million dollars or more.

The California Civil Rights Initiative campaign was nowhere near being able to pay this. It tried a volunteer signature-gathering effort, but it brought in only 150,000 signatures. It tried a direct-mail solicitation signed by Newt Gingrich, which got another 150,000. There was no choice but to hire a firm, but where would the money come from? All the time that Glynn Custred and Tom Wood were becoming famous, Arnie Steinberg and Larry Arnn were having donors slam doors in their faces.

The way you get initiatives in California on the ballot is by hitting up the business interests involved. The initiative process had been created as a means for people with no money to change the laws without having to go through the special-interest–dominated state legislature; but special interests came to have a much tighter hold on the initiative process than on the legislature. If you wanted to pass an initiative abolishing trailer-park rent control, you'd get contributions from trailer-park owners. The closest thing to an interest group the California Civil Rights Initiative had was the Republican Party, which was interested not out of passion about affirmative action but in the hope that its presence on the ballot would help more Republicans to be elected.

When Steinberg and Arnn, their backs to the wall, pleaded with the party for money, it didn't seem to work. The most powerful men in the national Republican Party were all edging away from them. They began resorting to a veiled threat: the emergence of the Initiative had brought a lot of kooks out of the woodwork, racists and militia leaders, and without Republican funds these people might take over and turn it all into a terrible embarrassment for the party. That didn't work. By the late summer of 1995, they decided to start the clock running, in the hope that the prospect of the Initiative's imminent demise would bring in the party. Their 150 days of signature-gathering began on September 24.

All the money they had on hand went to make a deposit with a company called American Petition Consultants, of Sacramento, so that it would send out signature-gatherers into the supermarket parking lots of California. But within only a few weeks, they had fallen behind on their payments, and at the end of October, American Petition Consultants stopped work and refused to start again unless it was paid. During the first half of November the famous California Civil Rights Initiative was clinically dead; precious days passed with no signature-gathering activity.

Then, in late November, Larry Arnn announced that Ward Connerly, Governor Wilson's ally, had become co-chairman of the California Civil Rights Initiative. Publicly, the story was that Connerly had accepted as a simple matter of conscience, and this was true as far as it went. But everybody understood that Connerly took his signals from Governor Wilson. What his arrival really meant was that Wilson had decided to get the Initiative on the ballot. Soon American Petition Consultants was back at work. The Initiative campaign was now subsumed under a larger force (Republican politics) with a different primary goal (electing Republican politicians). It wasn't going to be a pure principled argument about the nature of meritocracy in America anymore, because it hadn't been able to survive as that.

Eleanor Smeal, the national director of Feminist Majority, was a veteran of many crusades of the American left; from one of these, Senator Edward Kennedy's presidential campaign in 1980, she knew a political consultant in Washington named Robert Shrum. She arranged for Shrum to fly out to California and meet with Peg Yorkin and Kathy Spillar. He advised them to hire a full-time field director and recommended for the job a protégée of his named Patricia Ewing. The Feminist Majority people met her, liked her, and brought her in.

Shrum was a settled senior presence in Washington, a rumpled, balding, companionable man with a vast and well-maintained web of contacts. Ewing was younger, still in the stage of a strategist's career where you move to wherever the election is and go full tilt, living on cigarettes and burritos, until it's over. She loved the combat atmosphere of a campaign: she'd pace her office in her red cowboy boots, a mass of blond curls pinned to the top of her head, a phone glued to her ear, cursing, wheedling, shouting orders to subordinates. Both she and Shrum lived on their ability to win elections for Democrats; they had to perform or they were finished.

Shrum and Ewing thought of their party, sentimentally, as the good guys and the fight against the California Civil Rights Initiative as a good cause, but they both also thought the Initiative would be awfully tough to defeat.

Shrum talked himself into the idea that maybe he could beat it if he had a lot of money to work with—five million dollars, say, or even more, which could go into television advertising, the only way, he believed, to change Californians' minds. A few fund-raising trips to California demonstrated to him that getting that kind of money was impossible. So by the time Ewing got to Los Angeles, she and Shrum had quietly concluded that they were going to lose.

They began thinking of their real mission as something other than winning straight up, but nonetheless vitally important: preventing the California Civil Rights Initiative from becoming the next Proposition 13, something that would set the agenda for national politics and sweep Republicans to power all over the country. If they could accomplish this, it would well serve their careers, because they would have performed an immensely valuable service to the Democratic Party, the source of their livelihood; but they thought it would serve the country well, too.

How would they do it? Pat Ewing, who liked to think in military metaphors, believed that the key was to create confusion within the camp of the adversary. You looked for ways to play games with their minds. You sowed the seeds of dissension and doubt. You learned what the divisions were and found ways to heighten them. You peeled off their allies one by one. You altered the cost-benefit calculations. You created little problems, you kept them nervous and on edge, you threw off their judgment.

These were not the terms in which the Feminist Majority people thought. They wanted to march in the streets—which, Ewing believed, was exactly what Republicans hoped for. Even though Ewing was working out of the Feminist Majority office and being paid with Feminist Majority funds, her relations with the Feminist Majority people, particularly Kathy Spillar, quickly turned sour. In April 1996 there was a horrible all-day meeting devoted to arguing over who would be the public spokesman for the campaign, Ewing or Spillar.

The person in the campaign Pat Ewing drew close to was Connie Rice. They were about the same age, both single, both consumed with the fight against the Initiative. Both liked to think of themselves as political warriors, intensely savvy, practical, and committed. Military metaphors came easily to Connie's mind, too, since she was a military brat. When she needed a little boost to her spirits during some low moment, she would sneak out to see *Apollo 13* for the millionth time, and then strut into the Legal Defense Fund office and proclaim, "Failure is not an option!" Before long Pat Ewing and Connie had set up almost an organized opposition to the Feminist Majority people. Connie and Kathy Spillar got into an argument at a fund-raising party at Lorraine Sheinberg's house. There was another long, bitter meeting—two whole days this time—during which Spillar got so upset that she temporarily lost her sight.

Ewing desperately wanted to keep the Feminist Majority's busloads of student protesters off the television news and get about her business of playing with the Republicans' heads. There were several prongs to her plan of attack: to persuade the chairmen of big California corporations, with well-entrenched affirmative-action plans and lots of minority customers, that they should oppose the California Civil Rights Initiative; to use their opposition as a lever to move a few prominent moderate Republicans away from the Initiative, on the grounds that it was divisive; to highlight support for the Initiative by extremists like David Duke, the Louisiana Ku Klux Klan leader turned politician; to let the Republican high command in Washington, already extremely worried about their party's weakness among female voters, know that the clause about gender discrimination was making it unpopular among women in California. Above all this, glittering alone at the top of the tactical pile, was one more idea: to get to Colin Powell.

This was an idea that had occurred to both sides of the California Civil Rights Initiative campaign. Powell, recently retired after a military career in which he had been the architect of the American victory in the Persian Gulf War and then Chairman of the Joint Chiefs of Staff, was possibly the most admired man in the United States at that moment, certifiably moderate, and black. For many Americans, whatever Powell thought could stand as shorthand for the right thing to do. Powell had spent most of 1995 flirting with the idea of running for President and had then decided not to. Still, for Republicans in 1996 he was the dream vice presidential candidate who could carry any ticket to victory; merely his agreement to campaign would be a great boon. Once his position on the Initiative could be determined, no prominent Republican would want to contradict it.

Arnie Steinberg put a lot of effort into lobbying Powell. In July 1995 he was granted a very brief audience to make his pitch. He waited awhile and then wrote Powell a gently prodding note. Powell wrote back, somewhat cryptically: "I understand the CRI, but I still believe there are broader issues involved." That was a no.

Over the next few months, after Powell made several brief, hazy statements indicating that he supported affirmative action, it was decided within the opposition camp that Connie Rice should write him a letter asking for an opportunity to discuss the Initiative with him—Connie had a cousin, the similarly named Condoleezza Rice, who had worked closely with Powell in the White House in the 1980s. Powell wrote back saying he was supportive, he didn't want to do anything right away, but perhaps they could talk later.

Connie waited a few months and wrote him again, and he said she should come for a visit.

In April 1996, Connie and Elaine Jones, head of the Legal Defense Fund in New York, called on Colin Powell at his house in the Washington suburbs. By prearrangement, Jones, who was roughly Powell's age and was the first black woman graduate of the University of Virginia Law School, played the role of the compadre, the down-home, humble-origined, first-generation fellow barrier-breaker, while Connie played the bristlingly efficient young military officer. She knew how to do this by birthright; she actually prepared a Pentagon-style briefing, complete with flip charts, of the kind that her father used to present to generals. They spent the better part of a day with Powell. At the end he thanked them warmly and said he might or might not speak out against the Initiative. Connie left her briefing book with him.

Six weeks later, in a commencement address at Bowie State College in Maryland, Powell delivered a broadside against the California Civil Rights Initiative. "There are those who rail against affirmative action," he said. "They rail against affirmative action preferences, while they have lived an entire life of preference."

Connie's visit to Powell was Pat Ewing's idea of the perfect political move, a three-cushion shot. Connie and Elaine Jones had called on Colin Powell, without anyone knowing about it. No explicit deals had been made. Then Colin Powell gave his speech at Bowie State. Result: the collective mind of the Republican Party, and in particular the individual mind of Bob Dole, begins to feel a strange new doubt about the magic political potency of the affirmative-action issue. Dole shelved his bill to abolish affirmative action. The opposition had affected the Republicans' thinking without their even being aware of the chain of causation. All the Republicans knew was that they kept seeing polling about the gender gap, that Colin Powell was going around making fiery speeches, and that the California Civil Rights Initiative was feeling ungainly and troublesome.

After that Dole took a major dive on the issue. While campaigning as a presidential candidate he hardly ever brought up affirmative action, and when he did, he always seemed to mishandle it. He would sourly mumble his way through events for Proposition 209 (as the Initiative was called now that it was on the ballot) that his staff had arranged for him in California. He didn't seem to feel the substance of it—once, but only once, he managed to force the word "merit" out of his mouth, in a low voice that was difficult to hear—and he was alarmingly unguarded about discussing the political calculations, even saying publicly, proudly, that affirmative action was a good wedge issue for the Republican Party!

Colin Powell consented to give the keynote address at the Republican National Convention, and turned it into a flaming defense of affirmative action that went far beyond what any powerful Democrat had said. And Dole selected as his running mate Jack Kemp, the conservative, tax-hating former New York congressman and Secretary of Housing and Urban Development, who up to that point had been the Republican Party's most ardent supporter of affirmative action. Kemp's recantation of his previous views sounded manufactured, and during the campaign he was the furthest thing from a committed, effective advocate of Proposition 209. Like Dole's, his reluctance was palpable whenever he talked about it, and he always found a way to mangle the simple message of belief in a color-blind society that was supposed to accompany discussion of Prop 209. Once, for example, he said he favored Prop 209 because he supported the Supreme Court decision in the *Bakke* case, when the exact purpose of Prop 209 was to countermand that decision.

So the Republican Party had been neutralized. Meanwhile, Bob Shrum and Pat Ewing seemed to be in constant touch with high-level Democratic Party people in Washington—it was impossible to tell exactly how much, but they gave the impression that they were speaking regularly to the likes of George Stephanopoulos, or even to people above his level. Even after the disappointments from the party thus far, the hope inevitably began to awaken of a closer partnership between the campaign and the Democratic Party. President Clinton had made a stirring full-length speech in defense of affirmative action, after all. Since then his political position had become much stronger, especially in California, where polls showed him to be far in the lead. Thanks to the most elaborate fund-raising effort in the history of American politics, the Democratic Party was now flush with money. Was it so foolhardy to hope that the anti–Prop 209 campaign, now that it had Washington insiders at the helm, might be rescued with party money and a presidential commitment?

Pat Ewing let it be known that the biggest impediment to a full, warm White House embrace was the Feminist Majority crowd. For example, they had staged a widely televised event in Sacramento involving people dressed in black laying coffins on the steps of the state capitol building to symbolize the death of women's rights. This kind of loony-left tactic was the White House's worst nightmare. The feminists, for their part, began to wonder whether Ewing and Shrum were more loyal to the party establishment in Washington than to the campaign that was paying them.

In August 1996, another horrible meeting, held on a Sunday at a hotel near the Los Angeles airport, amounted to fourteen hours of pure lividity.

Connie accused the Feminist Majority people of insensitivity to blacks, and
Pat Ewing delivered a long litany of complaints, especially about her inabil-
ity to control how their position was presented to the press. By the end it had
been decided to set up three separate campaign bank accounts controlled by
three different people, but that was obviously a tiny solution futilely put in
place to solve an enormous problem.

Molly Munger missed the meeting at the airport hotel, but Connie filled
her in. Out of all the endless arguing, one phrase had stuck in Connie's mind.
Somebody from the Feminist Majority had said that Pat Ewing's real problem was that she couldn't focus on anything but "the electoral strategy." The
electoral strategy! This was a campaign, right? That was why they were all
here, right? So why was "the electoral strategy" a pejorative phrase? Pat
Ewing and Connie agreed on this, of course. Ewing was in touch with lots of
people in the political world. It was made known to her, and she made it
known to Connie and Molly, that the opposition campaign would get the
kind of major contributions that thus far hadn't come in if it didn't include
the Feminist Majority people. To be specific, the service employees' union
would give $100,000 if the Feminist Majority people weren't around.

There was nothing Molly would wish for more than that this situation
hadn't developed. In the 1970s, while Molly was working as a corporate
lawyer, the senior figures in Feminist Majority had campaigned endlessly
(though finally unsuccessfully) for the Equal Rights Amendment, spending
every day making another speech in another town and sleeping in another
motel room. In an indirect but undeniable way, their hard work had made
space for what Molly was doing. She owed them. And when the California
Civil Rights Initiative came along, they had immediately fought back—the
only people who did—and they had brought in Shrum and Ewing. The
Democrats had been condescending, distancing, and inactive, which made
Molly burn every time she thought about it.

She had learned something new, though, working on this campaign.
Molly liked to knit. Her previous work as a lawyer, she now thought, had
been like knitting something in a small, fine pattern: you used tiny, precise
needles and thin yarn and worked carefully alone for hours and at the end
you had a perfectly made square. Politics, on the other hand, was like knitting a big, loose comforter with thick yarn. It was messier and rougher and
went much more quickly; the satisfaction of getting everything exactly right
had to be sacrificed to make the bigger thing.

That Molly now had to make a choice she didn't want to make, and
hadn't expected to have to make—to decide whether to throw in her lot with
the feminists or the political professionals—was a particular, immediate

manifestation of something much larger, the failure of a social order. Molly was both a rational, systematic person and a passionate moralist. Was that a contradiction? If it was, she wasn't alone in embodying it. The American meritocracy as a whole did, too. It had been set up to be systematic and moral at the same time—moral, indeed, as a result of being perfectly systematic. But after fifty years, this perfect blend of qualities still hadn't been achieved, perhaps because it was unachievable: the project of deciding who gets slots in universities simply can't be made to function as the moral mainspring of a society. So questions of morality and social justice were left primarily to the elective political system on one hand, and to independent-movement groups like Feminist Majority on the other. In 1996, if you wanted to be a reformer, you had to choose between those two, and abandon a lifetime's hope that the meritocracy itself, if operated in just the right way, could perfect the United States.

Molly decided to go with the political system, even though it had disappointed her at every turn thus far. There wasn't finally any alternative—that was what she was learning. The founders of the American meritocracy had erred not only in expecting too much perfection of their system but also in assuming that one could successfully set up a new social order in the United States without public debate and consent. Those errors left their heirs in the position of being elaborately trained leaders with no followers. If people like Molly wanted to achieve their goals, they had to generate public support, and the only way to do that was in politics. You had an obligation, Molly felt, at least to try what was most likely to produce the result you were fighting for.

It fell to Molly to manage the endgame between the feminists and the political people. She still had credibility and respect on both sides, and she knew how to handle complicated disputes. She took a deep breath and asked Kathy Spillar if she and a few other people from the campaign could talk to her and Eleanor Smeal and Peg Yorkin about something confidential. They arranged a time one August evening at the Feminist Majority offices. After a little awkward small talk, Molly said: We need to be communicating here. She glanced at her colleagues. They gave her looks that said: Uh-uh, you do the talking. So Molly plowed on. The reason we're here, she said, is that the campaign as we've known it is over.

What do you mean? asked Eleanor Smeal.

Molly said she meant it was time for the opposition to Prop 209 to split into two separate groups, with the feminists in one and everybody else in the other. She was there to kick them out, for the good of the overall campaign.

Another difference between this and Molly's previous life was that, as a corporate lawyer, you never went into an important negotiation without having elaborately explored in advance every possible response to every possible point. This was a crucial moment in the opposition campaign, but there hadn't been any time to prepare for it. Molly just had to hope for the best.

Were Eleanor Smeal and Peg Yorkin and Kathy Spillar angry? Yes, they were angry, and they appeared to have been taken completely by surprise. As the meeting wore on, though, Molly sensed that they would accept the idea of the split, especially since the only real alternative was to spend the entire fall holding one poisonous all-day meeting after another. Toward midnight, as they were preparing to leave, Molly turned to Eleanor Smeal and said, in her customary brisk, cheerful way: Ellie, you're a class act, and when this is all over, I'm with you.

That didn't go over well. To the minds of the Feminist Majority people, Molly had gone to the enemy. It didn't matter if she was with them when this was all over—she wasn't with them now.

28
Defeat

The check from the service employees' union that was supposed to arrive immediately after the split didn't come.

Molly Munger, one of the world's more imperturbably positive people, fell into a funk that lasted for most of September. It wasn't a paralytic funk—she was frantically busy—but a feeling of deep annoyance she couldn't shake. This came from her dawning, if not yet fully accepted, realization that she'd been gamed. From the earliest days of the anti-Initiative campaign, various Democratic Party and White House figures had been hinting that a spigot of financial aid was about to be opened if only the campaign would do this or that. One of Bill Press's aides had once told Molly that even though the party wasn't helping now, "our pockets might become unstitched" later—that was the way it was typically phrased.

Most of the people in the anti–Prop 209 campaign didn't know exactly how the world of big-time politics worked. You maintained an appropriate veneer of cynicism, but peel that away and you had an idea that the Democratic Party might want to get involved in the campaign, since it involved a historic challenge to the party's number-one moral commitment and would have made sense even if the party hadn't actively (though subtly) promoted it. The exact mechanism by which Democrats would get the money to the opposition campaign wasn't clear. Were direct contributions made out of the party treasury? Would President Clinton appear at a fund-raising event? Would signals be sent to third parties, like the unions, to the effect that the White House looked favorably on contributions to the opposition campaign? It seemed clear that whichever it was, the presidential campaign, by now far ahead of the Republicans and flush with contributions, would get the money to the campaign against Prop 209 if it wanted to.

Instead, it seemed that the party conjured the apparition of cash whenever it wanted to influence the situation in its own interest—and then the apparition would vanish once the influence had been successfully exercised. When it might be in the President's interest to have a counter-initiative, there were signals about forthcoming money; then when the interest calculation in the White House changed, the money never came. When it was convenient for the White House to induce the factions that had disagreed so bitterly to work together again, vague, hopeful rumors arose about money; when the two sides mended fences, the money never came. When Washington became concerned that the feminists, with their penchant for staging televised demonstrations, might be turning off swing voters, the signal went out that if they were off-loaded before the fall campaign season it would mean funding; then, after Molly had done that unpleasant job for the good of the larger cause, the money never came.

Proposition 209 had slipped in the polls and was no longer ahead by the crushing 30-point margin that it once had. But none of the endless activities mounted against it mattered, because in the fall of a campaign year in California, only broadcast advertising counts, and the opposition campaign couldn't afford that. A busy traffic began in outraged stories about the financial perfidy of the White House.

Connie Rice had managed to get herself invited to a private event featuring Vice President Al Gore, and she asked him what the White House was doing to help defeat Prop 209. His answer seemed listless and perfunctory, and failed to motivate the contributors who were there. President Clinton, on one of his innumerable trips to California, had had a long, searching conversation while sitting in a hot tub with David Geffen, the richest man in the entertainment business and a big political contributor: the right signal at that moment could have unloosed an avalanche of funds from Geffen and his friends. Instead Geffen gave only $10,000 and then only because Peg Yorkin pressured him. The best story of all, the smoking-gun story, was that when Pat Ewing at a meeting had accused the state coordinator of the presidential campaign in California of having gone around telling important Democratic donors not to give to Defeat 209, the coordinator had gone into a long, indignant denial, at the climactic moment of which he turned to his assistant and asked her to affirm that everything he had just said was the gospel truth—and she wouldn't!

Molly began trolling the boardrooms of California for contributions. But every time she or Pat Ewing met with anyone and obtained a tentative commitment, Governor Wilson—the governor himself, not some underling—

would remind the potential contributor of how much business his company did with the state government, and of how heavily regulated it was by state agencies run by gubernatorial employees. The threats were that direct. And of course the contribution would dematerialize. The governor is a moral pygmy, one man told Molly, but he can cost me $250 million just by moving my regulation by two points. Another said that regulatory hearings involving his company were going on, and he had taken a look at his schedule and found that he would be extremely busy all fall, did Molly understand what he meant? As if to prove that Molly wasn't being paranoid, a few articles came out in the newspapers that confirmed her impressions: in one, a reporter overheard a conference call in which Wilson and Newt Gingrich pitched big contributors on the idea that to give to the Prop 209 campaign was to help all Republican candidates; in another, Wilson sent a letter to corporations warning them not to contribute to the other side.

Here, it seemed to Molly, was a rare case of the two major American political parties finding themselves in complete agreement. The Republican Party was deeply committed to preventing the Defeat 209 campaign from getting money to buy political advertising, and the Democratic Party was, too.

Kristin Luker, Jerry Karabel's wife, was pregnant, to the delighted surprise of both of them. In August 1996 Jerry and Krista became late-forties first-time parents, of twins. They took matching leaves of absence from their teaching jobs at Berkeley. For Jerry it was part paternity leave and part an opportunity to put more energy into the final phase of the Defeat 209 campaign. He didn't actually go out on the hustings; in fact he hardly left the house. But he operated a homey command post, juggling bottles, diapers, faxes, and phone calls, the house strewn with a wild miscellany of stuff (*Babyhood* by Penelope Leach, Otis Redding's Greatest Hits, polls, clippings, strollers), people from the campaign constantly dropping by with the latest intelligence reports.

Of all the astonishing things that had happened that political year, what Jerry found most astonishing was that President Clinton—Mr. Mend It Don't End It, Mr. Eloquent Defender of Affirmative Action—had still never officially come out against Proposition 209. It was true: you could look through his public statements and you wouldn't find anything.

An opportunity presented itself over the summer when Eva Paterson, leader of the opposition to Prop 209 in the Bay Area, was invited to a White House event, the kind where each guest gets to chat with the President for a minute or two. During her time, she told Clinton that her family came from Hope, Arkansas, the town where he was born, and that the President's grandfather had been the only white shopkeeper in town who would sell things to black families like hers. The President loved that. He gave Paterson more than her allotted time, and he made her feel the full depth and sincerity of his appreciation for the good work she and her colleagues were doing in the campaign against Proposition 209. He told her his position on it was well established in the public record. Later he even worked into a speech the anecdote about Paterson's family shopping at his grandfather's store.

When Paterson told all this to Jerry Karabel back in California, they looked again for the President's record of explicit opposition to Prop 209 and couldn't find it. Jerry had the idea that Paterson should write President Clinton a letter thanking him for his kind words while artfully attempting to get a written statement of his view of Prop 209. Miraculously, this ploy worked. "Proposals such as Proposition 209 that are designed to eliminate all affirmative action programs in public education, employment, and contracting are inconsistent with our national goal of ensuring equal opportunity, and contrary to all of our interests," the President wrote Paterson. "I assure you I will actively oppose this measure."

That was step one. Step two was to release the President's letter to Paterson to the press. But Jerry found that Pat Ewing was curiously unenthusiastic about this. Even though everybody in the moderate part of the opposition was supposed to love Ewing for having set in motion the divorce from the feminists, Jerry's relationship with her had never had any spark. Whenever he talked to her, he had the feeling that there was a big blinking neon sign over his head reading: PROFESSOR—HANDLE WITH EXTREME CAUTION. She seemed to have a patronizing, keep-you-at-arm's-length timbre in her voice, which denoted an impression on her part that he incarnated fuzzy-headed political impracticality. Meanwhile he had his own compensating suspicion of her, as a political operative for whom good relations with the Democratic politicians who were her future employers were more important than winning the campaign against Prop 209.

Karabel just couldn't persuade Ewing to release the President's letter to Eva Paterson in a way that would ensure that the press made a fuss over it. He went over her head and appealed directly to Shrum, but that didn't work either. Finally, the letter was released by the California office of the presidential campaign late on Friday afternoon of the Labor Day weekend, in a packet with several unrelated minor announcements. It therefore got no attention, which Jerry thought must have been just what the White House wanted.

In October, the long-expected money from the unions finally began to arrive. Between the service employees, the teachers, and the California Democratic Party, the opposition campaign received a little more than a million dollars, which meant that television advertising would be possible at last. Every Thursday all the leaders of the opposition campaign talked in a conference call; soon Jerry began hearing Pat Ewing and Bob Shrum describe with great enthusiasm a plan to bet all the money on a single roll of the dice. There would be only one ad, which would be about David Duke's support for Prop 209. Duke had showed up in California a few months earlier to participate in a debate about Prop 209; Shrum had dispatched a camera crew to cover it, and now, well pleased with his foresight, he wanted to turn the footage into a thirty-second television spot.

Jerry couldn't believe this. Anybody who looked at the polling data would see that they needed to cut into Prop 209's heavy support among whites, especially white men. Putting David Duke in the only ad would make them look like a polarizing, exaggerating, disingenuous bunch of left-wingers. Everybody knew that Prop 209 wasn't a Ku Klux Klan operation, and to suggest that it was would insult, not persuade, swing voters.

Okay: instead of just complaining fruitlessly in the conference calls, Jerry resolved to find a way to move the opinion of the campaign high command away from the Duke ad. An acquaintance of his named Shanto Iyengar, a professor of political science at UCLA, agreed, after a little prodding, to test all the opposition's possible ads with focus groups and in quick polls, free of charge. Iyengar was willing to do this because he was sympathetic to the campaign and because he thought he could get some good material for a book he was working on. Jerry presented the idea to his colleagues as a rare opportunity to get free market research from a leading expert.

Pat Ewing said: No, thanks. You have to trust your gut instinct in this business, especially when time and money are short, and she would just run the Duke ad without testing it. The professor wants to bring in another professor who wants to use the opposition campaign as a chance to get material for a book he's writing? She didn't think so.

Jerry was, fundamentally, a gentle and curious soul, but insofar as was possible for him, he spent the rest of the time until Election Day in a state of controlled rage. He'd call his friends and insistently, incredulously lay out the situation, asking rhetorically every unanswerable question he could think of about the Democrats' behavior. Proposition 209 was important. It was a big political showdown encompassing all the main questions about the structure of opportunity in the United States, the issue that lay at the pulsing innermost chamber of the life of the key society in the world. Dare one say that it was more important than who won this or that race for political office in November 1996? Why didn't anyone seem to be focusing on this with an all-out commitment of analytic intelligence?

Well, rather than distance himself and use his academic skills to criticize the campaign airily and dismissively, in the time-honored manner of the intellectual who loses a political battle, Jerry decided to use them to figure out how to change his colleagues' minds. Late at night, when the twins were asleep, he would construct alternate advertising scripts that might appeal to Shrum and Ewing. The best idea, he thought, would be something involving both President Clinton and Colin Powell.

From Powell they already had a wonderful sound bite: the Bowie State commencement speech. From the President, they had only his letter to Eva Paterson, which wasn't good television material. He needed to say something personally, on-camera. Then, fortuitously, he did. On the evening of October 16, the presidential candidates held their second debate, in California, in a format under which ordinary voters rather than journalists asked the questions. A lady got up and said, "My name is Tracy Saunders and my question is do you feel that America has grown enough and has educated itself enough to totally cut out affirmative action?" It sounded to Jerry like a plant from the Prop 209 campaign, but that was okay with him as long as it elicited a firm, definite presidential answer.

President Clinton stepped forthrightly out from behind his podium and toward the lady who asked the question. He set his jaw. He looked her straight in the eye. He said, "No, ma'am, I don't." Then he spent three or four minutes making the argument in favor of affirmative action that Jerry had been longing to hear from him.

But it was strange: when Jerry got hold of a videotape the next day and played the President's answer over and over, he found that he couldn't get a sound bite out of it. The President hadn't mentioned Prop 209. It just felt as if he had while you were watching the debate.

On October 31, with less than a week left in the campaign, the President came to California again. At a rally in Jack London Square in downtown Oakland, before a mostly black crowd in which a lot of Defeat 209 signs were visible, he finally said, in public, while being recorded, that he was against Prop 209. Jerry immediately composed a fax to Shrum, headed URGENT-URGENT-URGENT. He pulled out all the stops: "We must immediately reassess the situation with respect to the Duke ad and seize the opportunity given to us by Clinton's speech today. I believe we should immediately replace the Duke ad. . . . Failure to do this could be the margin by which we lose this historic election. And if this happens, we would all share the burden of responsibility for the disaster."

Shrum never got back to him.

Forced to give up his view of himself as a participant, not merely an observer, Jerry observed. His theory was this: President Clinton's victory in California was now assured beyond even the most nervous worrying of his most pessimistic aides. Therefore a little attention could be paid to other matters—not Prop 209, but the broader fortunes of the Democratic Party. The state assembly, which in 1994 had gone Republican for the first time in decades, was beginning to look recapturable. Three California congressional seats held by Republicans had come into the range of the Democrats. One way to tip the balance in these races would be to use Prop 209 to do what's known in the trade as "mobilizing the base," meaning, for Democrats, stimulating turnout by black and Latino voters (and for Republicans, by Christian conservatives). And what better way to do that than to put on the air a television ad that showed David Duke in a white hood, in front of a burning cross? It wouldn't make white swing voters change their minds about Prop 209, but it might well scare black voters enough to bring them to the polls, where they could be counted upon to vote for the local Democratic legislative and congressional candidates.

Jerry was supposed to be the guy who was against hierarchy, and he had put eight years of his life into fighting for a better, fairer hierarchy instead of trying to get rid of the whole idea. That was bad enough, but waging that battle and losing was even worse—and losing by virtue of being completely, humiliatingly ignored, both personally and conceptually, was worst of all.

Arnie Steinberg put together a series of television ads for the Prop 209 campaign that were in tone, though not of course in the position they advocated, just the kind that Jerry Karabel wanted the opposition to have. In each ad a person, usually either a white woman or a black man, shot in a soft, glowing light, would speak in a low-key, persuasive, sincere way about how Prop 209 would eliminate racial preferences and re-create the true American dream of a color-blind society. The ads were in no way negative or harsh or crudely racial. They took the high road. They appealed to the reasonable undecided voter. The only thing wrong with them was that Steinberg didn't have the money to run them. His total television budget was a minuscule $200,000.

Then, suddenly, strangely, at the end of October, Bob Dole's passionate opposition to affirmative action reappeared. On October 29, Dole flew to San Diego and delivered a major, formal address about the evils of affirmative action and the urgent necessity of Prop 209.

Dole's presidential candidacy was by that time a hopelessly lost cause. Steinberg surmised that the elders of the Republican Party had decided to make Prop 209 more visible in the hope that its popularity would rub off on Republican congressional and legislative candidates endangered by Dole's weakness. They had talked Dole, a loyal party man, into doing his part by putting Prop 209 at rhetorical center stage during the last week of the campaign, and they had found a million and a half dollars for a last-week advertising blitz on behalf of Prop 209.

The catch was that the Republicans wouldn't be spending the money to put Steinberg's ads on the air. Instead they would make new ads under the supervision of John Herrington, an automobile dealer who was the Republican state chairman and who was known to Steinberg, Glynn Custred, and Tom Wood as someone who profoundly didn't grasp the fundamentals of the Prop 209 campaign. Herrington made one ad with himself as the spokesman, a well-fed Republican white male, just the face the campaign didn't want. He made another featuring his secretary. A third made the argument that Martin Luther King, if he were still living, would favor Prop 209—a surmise that Custred and Wood had made in earlier days but stopped saying when it was established that King had actually favored affirmative action—so Herrington's King ad drew a quick barrage of criticism and he had to withdraw it, which was embarrassing. And every one of his ads made a big point of President Clinton's opposition to Prop 209. They all practically said out loud: We're not trying to win votes for Prop 209, we're trying to scare voters away from Democratic candidates in other races.

Steinberg had invested two years of his life in Prop 209. What was he supposed to do, meekly accept this ad campaign that turned all his work on its head? Well, he didn't. Instead he made his unhappiness known to anybody who would listen. Finally he announced he would go before the board of the California Republican Party and formally contest the way its advertising money was being spent. Ward Connerly, titular chairman of the Prop 209 campaign, dismissed Steinberg for insubordination.

It was a strange firing. Within a couple of days Steinberg and Connerly were back to speaking incessantly on the phone about campaign strategy. It was Steinberg's impression that he was the Republican equivalent of the Feminist Majority people: Connerly had been told that if he got rid of him, the party would become more generous with its funds.

What was most interesting about Steinberg's dismissal, though, was an article about it in the *Los Angeles Times*—especially a somewhat cryptic couple of sentences buried down near the end. George Skelton, the reporter who wrote it, a veteran with a reputation for being well plugged in, wrote: "Until now, there seems to have been a tacit nonaggression pact—subtly negotiated by Steinberg—between the 209 and Clinton camps. Clinton's support of affirmative action . . . would not be emphasized as long as the President did not raise big bucks for the anti-209 war chest." Skelton didn't say so, but anybody who knew what was what could figure out who Steinberg's contact in the other camp must have been: his old friend Bill Wardlaw, Democratic head of Clinton's campaign in California. Wardlaw would have gotten out of their pact political protection for the President; Steinberg would have gotten a reprieve from a significant opposition campaign.

The way events now played out lent plausibility to the notion that this agreement had in fact been made. Steinberg's ads never mentioned Clinton, and the opposition to Prop 209 never got any Democratic Party money. Then, as soon as Herrington's ads began to run, always mentioning the President, Democratic money began to flow into the coffers of the organized opposition to Prop 209. Steinberg himself didn't really bother to deny the story about the pact. He and Wardlaw talked all the time; they understood one another: there was a mutuality of interest between them.

But imagine if you were Molly Munger or Jerry Karabel, a battle-weary stalwart of the Defeat 209 campaign, and you found all this out on the very eve of the election. You had already been through the cycle of hope and despair enough times to have finally absorbed the truth that your party and your President had consistently led you on with artful signals of forthcoming support that evaporated like shimmering oases in the desert. You had come to realize that they cared about the Prop 209 campaign only insofar as it affected the electoral fortunes of Democratic candidates, especially President Clinton. Could it get any more disillusioning than that? Yes, it turned out, it could: your party and your President might actually have been in closer, smoother, and more efficient cooperation with the enemy all along than with the people who had spent two years putting heart and soul into saving affirmative action.

On the morning before Election Day, Bill Lee wandered into Molly's office at the Legal Defense Fund and raised an eyebrow. "Well?"

Bill was dressed customarily, in blue jeans torn at the knee and an old sweater. Molly had to make another speech that day, at a women lawyers' luncheon in Orange County, so she had a suit on. Their affect matched their clothes (and for that matter their personalities): Bill skeptical, Molly buoyant. "It's *close!*" she said.

"What does that mean? Too close to call?"

"Well," Molly said, "we did pretty well, considering." They both knew what was going to happen.

Molly had spent a great deal of her time during October doing what she would be doing today: driving around the Los Angeles basin in her BMW convertible to one or another Prop 209 event. It was a mildly surreal experience. She was required constantly to make confident predictions of victory that she knew were unrealistic, to talk about affirmative action as if it were a simple matter of justice when it was actually a not very satisfactory partial solution to a big problem, and to try not to let people see the bitterness that by now pervaded the world of people trying to defeat Prop 209.

Besides that, the spread and variety of Los Angeles were disorienting. The city where Molly had grown up had seemed to her to cohere. As compared with cities in the East, its poor sections hadn't been so poor and the rich sections hadn't been so inaccessible. Everybody had gone to public school and zoomed happily along the freeways. Unpretentiousness and lack of class consciousness had been great points of California pride. Now, in the fall of 1996, under the same bleaching sun and the same abrupt, sere mountains that denoted home, LA was different. The end of the Cold War had brought a severe recession to southern California, which was heavily dependent on the aerospace industry that Molly had served as a lawyer, but now it was over. People were building mansions in Beverly Hills and cutting brand-new suburbs into the hillsides. Her friends were sending their children to wonderful private schools and taking adventurous vacations. Then, as you traveled around, you'd see things that brought you up short, such as public schools that looked like decrepit holding pens. Los Angeles no longer seemed like a place that provided equal opportunity to everyone. It did not seem like a place that had an agreed-upon, well-functioning social compact. It did not seem like a place where people felt a real connection, let alone obligation, to anyone outside their immediate circle.

One day Molly drove out to Claremont—Larry Arnn territory—and debated Dinesh D'Souza, a well-known conservative author.

One day she went to a fund-raising breakfast on the West Side in West Los Angeles where George Stephanopoulos was the featured attraction.

One day she received an award for her contributions to the legal profession in Los Angeles.

One day she went to a big synagogue in the San Fernando Valley to hear Connie debate Eugene Volokh, a Russian émigré who was a law professor at UCLA and a strategist for the other side.

One night she went to a big, jam-packed, elaborately produced rally put on by "No on 209," the Feminist Majority group, at an auditorium on the West Side, where Anita Hill, the feminist heroine, was the top-billed speaker and everyone clasped hands and sang "We Shall Overcome" at the end.

One night she went to a fund-raiser at a Hollywood producer's house in Hancock Park, where she listened to California's two senators, Barbara

Boxer and Dianne Feinstein, speak confidently about how quickly the campaign against Prop 209 was closing the gap. In another room, on television, the vice presidential candidates were debating Prop 209: Vice President Gore said it was really an issue of a woman's right to choose. Jack Kemp ineffectually stammered out a reply. Eleanor Smeal of Feminist Majority glared at Kemp's head on the screen and said, "Keep talkin', ya dope! Keep doin' it! You're finished!"

One day Molly visited a middle school where the students were being taught from recycled work sheets because there was no money for textbooks.

Sometimes Molly worried that she was turning into a Los Angeles version of Prince Myshkin, the hero of one of her favorite novels, Dostoevsky's *The Idiot*—an innocent, positive-thinking young man (he carries around a parchment on which he has calligraphed the motto "Zeal overcomes all") who seems to generate a swirl of intense but indefinite activity around him wherever he goes.

On that morning before the election, Molly got in her BMW, put on her sunglasses, and drove down the Santa Ana Freeway to Orange County. The peak of the imitation Matterhorn at Disneyland glided spectrally by at the side of the road. She was thinking, thinking, thinking all the time about what to make of this experience she had had—thinking so all-consumingly that she missed her exit and had to turn around and drive back.

She got reoriented and found the place she was speaking with only a little bit of trouble. As soon as she walked in she could see that these were her people: women lawyers.

"This will be a nonpartisan speech," Molly said. Then she walked the audience through the whole story of her journey from legal glass-ceiling-breaker to civil-rights crusader. She had the audience: the women were nodding at every rhetorical beat, laughing at the jokes, applauding at the flourishes. She said she felt like Rip Van Winkle: she had put so many years into getting her career going and raising her children that she had hardly noticed what was going on in the outside world, and now she had awakened to find that American society had problems, pressing, scary problems, for women but not just for women, that people like them needed to address.

"How many of you would be willing to work in a new bipartisan group?" Molly asked. Every hand in the room went up. "Then pass me your business cards. Because we don't want this ride *ever* again."

At the end of Michael Young's *The Rise of the Meritocracy* comes the uprising of 2034, in which the low-IQ masses bloodily overthrow their meritocratic masters. That wasn't happening in the United States in 1996. The

meritocratic machinery was firmly in place. The first wave of its highest beneficiaries were now middle-aged, they occupied positions of responsibility,
and they were paying the system the ultimate tribute by trying to make sure
that their children (whether meritorious or not) would benefit from it, too.
They were in no danger whatsoever.

But they had not established themselves as an acknowledged American
leadership class, which was the original idea and was their own wish. That
was the lesson of the Prop 209 campaign. Most Americans just didn't accept
the idea of a formal, test-based meritocracy, leavened by affirmative action,
as the central organizing principle of their country's life. If any one category
of people ran America it was the Talents. The Mandarins themselves were
an elite of experts, highly competent and prosperous, but not generally
accepted as a natural aristocracy or a governing elite. They were substantially the authors of their own fate. Most of them devoted their lives mainly
to advancement—why should they be received as public servants if they
didn't comport themselves that way? Even Mandarins who ascended to real
public power did not, as had become painfully clear in the relationship
between the White House and the campaign against Proposition 209,
adhere to core principles first and careers second when a conflict arose
between the two.

Molly and Steve had both truly believed in the original vision. Steve
sometimes thought about writing a book that would argue, contrary to popular myth, that America had always done well when it addressed its difficulties by committing massive central-government resources: look at the
Panama Canal, the space program, the Second World War, and, in California, the freeways and the water system and the Master Plan. The same
approach could work again, only it had passed completely out of fashion.
America had channeled opportunity through the educational system and
then had failed to create schools and colleges that would work for everybody,
because that was very expensive and voters didn't want to pay for it.

Mandarins' natural tendency was either to get caught up in the busy-
ness of being an expert, even when it didn't advance their ideals, or to
pursue reform in a Mandarin manner, through lawsuits and regulatory
procedures. Molly and Steve both exemplified this tendency. While Steve
was composing in his mind his defense of big government, at work he was
defending the enormous brokerage house of Merrill Lynch against the
charge that it had induced the treasurer of Orange County, California, to
make excessively risky investments, which had gone sour and caused the
county to go bankrupt. The case was a direct result of public mistrust of
government: Orange County had gone into the financial markets in search

of money it couldn't get through taxation, because taxes were anathema to voters. Molly, for her part, had made the wrenching break from corporate law practice that Steve wasn't yet quite ready for, in order to go into public-interest law. One lesson for her of the campaign against Prop 209 was that the Legal Defense Fund was pursuing the right goal, equal opportunity, but that lawsuits—even more broadly, defenses of affirmative action—weren't the proper means.

Back when the second half of the twentieth century—modern, democratic, peaceful—was just coming into view, James Bryant Conant had believed with utter confidence that the United States could be made into a classless, perfectly mobile society through the construction of a great technical personnel system. Now, with the century's end coming into view, it was impossible for Molly, or anybody else, to say with a straight face that the country had become classless. The advent of a formal eudcational meritocracy might even have made it more class-bound, not less. It had become quite clear to Molly that endlessly fiddling with the system Conant and his allies had built was not the way to bring the realization of the democratic ideal. The plan for the system had been too hubristic—in particular, too optimistic about the loyalty of the American public to the meritocratic system as an instrument of justice. Democracy and meritocracy were separate projects, and people like Molly, who were primarily concerned with democracy, were going to have to find a new way of promoting it.

On election night the opposition, typically, held three separate victory parties. The feminists were at the Bubble Factory, Lorraine Sheinberg's production company on the West Side, surrounded by television crews who knew that celebrities would be there. The get-out-the-vote people were in the linoleum expanse of a union hall on the fringe of downtown Los Angeles. Defeat 209, the Democratic Party–allied group, was at the Biltmore Hotel, the traditional venue for southern California political events, where two rooms were reserved—a conference room downstairs for the press and a hospitality suite upstairs for the staff, equipped perfunctorily with televisions and a table holding a platter of vegetables and dip and a few bottles of wine.

Election nights are cruel and blunt. The Biltmore's main ballroom, rented by the Democratic Party, was packed with flush-faced young men and women in nice business suits. People would leave the ballroom in hilarious groups and ride up the elevators in pursuit of intoxication and sex. The Defeat 209 rooms, on the other hand, were dispirited and half empty. They had a feeling of being for the kind of virtuous "progressives" who always seemed to lose.

Connie Rice and Pat Ewing were dressed for the television cameras, grumbling. Stop Prop 209, the feminist group, had finally come up with enough money to put a few meager thirty-second television spots on the air during the last couple of days of the campaign. The ads showed a woman doctor having her white coat, her stethoscope, and finally her clothing roughly stripped away by burly male hands that came in from the sides of the screen. As Stop Prop explained in an accompanying press release: "As a gang of male voices yells 'Take it off! Take it all off!' the woman is stripped of her opportunities and her dignity, and is left vulnerable and humiliated. The 30-second spot ends with men's groping hands, the woman a victim of sexual harassment." The ad may not have moved voters, but it certainly summed up what had made trying to run a campaign with these people so maddening.

Connie said it was the last time she'd work in a political campaign. Pat Ewing said she was thinking of traveling in the Pacific islands for a while.

Like a weak breeze imperceptibly swaying a wheat field, a couple of rumors crossed the room to the effect that the vote on Prop 209 was too close to call. This produced a brief, languid stirring of excitement.

On the television sets in the hospitality suite, President Clinton came on to declare his victory. He was on an outdoor podium in Little Rock, under spotlights, in front of a huge joyous crowd in the streets. "The vital American center is alive and well!" he proclaimed, and went on to speak movingly and at length about the central importance of providing opportunity for all, especially through education, so that we as a nation could complete the unfulfilled promise of the American dream. He didn't mention meritocracy. He didn't mention affirmative action. He didn't mention Proposition 209.

After he was finished the televisions showed Ward Connerly, Glynn Custred, and Tom Wood in Sacramento declaring victory for Prop 209. Everybody in the Defeat 209 hospitality suite pretended not to watch.

At ten o'clock, Connie and Pat Ewing went downstairs to do their duty. Connie looked as if she might cry but then pulled herself together. "I'm here to declare victory," she said, in stentorian tones. "Please understand, they stood here eighteen months ago with 80 percent in the polls. You saw tonight, it was too close to call. Ladies and gentlemen, that is a victory!"

She had a point. Prop 209 won by only an eight-point margin, 54–46, and it lost among blacks, Latinos, Asians, and Jews; women were evenly split. The opposition had fought back and for the first time drummed up public political support for affirmative action. At least they had shown the Republicans they hadn't found an issue that would instantly make their candidates winners.

Molly decided to stay home instead of going to the Biltmore Hotel. She was exhausted, and she didn't feel right about what had happened.

Lisa Edwards, Molly's former babysitter in Pasadena, now an undergraduate at Berkeley, was worried about how Molly would take the election results, after all that draining effort, so she called the morning after to check. Molly was the same old Molly, bright and cheerful. She told Lisa she'd been meaning to give a call herself: the whole family was coming up to Berkeley soon because Nick was beginning to look at colleges and maybe they could spend some time together.

By the time Molly arrived in Berkeley, the situation was reversed. It was Lisa, not Molly, who had been dealt a big setback and who needed a shoulder to cry on.

Lisa was coming to the end of her undergraduate career at Berkeley. She had a highly specific ambition: to work at the Western Justice Center in Pasadena and devote herself to promoting legal mediation as a substitute for the adversary system. Maybe one day she could become director of the center. As a student intern she had done good enough work to have a standing job offer there. But first she wanted to get her law degree.

In the fall of 1996 Lisa's brother gave her seven hundred dollars to enroll in the Stanley Kaplan prep course for the Law School Aptitude Test. In class she was the star, the one who always knew the answers, but when the instructor began giving out practice questions—disaster. Everybody else would be done and Lisa would be struggling endlessly with the reading comprehension passages. The instructor told her, gently, that something must be wrong. She could have herself tested, and if she were judged to be learning-disabled she could take an untimed LSAT, on which she might be able to do well enough to get into law school. Otherwise, the reading comprehension passages were an insurmountable hurdle standing in the way of her becoming a lawyer.

Lisa called around to the members of her family, by way of mounting an inquiry into what was going on. It didn't take long for her to learn that she had a severe reading disability—and that she had had it all her life. Now it was embarrassingly obvious. How could she not have realized it? She had always been very bright and quick, talkative, and naturally good at math, but when she had to read anything longer than a sentence or two, she struggled. The words seemed to swim on the page, the black type dodging pinwheels of light. When she talked to her brother about the problem, he burst into tears, and then he reminded her that one of her early teachers had talked the family into buying a special reading machine. Her mother dug out all her old elementary-school report cards. Invariably they said she was outstanding at math and a poor reader.

Everything in her school career had conspired against Lisa's reading problem being recognized and confronted, let alone solved. Her parents were divorced. Her father was three thousand miles away in New Jersey. Her mother was depressed, distracted, and strapped, way past focusing intently on the children's lives. Nobody read to her or encouraged her to read. She was withdrawn and depressed. Her schools passed her from grade to grade because that was what they did with everyone; now she wondered whether the teachers had simply found it normal for a black student not to be able to read. In high school she had been put on the all-black slow-learner track, and given good grades. She learned little tricks to get by, like sounding out words one by one, or reading only the first and last sentence of every paragraph. When she began taking standardized tests midway through high school, her very high math scores got her placed in honors courses, and her very low reading scores somehow didn't attract notice. When she applied to Berkeley, a combination of her high math SAT score, good grades, and affirmative action got her in.

Showing Molly and Nick around Berkeley was upsetting to Lisa. She was playing the confident guide, when in fact she had been unable to negotiate her way through the university successfully. She knew that if she had been given the kind of attention as a child that white children in South Pasadena had gotten, at home and at school, she probably wouldn't be in this fix today. When she told Molly the whole sad story, Molly said that maybe she should think about not being a lawyer after all: lawyers did nothing but read, and she had so many other skills. Lisa didn't know what to do. It seemed cruel that she could not become a mediator of disputes just because of a handful of reading comprehension questions on the LSAT; but what bothered her far more was that American public education had pushed her along to its highest level while ducking its one most important task, making sure she could read fluently. What kind of system was that?

The morning after Proposition 209 passed, the American Civil Liberties Union filed suit in San Francisco to have it overturned.

A sympathetic federal judge issued an injunction against Prop 209's being put into effect; the injunction was overruled by the Ninth Circuit Court of Appeals; and the Supreme Court declined to hear an appeal, so all affirmative-action programs operated by the state of California were abolished. In the first admissions round without affirmative action, the University of California's law school at Berkeley enrolled one black law student, and Berkeley accepted 255 black undergraduates, down from 598 the year before.

Deval Patrick, Assistant Attorney General for Civil Rights, decided to leave the federal government. That set off a competition for his job. The civil rights organizations huddled, considered possible candidates, and settled on Bill Lee. They pushed hard for him, while political operatives in the Democratic Party promoted their own candidate, a woman named Judith Winston. Having lost every battle with the party for the past two years, the civil-rights people mysteriously won this one. In the fall of 1997, President Clinton nominated Bill.

Bill went from anonymity to being a regular name in the news. In the conservative press he was three-named Bill Lann Lee, the latest champion of quotas and preferences thrown up by the legal left. The White House, on the other hand, packaged him as the embodiment of the American Dream, who had gone from sorting dirty clothes in his parents' Harlem laundry to studying in the Ivy League: a healer, a pragmatist, a seeker of consensus.

Bill's confirmation hearing before the Senate Judiciary Committee had the crackle of a distinct Washington event. His whole family was there, and he was gotten up in a proper new business suit. Obviously he had been practicing. The quiet outrage that had propelled him through the Initiative campaign was not in evidence. Instead he presented himself as cautious and moderate. He smiled a lot.

In order to become the country's head enforcer of the civil-rights laws in 1997, it seemed, you had to have a position—or rather, you had to avoid having too clear a position—on the SAT. The fundamental conflict between handing out a chance to be well educated and to find a job on the basis of test scores and to try to achieve racial equality hadn't gone away—quite the opposite. It was the biggest, most obvious problem, so much so that in a confirmation hearing one had to pretend it wasn't there. Several senators asked Bill what he thought about standardized tests. Should the University of California use the SAT in admissions, for example? Bill said, very carefully, with an elaborate unenthusiastic blandness, that he was not against tests so long as the results were handled properly.

Orrin Hatch, chairman of the Judiciary Committee, a Republican from Utah who occupied a place on the leftward edge of the conservative wing of his party, refused to support Bill's nomination. When Congress recessed, President Clinton appointed him anyway, and he assumed his post in what seemed to be a state of permanent limbo.

Jerry Karabel finished his leave of absence and went back to teaching at Berkeley. He devoted a good part of his time to an endless round of conferences and strategy sessions and manifesto production on how to save affirmative action. But his main idea was to take a decided step back from all-consuming involvement in politics, which had been so unhappy an experience for him. He went up to the attic and hauled down the boxes of material for his book on admissions policy at Harvard, Yale, and Princeton, which had been sitting up there untouched ever since he and Krista had moved in, and got back to work as a sociologist.

Henry Chauncey, in his mid-nineties, was a miracle of geriatric robustness, constantly traveling, reading, corresponding, and telephoning from his base at a retirement community in Shelburne, Vermont. He appeared regularly at important events at ETS. Another of the duties he kept up with was tending to the Chauncey family grave site, where he would be buried. It sits just below the crest of the highest point in Indian Hill Cemetery, a large, venerable place just west of Middletown, Connecticut, which contains the substantial tombs of substantial nineteenth-century families of the Connecticut River valley.

The Chauncey plot is marked by an imposing brownstone mausoleum, with three crypts topped by linked Doric pediments. Each one has an arched doorway and, above it, in large block letters, the name of one branch of the family. The effect is aesthetically simple and severe but also grand, powerful, ambitious. The mausoleum commands a sweeping, lush view from the top of the hill, west, looking out across farms and towns and fading out into the endlessness of the new country. You stand there and think: Order, benign order, can be imposed upon this land.

.   .   .

Molly spent the year after the election trying to assimilate the meaning of it. It was a year like the year after the riots, when she'd been dramatically shown that her life didn't work but didn't know what to do with that information. Finally she decided to leave the NAACP Legal Defense Fund. In the spring of 1998, with the blessing of the civil-rights community, she and Connie Rice started a new organization called the Advancement Project. Connie left the Legal Defense Fund, and Steve left his law firm and joined them there.

You can tell from the name that Molly still held up individual opportunity as the highest goal—the Prop 209 campaign hadn't turned her into a Michael Young. What she had lost faith in was affirmative action. If people who cared about social justice, especially racial justice, built their cause around affirmative action, she feared they were destined to lose and lose and lose in perpetuity. It was the wrong fight to be in. The right fight was the fight to make sure that everybody got a good education and a chance to live a life of decency and honor, and that the country held together as a community. We were a long way from being in that condition—an amazingly long way, given the completeness of the country's rhetorical commitment to it. What really, as opposed to rhetorically, transfixed late-twentieth-century America was the precise calibration of a systematic national reward system, which was what the testing and education regime had become over half a century. But that was secondary and morally unimportant, especially if the people who got the best rewards weren't going to concern themselves with the good of the whole society.

Too bad that hadn't been clear from the start.

Meritocracy" is a curious word. Invented, by Michael Young, to denote a social order that he wanted to hold up as an object of horror, in the United States today it is received as the name of an inarguably sacred first principle: that our society rewards those who deserve and have earned advancement, rather than distributing reward by fiat in some way that involves the circumstances of birth. Moreover, people tend to assume casually that the system whose history I've given in these pages and in which we live our lives—a national regime of IQ-descended standardized tests that everyone takes and that lead the chosen few into the higher reaches of the university system—is the embodiment, and the only possible embodiment, of the principle of meritocracy.

Michael Young was dead set against the idea that giving rewards to the deserving could function as the premise of a good society. In the United States, equal opportunity for all seems far more worthy and workable as an ideal than it did to an English socialist in the 1950s. But from that it doesn't follow that the choice for Americans today is between a meritocracy organized around aptitude tests and "equality of result." There is much more space than we realize between the idea we've come to call meritocracy and the actual, specific American meritocracy we are living with.

The people at the top of a society almost always feel themselves to be genuinely superior to the rest, not just luckily born, and to have earned their place. Societies that we now think of as having been obviously more aristocratic than meritocratic—such as the United States between the world wars, or Victorian England— thought they were run by the people who deserved to be in charge. How could prosperous people in the past possibly have believed

Afterword: A Real Meritocracy

this about themselves? Usually they had participated in a limited-contest meritocracy, of the kind described, for example, in *Stover at Yale*: members of a small, highly restricted group compete all out for the best prizes, the winners feel justifiably entitled to them, and the great mass who could never enter the contest are off somewhere far away, invisible.

Today's upper-middle-class American Mandarins have taken on this set of attitudes. The notion that they are participating (and succeeding) in a great, broad, fair, open national competition is at the heart of their idea of themselves, and indeed you do have to be very intelligent and able to get the most prestigious of the billets distributed by the meritocratic machinery. Within every family, there is a variety of outcomes. But on the other hand the total range of possibilities for those born into the Mandarin class is pretty narrow, and so is the size of the opening to people who are not born in that class.

The advent of this particular system did not represent the country's embracing for the first time the idea of meritocracy—if meritocracy means equal opportunity, or rewards to the deserving, or careers open to talents. The idea of opportunity for everyone is woven deeply into the fabric of the United States, and it has been from the very beginning. Universal opportunity has been a theme in American writing and fable and rhetoric at every point in our history. The current system was a much more particular, even tendentious development, which in ensuing years we have wrongly conflated with the general principle.

The American meritocracy was founded on a linked chain of presumptions, which people aren't familiar with today because they weren't stated openly at the start. The first is that the system's main task should be to select a small number of people to form a new elite—the goal of giving opportunity to all Americans was added later, less as an essential element of the system's design than as a way of generating public support for it. The next presumption was that the means of selection should be intelligence tests, as a proxy for superior academic talent; the definition of "merit," in other words, is a purely intellectual, educational one. Finally, the purpose for which these students are being selected is to enter into the modern version of what Thomas Jefferson called "the offices of government"—that is, administrative and scholarly service to a modern bureaucratic state. What the founders of the system envisioned was closer to the elite civil-service system of a country like France or Japan than a meritocracy in the way the word is used today.

Over time the American meritocracy has evolved into a more general way of distributing opportunity to millions of people, fitting them into places in a highly tracked university system that leads to jobs and professions. And its assumed purpose has changed from being a way to obtain highly capable and well-trained public officials to a way of determining fairly who gets America's material rewards. These changes were, substantially, accidental, the result of the expansionist impulses within both ETS and the universities and of the privatism of American culture, but they have altered the moral calculus.

Let us say you wanted to design, from scratch, a system to distribute opportunity in the fairest possible way. Would you design the American meritocracy as it now exists? You would only if you believed that IQ test scores and, more broadly, academic performance are the same thing as merit. That's a defensible position, but it ought at least to show itself openly to be debated, rather than being presumed. If it did, the arguments against it would quickly emerge. Merit is various, not unidimensional. Intelligence tests, and also education itself, can't be counted on to find every form of merit. They don't find wisdom, or originality, or humor, or toughness, or empathy, or common sense, or independence, or determination—let alone moral worth. Perforce they judge people on their potential, not on their actual performance over the long term at the work for which they're being selected.

Indeed, to take the exercise a step further, let us say you were given the task of designing a system that would distribute opportunity in the most unfair possible way. A first choice could be a system in which all roles were handed down explicitly by inheritance. That would be a pernicious system— one that, thankfully, has never existed in the United States. The second most unfair system, though, could well be one that allowed for competition but insisted that it take place as early in life as possible and with school as the arena. The influences of parentage, of background culture and class, are at their highest and most explicit during a person's student years; although at every school there is an academic competition whose net result is to give some people the chance to move dramatically beyond their original circumstances, schools can't possibly function generally, in the words of James Bryant Conant, "to reorder the 'haves and have-nots' every generation to give flux to our social order." Education offers the hope—a hope explicitly, energetically, taken up by parents—of transferring status between generations, not of altering or upending it.

That our universities have evolved into a national personnel department represents the striking of a complicated bargain. They have gotten out of it the chance to be big and important—to be treated by the public, and not wrongly, as an object of yearning, an all-powerful arbiter of fates. They have lost a certain apartness from the world, a commitment to pure learning and scholarship, a freedom from instrumentalism. Universities are now political and economic institutions. It isn't a happenstance that the question of who gets to attend them has become the subject of election campaigns and Supreme Court cases. Because of the peculiar circumstances of the founding of the American meritocracy—the lack of public debate or assent (therefore the lack of general understanding about its purpose), the heavy reliance on mental tests as a selection device, the steady imperceptible segue in orientation from leadership training to reward distribution—the system seems to be one whose judgments are mysterious, severe, and final. The natural impulse is not simply to accept these judgments as fair. That is why, instead, people worry and squabble over them almost obsessively.

Conant believed that the system he was helping to set up would have the effect of reviving "the American radical tradition in education"—an idea that today seems touchingly, or even laughably, naive. There is now a sturdy and well-established conservative defense of the system, which argues that, however odd its evolution, it now works just fine: we're right to assign economic destinies through education and test scores, because that's the fairest way and the one most likely to promote the quality of sheer brainpower that fuels the modern American economy.

Within the universities themselves, the main sentiment is probably a somewhat oxymoronic liberal elitism—a fierce, competitive protectiveness toward their privileged position combined with discomfort over their role as a generator of wondrous economic advancement for their graduates. The argument that would accompany this sentiment, if it were precisely expressed, would be that while the system doesn't work—because it uses too narrow a criterion, produces an elite too confined in race and class, and imposes too few public obligations on those it favors—it could be made to function well by being restored to its original purpose. Diversify the elite through affirmative action; de-emphasize test scores in choosing the members; make them serve their country (which, after all, substantially pays for the education that launches them, even when it's at private universities) for extended periods. The founders of the American meritocracy would surely not view any of this as a betrayal of their intentions.

The arguments of both sides have something important in common, though, which is that they presume (as most discussions of meritocracy in America presume) that it's good for the country to have a designated, educationally derived elite. The question is whether to have one with a conservative or a liberal design. But there is another possibility, which would be for Americans to decline, to the greatest practicable extent, to use education to designate a national elite. Instead of our endeavoring to realize the dreams of Plato and Jefferson and Conant, we would reject those dreams as a workable basis of a good society, and side with John Adams: the ideal would be to have a society without a specially anointed group at the top of it. Adams was right to see immediately, when Jefferson suggested to him the idea of a natural aristocracy, that the project of picking just the right aristocrats for the United States is fundamentally quixotic, that it serves only to distract us from the obvious point: a democratic nation shouldn't have an aristocracy at all.

Every society of course has positions of authority and expertise that must be filled by people who can execute them well. But the central, original principle of the American meritocracy was different from this. It was that people should be chosen not for their suitability for specific roles but for their general worth, as if they were an updated Puritan elect. Hence it seemed right to select an American meritocracy by grades and test scores rather than by people's demonstrated abilities to do particular things, and to grant the high scorers a general, long-duration ticket to high status that can be cashed in anywhere. The reason for the crush at the gates of selective universities is that people believe admission can confer lifelong prestige, comfort, and safety, not just access to jobs with specific functions. To say that the project of picking the members of this elite properly, no matter how well it is done, cannot not confer an aura of justice on the whole society is not at all the same thing as to oppose selecting people for jobs on their merits. That is a good idea. So is the idea of a society that truly offers opportunity to all. But the idea of having a general-purpose meritocratic elite generated through university admissions is an idea we should abandon.

What would a United States that was a true meritocracy look like? It would be a society that gave everyone equal opportunity and gave jobs to those best able to perform them, but the restructuring that reaching these goals would entail would leave it looking quite different from the current American meritocracy. The essential functions and the richest rewards of money and status would devolve to people only temporarily, and strictly on the basis of their performances; there would be as little lifelong tenure on the basis of youthful promise as possible. The elite would be a group with a constantly shifting, rather than stable and permanent, membership. Successful people would have less serene careers, but this would give them more empathy for people whose lives don't go smoothly. Space in the Mandarin compound should be as small as possible and the space outside it as large as possible.

The institutions that would most dramatically change in this reimagining of what meritocracy means in America would be educational ones. John Gardner, in his little book entitled *Excellence*, published in 1961, a kind of manifesto for the current system, said in a tone of wondering disapproval:

"There was a time—a fairly recent time—when education was not a rigorous sorting-out process." The present meritocracy was devised by educator-planners who couldn't imagine any disadvantage to setting up school as the arena for determining individual destinies: that looked to them far more practical, more just, more efficient, and more conducive to social harmony than it has turned out to be. Their goal was to construct a competitive race that would begin in elementary school and be substantially over by the time one graduated from college or professional school. This was supposed to be the embodiment of the principle of equal opportunity: better to have schools making decisions about people's lives than leaving it to the disorganized market. Here is John Gardner again:

> The sorting out of individuals according to ability is very nearly the most delicate and difficult process our society has to face. Those who receive the most education are going to move into virtually all the key jobs. Thus the question "Who should go to college?" translates itself into the more compelling question "Who is going to manage the society?" That is not the kind of question one can treat lightly or cavalierly. It is the kind of question wars have been fought over.

But surely our guiding principle regarding education and opportunity ought to be precisely the opposite of the one implied in that passage. The chief aim of school should be not to sort out but to teach as many people as possible as well as possible, equipping them for both work and citizenship. Those who like to think of American life as a great race should think of the race as beginning, not ending, when school has been completed. The purpose of schools should be to expand opportunity, not to determine results.

If we define the main objective in this way, then the main problem becomes obvious: in the bad bottom tier of public schools, the ones where students don't even learn to read, we don't come anywhere near to providing equal educational opportunity. Our meritocracy was devised so as to nationalize education for the few of great gifts, identifying the best test scorers and whisking them away to good colleges and universities all over the country, while leaving education local for everyone else. Localism works reasonably well for most people, but it works very badly for students in those worst schools, most of which are in poor, all-minority neighborhoods. Those schools should be (and in fact are being) taken over by mayors and governors who ensure that they confer literacy and numeracy on their students. Decent schooling, the absolute prerequisite to a decent life in America today, should be thought of as something that government guarantees to every citizen as a matter of right. It shouldn't be left to local authorities to screw up, any more than flight safety should.

College is not so absolutely essential as basic early education is, but it has become steadily more important; people who don't go to college are now losing access to a place in the middle class. We should adopt the goal of sending most people all the way through college, just as, a hundred years ago, we adopted the then much more distant goal of sending most people all the way through high school. But we must remember that our current meritocratic system was not set up to do this. Its founders believed that even the small college population of the 1930s needed to be reduced, and the meritocracy was designed to evade entirely the question of the quality and consistency of American high schools.

To get more people through college, we shall have to establish greater national authority over education. High schools should prepare their students for college by teaching them a nationally agreed-upon curriculum. Tests for admission to college should be on mastery of this curriculum—not the SAT or some dreamed-of better, fairer alternative test of innate abilities. Test-prep should consist of mastering the high-school curriculum, not learning tricks to outwit multiple-choice aptitude exams.

It occurred to Conant back in the 1940s that there was some danger that in setting up a mechanism for picking, educating, and giving power to a small group of highly intelligent people, we might engender in them some of the superiority and selfishness he so much hated in the elite of the 1930s. So he insisted:

> If we are to continue to have an essentially free and classless society
> in this country, we must proceed from the premise that there are no edu-
> cational privileges, even at the most advanced levels of instruction. . . .
> As far as possible there should be no hierarchy of educational discipline,
> no one channel should have a social standing above the other.

Of course, this is another dream that didn't come true. Admission to a selective college is treated by Americans largely as a matter of a competititon for, precisely, "educational privileges" and "a social standing above the other," to an extent that would horrify Conant. The only way to undo the class-creating aspect of college admissions is to close the gap that Conant and his associates wanted to open, between the more and less selective colleges. The better and more equal the high schools are, the more universal college is, and the less territory in the posteducation world is reserved in advance for high-aptitude, high-grade Mandarins, the less important admission to a selective college will become.

It's a given by now that it matters a great deal *whether* you went to college; it doesn't, however, have to be supremely important *where* you went to college. Americans' preoccupation with admission to selective colleges has gone past the bounds of rationality. We don't have a radical undersupply of higher education, as in East Asia, and we don't have an informal tradition of the nation's best jobs being closed to people who didn't go to a certain handful of colleges, as in England. Nonetheless, the gap in graduates' life-fates between all colleges and selective colleges is increasing. Closing it will make the United States a better country and one that more fully uses the talents of its people. The culture of frenzy surrounding admissions is destructive and anti-democratic; it warps the sensibilities and distorts the education of the millions of people whose lives it touches.

The idea of educating everyone at public expense ranks with political democracy as one of the United States' great original social contributions. Both ideas rest on a belief that ordinary people are capable of more than the leaders of previous societies would have thought possible. The best and most distinctive tradition in American education is the tradition of pushing to educate more people. That is what Thomas Jefferson was doing when he tried unsuccessfully to establish public elementary schools in Virginia; it is what Horace Mann did when he finally got taxpayers to support public schools in Massachusetts; it was the effect of the GI Bill.

Our apparatus of meritocracy is not part of this tradition. Rather, it belongs to an older, less distinctively American tradition of using tests and education to select a small governing elite. The founders of the American meritocracy were not supporters of an expanded, opportunity-oriented (rather than selection-oriented) educational system, and they were certainly not the originators of the idea of equal opportunity. They did, however, believe they were destroying a nascent class system and building a fluid, mobile society. In retrospect, this was vainglorious—you can't undermine social rank by setting up an elaborate process of ranking. Fifty years later, their creation looks more and more like what it was intended to replace.

The plurality of the primary archival material I'll refer to here is in the archives of the Educational Testing Service. I've tried to put each reference in a form that would make it as easy as possible for somebody else to find the document I've quoted from. Therefore I've followed the ETS archives' schema of collections. The Henry Chauncey Papers are mainly from Chauncey's long period as president of ETS. The Chauncey Merger File is a separate collection of papers pertaining to the creation of ETS in the 1940s. The Oral History Collection is a set of interviews with pioneer figures in educational testing, conducted mainly by Gary Saretzky of the ETS archives. The William W. Turnbull Papers are the equivalent of the Henry Chauncey Papers for Chauncey's successor as president. The ETS archives has also assembled collections of papers for the early testers Carl C. Brigham and Ben D. Wood.

The Chauncey Family Archives were put together by Henry Chauncey personally, with the help of an archivist, and are currently in his possession. But he has made plans to transfer them to the ETS archives. I've used his method of reference for these papers, which I assume the ETS archives will adopt. In addition, over the years of working on this book I have carried on a substantial correspondence with Chauncey, much of it consisting of his clarifying or elaborating on details in the history of testing. Especially noteworthy in this material is a 137-page handwritten manuscript that he produced in 1997, at the age of ninety-two, called "Recollections of Testing in Early Days." I will find a way to make these letters, along with other correspondence, interviews, and private papers that I refer to below but that can't be used by others because they're in my personal files, available to researchers by depositing them in a library.

BOOK ONE

4: "Finally, I decided to take the plunge": Henry Chauncey's notebook for February 4, 1945, page 46. Henry Chauncey Papers, Box 95, Folder 1067, Frame 00145.

6: differences between the college-educated and non-college-educated: I refer below (note for page 274) to some of the economic literature on this. On attitudinal differences, an interesting document is "Democracy's Next Generation II: A Study of American Youth on Race," a 1992 report by People for the American Way based on a poll conducted by Peter D. Hart Research.

8: extirpation of any accent: As an example, John Morton Blum, in the 1930s a Harvard undergraduate protégé of Henry Chauncey's, today a professor emeritus of history at Yale, was given elocution lessons as a student at a New England boarding school so as to be ridded of his Bronx Jewish accent. Author's interview with Blum.

   percentage of teenagers graduating from high school and entering college: National Center for Education Statistics, *Digest of Education Statistics 1995*, Government Printing Office, 1995, pages 17–18.

9: German-style research universities: See Richard Hofstadter and Walter P. Metzger, *The Development of Academic Freedom in the United States*, Columbia University Press, 1955, pages 367–383.

10: Chauncy family history: See William Chauncey Fowler, *Memorials of the Chaunceys, Including President Chauncy and His Ancestors and Descendants*, republished with revisions by Stanley T. Dunn, Cook-McDowell Publications, 1981.
   "deeply bewailed his sinful compliance": Fowler, *Memorials of the Chaunceys*, page 14.
   "dipt and not sprinkled": Ibid., page 14.
   "had given his head to the block": Ibid., page 18.
   "forbear to disseminate": Ibid., page 19.
   Halfway Covenant: See Perry Miller, *Errand into the Wilderness*, Harvard University Press, 1956. On Puritan matters, the author's conversations with Andrew Delbanco and Alan Heimert were also very helpful.

11: "aimed at putting their Passions into a Ferment": Charles Chauncy, *Seasonable Thoughts on the State of Religion in New England*, Rogers and Fowle, 1743, page 93.
   "the WASP ascendancy": This term is used throughout in Joseph Alsop with Adam Platt, *I've Seen the Best of It: Memoirs*, W. W. Norton, 1992.
   "Be assured that I have not been influenced": Henry Chauncey, letter to Joseph W. Alsop, March 8, 1835, typed and given to author by Henry Chauncey.

12: Egisto Fabbri Chauncey: Henry Chauncey wrote and privately published a memoir of his father: Henry Chauncey, *A Life of Faith in God and Service to His Fellow Men*, The Grapevine Press, 1991.
   "People are reading:" "Mother Stork's Baby Book," 1905, kept by Edith Taft Chauncey. Chauncey Family Archives, Box 1, Folder 1.

13: growth in Episcopal Church membership: T. J. Jackson Lears, *No Place of Grace: Antimodernism and the Transformation of American Culture, 1880–1920*, Pantheon, 1981, page 198.
   history of Groton School: See Frank D. Ashburn, *Peabody of Groton: A Portrait*, The

Riverside Press, 1967. There is also some material on Groton in E. Digby Baltzell, *Philadelphia Gentlemen*, The Free Press, 1958, and P. W. Cookson, Jr., and Caroline Hodges Persell, *Preparing for Power: America's Elite Boarding Schools*, Basic Books, 1985. Also author's interviews with Douglas Brown, Egisto Chauncey, Henry Chauncey, Henry Chauncey, Jr., A. Wright Palmer, William Polk, and Allen Wardwell.

14: "Bethlehem was a little town": Ashburn, *Peabody of Groton*, page xiii.

15: "to serve is to reign": The strictest literal translation would be something like "who serves is ruler," and some Grotonians prefer "to serve Him is to reign." The old, traditional translation was in general use back in Chauncey's student days and has since become embarrassing and isn't heard around the school as much.

"The highest honor": Ashburn, *Peabody of Groton*, page 98.

"Now one of my biggest ideas": Notes by Henry Chauncey, dated 1924. Chauncey Family Archives, Box 8, Folder 2.

16: arrangement with Clarence Dillon: Clarence Dillon, letter to Henry Chauncey, December 9, 1926. Chauncey Family Archives, Box 3, Folder 13.

17: Alfred Binet and the early history of intelligence testing: Excellent, but skeptical, accounts can be found in Stephen Jay Gould, *The Mismeasure of Man*, W. W. Norton, 1981, and Daniel J. Kevles, *In the Name of Eugenics: Genetics and the Uses of Human Heredity*, Harvard University Press, 1985. For a much more sympathetic treatment of the development of IQ testing, see Arthur Jensen, *Bias in Mental Testing*, The Free Press, 1980, and *The g Factor: The Science of Mental Ability*, Praeger, 1998.

Lewis Terman and Edward Thorndike: See Henry L. Minton, *Lewis M. Terman, Pioneer in Psychological Testing*, New York University Press, 1988. I'm not aware of a biography of Thorndike, but he published widely. See, for example, his *Educational Psychology*, Science Press, 1903, and *Individuality*, Houghton Mifflin, 1911.

19: "There were personal relationships involved": Henry Aaron Yeomans, *Abbott Lawrence Lowell, 1856–1943*, Harvard University Press, 1948, page 84.

"greatest of all forward passes": George H. Mitchell, letter to Henry Chauncey, May 23, 1969. Henry Chauncey Papers, Folder 368, Frame 00488.

20: "I am interested in the complete reorientation": Henry Chauncey, letter to William S. Learned, January 14, 1932. Henry Chauncey Papers, Folder 1.

21: James Bryant Conant: The definitive biography is James Hershberg, *James B. Conant: Harvard to Hiroshima and the Making of the Nuclear Age*, Alfred A. Knopf, 1993. An interesting unpublished doctoral dissertation on Conant is Jean Amster, "Meritocracy Ascendant: James Bryant Conant and the Cultivation of Talent," Graduate School of Education, Harvard University, 1990.

22: progressive education and the Eight-Year Study: For general background on this, see Wilford M. Aikin, *The Story of the Eight-Year Study with Conclusions and Recommenda-*

tions, Harper & Brothers, 1942. The director of the study was Ralph W. Tyler, an important figure in educational testing who had a long and varied career and was an early critic of ETS. There is an interview with Tyler in the Columbia University Oral History Collection (Carnegie Corporation Project), and another one in George F. Madaus and Daniel L. Stufflebaum, editors, *Educational Evaluation: Classic Works of Ralph W. Tyler*, Kluwer Academic Publishers, 1989.

the Pennsylvania Study: William S. Learned and Ben D. Wood, *The Student and His Knowledge*, Carnegie Foundation for the Advancement of Teaching, 1938.

23: the views of Francis Galton: Francis Galton, *Hereditary Genius: An Inquiry into Its Laws and Consequences*, Macmillan, 1869.

The Bell Curve: Richard J. Herrnstein and Charles Murray, *The Bell Curve: Intelligence and Class Structure in American Life*, The Free Press, 1994. For the author's detailed comments on this work, see Nicholas Lemann, "Is There a Cognitive Elite in America?" in Bernie Devlin, Stephen E. Fienberg, Daniel P. Resnick, and Kathryn Roeder, editors, *Intelligence, Genes, & Success: Scientists Respond to* The Bell Curve, Copernicus, 1997, and Nicholas Lemann, "The Bell Curve Flattened," *Slate*, January 16, 1997 (http://www.slate.com/features/bellcurve/bellcurve.asp).

24: "the Psychological Battalion of Death": Walter Lippmann, "A Defense of Education," *The Century Magazine*, May 1923, page 103.

E. F. Lindquist: See Julia J. Peterson, *The Iowa Testing Programs: The First Fifty Years*, University of Iowa Press, 1983. Also author's interview with William E. Coffman.

25: "excellent and beneficial for one particular type": H. E. Hawkes, E. F. Lindquist, and C. R. Marm, *The Construction and Use of Achievement Exams: A Manual*, Houghton Mifflin, 1936, page 476.

"not for a test that would skim the cream": E. F. Lindquist, "The Iowa Testing Programs—A Retrospective View," *Education* magazine, September–October 1970.

27: Lowell and the Jewish quota: Yeomans, *Abbott Lawrence Lowell*, page 209.

28: College Entrance Examination Board: The Board's somewhat dull official history is Claude M. Fuess, *The College Board: Its First Fifty Years*, Columbia University Press, 1950. Also see Michael Schudson, "Organizing the 'Meritocracy': A History of the College Entrance Examination Board," *Harvard Educational Review*, February 1972.

29: Carl Brigham: Research material on Brigham is spotty, but the Educational Testing Service archives has assembled what is available—mainly Brigham's correspondence with other psychologists and eugenicists—in its Carl Campbell Brigham Papers. The ETS archives' Oral History Collection's interviews with Chauncey Belknap (a Princeton classmate), Cecil R. Brolyer (Brigham's research assistant), John Stalnaker (Brigham's assistant at the College Board), and Ben D. Wood (Brigham's archrival) also contain interesting material on Brigham.

Madison Grant and Charles W. Gould: Grant's best-known book is Madison Grant, *The Passing of the Great Race*, Arno Press, 1970 (originally published 1918). Gould's only book is Charles Winthrop Gould, *America: A Family Matter*, Charles Scribner's Sons, 1920. Brigham, in the introduction, called his book *A Study of American Intelligence* "a companion volume" to this work (Brigham, *A Study of American Intelligence*, page vi). Another popular eugenicist Brigham referred to favorably in his correspondence was Lothrop Stoddard, author of *The Rising Tide of Color Against White World Supremacy*, Charles Scribner's Sons, 1923, and *The Revolt Against Civilization: The Menace of the Under Man*, Charles Scribner's Sons, 1922.

"I am not afraid to say anything that is true": Carl Brigham, letter to Robert Yerkes, July 16, 1922. Carl Campbell Brigham Papers (at the Educational Testing Service archives), box labeled "Brigham Literature," folder labeled "Brigham Correspondence from the Yerkes Paper, Yale."

30: Brigham's book: Carl C. Brigham, *A Study of American Intelligence*, Princeton University Press, 1923.

"Our figures, then, would rather tend to disprove": Brigham, *A Study of American Intelligence*, page 190.

"American intelligence is declining": Ibid.,

31: "breaks down as a finely differentiating instrument": Carl C. Brigham, "A Report on the Use of Intelligence Tests in Predicting Marks in Military Science," December 1, 1924. Carl Campbell Brigham Papers, Box 1, folder labeled "United States—War Department."

items from the first SAT: Carl C. Brigham, *A Study of Error: A Summary and Evaluation of Methods Used in Six Years of Study of the Scholastic Aptitude Test of the College Entrance Examination Board*, College Entrance Examination Board, 1932, pages 40–41 (first two items), 213 (third item).

32: early validity coefficients for intelligence tests: Paul S. Burnham (the head testing man at Yale), oral history interview, April 8, 1985, page 16, Oral History Collection, ETS archives.

"social distractions": Carl C. Brigham, "A Report on the Use of Intelligence Tests in Predicting Marks in Military Science," December 1, 1924. Carl Campbell Brigham Papers, Box 1, folder labeled "United States—War Department."

earliest uses of the SAT: See Brigham, *A Study of Error*, page 331; Paul Burnham, oral history interview, April 8, 1985, Oral History Collection, ETS archives; Brigham, "A Report on the Use of Intelligence Tests in Predicting Marks in Military Science," December 1, 1924. Carl Campbell Brigham Papers, Box 1, folder labeled "United States—War Department."

33: Brigham declining to speak at Terman's conference: Carl C. Brigham, letter to Lewis Terman, December 27, 1927. Carl Campbell Brigham Papers, Box 3, folder labeled "Brigham-Terman Letters."

Brigham's public recantation: Gary Saretzky, unpublished biographical note on Carl Brigham, page 9. In the ETS archives.

"pretentious": Carl Brigham, "Intelligence Tests of Immigrant Groups," *Psychological Review*, Volume 37, No. 2 (1930).

dividing the SAT score into two parts: Cecil R. Brolyer, oral history interview, June 13, 1984, page 33. Oral History Collection, ETS archives.

"the more I work in this field": Carl C. Brigham, letter to Charles B. Davenport, December 8, 1929. Carl Campbell Brigham Papers, Box 2, folder labeled "Brigham/Davenport Correspondence."

34: "The test movement came to this country": Carl C. Brigham, "Manuscript for Article on Board Examinations Taken by West Point and Annapolis," handwritten, dated 1934–35, page 17. Carl Campbell Brigham Papers, Box 1, folder labeled "MSS 4."

"ready method of interview": Brigham, "Manuscript for Article on Board Examinations," page 16.

"Practice has always outrun theory": Ibid., page 2.

35: "In all too many of the social science fields": Henry Chauncey, notebook entry for August 28, 1948. Henry Chauncey Papers, Box 95, Folder 1068, Frame 00286.

Ben Wood's early life: Wood himself wrote a 73-page typescript memoir in 1982 called "The Early Life of Ben D. Wood." In author's personal files. See also Ben D. Wood, oral history interview, May 8, 1978. Oral History Collection, ETS archives.

"marsupial sanctuary": "The Early Life of Ben D. Wood, page 7.

Thorndike's racial theories: See, for example, the chapter called "The Influence of Remote Ancestry or Race" pages 206–224, in Edward L. Thorndike, *Mental Work and Fatigue*, and *Individual Differences and Their Causes*, Teachers College, Columbia University, 1914.

36: "self-education": Learned and Wood, *The Student and His Knowledge*, page 48.

"Another point on which I think we should force the radicals": Ben D. Wood, letter to Herbert Hawkes, October 5, 1933. Ben D. Wood Papers (in the ETS archives), Folder 64, Frame 005527.

37: Reynold B. Johnson: A decent source on his life is Reynold B. Johnson, oral history interview, October 27, 1977. Oral History Collection, ETS archives.

Johnson wanting a job: Reynold Johnson, letter to J. E. Holt, March 8, 1934. Ben D. Wood Papers, File 463.

Johnson selling the rights to IBM: Reynold Johnson, letter to G. W. Baehne, July 14, 1934. Ben D. Wood Papers, File 463.

Wood's letter to Thomas Watson: Ben D. Wood, letter to Thomas J. Watson, August 4, 1934. Ben D. Wood Papers, File 463.

39: James Tobin: Author's interview with Tobin.

CONANT PRIZE SCHOLARS NOT BOOK WORMS: *The Harvard Crimson*, December 9, 1935.

the Scholarship Examinations: Henry Chauncey, "Origin of the Present College Board Admission Testing Program," undated, unpublished manuscript, in author's personal files.

40: "it is probably simpler to teach cultured men testing": Carl Brigham, "The Place of Research in a Testing Organization," *School and Society*, December 11, 1937, pages 756–759.

Brigham's letter to Conant: Carl C. Brigham, letter to James Bryant Conant, January 3, 1938. Carl Campbell Brigham Papers, Box 1, folder labeled "Brigham, Dr. Carl C. (deceased)."

41: Brigham's apology: Carl C. Brigham, letter to James Bryant Conant, February 1, 1938. Carl Campbell Brigham Papers, Box 1, folder labeled "Brigham, Dr. Carl C. (deceased)."

number of takers of the SAT: "Scholastic Aptitude Test Candidates, 1926–1940." Henry Chauncey Papers, Folder 793.

43: Jefferson's letter to Adams: Lester J. Cappon, editor, *The Adams-Jefferson Letters: The Complete Correspondence Between Thomas Jefferson and Abigail and John Adams*, University of North Carolina Press, 1959, pages 387–392.

"there are too many rather than too few": James Bryant Conant, "The Future of Our Higher Education," *Harper's*, May 1938, page 566.

44: "twenty of the best geniuses": Thomas Jefferson, *Notes on the State of Virginia*, in *Thomas Jefferson: Writings*, Library of America, 1984, page 272.

"I was never so tactless": James Bryant Conant, *Thomas Jefferson and the Development of American Public Education*, University of California Press, 1962, page 54.

"a golden or silver parent": Plato, *The Republic*, Modern Library, 1982, page 125.

examination systems in other countries: The literature on this is enormous. Two useful surveys, despite the tendentious titles, are: Ichisada Miyazaki, *China's Examination Hell: The Civil Service Examinations of Imperial China*, Yale University Press, 1981, and Ronald Dore, *The Diploma Disease: Education, Qualification, and Development*, George Allen & Unwin, 1976. Also see *Testing in American Schools: Asking the Right Questions*, U.S. Office of Technology Assessment, 1992, Chapter 5.

45: "The existence of an upper class is not injurious": Ralph Waldo Emerson, "Aristocracy," in *The American Transcendentalists*, Anchor Press, 1957.

46: "Your distinction between natural and artificial aristocracy": Cappon, *The Adams-Jefferson Letters*, pages 397–402.

Conant's unpublished book: James Bryant Conant, *What We Are Fighting to Defend*, unpublished, undated manuscript. In the papers of James B. Conant, Box 30, Harvard University Archives.

"a new type of social instrument": Ibid., Chapter 6: "The Role of Public Education," page 2.

47: "We must proceed from the premise": Ibid., pages 20–21.

data on social mobility: Again, there is a vast literature. The classic works are Seymour Martin Lipset and Reinhart Bendix, *Class, Status, and Power: Social Stratification in Comparative Perspective*, The Free Press, 1967; Peter Blau and Otis Dudley Duncan, *The American Occupational Structure*, Wiley, 1967; Christopher Jencks, *Inequality: A Reassessment of the Effect of Family and Schooling in America*, Basic Books, 1972, and *Who Gets Ahead? The Determinants of Economic Success in America*, Basic Books, 1979;

and David L. Featherman and Robert M. Hauser, *Opportunity and Change*, Academic Press, 1978. For a specific refutation of the "Turner thesis" that mobility was especially high in frontier days, see Edward Pessen, *Riches, Class, and Power Before the Civil War*, D. C. Heath, 1973.

48: Turner's invention of "social mobility": This connection was made in Christopher Lasch, *The Revolt of the Elites and the Betrayal of Democracy*, W. W. Norton, 1995, page 73.

"Even in the dull brains": Frederick Jackson Turner, *The Frontier in American History*, Holt, Rinehart, and Winston, 1962, page 278.

"our newly erected system of public education": Conant, "Education for a Classless Society," page 600.

Horace Mann: The standard biography is Jonathan Messerli, *Horace Mann: A Biography*, Alfred A. Knopf, 1972.

statistics on high-school graduation: *Digest of Education Statistics 1995*, pages 17–18.

49: "the powers of government to reorder": James Bryant Conant, "Wanted: American Radicals," *The Atlantic Monthly*, May 1943, page 41.

"Abilities must be assessed": Conant, "Education for a Classless Society," page 600.

"a fanatical believer in equality": Conant, "Wanted: American Radicals," page 43.

Conant displeasing his superiors: Hershberg, *James B. Conant*, pages 175–178. The most displeased, Hershberg tells us, was Thomas W. Lamont, the banker and associate of J. P. Morgan.

50: "the taxpayer has a duty": James Bryant Conant, *Education and Liberty: The Role of Schools in a Modern Democracy*, Harvard University Press, 1952, page 32.

"The first thing that strikes one": Alexis de Tocqueville, *Democracy in America*, Perennial Library, 1978, page 627.

"at the age when one might have a taste for study": Ibid., page 55.

Edward Bok: See Edward Bok, *The Americanization of Edward Bok*, Charles Scribner's Sons, 1920.

51: "I don't want to be a boy": Theodore Dreiser, *The Financier*, Meridian, 1986, page 15.

"It is not book-learning young men need": Elbert Hubbard, *A Message to Garcia and Thirteen Other Things*, The Roycrofters, 1901, page 10.

"Mr. Carnegie has given no money to universities": Elbert Hubbard, *Little Visits to the Homes of Great Business Men: Andrew Carnegie*, The Roycrofters, 1909, page 56.

"The West was another name for opportunity": Turner, *The Frontier in American History*, page 212.

"a mobile mass of freely circulating atoms": Ibid., page 286.

52: "Education is not only a moral renovator": Horace Mann, "Annual Report as Secretary of the Massachusetts State Board of Education, 1941," in *Life and Works of Horace Mann*, Lee and Shepard, 1891, Volume 3, page 92.

"henceforth educated people must labor": Abraham Lincoln, "Address to the Wisconsin State Agricultural Society," September 30, 1859, in *Abraham Lincoln: Speeches and Writings*, Library of America, 1989, page 98. This long speech is well worth reading in full as probably Lincoln's most sustained statement on the subject of opportunity in America.

54: College Board officials on Pearl Harbor day: Henry S. Dyer, oral history interview, September 23, 1978, page 8. Oral History Collection, ETS archives.

55: "Write to me at once": John Stalnaker, letter to Henry Chauncey, February 1, 1943. Henry Chauncey Papers, Folder 1.

57: "He plans 'em": "Song for CEEB farewell dinner for HC," 1944. Chauncey Family Archives, Box 5, Folder 35.

58: The College Board job won: "HC's notes on job decision," 1945. Henry Chauncey Papers, Folder 8.
    "The stage of development": Henry Chauncey, notebook entry for February 21, 1945. Henry Chauncey Papers, Box 95, Folder 1067, Frame 00150.
    History of the GI Bill: The best sources are Keith W. Olson, *The G. I. Bill, the Veterans, and the Colleges*, University Press of Kentucky, 1974, and Michael J. Bennett, *When Dreams Came True: The G.I. Bill and the Making of Modern America*, Brassey's, 1996.

59: "in this war we have had a much greater load": Testimony of Warren H. Atherton, national commander, American Legion, in "Hearings Before a Subcommittee of the Committee on Finance, United States Senate, Seventy-eighth Congress, Second Session, on S. 1617," Government Printing Office, 1944, page 5.
    "the demobilization of our armed forces": Conant, "Wanted: American Radicals," page 41.

60: "Equality of opportunity in the early days of our country": Henry Chauncey, letter to the editor, *The Boston Globe*, February 12, 1945. Henry Chauncey Papers, Box 47, Folder 1041.

61: "I am sure that you are going to be in New York": Devereux Josephs, letter to Henry Chauncey, June 8, 1945. Chauncey Merger File, Box 1, folder labeled "Correspondence 1944–45."
    "Can you not arrange to take time": William S. Learned, letter to Henry Chauncey, October 18, 1945. Chauncey Merger File, Box 1, folder labeled "Correspondence 1944–45."
    "No college will quickly turn down": Henry Chauncey, "A few notes on my conversation with Provost Paul Buck in regard to the Board's taking over the GRE," February 25, 1946. Chauncey Merger File, Box 1, Folder 2.
    "He spoke with great conviction": Henry Chauncey, notes on meeting with James Bryant Conant, March 21, 1946. Chauncey Merger File, Box 1, Folder 2.

62: "Even if we were to decide to go ahead": Henry Chauncey, "Verbatim notes of telephone conversation with Charles Dollard, April 5, 1946." Chauncey Merger File, Box 1, Folder 2.

63: "When an organization of this sort becomes big and powerful": Henry S. Dyer, letter to Paul S. Buck, October 15, 1946. Chauncey Merger File, Box 1, Folder 3.

"In general, I found Mr. Conant very reassuring": Henry Chauncey, "Memorandum of conference with Mr. Conant," October 18, 1946. Chauncey Merger File, Box 1, Folder 3.

Josephs bribing Zook: Author's interviews with Henry Chauncey.

ACE COMMITTEE WILLING ACCEPT: Charles Dollard, telegram to Henry Chauncey, April 17, 1947. Chauncey Merger File, Box 1, Folder 5.

64: "Counsel of fear": Henry Chauncey, "Notes on Outcome of Oct. 9 Meeting," October 10, 1947. Chauncey Merger File, Box 1, Folder 8.

University presidents coming to College Board meeting: Author's interviews with Henry Chauncey.

The Zook report: President's Commission on Higher Education, *Higher Education for American Democracy*, Harper & Brothers, 1948.

66: "It seems to me": Edward S. Noyes, letter to Devereux Josephs, October 30, 1947. Chauncey Merger File, Box 1, Folder 8.

"It was in the spirit of self-denial": Henry Chauncey, letter to Gary Saretzky, April 10, 1992, in author's files.

Davis-Havighurst article: W. Allison Davis and Robert J. Havighurst, "The Measurement of Mental Systems (Can Intelligence Be Measured?)" *The Scientific Monthly*, April 1948.

"a very narrow range": Ibid., page 307.

"a teacher's rating of a pupil": Ibid., page 311.

"They take the extreme": Henry Chauncey, notebook entry for July 31, 1948. Henry Chauncey Papers, Box 95, Folder 1068, Frame 00250.

67: "If ability has any relation": Ibid.

"The Dawn of Social Science": Henry Chauncey, notebook entry for July 17, 1948. Henry Chauncey Papers, Box 95, Folder 1068, Frame 00229.

68: "We seem . . . to have arrived": Ibid.

"Psychology, the Cinderella": Henry Chauncey, notebook entry for November 22, 1948. Henry Chauncey Papers, Box 95, Folder 1068, Frame 00310.

"the social sciences are at last": Ibid.

"Our mores should not be derived": Henry Chauncey, notebook entry for October 5, 1948. Henry Chauncey Papers, Box 95, Folder 1069, Frame 00338.

"hierarchy of values": Henry Chauncey, notebook entry for February 13, 1950. Henry Chauncey Papers, Box 95, Folder 1069, Frame 00415.

69: "Only Plato had the answer": Henry Chauncey, notebook entry for December 26, 1949. Henry Chauncey Papers, Box 95, Folder 1069, Frame 00401.

"occupy a position of power": Walter Lippmann, "A Future for the Tests," *The New Republic*, November 29, 1922.

"What I hope to see established": Henry Chauncey, notebook entry for June 18, 1950. Henry Chauncey Papers, Box 95, Folder 1070, Frame 0467.

71: "Basically I favor a rather drastic cut back": Robert Merry, letter to Henry Chauncey, February 28, 1950. Henry Chauncey Papers, Folder 623, Folder 02172.

"One can certainly get an idea of the frustration": Henry Chauncey, memorandum of conversation with Emmett Welch of the National Security Resources Board, November 17, 1949. Henry Chauncey Papers, Folder 834, Frame 00145.

"After several years of reconnoitering": Henry Chauncey, memorandum to William W. Turnbull, January 3, 1950. Henry Chauncey Papers, Folder 725, Frame 00684.

72: "We are not impressed": Robert L. Clark, letter to Stuart Symington (Director of Manpower Office, National Security Resources Board), June 18, 1950. Henry Chauncey Papers, Box 79, Folder 834.

"He was about fifteen minutes behind-hand": Henry Chauncey, memorandum of conversation with Stuart Symington, July 6, 1950. Henry Chauncey Papers, Box 79, Forder 834.

the debate over the draft: An excellent monograph on the subject, from which much of my account is drawn, is Thomas J. Frusciano, "Student Deferment and the Selective Service College Qualification Test," Educational Testing Service Research Reports, 1980. Also useful is Hershberg, *James B. Conant*, Chapter 27.

73: "Hershey . . . emphasized": Henry Chauncey, memorandum to Selective Service Scientific Committees, January 3, 1949. Henry Chauncey Papers, Folder 869, Frame 00676.

"We, the citizens": Report of the six scientific advisory committees to the Selective Service System, December 18, 1950. Henry Chauncey Papers, Folder 869, Frame 00810.

"The test should not be looked upon or referred to": Henry Chauncey, undated draft of a letter to General Lewis B. Hershey. Henry Chauncey Papers, Folder 870, Frame 00880.

Chauncey's changes to Hershey's plans: See Henry Chauncey, undated draft of a letter to Lewis B. Hershey, Henry Chauncey Papers, Folder 870, Frame 00880; Henry Chauncey, undated draft of a letter to Lewis B. Hershey, Henry Chauncey Papers, Folder 870, Frame 00845; Henry Chauncey, memorandum of a conversation with Lewis B. Hershey, January 31, 1949, Henry Chauncey Papers, Folder 869, Frame 00688.

75: PRESIDENT TRUMAN ADVOCATES: Editorial cartoon from *The Sacramento Bee*, April 9, 1951. In ETS Clipping File, Box 1, Folder 11.

THE AVERAGE GUY: Editorial cartoon from *The Philadelphia Inquirer*, undated (1951). In ETS Clipping File, Box 1, Folder 11.

76: scores of Southerners: Frusciano, "Student Deferment and the Selective Service College Qualification Test," page 37. See also Henry Chauncey, memorandum to William W. Turnbull, December 31, 1951, Henry Chauncey Papers, Folder 72; Henry Chauncey, memorandum of a conversation with "Mr. Adams of *U.S. News*," April 3,

1951, Henry Chauncey Papers, Folder 870, Frame 00861; and Paul Diederich, memorandum to Henry Chauncey, May 16, 1951, page 2, Henry Chauncey Papers, Folder 870, Frame 00873.

Chauncey and Edwin James: Henry Chauncey, "Notes of meeting with Edwin James of New York Times—April 18, 1946." Henry Chauncey Papers, Box 1, Folder 26.

77: ETS's first professional public-relations consultant: The man's name was Raymond Miller. See Jack Rimalover, memorandum to Henry Chauncey, September 18, 1951. Henry Chauncey Papers, Folder 371.

THEY KNOW ALL THE ANSWERS: *Collier's*, May 19, 1951.

"Now ETS is recognized": " 'And the Last Shall Be First,' " *Pathfinder*, August 8, 1951.

profit on the contract: Henry Chauncey, oral history interview, Part Six, November 8, 1977, page 11. Oral History Collection, ETS archives.

78: "wasn't a vital part of my undertaking": James Bryant Conant, oral history interview, April 13, 1967, page 69. Carnegie Corporation Project, Columbia University Oral History Collection.

79: "The present thinking is": Henry Chauncey, memorandum of conversation with General Lewis B. Hershey, June 24, 1952. Henry Chauncey Papers, Folder 870, Frame 00939.

"During the Korean crisis": Earl Newsom (another ETS public-relations consultant), "The Educational Testing Service and the Public," unpublished report from 1957. William W. Turnbull Papers, Folder 1032.

81: "If you were given certain topics": "A Study of Values," undated test taken by Henry Chauncey. Henry Chauncey Papers, Folder 182.

82: "It seems to me that in the personality domain": Henry Chauncey, memorandum to the file, July 9, 1952. Chauncey Family Archives, Box 8.

83: "It's an objective fact": Laurie Chauncey, letter in *The Ladies' Home Journal*, November 1957. Chauncey Family Archives, Laurie Chauncey Papers, Box 3, Folder 5.

84: "He'd say, 'I'll call him up!' ": Author's interview with John Hollister.

85: enrollment in higher education: The raw numbers can be found, in a great variety of forms, in *Digest of Education Statistics 1995*, pages 11–24 and 174–227. For a descriptive account, see Christopher Jencks and David Riesman, *The Academic Revolution*, University of Chicago Press, 1968.

"Realistically I can see no way": Robert Merry, letter to Henry Chauncey, April 20, 1955. Henry Chauncey Papers, Folder 623, Frame 02239.

86: predictive validity: It should be no surprise that there is a great deal of material in the ETS archives on this question, which is the organization's bread and butter. For references to very high early validities, see Paul Burnham, oral history interview, April 8, 1985, page

16. Oral History Collection, ETS archives. Also Carl Brigham, "A Report on the Use of Intelligence Tests in Predicting Marks in Military Science," December 1, 1924. Carl C. Brigham Papers, Box 1, folder labeled "United States—War Department." For a good survey of contemporary validity studies, see Warren Willingham, Charles Lewis, Rick Morgan, and Leonard Raunist, *Predicting College Grades: An Analysis of Institutional Trends over Two Decades*, Educational Testing Service, 1990.

    percent of the variance: The basic correlation coefficient between an independent and a dependent variable is called r. The percent of variance in the dependent variable (in this case, first-semester grades) produced by the independent variable (in this case, SAT scores) is derived by multiplying r by itself to produce r squared. So if the correlation coefficient between SAT scores and first-semester grades is .4, the percent of the variance in grades explained by SAT scores will be .4 squared, or .16.

87: the Rorschach test and Johnson O'Connor: Author's interviews and correspondence with Henry Chauncey; also Henry Chauncey, "Recollections of Testing in Early Days," handwritten, unpublished manuscript, 1997, in author's personal files.

    test of practical judgment: Author's interviews and correspondence with Henry Chauncey, and Chauncey, "Recollections."

    TV quiz shows: Henry Chauncey, memorandum to John Cowles, Richard Sullivan, and William W. Turnbull, July 20, 1950. Henry Chauncey Papers, Folder 371. Also John S. Helmick, memoranda to William W. Turnbull, September 22, 1961, and October 5, 1961. William W. Turnbull Papers, Folder 1410.

88: test of persistence: Author's interviews and correspondence with Henry Chauncey, and Chauncey, "Recollections."

    Henry Murray: A fascinating biography, focusing mostly on Murray's affair with Christiana Morgan, is Forrest G. Robinson, *Love's Story Told: A Life of Henry A. Murray*, Harvard University Press, 1992.

    description of Thematic Apperception Test: Henry A. Murray, M.D., *Thematic Apperception Test*, Harvard University Press, 1943.

89: Murray's work for the OSS: Author's interviews and correspondence with Henry Chauncey.

    "After our two days with Harry Murray": Henry Chauncey, memorandum to William W. Turnbull, January 3, 1950. Henry Chauncey Papers, Folder 725, Frame 00684.

90: the Picture Apperception Test: Author's interviews and correspondence with Henry Chauncey, and Chauncey, "Recollections."

    "Sylvan and the psychometricians": Chauncey, "Recollections."

    ETS's work for the Central Intelligence Agency: William W. Turnbull, untitled memorandum dated October 12, 1957. William W. Turnbull Papers, Folder 1422. See also David L. Fox, "CIA Funding Through the Navy," September 20, 1977. William W. Turnbull Papers, Folder 1422.

91: Isabel Briggs Myers: For a history of the test, see Frances Wright Saunders, *Katharine and Isabel: Mother's Light, Daughter's Journey*, Consulting Psychologists Press, 1991.

Consulting Psychologists Press, which owns the copyright to the Myers-Briggs Type Indicator, has also republished several works by Isabel Briggs Myers, including *Gifts Differing: Understanding Personality Type* (1993) and *Introduction to Type: A Description of the Theory and Applications of the Myers-Briggs Type Indicator* (1993).

"It's almost like astrology": Author's interview with Norman Freeberg, an ETS executive whose area of special expertise is industrial testing.

"a platform along with aptitude test scores": Henry Chauncey, "Memorandum of Conference with Mrs. Myers," May 3, 1961, page 3. Henry Chauncey Papers, Folder 641.

92: "he assumed a role not unlike a New York dramatic critic": Isabel Briggs Myers, letter to Henry Chauncey, August 30, 1961, page 2. Henry Chauncey Papers, Folder 641.

"she seems to be trying for the first time": J. A. Davis, memorandum to Henry Chauncey and William W. Turnbull, June 2, 1965. Henry Chauncey Papers, Folder 641, Frame 02002.

ETS ending the contract with Myers: Author's interview with Winton Manning.

93: Ideas, Things, Men, and Economic Symbols: Author's correspondence with Henry Chauncey.

David Rockefeller: David Rockefeller, letter to Barklie Henry, July 12, 1954. Henry Chauncey Papers, Folder 320.

John Hay Whitney: Henry Chauncey, memorandum of conversation with John Hay Whitney, May 28, 1954. Henry Chauncey Papers, Folder 320.

Benjamin Buttenweiser: Henry Chauncey, memorandum of conversation with Benjamin Buttenweiser, March 24, 1954. Henry Chauncey Papers, Folder 319.

Devereux Josephs: Henry Chauncey, memorandum of conversation with Devereux Josephs, June 30, 1953. Henry Chauncey Papers, Folder 321.

"dragging my feet on this project": Richard Sullivan, memorandum to William W. Turnbull, March 26, 1953. Henry Chauncey Papers, Folder 723, Frame 00369.

"I think we might begin a low pressure campaign": Henry S. Dyer, memorandum to Henry Chauncey, May 19, 1955. Henry Chauncey Papers, Folder 57.

94: Chauncey offering Lindquist a job: Henry Chauncey, memorandum of conversation with E. F. Lindquist, January 28, 1948. Henry Chauncey Papers, Folder 601, Frame 00158. Also Robert Merry, letter to Henry Chauncey, February 16, 1948. Henry Chauncey Papers, Folder 623, Frame 02096.

Lindquist's view of ETS: Author's interviews with Henry Chauncey, William E. Coffman, Richard Pearson, and Ben Schrader. See also B. E. Bergesen, Jr., oral history interview, November 20, 1984, page 24. Oral History Collection, ETS archives.

95: articles about the Test of Developed Ability: Henry S. Dyer and William E. Coffman, "The Tests of Developed Ability," *College Board Review*, Winter 1957.

"the TDA battery as a whole": Frank H. Bowles, *Admission to College: A Perspective for the 1960s*, College Entrance Examination Board, 1959, page 68.

97: Science Research Associates: Author's interviews with Henry Chauncey, Irving Harris, and John Hollister.

John Stalnaker's dealings with ETS: See, for one of many possible examples of the testiness of this relationship, Henry Chauncey, memorandum of conversation with John Stalnaker, September 30, 1959. Henry Chauncey Papers, Folder 662, Frame 01579.

98: "mammoth agency": Henry Chauncey, letter to John Stalnaker, November 29, 1959. Henry Chauncey Papers, Folder 662, Frame 01705.

"You might find it interesting": Robert Sullian, memorandum to "Mr. Bartnik," October 29, 1951. Henry Chauncey Papers, Folder 761, Frame 01688.

"Nothing remotely compared to ETS": Richard Sullivan, memorandum to Henry Chauncey, September 15, 1954. Henry Chauncey Papers, Folder 870, Frame 00966.

"a Jewish crowd": A. Glenwood Walker, memorandum to Robert Sullian, undated (received at ETS October 11, 1954). William W. Turnbull Papers, Folder 1405.

"Spencer's weaknesses are power and money": Henry Chauncey, memorandum of conversation with "Mr. Cummings," a former vice president of Science Research Associates, October 14, 1954. Henry Chauncey Papers, Folder 870, Frame 00979.

99: Chauncey's suspicion: Henry Chauncey, memorandum of conversation with John Stalnaker, December 23, 1958. Henry Chauncey Papers, Folder 662, Frame 01648.

"the situation may be more complex than that": Ibid.

Newton Minow: Author's interviews and correspondence with Henry Chauncey.

Chauncey's meeting with Frank Thompson: Henry Chauncey, memorandum of conversation with Frank Thompson, May 24, 1962. Henry Chauncey Papers, Folder 791, Folder 02021. The official Thompson called was Henry Fowler, Under Secretary (and later Secretary) of the Treasury. Chauncey wrote a memorandum summarizing the history of the IRS investigation of ETS's tax status, dated April 25, 1963, which is in the Henry Chauncey Papers, Folder 67.

100: "Hoffmann is a very bright mathematical physicist": Henry Chauncey, "Memorandum for Mr. Turnbull," December 6, 1955. Henry Chauncey Papers, Folder 503.

"You say that among all the questions": Banesh Hoffmann, letter to Richard Pearson, February 8, 1956, page 8. Henry Chauncey Papers, Folder 503.

"the bright student": Ibid., page 2.

"the situation seems to me appalling": Ibid., page 1.

101: The Tyranny of Testing: Greenwood Press, 1978.

102: "Had it not been for our recent conversations": Henry Chauncey, letter to John W. Gardner, January 17, 1957. Henry Chauncey Papers, Folder 164.

"the negative attitude toward ETS": Henry Chauncey, memorandum of conversation with John W. Gardner, April 19, 1955. Henry Chauncey Papers, Folder 164.

"He felt that the job was largely one of immunizing": Henry Chauncey, memorandum of conversation with John W. Gardner, May 22, 1957. Henry Chauncey Papers, Folder 164.

Gardner's studies of standardized testing: Bernard Berelson, oral history interview, May 8, 1967. Carnegie Corporation Project, Columbia University Oral History Collection.

"Up to the present year": "Growth and Change in College Admissions Testing," unsigned, undated confidential report, page 14. Henry Chauncey Papers, Folder 189.

103: "The emphasis in the ACT literature": Ibid., page 15.

"We will deal with the great unwashed": Ibid.

"high pressure": Ibid., page 19.

"harsh misrepresentations": Ibid., page 15.

"commercially, rather than educationally": Ibid., page 19.

"I believe it to be ungentlemanly": Undated, unsigned letter, probably from September 1959. Henry Chauncey Papers, Folder 173. Another copy is in the William W. Turnbull Papers, Folder 368. It appears that somebody at ETS drafted this letter to be sent to college admissions directors, who would then retype it, sign it, and send it to the members of the American Psychological Association's professional ethics and conduct committee.

104: experimental use of the SAT at the University of California: Richard Pearson, memorandum to Henry Chauncey, November 16, 1954. Henry Chauncey Papers, Folder 881, Frame 01027. An excellent overall source on University of California admissions is John A. Douglas, "Setting the Conditions of Undergraduate Admissions: The Role of California Faculty in Policy and Process," a report to the Task Force on Governance, University of California Academic Senate, February 10, 1997.

105: Walker in Socorro, New Mexico: Author's interview with Richard Pearson.

106: "For over a week": A. Glenwood Walker, letter to Richard Sullivan, June 3, 1952. Henry Chauncey Papers, Folder 71.

"I have just about had 'it' ": A. Glenwood Walker, letter to Henry Chauncey, October 25, 1952. Henry Chauncey Papers, Folder 158.

Walker's offer from SRA: Richard Sullivan, memorandum to Henry Chauncey, June 1, 1950. William W. Turnbull Papers, Folder 1405.

"I've stayed with ETS": A. Glenwood Walker, letter to Richard Sullivan, December 6, 1953. William W. Turnbull Papers, Folder 1405.

"Would you rather spit on the Bible": There is an entire folder devoted to ETS's troubles with the right wing in the William W. Turnbull Papers, Folder 1416. See, especially, Robert Lambert, memorandum of a meeting at the California State Department of Education, June 30, 1961.

ETS's problems in San Diego and Bakersfield: Ibid. and Robert Lambert, "That Subversive STEP Social Studies Test," February 16, 1962.

107: "If a copy of the list": A. Glenwood Walker, letter to Henry Chauncey, October 31, 1952. Henry Chauncey Papers, Folder 158.

offer of California Test Bureau stock to Chauncey: Helen Roberts, letter to Henry Chauncey, April 14, 1953. Henry Chauncey Papers, Folder 158.

"A list of CTB stockholders": Richard Sullivan, letter to A. Glenwood Walker, November 12, 1952. Henry Chauncey Papers, Folder 158.

"Just as a friend": Richard Sullivan, letter to John Caffrey, June 11, 1956. William W. Turnbull Papers, Folder 1406.

"For heaven's sake": Richard Sullivan, letter to A. Glenwood Walker, October 22, 1953. William W. Turnbull Papers, Folder 1405.

108: "Clark Kerr spoke to me twice": Henry Chauncey, memorandum to William W. Turnbull, November 13, 1953. Henry Chauncey Papers, Folder 72.

110: Stanley Kaplan: Author's interviews with Fred Danzig, Donald Halperin, Stanley Kaplan, and Barry Wexler.

111: "Bernard can get the best marks in school": Arthur Miller, *Death of a Salesman: Certain Private Conversations in Two Acts and a Requiem*, Penguin Books, 1985, page 32.

113: Abe Lass's meeting with William Turnbull: Abraham Lass, oral history interview, March 6, 1978, page 5. Oral History Collection, ETS archives.

"We were a little rougher": Ibid., page 15. Oral History Collection, ETS archives.

114: "From time to time I have reacted": Robert L. Ebel, memorandum to Henry Chauncey, April 20, 1961. Henry Chauncey Papers, Folder 58.

116: "You need a *fault* to have a good society": Author's interview with Michael Young. *New Fabian Essays*: R. H. S. Crossman, editor, Turnstile Press, 1952.

117: "rule not so much by the people": Young, *The Rise of the Meritocracy*, Transaction Publishers, 1994, page 11.

"Intelligence tests . . . were the very instrument": Ibid., page 63.

118: "the lower classes no longer have the power": Ibid., page 179.

119: "wrest nationhood from polyglot chaos": Ibid., page 33.

"Professor Conant . . . is simply asking for the impossible": Ibid., page 40.

American figures reading *The Rise of the Meritocracy*: Author's interviews with Henry Chauncey, John Gardner, and Clark Kerr.

Young's letter to Chauncey: Sasha Moorman and Michael Young, letter to Henry Chauncey, December 21, 1959. Henry Chauncey Papers, Folder 36.

119–120: Conant and public-school tracking: See James Bryant Conant, *The American High School Today*, McGraw-Hill, 1959.

120: "I tend to be a little wary": Henry Chauncey, letter to Gregory Anrig, May 23, 1992. Personal files of Gary Saretzky, folder labeled "Henry Chauncey Correspondence," ETS archives. The subject of the letter is the author's request for access to Chauncey's papers.

"The democracy of merit on the campus": William S. Learned, "Variability in Education," *Thirtieth Annual Report of the Carnegie Foundation for the Advancement of Teaching*, 1935, page 72.

"The book is an amusing and effective sermon": Gardner, *Excellence*, page 114.

121: "the structuring of the labor force": Clark Kerr, John T. Dunlop, Frederick H. Harbison, and Charles A. Myers, *Industrialism and Industrial Man: The Problems of Labor and Management in Economic Growth*, Harvard University Press, 1960, page 8.

"education becomes one of the principal means": Ibid., page 37.

Kerr's inauguration: Mary Clark Stuart, "Clark Kerr: Biography of an Action Intellectual," unpublished doctoral dissertation at the University of Michigan, 1980, page 137.

"universities today are at the vital center": Clark Kerr, "Education for the Twenty-first Century," inaugural address given at the University of California, Riverside, October 1, 1958, page 4. In author's personal files.

"we must again concern ourselves with educating an elite": Ibid., page 16.

122: "Henry Chauncey's son": Author's interviews with Henry Chauncey, Jr.

BOOK TWO

125: History of the University of California: The best source is Verne A. Stadtman, *The University of California, 1868–1968*, McGraw-Hill, 1970.

regents approving the hiring of coaches: See, for example, the minutes of the Regents of the University of California's Committee on Educational Policy for January 21 and March 17, 1960, at both of which coaching changes preceded the Master Plan on the agenda. In the archives of the Regents of the University of California, Oakland, California.

the Universities of Michigan and Wisconsin: See Lawrence A. Cremin, *American Education: The Metropolitan Experience, 1876–1980*, Harper & Row, 1988, pages 242–255.

"a reverberating voice": Stadtman, *The University of California*, page 258.

126: Sproul considering becoming a bank president: Ibid., pages 279–280.

Clark Kerr's early life: Stuart, "Clark Kerr" is an excellent source. Also, author's interviews with Clark Kerr.

127: "at least five and maybe even ten years": Author's interviews with Clark Kerr.

128: Kerr refusing to support Upton Sinclair: Author's interview with Dean McHenry.

The Berkeley loyalty oath controversy: There is a full account in Stuart, "Clark Kerr"; another one in Stadtman, *The University of California*; and another one in Ellen W. Schrecker, *No Ivory Tower: McCarthyism and the Universities*, Oxford University Press, 1968.

129: Kerr's house and his management techniques: Stuart, "Clark Kerr," pages 166–167.

130: reports on the future of California higher education: The most important of these were the Suzzallo Report of 1933 (named after Henry Suzzallo, president of the Carnegie

Foundation for the Advancement of Teaching, the funder), the Strayer Report of 1948 (named after George Strayer, head of a gubernatorial task force), and the McConnell Report of 1955 (named after T. R. McConnell, former chancellor of the University of Buffalo, the head of the supervising committee).

131: Kerr's work on the Master Plan: Specific sources for this account are noted below. More generally, it comes from author's interviews with Robert Baumann, Patrick Callan, William Coblentz, John T. Dunlop, Frederick Dutton, Marian Gade, Louis Heilbron, Clark Kerr, Seymour Martin Lipset, Dean McHenry, and Kevin Starr. Also helpful were Stadtman, *The University of California*, Chapters 23 and 24, and Clark Kerr, "The Master Plan," a chapter from an unpublished book manuscript, dated 1993, in author's personal files.

"pulled the double cross": Dean McHenry, memorandum to "Gloria," March 14, 1959. University of California President's Files for Clark Kerr, Box 994, folder labeled "Master Plan Survey, McHenry Confidential Materials, 1959–60." Bancroft Library, University of California at Berkeley.

"We cannot allow": Dean McHenry, memorandum to Clark Kerr, March 17, 1959. U of C President's Files, Box 994, folder labeled "Master Plan Survey, McHenry Confidential Materials, 1959–60."

132: "The American norms of equality": Seymour Martin Lipset, memorandum to Clark Kerr, November 5, 1959. U of C President's Files, Box 994, folder labeled "Master Plan Survey, McHenry Confidential Materials, 1959–60."

"Within the bounds of polite language": Herman A. Spindt, letter to Clark Kerr, November 23, 1959. U of C President's Files, Box 994, folder labeled "Master Plan Survey, McHenry Confidential Materials, 1959–60."

"As you say, I had hoped": Clark Kerr, memorandum to Herman A. Spindt, December 3, 1959. U of C President's Files, Box 994, folder labeled "Master Plan Survey, McHenry Confidential Materials, 1959–60."

133: "You don't have a chance": Author's interviews with Clark Kerr.
"the long auto ride of Glenn Dumke": Author's interviews with Clark Kerr.

134: "It is tragic": Frederick G. Dutton, memorandum to Governor Edmund G. Brown, December 11, 1959. Edmund G. Brown Papers, Box 380, folder labeled "Board of Regents, October–December 1959." Bancroft Library, University of California at Berkeley.

"the top students": Don B. Leiffer, memorandum to Governor Edmund G. Brown, January 8, 1960, page 2. Edmund G. Brown Papers, Box 380, folder labeled "Education, January 1960." Bancroft Library, University of California at Berkeley.

135: "Master Planner":"Master Planner," *Time*, October 17, 1960.
135: "Fever of a Mass Thrust for Knowledge": "Fever of a Mass Thrust for Knowledge," *Life*, October 19, 1962.

"Rah! Rah! Rah!": Lois Dickert and Art Seidenbaum, "Rah! Rah! Rah! College for Everybody!" *McCall's*, May 1964.

"In short, a remarkable man": "Clark Kerr," unsigned memorandum, May 7, 1962.

Office Files of John Macy, Container 306, folder labeled "Kerr, Clark D-Calif." Lyndon B. Johnson Presidential Library.

Time's cover story on the University of California at Irvine: "The Man with the Plan," *Time*, September 6, 1963.

136: "I thought that was *phony*": Author's interviews with Clark Kerr.

Kerr's friend's visit to Berkeley: Author's interview with Eli Ginzberg.

Conant's lectures at Berkeley: James Bryant Conant, *Thomas Jefferson and the Development of American Public Education*, University of California Press, 1962.

137: "Over the past twenty-five years": Ibid., page 54.

"something approaching a caste system": Ibid., page 60.

"What the nation today requires": Ibid., page 61.

Kerr's lectures at Harvard: Clark Kerr, *The Uses of the University*, Harvard University Press, 1982.

138: "an institution unique in world history" and "a prime instrument of national purpose": Ibid., page 87.

"the focal point for national growth": Ibid., page viii.

"an imperative rather than a reasoned choice": Ibid., page 6.

"*The Uses of the University* is the work of a deeply satisfied man": Edgar Z. Friedenberg, "L.A. of the Intellect," *The New York Review of Books*, November 6, 1963, page 11.

"multiversity": Kerr, *The Uses of the University*, page 6.

"the resultant student sense of neglect": Ibid., page 104.

139: "The great university is of necessity elitist": Ibid., page 121. A possibly even more exuberantly confident expression of Kerr's views when he was at the peak of his influence is Clark Kerr, "Education: Genie or Master?" an address to the American Philosophical Society, April 24, 1964. In author's personal files.

140: education and early career of Sam Chauncey: Author's interviews with Henry Chauncey, Jr.

141: the old Yale: Author's interviews with John Morton Blum, William F. Buckley, Jr., McGeorge Bundy, Henry Chauncey, Jr., Inslee Clark, Arthur Howe, Paul Moore, Jr., William Stack, Eustace Theodore, and James Tobin.

Whitney Griswold's schedule: Author's interviews with Henry Chauncey, Jr.

142: William F. Buckley, Jr.'s, testimony in Hartford: Author's interview with William F. Buckley, Jr.

143: *Stover at Yale*: Owen Johnson, *Stover at Yale*, Little, Brown and Company, 1931.

"Wookey, the little freshman": Ibid., page 295.

"It's the one place": Ibid., page 10.

"stands as a reward of merit here": Ibid., page 343.

"ambition and industry and character": Ibid., page 373.

144: "I'm not satisfied with Yale": Ibid., page 386.
life and views of Arthur Howe: Author's interview with Arthur Howe.

145: James Tobin's views on Yale admissions: Author's interview with James Tobin.

146: "what you'd now call nerds": Author's interview with Arthur Howe.
"Sometimes I lie awake nights": Katharine T. Kinkead, *How an Ivy League College Decides on Admissions*, W. W. Norton, 1961, page 26.

147: "Four Negro boys": Author's interviews with Henry Chauncey, Jr.

148: Brewster's class at Yale: Geoffrey Kabaservice, Brewster's biographer, compiled these figures. Kabaservice also allowed the author to read a draft chapter, titled "Meritocracy and Yale's Road to Coeducation," from the biography. In author's personal files.
life and views of Inslee Clark: Author's interview with Clark.

149: "Do you see yourself as an architect": Author's interview with Inslee Clark.
"Where the hell have you guys been": Author's interview with Inslee Clark.
changes in Yale admissions statistics: Thomas Herman, "Class of '70 Reflects Admissions Changes," *Yale Daily News*, summer issue, 1966.
mean SAT verbal score . . . of Clark's first class: Paul S. Burnham, "Summary of Research Output, 1959–1971," Yale University Office of Educational Research, page 4. Yale University Archives.
change in percentage of alumni sons: Author's interview with Inslee Clark.

150: "The son of an alumnus": William F. Buckley, Jr., "What Makes Bill Buckley Run," *The Atlantic Monthly*, April 1968, page 66.
"Look around this room": Author's interview with Inslee Clark.
"Yale is first and foremost": Admissions Policy Advisory Board, memorandum to Kingman Brewster and Inslee Clark, December 15, 1965, page 2. In author's personal files.

151: "It is just as well to be candid": Admissions Policy Advisory Board, "Second Report," memorandum to Kingman Brewster and Inslee Clark, undated, page 6. In author's personal files.
"The only preference by inheritance": Kingman Brewster, draft of letter to John Muyskens, undated, page 8. In author's personal files.
"We want Yale men to be leaders": Ibid., page 1.
"we undoubtedly made some mistakes": Kingman Brewster, "Admission to Yale: Objectives and Myths," *Yale Alumni Magazine*, October 1966, page 33.
"movers and doers": Ibid., page 31.
"the intellectual potential": Brewster, letter to Muyskens, page 3.

152: "It seems to me that this ethic": Brewster, "Admission to Yale," page 31.

153: "to see to it that every effort be made": John Perry Miller, *Creating Academic Settings: High Craft and Low Cunning: Memoirs*, J. Simeon Press, 1991, page 216.

Kingman Brewster's grave: Author's interviews with Henry Chauncey, Jr., and visits to the grave site.

155: "To be practical": Conant, "Wanted: American Radicals," page 41.

156: fair employment practices commissions, the Motorola case, and quotas: Hugh Davis Graham, *The Civil Rights Era: Origins and Development of National Policy*, Oxford University Press, 1990, Chapters 4 and 5.

157: "threw merit and ability out the window": *Congressional Record*, April 20, 1964, page 8448.
"I point out that the college entrance examinations": *Congressional Record*, June 11, 1964, page 13492.

159: ETS and the Coleman Report: Good general sources were the author's interviews with Alfred Beaton, Henry Chauncey, and Robert Solomon. Sources for specific figures and quotations are noted below.
"a test of skills that you couldn't connect": Author's interviews with Robert Solomon.

160: nonparticipation in the Coleman Report: Author's interview with Alfred Beaton.
"we really thought that the Northeastern Negro": Author's interview with Alfred Beaton.
"Differences between schools account": James S. Coleman et al., *Equality of Educational Opportunity*, Government Printing Office, 1966, page 22.
"Most of the single variable comparisons": Henry S. Dyer, memorandum to Robert Solomon, May 3, 1966. Henry Chauncey Papers, Folder 844, Frame 01191.
"bias would probably have the effect": Henry S. Dyer, "Some Implications of the Civil Rights Survey," October 14, 1966, page 1. Henry Chauncey Papers, Folder 844, Frame 01209.
"tends to depress the effect": Frederick Kling, memorandum on the Coleman Report, October 18, 1966. Henry Chauncey Papers, Folder 844, Frame 01217.
Beaton's technical report: Alfred E. Beaton, "Some Considerations of Technical Problems in the Educational Opportunity Survey," ETS Reach Reports, 1968. See also George W. Mayeske et al., *A Study of Achievement in Our Nation's Students*, Government Printing Office, 1973, which is another analysis of the Coleman Report data that places much greater weight than Colemen did on school factors.

161: Daniel Patrick Moynihan and the Coleman Report: see Thomas F. Pettigrew and Daniel P. Moynihan, memorandum to Dean Theodore Sizer, September 15, 1966. Henry Chauncey Papers, Folder 844. As an example of the way the report was being read and used, the letter says, "Coleman has indicated to us in conversation that he feels the report is potentially the strongest case for school integration yet made."
"The most important contribution of the survey": Dyer, "Some Implications of the Equal Opportunity Survey," page 5.
"I was searching for something that would give a sense of positiveness": Hobart Tay-

lor, Jr., oral history interview, January 6, 1969, page 12. Oral history collection, Lyndon B. Johnson Presidential Library.

163: "Rights Groups Fear Easing": John Herbers, "Rights Groups Fear Easing of U.S. Enforcement Role," *The New York Times*, October 17, 1965, page 1.

164: "The average business guy wants to know": Author's interview with Edward Sylvester.

166: Kerr and the California Fair Employment Practices Commission: Cartons 534 and 686 of the papers of Edmund G. Brown are substantially devoted to correspondence about this. See, especially, Clark Kerr, letter to William L. Becker, November 21, 1963. Brown Papers, Carton 534, folder labeled "FEPC, July–August." Bancroft Library, University of California at Berkeley.

The events of 1964 at Berkeley: There are several books on the subject, including Seymour Martin Lipset and Sheldon S. Wolin, editors, *The Berkeley Student Revolt: Facts and Interpretations*, Anchor, 1965; Max Heinrich, *The Spiral of Conflict: Berkeley 1964*, Columbia University Press, 1971; and Hal Draper, *Berkeley: The New Student Revolt*, Grove Press, 1965; also, author's interviews with William Coblentz, John T. Dunlop, Frederick Dutton, Marian Gade, Clark Kerr, and Seymour Martin Lipset.

169: the Goldwater and Reagan campaigns: Matthew Dallek gave the author portions of his unpublished undergraduate honors essay from Columbia University on the rise of the conservative movement in California, which was helpful for this passage. In author's personal files.

170: dinner at H. R. Haldeman's house: Author's interviews with William Coblentz and Frederick Dutton.

171: the University of California requiring the SAT of all applicants: John A. Douglas, "Setting the Conditions of Undergraduate Admissions: The Role of California Faculty in Policy and Process," a report to the University of California Academic Senate, February 10, 1997, pages 39–43.

172: "The University of California is the largest": Robert Lambert, "Trip Report" on visit to the University of California, Berkeley, February 9, 1962, page 3. William W. Turnbull Papers, Folder 1411.

174: early life of Don Nakanishi: Author's interviews with Nakanishi.

176: "The learned class may still be subdivided into sections": Thomas Jefferson, letter to Peter Carr, September 7, 1814, in *Thomas Jefferson: Writings*, Library of America, 1984, page 1348.

Yale student life in the mid-1960s: Author's interviews with Henry Chauncey, Jr., Bill Lee, Don Nakanishi, Daniel Singer, Steven Weisman, Alice Young, and Nancy Young.

177: Asian-Americans in Los Angeles: Author's interviews with Ronald Cheng, John Kojaku, Robert Kwan, Don Nakanishi, Lawrence Ng, Paul Okada, Christopher Otsuki, Phyllis Rothrock, and Terry Tang. A long memorandum written for the author by Robert Kwan was also very helpful. In author's personal files. Also, Sucheng Chan, *Asian-Americans: An Interpretive History*, Twayne Publishers, 1991.

178: life and attitudes of John Young: Author's interviews with John Young, Alice Young, Nancy Young, and Peter Young.
"Study and learn in what way they may fail": Author's interview with John Young.
"because I wanted to be *better*": Author's interview with John Young.

180: life and attitudes of Bill Lann Lee: Author's interviews with Lee.

183: Sam Chauncey and the ethnic student groups: Author's interviews with Henry Chauncey, Jr.

185: Career decisions of Alice, Nancy, and Peter Young: Author's interviews with Alice Young, Nancy Young, and Peter Young.

188: "Molly, with her shiny blond hair": Jill Abramson and Barbara Franklin, *Where They Are Now: The Story of the Women of Harvard Law 1974*, Doubleday, 1986, page 149.

189: the life of Charles Munger: Author's interview and correspondence with Charles Munger.

190: life and attitudes of Nancy Huggins: Author's interview with Nancy Huggins Freeman.

193: life and attitudes of Molly Munger: Author's interviews with Molly Munger. Also, author's interviews with Alice Ballard, Gordon Grand, Stephen English, Nancy Freeman, J. Tomlinson Hill, Bill Lee, Charles Munger, and Constance Rice. There is much of Molly Munger here, so it's worth saying that unless otherwise noted, all passages about her are drawn from the author's interviews with her.

194: the life of Alice Ballard: Author's interviews with Alice Ballard and Frederick Ballard
E. Digby Baltzell: See E. Digby Baltzell, *The Protestant Establishment: Aristocracy and Caste in America*, Random House, 1964.

199: The NAACP Legal Defense and Education Fund, Inc.: See Juan Williams, *Thurgood Marshall: American Revolutionary*, Times Books, 1998; Jack Greenberg, *Crusaders in the Courts: How a Dedicated Band of Lawyers Fought for the Civil Rights Revolution*, Basic Books, 1994; and Richard Kluger, *Simple Justice: The History of Brown v. Board of Education and America's Struggle for Equality*, Alfred A. Knopf, 1975.

200: The life of Arthur Fletcher: Author's interview with Arthur Fletcher. Graham, *The Civil Rights Era*, Chapters 11 and 13, has a detailed history of the Philadelphia Plan and affirmative action during the Nixon Administration. Another account is in John David

Skrentny, *The Ironies of Affirmative Action: Politics, Culture, and Justice in America*, University of Chicago Press, 1996, Chapter 7.

"mad son of a bitch": Author's interview with Arthur Fletcher.

201: "When I was a plumber": John D. Ehrlichman, notes on a meeting with Richard Nixon, Bryce Harlow, and Ronald Ziegler, December 23, 1969. Nixon Presidential Materials Project (at the National Archives), White House Special Files, Staff Member and Office Files, John Ehrlichman Box 3, folder labeled "JDE Notes of Meetings with the President, 4 of 4."

statistics on Philadelphia building-trades unions: Arthur A. Fletcher and John L. Wilks, "Order to Heads of All Agencies," September 23, 1969. In author's personal files.

"A wedge has been driven": "Plan: Philadelphia Plan," unsigned memorandum, December 23, 1969. Nixon Project, Leonard Garment Box 143, folder labeled "Philadelphia Plan 2 of 2."

"The key issue is that we have laid bare": John R. Price, memorandum to John D. Ehrlichman, December 22, 1969. Nixon Project, Leonard Garment Box 143, folder labeled "Philadelphia Plan 1 of 2."

202: "Fletcher's basic problem": Frederick R. Malek, memorandum to John D. Ehrlichman, September 24, 1971. Nixon Project, Confidential Files Box 20, folder labeled "CF FG Department of Labor (1971–1974)."

pamphlets for the Republican Convention: Author's interview with Arthur Fletcher.

203: articles by Arthur Jensen: The best-known of Jensen's many articles is Arthur Jensen, "How Much Can We Boost IQ and Scholastic Achievement?"*Harvard Educational Review*, Volume 39 (1969), pages 1–123.

article by Richard Herrnstein: Richard Herrnstein, "I.Q.," *The Atlantic Monthly*, September 1971.

memo from six Jewish organizations: "Preferential Treatment and Other Improper Procedures in Admissions and Employment at Colleges and Universities: Illustrative Instances," memorandum from six Jewish organizations to the Secretary of Health, Education and Welfare, August 8, 1972. Nixon Project, Leonard Garment Box 145, folder labeled " 'Quota' Policy (2 of 3)."

204: Griggs case: *Griggs* v. *Duke Power*, 401 U.S. 424 (1971).

205: the life of William O. Douglas: See William O. Douglas, *Go East, Young Man: The Early Years: The Autobiography of William O. Douglas*, Random House, 1974. Also, author's interview with Ira Ellman.

206: "there really was some kind of quota here": "IE" (Ira Ellman), Supplemental Memo on Mootness, November 8, 1973. Papers of William O. Douglas, Library of Congress, Manuscript Division, Carton 1655, No. 73-235.

"I don't know about these tests": Author's interview with Ira Ellman.

"by no means objective": William O. Douglas, draft opinion in *DeFunis* v. *Odegaard*, Draft 1, page 1. Douglas Papers, Carton 1655, No. 73-235.

LSAT's predictiveness of blacks' law school grades: See ETS research report LSAC-77-03, 1977, which discusses this.

"The democratic ideal": Douglas, Draft 1, page 3.

"those clearly qualified": Douglas, Ibid.

"I might not be around next time": Author's interview with Ira Ellman.

207: "allow racial groups into graduate schools": William O. Douglas, draft opinion in *DeFunis* v. *Odegaard*, Draft 3, page 13. Douglas Papers, Carton 1655, No. 73-235.

"racial classifications cannot be used": William O. Douglas, draft opinion in *DeFunis* v. *Odegaard*, Draft 4, page 18. Douglas Papers, Carton 1655, no. 73-235.

"the essence of the policy here": William O. Douglas, draft opinion in *DeFunis* v. *Odegaard*, Draft 5, page 21. Douglas Papers, Carton 1655, No. 73-235.

"say the last twenty seats": William O. Douglas, draft opinion in *DeFunis* v. *Odegaard*, Draft 6, page 22. Douglas Papers, Carton 1655, No. 73-235.

"insofar as the LSAT tests": William O. Douglas, draft opinion in *DeFunis* v. *Odegaard*, Draft 9, Rider 15. Douglas Papers, Carton 1655, No. 73-235.

"The opinion you wrote": Author's interview with Ira Ellman.

"The purpose of the University of Washington": William O. Douglas, draft opinion in *DeFunis* v. *Odegaard*, Draft 11, page 23. Douglas Papers, Carton 1655, No. 73-235.

208: "He changed the bottom line": Author's interview with Ira Ellman.

Bakke case: *Regents of the University of California* v. *Bakke*, 438 U.S. 265 (1978).

209: amicus curiae briefs and research papers in connection with the Bakke case: There are interesting amicus curiae briefs in the case record from the deans of the University of California's law schools, jointly from Columbia, Harvard, Stanford, and the University of Pennsylvania, and from the NAACP Legal Defense and Education Fund, Inc. In the Columbia-Harvard-Stanford-Penn brief, a short appendix called "Harvard College Admissions Program," which heavily quotes Henry Chauncey's old colleague Wilbur J. Bender, appears to be the source for the "diversity" standard that Justice Powell settled on in his decisions. In the Legal Defense Fund Brief, Appendix B, *"De Jure* Segregation in California Public Education," was written by Bill Lann Lee. In the William W. Turnbull Papers, Folders 374 and 375 are devoted to the study Clark Kerr commissioned from ETS in connection with the Bakke case. In the ETS archiveís.

Bill Lee's findings on California public education: See the Legal Defense Fund amicus curiae brief, Appendix B.

210: reactions of ETS staff and Bill Lee to the *Bakke* decision: Author's interviews with Bill Lee and Winton Manning.

211: *A Theory of Justice*: John Rawls, *A Theory of Justice*, Harvard University Press, 1971. See especially pages 106–107, in which Rawls discusses—in fact, opposes—meritocracy.

212: Alice Young's legal career: Author's interviews with Alice Young.

213: Molly Munger's legal career: Author's interviews with Molly Munger.

215: the life of Stephen English: Author's interview with Stephen English.

218: *"Something that's terrible is coming"*: William W. Turnbull, undated, unpublished poem. William W. Turnbull Papers, Folder 2392.

enrollment in higher education: *Digest of Education Statistics 1995*, pages 175–177.

"I think it's not too much to say": John D. Millett, remarks given at a retirement dinner for Henry Chauncey, May 3, 1970. Henry Chauncey Papers, Folder 183, Frame 00534.

219: the life of William Turnbull: William W. Turnbull, oral history interviews of April 7, 1983, and August 5, 1983. Oral History Collection, ETS archives. Also, author's interviews with David Brodsky, Henry Chauncey, John Hollister, Winton Manning, Richard Pearson, Robert Solomon, Mary Turnbull, and E. Belvin Williams.

"a rather orderly, quantifiable approach": William W. Turnbull, oral history interview, April 7, 1983, page 3. Oral History Collection, ETS archives.

220: "Educational Statesmen of the Century": Ben D. Wood, letter to William W. Turnbull, November 3, 1970. William W. Turnbull Papers, Folder 2499.

attacks on ETS during the 1970s: Steven Brill, "The Secrecy Behind the College Boards," *New York*, October 7, 1974; James Fallows, "The Tests and the Brightest," *The Atlantic Monthly*, February 1980; David Owen, *None of the Above: Beyond the Myth of Scholastic Aptitude*, Houghton Mifflin, 1985; Steven Levy, "E.T.S. and the 'Coaching' Cover-Up," *New Jersey Monthly*, March 1979.

221: life and attitudes of Ralph Nader: Author's interview with Ralph Nader.

222: life of Allan Nairn: Author's interview with Allan Nairn.

223: William Turnbull's dealings with Ralph Nader: Author's interviews with Henry Chauncey. A deeply ingrained suspicion of outsiders, especially journalists, persists at ETS. Here is an example. In March 1993 the author, then at work in the ETS archives, received in the mail a copy of a memorandum titled "Media Alert" dated February 26, 1993, and with more than thirty officials of the College Board listed at the top to whom it was supposed to be distributed. The memorandum reports on a telephone call from Warren Day, head of public relations at ETS, to his counterpart at the College Board to warn him about the author: "Warren says the guy is somewhat devious, given to calling people directly and giving the impression it was at the suggestion of someone else who may or may not have suggested it. Similarly, he feigns ignorance with successive interviewees of material he has already discussed and gotten answers about with other interviewees. All of which is to say almost anyone can expect to hear from him, and probably without prior contact with Public Affairs. Of course if he calls Public Affairs we will handle the matter as a normal media inquiry and cooperate as needed." The memorandum was mailed to the author from a general mail facility in New Jersey so that it would have no traceable postmark. In author's personal files.

the Federal Trade Commission's investigation: See "Staff Report of the Federal Trade Commission Investigation of Coaching for Standardized Admission Tests," Boston Regional Office, Federal Trade Commission, 1979. This report was never published; the author obtained it through a Freedom of Information Act request. In author's personal files.

congressmen thinking of holding hearings: Benjamin Rosenthal, letter to William W. Turnbull, April 5, 1976. William W. Turnbull Papers, Folder 618. David Brodsky, memorandum to William W. Turnbull, March 26, 1976. William W. Turnbull Papers, Folder 618 (this entire folder, called "Congressional Inquiries," is relevant). Also, author's interviews with Winton Manning and Robert Solomon.

thirty-seven truth-in-testing bills: Author's interview with David Brodsky.

Nader not returning Turnbull's calls: Author's interviews with Henry Chauncey.

Turnbull's answers to criticisms of ETS: Folder 324 in the William W. Turnbull Papers, "Notes for a Book by WWT," is the best source here. Turnbull never wrote the book.

the California truth-in-testing bill: Folder 1810 in the William W. Turnbull Papers, "Legislation, California," is entirely devoted to this.

career and attitudes of Kenneth LaValle: Author's interview with LaValle.

224: the New York truth-in-testing bill: This account comes generally from the author's interviews with David Brodsky, John Katzman, Kenneth LaValle, Mary Anne McLean, Allan Nairn, Ralph Nader, Donald Ross, Robert Schaeffer, Robert Solomon, Mary Turnbull, and E. Belvin Williams. See also "Truth-in-Testing: A Study in Educational Reform," a report by Senator Kenneth LaValle, 1984. In author's personal files.

"ETS is one of the most extravagantly administered institutions": "Minutes of Proceedings at a Joint Public Hearing of the Senate and Assembly Standing Committees on Higher Education," May 9, 1979, page 88. Office files of Senator Kenneth LaValle.

E. Belvin Williams on the *Today* show, and William Turnbull's reaction: Author's interviews with E. Belvin Williams and Winton Manning.

testimony of Donald Halperin: "Minutes of Proceedings," page 24; also, author's interview with Donald Halperin.

225: opposition to the truth-in-testing bill: All these opponents' letters are in the office files of Senator Kenneth LaValle in Albany.

226: "I only wish that all of you could take a little field trip": Official transcript of New York State Assembly debate on Senate Bill No. 5200-A, June 16, 1979, page 10204.

"Now, you know this State was the first State": Ibid., page 10207.

lobbying of Hugh Carey: Author's interviews with Mary Anne McLean, Allan Nairn, and Donald Ross.

LaValle's invitation to ETS: Author's interviews with Kenneth LaValle and Mary Anne McLean.

227: Stanley Kaplan's rapprochement with ETS: Author's interviews with Stanley Kaplan. In recent years, Kaplan's company has fallen out with ETS again. ETS sued Kaplan in 1996, accusing it of copyright violation after Kaplan staged a demonstration of how easy it would be to cheat on the first computer-administered standardized test, a

Graduate Record Exam, by sending ringers to take the test in order to prove that the questions were too similar from one administration to another.

Allan Nairn's report on ETS: Allan Nairn and Associates, *The Reign of ETS: The Corporation That Makes Up Minds*, The Ralph Nader Report on the Educational Testing Service, 1980.

228: "It's unrelievedly bad": William W. Turnbull, "Nader/Nairn Report," undated handwritten notes. William W. Turnbull Papers, Folder 324.

life and attitudes of John Katzman: Author's interviews with John Katzman.

229: "It had the sheen of being for losers": Author's interviews with John Katzman.

"We'd send people in to take tests": Author's interviews with John Katzman.

"the substantial weakening, if not the destruction": William W. Turnbull, oral history interview, August 5, 1983, page 16. Oral History Collection, ETS archives.

230: "bulldog commitment": Author's interview with Ralph Nader.

Nader's comments to Turnbull: William W. Turnbull, oral history interview of August 5, 1983, page 17. Oral History Collection, ETS archives.

"Let's say the country desperately needs community organizers": Author's interview with Ralph Nader.

William Turnbull's drinking problems: Author's interviews with Henry Chauncey and E. Belvin Williams; also, Mary Turnbull, letter to Henry Chauncey, May 10, 1983. Chauncey Family Papers, Box 2, Folder 64.

"We've got troubles": Author's interviews with Henry Chauncey.

231: life and attitudes of Gregory Anrig: Author's interview with Gregory Anrig.

Anrig's lack of familiarity with psychometrics: Author's interviews with Winton Manning and E. Belvin Williams.

BOOK THREE

235:"Molly Munger . . . is determined": Abramson and Franklin, *Where They Are Now*, Doubleday, 1986, page 194.

236: Alice Young's maternity leave: Author's interviews with Alice Young.

"I called you three times yesterday": Author's interview with Nancy Young.

lawsuit against the Pasadena school system: The case is *Spangler* v. *Pasadena City Board of Education*, 311 F.Supp. 501 (1970).

Nina and Lisa Edwards: This account is drawn from the author's interviews with Lisa Edwards, Molly Munger, and Shandra Rowe.

238: Proposition 13: A good source on the subject is Robert Kuttner, *Revolt of the Haves: Tax Rebellions and Hard Times*, Simon & Schuster, 1980.

241: Changes in immigration policy and Asian-American population growth: A good overall source is Chan, *Asian-Americans*.

242: Test of English as a Foreign Language and cheating schemes: Author's interviews with Shirley Kane-Orr and Russell Webster, ETS executives in charge, respectively, of test security and TOEFL.

243: University of California at Irvine: Samuel Clyde McCullough, "Instant University: The Founding and Growth of the University of California, Irvine, 1962–1993," unpublished book manuscript, in author's personal files. Also author's interviews with McCullough, Clark Kerr, and Don Nakanishi.

Increase in applications to Berkeley: Good sources are John Aubrey Douglas, "Anatomy of Conflict: Making and Unmaking of Affirmative Action at the University of California," unpublished manuscript dated June 23, 1997, in author's personal files; John A. Douglas, "Setting the Conditions of Undergraduate Admissions: The Role of California Faculty in Policy and Process," a report to the Task Force on Governance, University of California Academic Senate, February 10, 1997; and "Freshman Admissions at Berkeley: A Policy for the 1990s and Beyond," a report of the committee on admissions and enrollment, Berkeley division, Academic Senate, University of California, 1989 (otherwise known as the Karabel Report). Also, author's interviews with Patrick Callan, Troy Duster, Patrick Hayashi, Jerome Karabel, Bob Laird, Don Nakanishi, and Genaro Padilla.

244: Don Nakanishi and Asian-American admissions: See Don Nakanishi, "A Quota on Excellence? The Asian American Admissions Debate," *Change*, November–December 1989. Also author's interviews with Nakanishi.

Ronald Reagan and the *Bakke* decision: Author's interview with W. Bradford Reynolds.

Changes in Berkeley's affirmative-action policy: "Freshman Admissions at Berkeley," and author's interviews with Jerome Karabel and Don Nakanishi.

245: federal investigation of Asian-American admissions policy: John E. Palomino, letter to Dr. Chang-Lin Tien, March 1, 1996, is the Justice Department's final report of the whole matter, and a useful account. In author's personal files.

Jerome Karabel: The account of Karabel's life and his views come from the author's interviews with him. These interviews are also, except where noted, the source for all subsequent passages about his political activities, his thoughts, and his reactions to events.

Henry Goddard and Vineland: See Gould, *The Mismeasure of Man*, pages 158–174, and Kevles, *In the Name of Eugenics*, pages 76–84.

249: Karabel's article on open admissions: Jerome Karabel, "The Politics of Structural Change in American Higher Education: The Case of Open Admissions at the City University of New York," in Harry Hermanns et al., editors, *The Compleat University: Break from Tradition in Germany, Sweden, and the U.S.*, Schenkman Publishing, 1983.

250: Karabel's article on professional basketball: Jerome Karabel and David Karen, "Color on the Court," *In These Times*, February 10–16, 1982

Books by Kristin Luker: Kristin Luker, *Taking Chances: Abortion and the Decision Not to Contracept*, University of California Press, 1975; *Abortion and the Politics of*

Motherhood, University of California Press, 1984; *Dubious Conceptions: The Politics of Teenage Pregnancy*, Harvard University Press, 1996.

251: Changes in Berkeley admissions policy: "Freshman Admissions at Berkeley"; Douglas, "Setting the Conditions"; and author's interviews with Karabel and Douglas.

articles in conservative magazines: See, for example, John H. Bunzel, "Affirmative-Action Admissions: How It 'Works' at UC-Berkeley," *The Public Interest*, Fall 1988. Dinesh D'Souza, *Illiberal Education: The Politics of Race and Sex on Campus*, the Free Press, 1991, has a chapter on Berkeley.

252: recommendations in Karabel Report: "Freshman Admissions at Berkeley," pages 29–44.

Karabel's book on community colleges: Steven Brint and Jerome Karabel, *The Diverted Dream: Community Colleges and the Promise of Educational Opportunity in America, 1900–1985*, Oxford University Press, 1989.

Nakanishi's tenure battle at UCLA: A large portion (eight articles in all) of an issue of the *Amerasia Journal* is devoted to this: *Amerasia Journal*, volume 16, number 1 (1990), pages 61–172. Also author's interviews with Nakanishi.

253: after-graduation experiences of Asian-Americans: Author's interviews with Ronald Cheng, Rockwell Chin, Georgiana Dwight, Howrani Dwight, John Kojaku, Robert Kwan, Lucille Leong, Don Nakanishi, Lawrence Ng, Paul Okada, Christopher Otsuki, Terry Tang, Alice Young, Nancy Young, and Peter Young.

"You need to get some lead in your pencil": Author's interview with Lawrence Ng.

254: Bill Lee's moving to Los Angeles: Author's interviews with Bill Lee.

255: career of Charles Munger: Author's interview and correspondence with Charles Munger. Also see Robert Lenzner and David S. Fondiller, "The Not-So-Silent Partner," *Forbes*, January 22, 1996.

257: career of Molly Munger: As in Book Two, the account of Munger's life and her views come from the author's interviews with her. These interviews are also, except where noted, the source for all subsequent passages about her political activities, her thoughts, and her reactions to events.

263: Los Angeles riot: An excellent book on the subject is Lou Cannon, *Official Neglect: How Rodney King and the Riots Changed Los Angeles and the LAPD*, Times Books, 1997.

265: Soon Ja Du case: Ibid., pages 108–120 and 148–173.

John Muir High School: Author's interviews with Molly Munger and Eddie Newman, the school's principal.

269: career of Winton Manning: Author's interviews and correspondence with Winton Manning.

270: the Commission on Tests: Author's interviews with Winton Manning and Richard Pearson, and correspondence with Pearson.

"I saw testing as a grand, rational system": Winton H. Manning, "From Procrustes to Prometheus: Constructing a New Ethical Foundation for Assessment," unpublished manuscript dated June 1993, page 7. In author's personal files.

271: "Class in the Guise of Merit": Nairn and Associates, *The Reign of ETS*, Chapter 5.

272: Manning's chart of MAT scores: Winton H. Manning, "Identifying Talented Minority Students: A Preliminary Investigation of the MAT," unpublished manuscript, 1989. In author's personal files.

"He would use the powers of government": Conant, "Wanted: American Radicals," page 41.

274: the labor economics of higher education: See Richard B. Freeman, *The Overeducated American*, Academic Press, 1976; and, for the more recent view that a college education produces a very high economic return, Frank Levy, *Dollars and Dreams: The Changing American Income Distribution*, W. W. Norton, 1988, and Frank Levy and Richard J. Murnane, *Teaching the New Basic Skills: Principles for Educating Children to Thrive in a Changing Economy*, The Free Press, 1996.

275: Manning's meeting with Messick and Cole: Author's interviews with Winton Manning. Messick died in 1998. Cole defends her cutting off of funds for Manning's research in this way: "I questioned his measure [the MAT] because he was promoting it for potential use by colleges without adequate data to support it; it eliminated racial differences artificially, because he used race directly in the equations; and he told Sam Messick and me that he had no intention of revealing the underlying approach to the public since that would make it more difficult for colleges to defend its use." Nancy Cole, letter to author, April 29, 1999. In author's personal files. Manning says he was promoting a field test of the MAT, not a general introduction; that he used race directly in some of his calculations and not in others; and that Cole wanted him to turn over his equations to colleges not in the spirit of making information publicly available but as a substitute for continued development of the MAT. Author's interviews and correspondence with Winton Manning.

"It was the most stark example": Winton H. Manning, letter to author, June 22, 1993. In author's personal files.

276: "Or is it too politicially sensitive?": Winton H. Manning, "Genetic Analysis of Cognitive Abilities," memorandum to Warren Willingham, November 16, 1992. In author's personal files.

Manning's long philosophical treatise: Manning, "From Procrustes to Prometheus."

277: "we have learned that there is not large-scale, consistent bias": Nancy Cole, "Bias in Testing," *American Psychologist*, October 1981, page 1070.

"selecting equal proportions": Ibid.

278: attempts to persuade Ronald Reagan to abolish affirmative action: Author's interviews with C. Boyden Gray, Michael Horowitz, and W. Bradford Reynolds. Horowitz, as an official of the Office of Management and Budget, wrote a lengthy critique of affirmative action that he appended to the official United States Budget for fiscal year 1986. See "Special Analysis J" in *Special Analysis, Budget of the United States Government, Fiscal Year 1986*, Government Printing Office, 1985. Also see Gary L. McDowell, "Affirmative Inaction: The Brock-Meese Standoff on Federal Racial Quotas," *Policy Review*, Spring 1989, a detailed account in a conservative magazine.

attempts to persuade George Bush to abolish affirmative action: Author's interviews with C. Boyden Gray, Michael Horowitz, and W. Bradford Reynolds.

279: Supreme Court decisions on affirmative action: The Croson case is *City of Richmond v. J. A. Croson Co.*, 488 U.S. 469 (1989); the Wards Cove Case, *Wards Cove Packing* v. *Atonio*, 490 U.S. 643 (1989); and the Metro Broadcasting case, *Metro Broadcasting, Inc.* v. *FCC*, 497 U.S. 547 (1990).

the 1991 Civil Rights Act: For a summary of its history and main provisions, see "Compromise Civil Rights Bill Passed," 1991 *Congressional Quarterly Almanac*, pages 251–252.

280: "Each segment of California higher education": "Freshman Admissions at Berkeley," page 11.

Glynn Custred's reaction to California affirmative-action policies: Author's interviews with Custred.

282: career and attitudes of Tom Wood: Author's interviews with Wood.

Wood's job interview at San Francisco State: Tom Wood, memorandum to Glynn Custred, Joe Gelman, and Arnold Steinberg, April 9, 1995. This is a candid, private account by Wood of an incident much reported in the press at the time. California Civil Rights Initiative Papers (author's name for a collection of papers made available by a confidential source). In author's personal files.

283: Custred and Wood's early efforts to promote their initiative: Author's interviews with Custred and Wood. For a useful, blow-by-blow history of the initiative, see Lydia Chávez, *The Color Bind: California's Battle to End Affirmative Action*, University of California Press, 1998.

285: career and attitudes of Joe Gelman: Author's interviews with Gelman.

career and attitudes of Larry Arnn: Author's interviews with Arnn.

career and attitudes of Arnold Steinberg: Author's interviews with Steinberg.

287: Bill Lee's attitude toward the California Civil Rights Initiative: Author's interviews with Lee.

career and attitudes of Constance Rice: Author's interviews with Rice.

290: Wood's contacts with Michael McConnell, Richard Epstein, and Lino Graglia: Author's interviews with Wood and Glynn Custred; also Michael McConnell, memorandum to Tom Wood, June 26, 1995. In California Civil Rights Initiative Papers. In this memo McConnell argues that the Initiative should not explicitly forbid discrimination on the basis of religion, because "I fear that the inclusion of the term 'religion' could be taken to outlaw legitimate religious accommodations, for example, allowing state employees to take unpaid leave for celebration of religious holy days, or allowing religious employees to deviate in unobtrusive ways from a uniform requirement." Epstein's main contribution to the wording of the Initiative, according to Wood, was in arguing successfully that private institutions should be exempted, on the grounds that racial and gender discrimination by private institutions ought to be legal. The way the Initiative was initially written by Wood, it would have outlawed affirmative action everywhere in California—at Stanford University and Pacific Gas & Electric as well as in state government.

Epstein's book: Richard Epstein, *Forbidden Grounds: The Case Against Employment Discrimination Laws*, Harvard University Press, 1992. See especially Chapter 14, "Bona Fide Occupational Qualifications," pages 283–312.

291: career of Erroll Smith: Author's interview with Smith.

293: William Wardlaw's political views: Author's interview with William Wardlaw.

294: donation from Howard Ahmanson: Arnold Steinberg, memorandum to Larry Arnn, April 11, 1995. In California Civil Rights Initiative Papers. Also author's interviews with Steinberg, Arnn, and Joe Gelman.

findings of Steinberg's poll: A thick binder of the poll results, dated February 11–21, 1995, is in the group of documents I've called the California Civil Rights Initiative Papers. There is also a facinating and comprehensive private 200-page "Campaign Plan" produced by Steinberg later, in the spring of 1996, which contains a complete history of the Initiative from his perspective. In author's personal files.

career and attitudes of Peg Yorkin: Author's interview with Peg Yorkin.

295: career and attitudes of Bill Press: Author's interview with Bill Press.

296: "Mr. President, is it true": *Public Papers of the Presidents of the United States, Administration of William J. Clinton, 1995*, Government Printing Office, 1996, page 263.

"Do they work? Are they fair?" Ibid.

attitude of White House staff toward the press conference: Author's interviews with Christopher Edley and William Galston.

"I have ordered a review": *Administration of William J. Clinton, 1995*, page 293.

297: career and attitudes of Christopher Edley, William Galston, and George Stephanopoulos: Author's interviews with Edley, Galston, and Stephanopoulos. Also see Christopher Edley, Jr., *Not All Black and White: Affirmative Action, Race, and American Values*, Hill and Wang, 1996.

Jesse Jackson's contemplation of a presidential race: Author's interviews with Penda Hair, Wade Henderson, and Ralph Neas.

Custred and Wood's meetings in Washington: Author's interviews with Custred and Wood. Also, regarding Rupert Murdoch, Arnold Steinberg, memorandum to Joe Gelman, April 6, 1995. In California Civil Rights Initiative Papers.

298: "Let me close with a few words": *Administration of William J. Clinton, 1995*, page 501. "We don't have to retreat": Ibid., page 503.

299: reactions of Molly Munger, Bill Press, and George Stephanopoulos to President Clinton's speech: Author's interviews with Munger, Press, and Stephanopoulos.

300: "their relationship with the powers-that-be": Jerome Karabel, "Toward a Theory of Intellectuals and Politics," *Theory and Society*, Volume 25 (1996), page 208. "suspicion and dissent": Ibid., page 209

301: "a debacle for the Democratic Party": Jerome Karabel, memorandum to George Stephanopoulos, March 30, 1995, page 1. In author's personal files.

303: the Initiative's Web site and King's views on affirmative action: The Web site is no longer active. On King, see Eric Foner, "Stolen Dream: Would King Really Be Against Affirmative Action?" *Slate*, July 26, 1996 (http://www.slate.com/HeyWait/96–07-26/HeyWait. asp).

304: Custered and Wood's meetings with Democrats: Glynn Custred, memorandum to Larry Arnn, Joe Gelman, Arnold Steinberg, and Tom Wood, April 10, 1995 (regarding Will Marshall of the Progressive Policy Institute); Tom Wood, memorandum to Arnold Steinberg, April 12, 1995 (regarding William Galston of the White House staff, Will Marshall, and Al From of the Democratic Leadership Council). In California Civil Rights Initiative Papers. Also author's interviews with Custred and Wood.

Steinberg's contacts with Democrats: Arnold Steinberg, memorandum to Larry Arnn, Glynn Custred, and Joe Gelman, June 16, 1995 (regarding his meeting with Jesse Jackson); Steinberg, memorandum to Gelman, January 24, 1995 (regarding Democratic congressmen Howard Berman and Gary Condit); Steinberg, memorandum to Gelman, February 1, 1995 (regarding "Klein," who is quoted as an authority on what President Clinton might do—possibly Joel Klein, then a member of the White House staff, later Assistant Attorney General for Antitrust); Steinberg, memorandum to Wood, February 14, 1995 (regarding Bill Press); Steinberg, memorandum to Gelman, March 15, 1995 (regarding Stanley Greenberg, Democratic poll-taker). All in California Civil Rights Initiative Papers. Also author's interviews with Steinberg.

"Glynn Custred—all of you ought to take his class": The author heard a tape of Brown's remarks made by a volunteer in the campaign for the Initiative named Peggy Thibodeau, who had copied a tape made by somebody in the class, which was circulated widely among supporters of the Initiative.

activities and views of Scott Taylor: Author's interviews with Scott Taylor, Larry Arnn, Glynn Custred, Joe Gelman, Arnold Steinberg, and Tom Wood.

305: White House discussions of the location for President Clinton's speech: Author's interview with Christopher Edley.

faxes from Dick Morris: Author's interviews with Christopher Edley, John Emerson, William Galston, and George Stephanopoulos.

306: impact of the *Adarand* decision: Author's interviews with William Galston and George Stephanopoulos. Just after these events, Galston wrote an interesting paper on affirmative action that provides a look at his thinking on the subject: William A. Galston, "An Affirmative Action Status Report: Evidence and Options," unpublished paper prepared for the Aspen Institute Domestic Strategy Group, August 1995. In author's personal files.

account of the final work on the affirmative-action speech: Author's interviews with Donald Baer, Christopher Edley, William Galston, and George Stephanopoulos.

307: "But let me be clear": "Remarks by the President on Affirmative Action," July 19, 1995, official White House text, page 10.

310: writings of Michael Lind: See especially Lind's account of his break from the conservative movement, Michael Lind, *Up from Conservatism: Why the Right Is Wrong for America*, The Free Press, 1996.

311: "the Karabel matrix": Author's interview with Ward Connerly.

312: Karabel's figures: Two memoranda written by Karabel that cover the same material, though they were written after the event described here, are Jerome Karabel, "Research Findings, Strategy, and Message," July 24, 1996, and "Polling Results and Implications for Anti-209 Message," September 4, 1996. In author's personal files.

314: signature-gathering for a California initiative: Author's interviews with Michael and William Arno and with Joe Gelman.

results of volunteer and direct-mail efforts: Author's interviews with Michael and William Arno, Glynn Custred, Joe Gelman, Arnold Steinberg, and Tom Wood.

315: American Petition Consultants stopping work: Michael Arno, letter to Joe Gelman, October 23, 1995. California Civil Rights Initiative Papers.

careers and views of Robert Shrum and Pat Ewing: Author's interviews with Shrum and Ewing.

316: Spillar's quarrels with Ewing: Author's interviews with Kathy Spillar, Pat Ewing, Molly Munger, Constance Rice, and Peg Yorkin.

317: "I understand the CRI": Colin Powell, letter to Arnold Steinberg, September 8, 1995. In California Civil Rights Initiative Papers.

318: Connie Rice's visit to Colin Powell: Author's interviews with Molly Munger.

"There are those who rail": Colin L. Powell, "America's Last Best Hope," pamphlet printed by Bowie State University, 1996, page 10.

Dole's attitude toward affirmative action: Author's interviews with Dennis Shea, Glynn Custred, Arnold Steinberg, and Tom Wood.

319: Kemp and affirmative action: An anecdote that may be of interest here is that after the emergence of the California Civil Rights Initiative but before his vice presidential nomination, Kemp telephoned the author, who had interviewed him once and had written on the subject, to say that he was planning to give a speech in support of affirmative action and wanted to rehearse his arguments. An amiable conversation ensued, in which there was no hint on Kemp's part that he was contemplating a renunciation of his support for affirmative action.

320: promised contribution from the service employees' union: Author's interviews with Pat Ewing and Molly Munger.

321: leaders with no followers: One of the most interesting discussions of this question, written long before the events described here, is Ralph H. Turner, "Modes of Social Ascent Through Education: Sponsored and Contest Mobility," *American Sociological Review*, volume 25 (1960), pages 121–139. Turner posits that "*contest* mobility is a system in which elite status is the prize in an open contest and is taken by the aspirants' own efforts," whereas "under *sponsored* mobility, elite recruits are chosen by the established elite or their agents, and elite status is *given* on the basis of some criterion of supposed merit and cannot be *taken* by any amount of effort or strategy." Turner identifies contest mobility with the United States and sponsored mobility with England. But he assumes that Americans get ahead through no organized process. The advent of ETS has created an American version of sponsored mobility, but the allegiance of the country as a whole is still with contest mobility—hence the lack of wide acceptance of the meritocratic Mandarins as national leaders.

the meeting to divide the opposition into two groups: Author's interviews with Molly Munger and Peg Yorkin.

323: "our pockets might come unstitched": Author's interviews with Molly Munger

the White House and funding for the anti-Prop 209 campaign: After the 1996 elections, a congressional investigation into fund-raising in the Democratic presidential campaign produced a bit of information that would seem to support the idea that the White House could have gotten a good deal of money into the hands of the anti-Prop 209 campaign if it had wanted to. On October 22, 1996, at a fund-raising event in Coral Gables, Florida, a man named R. Warren Meddoff managed to slip into President Clinton's hand a business card on which he had written: "My associate has $5 million he wants to contribute to your campaign." On October 29, the White House deputy chief of staff, Harold Ickes, called Meddoff from Air Force One. Meddoff said he wanted to make contributions that would be understood as going to the campaign, but would be tax-deductible. Two days later, Ickes sent Meddoff a fax directing him to wire-transfer $250,000 to Defeat 209, care of a Sacramento bank account. Pat Ewing's name is listed on the fax, and in Ickes' handwritten notes, as the "contact" for this contribution. Meddoff testified in the U.S. Senate that Ickes called him back later the same day and instructed him to destroy the fax, and that he never made the contribution; the point of the story is just that the White House did in fact at least think about directing contributions to the anti-Initiative campaign, but not until it was too late to make much difference.

326: "Proposals such as Proposition 209": Bill Clinton, letter to Eva Paterson, August 22, 1995. In author's personal files.

328: "My name is Tracy Saunders": This quotation is taken from the transcript of the debate printed in *The New York Times*, October 17, 1996, page B11.

"We must immediately reassess": Jerome Karabel, memorandum to Robert Shrum et al., October 31, 1996, page 2. In author's personal files.

330: Connerly and Steinberg speaking on the phone: For example, the author was at Steinberg's house the week after his firing, and Connerly called twice during his interview with Steinberg.

"Until now, there seems to have been": George Skelton, "Can the GOP Sail to Victory on Prop 209?" *Los Angeles Times*, October 24, 1996, page A-3.

331: Conversation between Bill Lee and Molly Munger: The author was present.

333: "Keep talkin', ya dope!": The author was present.

"Zeal overcomes all": Fyodor Dostoevsky, *The Idiot*, Signet Classics, 1989, page 54.

"This will be a nonpartisan speech": The author was present.

334: Steve English's idea for a book: Author's interview with Steven English.

335: election-night scene at the Biltmore Hotel: The author was present.

"As a gang of male voices": A transcript is in "Stop Prop 209 Releases TV Ad in a Final Push: Ad Dramatizes Women's Losses If Prop 209 Passes," November 1, 1996. In author's personal files.

338: Lisa Edwards' discovery of her reading disability: Author's interviews with Lisa Edwards.

339: Bill Lann Lee's confirmation hearing: The author was present.

340: Henry Chauncey's grave site: Author's interviews with Henry Chauncey, and visits to Indian Hill Cemetery.

AFTERWORD

344: "the offices of government": Thomas Jefferson, letter to John Adams, October 28, 1813, In Lester J. Cappon, editor, *The Adams-Jefferson Letters: The Complete Correspondence Between Thomas Jefferson and Abigail and John Adams*, University of North Carolina Press, 1959, page 388.

345: "to reorder the 'haves and have-nots' ": James Bryant Conant, "Wanted: American Radicals," *The Atlantic Monthly*, May 1943, page 41.

346: "the American radical tradition": James Bryant Conant, "What We Are Fighting to Defend," unpublished, undated book manuscript, Chapter VI, page 4. Harvard University Archives, Papers of James B. Conant, Box 30, folder labeled "What We Are Fighting to Defend: Draft (2 of 2)."

liberal elitism: This position is publicly stated less often than you'd think, partly because its natural purveyors, university presidents, are constrained by such pressures as the need constantly to raise money and the threat of reverse-discrimination lawsuits. Its best spokesman is Conant's successor-at-one-remove as president of Harvard, Derek Bok, though even his voice was fairly muted until he had retired. See Derek Bok, *The Cost of Talent: How Execuives and Professionals Are Paid and How It Affects America*, The Free Press, 1993, and William Bowen and Derek Bok, *The Shape of the River: Long-Term Consequences of Considering Race in College and University Admissions*, Princeton University Press, 1993.

347: "There was a time": John W. Gardner, *Excellence: Can We Be Equal and Excellent Too?* Harper & Brothers, 1961, page 63.

"The sorting out of individuals": Ibid., page 71.

349: "If we are to continue". Conant, "What We Are Fighting to Defend," Chaper VI, pages 20–21.

350: "the gap . . . is increasing": See Dominic G. Brewer, Eric R. Eider, and Ronald G. Ehrenberg, "Does It Pay to Attend an Elite Private College? Cross-Cohort Evidence on the Effects of College Type on Earnings," *The Journal of Human Resources*, Winter 1999. But this is a question still being debated. For the opposite position, see, for example, Andrew Hacker, *Money: Who Has How Much and Why*, Scribner, 1997.

A c k n o w l e d g m e n t s

What you need first to write a book like this is the generous cooperation of the people who become the main characters. My first and greatest debt is to them, for their gift of time, patience, and trust in telling me the stories of their lives: Alice Ballard, Henry Chauncey, Sam Chauncey, Lisa Edwards, Jerome Karabel, Clark Kerr, Bill Lann Lee, Molly Munger, Don Nakanishi, and Alice Young, along with the associated friends, relatives, and colleagues of theirs who appear in these pages. Two people who aren't mentioned in the book were particularly copious and helpful when I repeatedly interviewed them: Robert Kwan, in Los Angeles, and Dr. Daniel Singer, in Boston.

I spent the first period of my research in the archives of the Educational Testing Service in Princeton, New Jersey. The late Gregory Anrig, then president of ETS, granted my request for access to the archives, with the assent of Henry Chauncey regarding his papers. Eleanor Horne, a special assistant to Anrig, and Daniel Yankelovich, an ETS board member, were crucial in persuading him to look favorably on my request.

The three staff members of the ETS archives at the time I was working there were Gary Saretzky, the head archivist, Tim Corlis, and Liz Blasco. They patiently guided me through the voluminous papers of Chauncey, William Turnbull (his successor as president of ETS), Carl Campbell Brigham (author of the SAT), and Ben D. Wood (a key early figure in educational testing), all of which are housed there. The ETS archives are also home to an oral-history collection on testing, the papers pertaining to the merger of testing agencies that created ETS, a half-century's worth of news clippings about testing, and a reference library on testing and education. The history of educational testing has never been recorded in any one place, and it would have been impossible to put it together for this book without the use of the ETS archives and the archivists' constant help. At the ETS public relations department, Warren Day, head of the department, and Tom Ewing have my thanks for setting up my interviews with ETS staff members.

Henry Chauncey has also created, with the help of a professional archivist, Tammy Gobert, an indexed collection of papers on the history of his family from the seventeenth century to the present. He gave me full access to these papers, which I refer to in the endnotes as the Chauncey Family Archives (as opposed to the Henry Chauncey Papers, housed at ETS).

Several other archives yielded primary source material for this book, and I owe thanks to their staffs: the Yale University Archives, the Harvard University Archives (home of the James Bryant Conant papers), the Columbia University Oral History Collection (home of a project on the history of the Carnegie Corporation), the Lyndon Baines Johnson Presidential Library in Austin, Texas, the Nixon Presidential Materials Project at the National Archives in College Park, Maryland, the Library of Congress (home of the William O. Douglas papers), and Bancroft Library at the University of California (home of the office papers of Clark Kerr and Governor Edmund G. Brown, Sr.)

I used a few collections of papers that, like the ETS archives, required special permission as a condition of access. Jack Pelatson, then president of the University of California, let me see the meeting records of the university's Board of Regents. New York State Senator Kenneth LaValle allowed me to go through his office files on the New York Truth in Testing Act of 1980. And a source I can't name let me read a collection of memoranda and correspondence written by the organizers of the Proposition 209 campaign in California. (I refer to these in the endnotes as the California Civil Rights Initiative Papers.) Finally, Arthur Levine, president of Teachers College at Columbia University, several times granted me temporary privileges at the first-rate library there.

The following people made available to me various unpublished works they had written and related research materials: Matthew Dallek (on conservative politics in California in the 1960s), John Aubrey Douglas (on University of California admissions), Geoffrey Kabaservice (on Yale University and Kingman Brewster), Clark Kerr (chapters from a memoir-in-progress), and James Tobin (on Yale admissions). All of these materials were useful, and giving me the chance to read them was in every case an act of generosity for which I am grateful.

I've had the help of several generations of research assistants. Three worked for me full-time for a year each: Meg Jacobs, Justin Powell, and Julian Barnes. I also had the part-time help of Jerome Chou, Judy Davis, Brooke Douglas, Anne Gilbert, David Michaels, Sam Seidel, Ira Stoll, and Seth Stuhl. I couldn't have written this book without their help and friendship.

Several friends who are also magazine editors read a first draft of the manuscript and gave me detailed, indispensable advice on matters of prose and structure: Byron Dobell, James Fallows, Michael Kinsley, and Robert Vare. Judith Shulevitz, who will be my wife within a few weeks of the publication of this book, read and reread and talked through the manuscript more than anyone else, and was encouraging in every possible other way, too.

Another set of people provided me with guidance, advice, criticism of drafts, and encouragement on the intellectual aspects of the book. First on the list is Robert K. Merton. In the early going I came across his famous essay "Social Structure and Anomie," called Merton up, and asked if I could come see him. He agreed, and over the next few years he acted as an informal tutor to me on matters of social theory. Merton's idea of "opportunity structure" is really the underpinning of this book, though the phrase itself hardly appears in it. I also got invaluable conceptual guidance from Alan Brinkley, Andrew Delbanco, Herbert Gans, Andrew Hacker, Robert Hauser (who read and commented extensively on the whole manuscript), Christopher Jencks, Nira Kaplan, Mark Kelman, Frank Levy, Lawrence Mead, Charles Peters, David Riesman, Isabel Sawhill, Robert Wiebe, and Garry Wills.

William Whitworth, my editor for fifteen years at *The Atlantic Monthly*, allowed me to pursue the line of inquiry that led to this book with complete freedom and lack of time pressure. At key moments he gently guided me away from potential difficulties, and he published several early versions of sections of the book. My agent, Amanda Urban, deftly managed the business side of the operation. Linda Healey oversaw the long research phase of my work on the book with unflagging intelligence and encouragement. The actual editing was done by the incomparable Elisabeth Sifton. I don't think I've ever seen anybody edit anything as well as she edited this book. I imagine there are few sentences in all these pages that haven't profited from her reading them. Endless thanks to her.